All Will Stand – A Collection of Articles from the Ministry Website

By Timothy Medsker

All Will Stand – A Collection of Articles from the Ministry Website

Copyright © 2021 Timothy Medsker; Fresh Media LLC

All rights reserved. Except for the use in any review, the reproduction or utilization of this work in whole or in part in any form by any electronic, mechanical or other means is forbidden without the express permission of the author.

All Scripture taken from the VW Edition (www.a-voice.org), with permission.

www.allwillstand.org

First Edition

ISBN 978-0-9906958-9-9

"So then each of us shall give account concerning himself to God." Romans 14:12

"And I saw the dead, small and great, standing before God. And books were opened. And another book was opened, which is the Book of Life. And the dead were judged according to their works, out of the things which were written in the books." Revelation 20:12

All Will Stand — A Collection of Articles from the Ministry Website

Contents		**Page**
Preface		6
Article 1	Death Defying	7
Article 2	Yet a Little While	9
Article 3	To Be Like Him	11
Article 4	Grow in Christ!	15
Article 5	Are You Listening & Obeying?	20
Article 6	Memorial Day	22
Article 7	Nothing New Under the Sun	25
Article 8	Fear of God	27
Article 9	Will you (or can you?) Wait any Longer?	32
Article 10	What is Wisdom?	36
Article 11	Separated Unto God	42
Article 12	Heaven or Hell?	46
Article 13	Who Will Remember You? – Vanity	51
Article 14	If Today were the Last Day?	55
Article 15	Don't Join Us!!!	58
Article 16	What is Truth?	61
Article 17	All to Stand	66
Article 18	Lies	72
Article 19	Trappings!	77
Article 20	The Path is Narrow	82
Article 21	Tragedies	86
Article 22	Evidence Around Us	88
Article 23	Trendy	90
Article 24	A Perishing World	92
Article 25	Take a Moment	95
Article 26	In a Twinkling of an Eye	99
Article 27	The Night is Far Spent	101
Article 28	The Collective	103
Article 29	As He Says	109
Article 30	God Sees You	111
Article 31	Lone Wolves?	113

Contents   Page

Article 32	They Forgot About God	117
Article 33	What's Next?	123
Article 34	The Deception is Great!	129
Article 35	What is Your Soul Worth?	133
Article 36	Ineffective Christianity	136
Article 37	At Any Moment	141
Article 38	They Took the Bait	143
Article 39	Intolerant	146
Article 40	Enslavement	149
Article 41	As Little Children	161
Article 42	Following Who?	165
Article 43	First in Line	169
Article 44	No Place for Them	172
Article 45	They Didn't Make It	177
Article 46	Freedom	183
Article 47	What Will You Do?	186
Article 48	Atrocities	190
Article 49	Is it Finally the End?	194
Article 50	Willfully Ignorant	198
Article 51	Christians – Get Up!	201
Article 52	Proud to Defy God?	205
Article 53	Unfortunate Ones	210
Article 54	Lights Out?	217
Article 55	Where have all of the Preachers Gone?	224
Article 56	Alarm Bells	227
Article 57	The Broad Path	231
Article 58	Pounding the Pulpit	236
Article 59	Slaves to Sin	239
Article 60	To the Oppressed of the World	246
Article 61	Garbage Heap	262
Article 62	Don't Wait	268
Article 63	In a Moment	277
Article 64	Warn Them!	282
Article 65	Set in Order	287
Article 66	Place of Torment	291
Article 67	Threats	299
Article 68	Knowledge Shall Be Increased	306
Article 69	They Believe Others	311
Article 70	Slothful	317
Article 71	Word by Word	322
Article 72	One Chance	341
Article 73	Controversy with the Nations	345
Article 74	Fearmongers	353
Article 75	Know No Evil	360

Preface

It seemed good for me to put into a book format a collection of articles that have been published on All Will Stand's ministry's website, www.AllWillStand.org. For men certainly need to be warned of the reality of this world. They need to be warned to turn from sin and to turn to Christ.

"Him we preach, warning every man and teaching every man in all wisdom, that we may present every man complete in Christ Jesus. To this end I also labor, striving according to His working which works in me mightily." Colossians 1:28-29

Over the years the algorithms that decide what is found on a search engine has changed to the point that material that someone decides not to like is able to be hidden, in essence blacklisting websites or sending people to other websites. Now the reality is that such a small ministry as All Will Stand has never considered being on the first page of the search results anyway, but we live in a time where censorship is certainly happening on the internet.

All Will Stand maintained a social media account on a popular website and we believe that our account was shadow-banned. Though our reach was never great, the amount of views greatly diminished around the time of things being publicly censored prior to the 2020 election was quite apparent. Unfortunately a test a few months ago proved this to still be the case when several articles were posted with links and had no impressions made whatsoever.

While there is still time and before censorship increases, it seems good to publish these articles that they might do whatever the purpose of Him who Created us will have them do. As a Believer, I do as the Lord leads, the results are His.

You can visit the website at www.AllWillStand.org

In Christ,

Tim Medsker

Tim Medsker

Death Defying

The other day I watched some videos on parkour or freerunning. This is a new hit with many younger people, mostly in Europe and Russia but also in the United States. The concept is simple, find the shortest route between two points and take it. If this includes climbing over buildings, jumping from rooftop to rooftop or doing many other such maneuvers, so be it. Some of the videos online show much skill and indeed some of these young people have had gymnastics training.

To take matters even further there are also a sect of these youth who will climb radio towers, using no safety equipment, and once at the top they will take and climb over the edge, doing pushups or hanging from the steel frame in a death defying act. When questioned about it most will give an answer that they enjoy the thrill and the rush of doing such things.

If one digs a little deeper you will find that there are news articles that some of these participants do not make the jump across the buildings. Others fall to their death, some break their necks or injure themselves very badly. This is the side that you do not typically see when you watch a carefully crafted video showing only the successes of the group in what appears to be movie style moves. People have often done things like this, though this newest trend is much more dangerous than things of the past.

There have always been people who have done skydiving, extreme boat racing, mountain climbing, etc. It is not the scope of this article to determine what a Believer may or may not do in terms of outdoor activities. A Believer who is living righteously ought to know in their heart what is acceptable to Him or not. There are also such careers that can have heavy risks, such as police, military, inner city taxi cab drivers and private plane pilots, to name a few. I've read of an instance of a man whose job in the Israeli military was to diffuse landmines. His testimony consists of how he was called for duty many times during his years and watched as his friends/coworkers would not be so lucky, but would get blown up, either being massively injured or dying in the process. However, God watched over him and through His grace he succeeded in completing the tasks assigned to him during his military duties required of him.

However, dear reader, are you inadvertently doing death defying activities?

"There is a way which seems right to a man, but the end of it is the ways of death." Proverbs 14:12

Most people wouldn't participate in the above activities mentioned but yet they try to defy the Most High God. They refuse to listen to Him and refuse to repent and accept Salvation that is offered freely through His Son, Jesus Christ.

"But the free gift is not like the offense. For if by the one man's offense many died, much more the grace of God and the gift by the grace of the one Man, Jesus Christ, abounded to many." Romans 5:15

If you are one who goes about your life ignoring God, be ASSURED you are defying death each and every day. Every breath that you take is one more breath that you defy the Most High God and you WILL be held accountable. You will NOT be able to defy death, for there is NO defying death before your Creator.

"For it is written: As I live, says the Lord, Every knee shall bow to Me, and every tongue shall confess to God. So then each of us shall give account concerning himself to God." Romans 14:11-12

Whether or not you choose to acknowledge this fact, you will indeed stand before Him and you will be judged. If you have not accepted Jesus Christ as your Savior, you will be cast into the Lake of Fire.

"And anyone not found written in the Book of Life was cast into the Lake of Fire." Revelation 20:15

There is no skirting around it, no amount of skill that will prevent this from happening or any amount of worldly training that will prevent this outcome.

The facts are simple, either you accept Jesus as your Savior and serve the Most High God or you die the death and will spend eternity in punishment for doing so.

"And as it is appointed for men to die once, and after this the judgment..." Hebrews 9:27

Amen!

Yet a Little While

"For yet a little while, and the wicked shall be no more; indeed, you shall diligently consider his place, and it shall be no more." Psalms 37:10

How much longer will we, who are Believers, have to contend with those who plot to destroy the earth? The ones who subvert everything they can. These men of evil plots purposefully dumb down societies with education, junk food, chemicals in the water, vaccinations, chemtrails, media, television, entertainment and various other means. These same men also promote false doctrines, increase violence in societies, wars and help cause pestilences in various places. Who are these men?

These are those who have aligned themselves with Satan, they have made a 'deal' with him…

"Again, the devil takes Him up on an exceedingly high mountain, and shows Him all the kingdoms of the world and their glory. And he says to Him, All these things I will give to You if You will fall down and do homage to me." Matthew 4:8-9

…and are preparing to make war against God.

"For they are spirits of demons, performing signs, which go forth to the kings of the earth and of the whole world, to gather them to the battle of that great day of God Almighty. Revelation 16:14

"And they gathered them together to the place called in Hebrew, Armageddon." Revelation 16:16

These are those who use puppet governments to create bureaucracy to further Satan's realm…

"For we do not wrestle against flesh and blood, but against rulers, against authorities, against the world's rulers of the darkness of this age, against spiritual wickedness in the heavenlies." Ephesians 6:12

…and use many men as their fronts for their evil plot. They do not fear the Most High God, their Creator, but they will.

"Do you indeed speak justice, O silent ones? Do you judge with equity, O sons of men? Indeed, in heart you work injustice; you weigh out the violence of your hands in the earth. The wicked are estranged from the womb; they go astray from the belly, speaking lies. Their poison is like the poison of a serpent, like the deaf cobra that stops its ear, which will not heed the charmer's voice, who charms so skillfully. O God, break their teeth in their mouth; break out the fangs of the young lions, O Jehovah. Let them flow away like waters that move along. When he bends his bow to shoot arrows, let them be as though they were cut off. Let them be as a snail that melts away; as a stillborn child of a

woman, that has not seen the sun. Before your pots can feel the thorns, whether green or glowing, He shall sweep it away. The righteous shall rejoice when he sees the vengeance; he shall wash his feet in the blood of the wicked. And man shall say, Truly, there is a reward for the righteous; truly, there is a God who judges in the earth." Psalms 58

Though these men think they are unstoppable, indeed God will stop them. Their work will be halted! Him who they do not fear is He who will stop them. Though they stop God from being spoken about in public schools, though they push agendas such as sodomite marriage, though they try to united the world religions, their works will be halted! Though they prepare to further enslave mankind and fulfill the prophecies that God foretold in the Holy Scriptures, there is an end to them.

"But the wicked shall perish, and the enemies of Jehovah shall be as prized lambs; they are consumed; like smoke they vanish." Psalms 37:20

"Do not be led astray, God is not mocked; for whatever a man sows, that he will also reap." Galatians 6:7

EVERY man will give an account of himself!

"So then each of us shall give account concerning himself to God." Romans 14:12

Each man will stand before the Most High God and if his name is not found in the Book of Life *(Revelation 20:12)* then they will be cast into the Lake of Fire *(Revelation 20:14)*.

God will put an end to their works. Mankind does not seek after the Most High, they are deserving.

"God looked down from Heaven upon the children of mankind to see if any was circumspect, seeking God. Every one of them has turned back; they have all together become corrupt; not one is doing good, no, not even one. Have the workers of iniquity no knowledge? They eat up my people as they eat bread; they have not called upon God." Psalms 53:2-4

Amen!

To Be Like Him

What is the ultimate goal or rather what should the ultimate goal of Christians around the world be? Shouldn't our goal be to be like Him, the author and finisher of our faith?

"Therefore we also, since we are surrounded by so great a cloud of witnesses, let us lay aside every weight, and the sin which so persistently harasses us, and let us run with perseverance the race that is set before us, looking unto Jesus, the author and finisher of our faith, who for the joy that was set before Him endured the cross, despising the shame, and has sat down at the right hand of the throne of God." Hebrews 12:1-2

"But we all, with unveiled face, beholding as in a mirror the glory of the Lord, are being transformed into the same image from glory to glory, just as by the Spirit of the Lord." 2nd Corinthians 3:18

"Beloved, now we are children of God; and it has not yet been revealed what we shall be, but we know that when He is revealed, we shall be like Him, for we shall see Him as He is." 1st John 3:2

"But no, rather, I also count all things loss for the excellence of the knowledge of Christ Jesus my Lord, for whom I have suffered the loss of all things, and count them as refuse, that I may gain Christ and be found in Him, not having my own righteousness, which is from the Law, but that which is through the faith of Christ, the righteousness which is from God by faith; that I may know Him and the power of His resurrection, and the fellowship of His sufferings, being conformed to His death, if, by any means, I may attain to the resurrection from the dead. Not that I have already attained, or am already perfected; but I press on, that I may lay hold, since Christ Jesus has also laid hold of me. Brethren, I do not count myself to have laid hold; but one thing I do, forgetting those things which are behind and stretching forward to those things which are ahead, I press toward the goal for the prize of the upward call of God in Christ Jesus." Philippians 3:8-14

The goal of a true Believer should be to become like Christ. Why? What does that mean? Let's expound on the topic.

When a sinner comes to repentance and in faith receives Christ as their Savior, did not they forsake the former things in their lives?

"But Jesus said to him, No one, having put his hand to the plow, and looking back, is fit for the kingdom of God." Luke 9:62

Did we not die to our foolish, sinful lives and become alive in Christ?

"Likewise you also, reckon yourselves to be dead indeed to sin, but alive to God in Christ Jesus our Lord." Romans 6:11

"And you being dead in trespasses and sins, in which you formerly walked according to the course of this world, according to the ruler of the authority of the air, the spirit who now works in the sons of disobedience, among whom also we all formerly conducted ourselves in the lusts of our flesh, fulfilling the desires of the flesh and of the mind, and were by nature children of wrath, just as the others; but God, who is rich in mercy, because of His great love with which He loved us, even when we were dead in trespasses, made us alive together with Christ (by grace you are saved), and raised us up together, and made us sit together in the heavenlies in Christ Jesus, that in the ages to come He might display the exceeding riches of His grace in His kindness toward us in Christ Jesus. For by grace you are saved through faith; and that not of yourselves, it is the gift of God; not of works, that no one should boast. For we are His workmanship, created in Christ Jesus unto good works, which God prepared beforehand that we should walk in them. Therefore remember that you, being Gentiles in the flesh; who are called uncircumcision by what is called the circumcision made in the flesh by hands; that at that time you were without Christ, being aliens from the commonwealth of Israel and strangers from the covenants of promise, having no hope and without God in the world. But now in Christ Jesus you who once were far off have been made near by the blood of Christ. For He Himself is our peace, who has made both one, and has broken down the middle wall of separation, having abolished in His flesh the enmity, that is, the Law of commandments contained in ordinances, that He might create in Himself one new man from the two, thus making peace, and that He might reconcile them both to God in one body through the cross, thereby putting to death the enmity. And He came and preached peace to you who were afar off and to those who were near. For through Him we both have access by one Spirit to the Father. Now, therefore, you are no longer strangers and foreigners, but fellow citizens with the saints and members of the household of God, having been built on the foundation of the apostles and prophets, Jesus Christ Himself being the chief corner stone, in whom the whole building, being joined together, grows into a holy temple in the Lord, in whom you also are being built together into a dwelling place of God in the Spirit." Ephesians 2

We were dead! You thought you were alive, but you were dead! Dead in your sins, dead in your trespasses against an almighty Creator!

When we lived before being Saved, what did we live for, or to whom? Did we not live to fulfill our own lusts? Think about it.

The Holy Scriptures speaks of being Born Again, think of that for a minute, being Born Again.

"Jesus answered and said to him, Truly, truly, I say to you, unless one is born from above, he is not able to see the kingdom of God." John 3:3

All, every person on the face of this earth, are born once. But, in order to become a Christian, to truly serve the Most High God, to become holy, separate, righteous and a follower of Jesus, we MUST be born from above. For our nature, prior to Christ, was that of sin. Without Him, there was no hope, without Him we were not made alive.

"for all have sinned and fall short of the glory of God" Romans 3:23

"For the wages of sin is death, but the gift of God is eternal life in Christ Jesus our Lord." Romans 6:23

When we became Saved, we became free men. Not in the sense of rights that man is used to, but we are free from the enslavement of sin and slaves to Christ.

"But now having been set free from sin, and having become slaves to God, you have your fruit unto sanctification, and the end, eternal life." Romans 6:22

"For he who is called in the Lord while a slave is the Lord's freedman. Likewise he who is called while free is Christ's slave." 1st Corinthians 7:22

We have died to our self, self-esteem is out the window, or should be. Our fleshly desires should be replaced with walking in the Spirit and doing the things that please Him, as Christ did as an example to us, while He walked upon the earth in human form.

"I say then: Walk in the Spirit, and you shall not fulfill the lust of the flesh. For the flesh lusts against the Spirit, and the Spirit against the flesh; and these are contrary to one another, so that you do not do the things that you wish." Galatians 5:16-17

"If we live in the Spirit, let us also walk in the Spirit." Galatians 5:25

As Christians, then our goal needs to be to be like Him. Christ has set the example to follow.

"I am able to do nothing from Myself. As I hear, I judge; and My judgment is just, because I do not seek My own will but the will of the Father who sent Me." John 5:30

"And He who sent Me is with Me. The Father has not left Me alone, for I always do those things that please Him." John 8:29

What is our responsibility towards the Most High? How are we to become like Christ?

"And do not be conformed to this world, but be transformed by the renewing of your mind, that you may prove what is that good and acceptable and perfect will of God." Romans 12:2

"Therefore, if anyone is in Christ, he is a new creation; the old things have passed away; behold, all things have become new." 2nd Corinthians 5:17

"These things I have spoken to you, that in Me you may have peace. In the world you have affliction; but be of good courage, I have overcome the world." John 16:33

In Conclusion:

"He who says he abides in Him ought himself also to walk just as He walked." 1st John 2:6

How are we to know how to walk, how to live holy and righteous lives, what examples Christ set for us? We must put on the armor of God, drink the milk of the Word and live Godly lives, in prayer, walking as He walked. We must strengthen ourselves daily and examine ourselves frequently so that we can be assured of our faith and walk properly before God amongst both the living and the dying.

"Finally, my brethren, be strong in the Lord and in the power of His might. Put on all the armor of God, that you may be able to stand against the wiles of the devil. For we do not wrestle against flesh and blood, but against rulers, against authorities, against the world's rulers of the darkness of this age, against spiritual wickedness in the heavenlies. Therefore take up all the armor of God, that you may be able to resist in the evil day, and having done all, to stand. Stand firm therefore, having girded your waist with truth, having put on the breastplate of righteousness, and having shod your feet with the preparation of the gospel of peace; above all, taking the shield of faith with which you will be able to quench all the fiery darts of the wicked one. And take the helmet of salvation, and the sword of the Spirit, which is the Word of God; praying always with all prayer and supplication in the Spirit, being watchful to this end with all perseverance and supplication for all the saints; and for me, that utterance may be given to me, that I may open my mouth boldly to make known the mystery of the gospel, for which I am an ambassador in chains; that in it I may speak boldly, as I ought to speak." Ephesians 6:10-20

"as newborn babes, desire the pure milk of the Word, that you may grow thereby" 1st Peter 2:2

"Examine yourselves as to whether you are in the faith. Test yourselves. Do you not know, yourselves, that Jesus Christ is in you; unless indeed you are ones failing the test?" 2nd Corinthians 13:5

Amen!

Grow in Christ!

What is it to be a Christian? What is expected out of the Believer?

When someone comes to Jesus, in repentance towards God through the blood of Christ, believing into Him, change happens, Salvation is granted and with that the new Believer is also a new creature.

"...testifying both to Jews, and also to Greeks, repentance toward God and faith toward our Lord Jesus Christ." Acts 20:21

"Therefore, if anyone is in Christ, he is a new creation; the old things have passed away; behold, all things have become new." 2nd Corinthians 5:17

There is a renewing of the mind and with this renewing of the mind a renewing of the direction and purpose of our lives.

"And do not be conformed to this world, but be transformed by the renewing of your mind, that you may prove what is that good and acceptable and perfect will of God." Romans 12:2

"If then you are raised with Christ, seek those things which are above, where Christ is, sitting at the right hand of God. Set your mind on things above, not on the things of the earth; for you died, and your life is hidden with Christ in God." 1st Corinthians 3:1-3

No longer are we to seek our own, but we are to seek His will, we are to follow Jesus, serving the Most High God.

"Then Jesus said to His disciples, If anyone desires to come after Me, let him deny himself, and take up his cross, and follow Me." Matthew 16:24

"For to this you were called, because Christ also suffered for us, leaving us an example, that you should follow His steps..." 1st Peter 2:21

What then, how is it that a Believer does not produce excellent fruit?

"You will know them from their fruits. Do men gather grapes from thornbushes or figs from thistles? Even so, every good tree produces excellent fruit, but a corrupt tree produces evil fruit. A good tree is not able to produce evil fruit, nor is a corrupt tree able to produce excellent fruit. Every tree that does not produce excellent fruit is cut down and thrown into the fire. Therefore from their fruits you will know them." Matthew 7:16-20

I speak from experience, knowing the temptations that happen to all of us. The problem lies with our hearts, it is an inner conflict of the flesh verses the spirit. How ought we to live?

"Jesus said to him, You shall love the Lord your God with all your heart, with all your soul, and with all your mind. This is the first and great commandment. And the second is like it: You shall love your neighbor as yourself." Matthew 22:37-39

"Therefore, having these promises, beloved, let us cleanse ourselves from all defilements of the flesh and spirit, perfecting holiness in the fear of God." 2nd Corinthians 7:1

"Therefore gird up the loins of your mind, be sober, and rest your hope fully upon the grace that is to be brought to you at the revelation of Jesus Christ; as obedient children, not conforming yourselves to the former lusts in your ignorance; but as He who called you is holy, you also become holy in all conduct, because it is written, Be holy, because I am holy." 1st Peter 1:13-16

God says, *"Come now and let us reason together, says Jehovah: Though your sins are as scarlet, they shall be as white as snow; though they are red like crimson, they shall be as wool." (Isaiah 1:18)*, so where lies the problem? Do we not believe that we are fellow partakers through Christ? Where is the growth that a Christian is to experience, are we growing in Christ?

"But grow in the grace and knowledge of our Lord and Savior Jesus Christ. To Him be the glory both now and forever. Amen." 2nd Peter 3:18

Are we feeding ourselves? Are we yet living in sin? Are we distracted? Are our hearts right before the Almighty, the just Judge before whom we will all stand?

Jesus said, *"Man shall not live by bread alone, but by every Word that comes forth from the mouth of God." Matthew 4:4b*

"For we must all appear before the judgment seat of Christ, that each one may receive the things done in the body, according to what he has done, whether good or bad." 2nd Corinthians 5:10

Consider your ways carefully, examine yourselves. Understand what is expected of a Christian and diligently pursue it.

"Examine yourselves as to whether you are in the faith. Test yourselves. Do you not know, yourselves, that Jesus Christ is in you; unless indeed you are ones failing the test?" 2nd Corinthians 13:5

"Do you not know that those who run in a race all run, but one receives the prize? Run in such a way that you may obtain it." 1st Corinthians 9:24

God did not call us to continue on with our lives while including Christ into them, rather through Jesus we are called to be His servants, our lives dedicated to serving Him and doing His will.

"You shall walk after Jehovah your God and fear Him, and keep His commandments and obey His voice, and you shall serve Him and cleave unto Him." Deuteronomy 13:4

"I have been crucified with Christ; it is no longer I who live, but Christ lives in me; and the life which I now live in the flesh I live by the faith of the Son of God, who loved me and gave Himself for me." Galatians 2:20

It is no longer our purpose in life to chase dreams and fulfill vain desires, but rather to do the will of God, the Almighty Creator, from whom we were carefully crafted in the womb.

"Only fear Jehovah, and serve Him in truth with all your heart; for consider what great things He has done for you." 1st Samuel 12:24

"My frame was not hidden from You when I was made in secret, and skillfully wrought in the lowest parts of the earth. Your eyes saw my embryo, and in Your book I was enrolled, and all my days had been preordained, when as yet there was nothing." Psalms 139:15-16

No longer should we be slaves to sin, but rather slaves to Christ.

"But God be thanked that though you were slaves of sin, yet you obeyed from the heart that form of doctrine which was delivered to you. And having been set free from sin, you became slaves to righteousness." Romans 6:17-18

Even in this late hour, let our fruit grow graciously, due to the mercy of God who gave His only Son that we might have life.

"Therefore bring forth fruits worthy of repentance..." Matthew 3:8

"For God so loved the world that He gave His only begotten Son, that everyone believing into Him should not perish but have eternal life. For God did not send His Son into the world to judge the world, but that the world through Him might be saved." John 3:16-17

Let our focus rest on Him who is the author and finisher of our faith.

"...looking unto Jesus, the author and finisher of our faith, who for the joy that was set before Him endured the cross, despising the shame, and has sat down at the right hand of the throne of God." Hebrews 12:2

"Do not be led astray, God is not mocked; for whatever a man sows, that he will also reap. For he who sows to his flesh will of the flesh reap corruption, but he who sows to the Spirit will of the Spirit reap eternal life." Galatians 6:7-8

Let us have assurance of our calling in Christ, resting securely in His merciful might.

"Therefore, brethren, be even more diligent to make sure of your calling and election, for if you do these things you will not ever stumble; for so an entrance into the eternal kingdom of our Lord and Savior Jesus Christ will be richly supplied to you." 2nd Peter 1:10-11

"Therefore gird up the loins of your mind, be sober, and rest your hope fully upon the grace that is to be brought to you at the revelation of Jesus Christ;" 1st Peter 1:13

Examine yourself and consider carefully. What restrains you from doing His will, what causes you to backslide and not continue forward?

"Therefore, my beloved brethren, be steadfast, immovable, always abounding in the work of the Lord, knowing that your labor is not in vain in the Lord." 1st Corinthians 15:58

You are in a race and in that race you must press on.

"Therefore I run in this manner: not with uncertainty. Thus I fight: not as one who beats the air. But I discipline my body and bring it into subjection, lest, when I have preached to others, I myself should become disqualified." 1st Corinthians 9:26-27

"I have fought the good fight, I have finished the course, I have kept the faith." 2nd Timothy 4:7

"For He says: In an acceptable time I have heard you, and in a day of salvation I have helped you. Behold, now is the accepted time; behold, now is the day of salvation." 2nd Corinthians 6:2

Do not delay! Understand the magnitude of the blessing that God has bestowed upon us, understand the seriousness of following Christ and the indescribable gift that we have received through His blood.

"Blessed be the God and Father of our Lord Jesus Christ, who has blessed us with every spiritual blessing in the heavenlies in Christ, just as He chose us in Him before the foundation of the world, that we should be holy and without blemish before Him in love, having predestined us to adoption as sons by Jesus Christ to Himself, according to the good pleasure of His will, to the praise of the glory of His grace, by which He has made us accepted in the Beloved. In Him we have redemption through His blood, the remission of sins, according to the riches of His grace which He made to abound toward us in all wisdom and understanding, having made known to us the mystery of His will, according to His good pleasure which He purposed in Himself, that in the dispensation of the fullness of the times He might sum up in one all things in Christ, both which are in Heaven and which are on earth; in Him." Ephesians 1:3-10

"Thanks be to God for His indescribable gift." 2nd Corinthians 9:15

"Of how much worse punishment, do you suppose, will he be thought worthy who has trampled on the Son of God, counted the blood of the covenant by which he was sanctified a common thing, and insulted the Spirit of Grace?" Hebrews 10:29

Amen!

Are You Listening & Obeying?

"To whom shall I speak, and give warning, that they may hear? Behold, their ears are uncircumcised, and they cannot give heed. Behold, the Word of Jehovah is a reproach to them; they have no delight in it." Jeremiah 6:10

Who listens nowadays? The world is full of God's message of Salvation through Jesus Christ. The Gospel has been preached to every country in the world. The United States is full of churches, numerous churches large and small in every city. Who listens to God, of those who listen, who obeys?

Why has such a simple message of Salvation through repentance and faith into Jesus Christ, our Savior, been so difficult for many to understand? Why is it so difficult for those who are in the church, those who name the name of Christ and call themselves Christians to keep God's message to humanity pure and simple. Is it too difficult?

Instead some churches pile on burdens to people, making the way of God to be through works, which is not how one gets to Heaven. Others, more frequently found in the United States and indeed much of the world now, do the opposite and simple water down God's Word so much that people never find Salvation through the preacher. Where are the preachers that speak the truth, where are the ones who are truly called of God into the ministry of Jesus Christ our Lord and Savior?

"He who is of God hears God's Words; therefore you do not hear, because you are not of God." John 8:47

Most of these churches are not Churches, they do not preach the full Word of God, oftentimes the perversions of the Holy Scriptures that they use are so far off from the truth it is nearly impossible for those attending to come to a full true knowledge of Salvation in Jesus Christ. Yet, despite all of this, these people do not want to hear. Is there yet a famine for the Word of God?

"Behold, the days are coming, declares the Lord Jehovah, that I will send a famine into the land, not a famine for bread, nor a thirst for water, but rather a famine for hearing the Words of Jehovah." Amos 8:11

We are certainly getting close, but there is no excuse. Those who truly are seeking after Him, will find Him.

"And you shall seek Me and find Me, when you search for Me with all your heart." Jeremiah 29:13

God is not far in terms that man cannot find Him. As long as the Rapture hasn't occurred, there are still His workers down here, warning and pleading with individuals to accept the free gift of Salvation. There are websites with God's truth, sermons online where one can find godly pastors and yes, at the moment there are still true Churches here and there scattered across the country. If an individual is truly seeking the Most High God they will find Him and they will be pointed to His Son, Jesus Christ.

Amen!

Memorial Day

This Memorial Day I think it would be fitting to remember an America that once at least adhered to much of God's laws.

An America where there was no debate over sodomite marriage. Who would have dared in 1950 to promote from coast to coast marriage outside of God's purpose?

An America where public school students were not subjected to having the opposite sex use their locker rooms and rest rooms. An America where boys were boys and girls were girls, not an America where a child is taught at a young age to decide what sex they are, not based on actual gender, but a supposed preference. An America where liberals wouldn't criticize parents for putting newborns in blue or pink based off of their sex. Shame on California and Colorado (and where ever else this goes on).

An America where our public schools have 'centering rooms', which are really padded rooms with no windows, to lock children in ALL day long, some of which have the air conditioning on to make it cold. In these rooms a teacher will wear a jacket as the youngster is shivering with their arms in their shirt, mocking them.

An America where businesses where closed on Sundays. At least the people had respect to set aside one day to their Creator, whether or not they followed Him, they at least acknowledged the One whom they will give an account to.

An America where people didn't decide to riot for something to do or gangs of youth didn't use social media to plot their next mass theft of a local market, retail store or an entire block of unsuspecting people.

An America where our younger people didn't turn to meth and other drugs because they are bored and looking for something to do.

An America where women (and men) dressed modestly and didn't walk around like harlots, as if there was nothing wrong with the way they dressed and the attention they garnered. Do they even know that the modest woman nowadays is the one who gets the attention?

An America where people were not completely filled with entertainment and electronic gadgets. A country where people had time to consider God and His Way, instead of endless amounts of nonsense text messages and tweets to respond to.

An America where a man could walk down the street carrying a holstered handgun on his hip, without the stares and gawks of people wishing it was fully illegal. These same people who feel threatened due to a holstered gun are violent in mind and can not get enough violence in their music, television and movies.

An America where children are taught the fundamentals of reasoning (math, reading, writing, true science), not an America where children are taught thought patterns, self-esteem, social and economic dependence, essentially to be slaves.

An America where families gathered around the dinner table and still remembered that it was God who provided. Not an America where people get their monthly government stipend and are now throwing out the kitchen table to replace it with entertainment and couches, with no social interaction of even their own kin.

An America that knew what was right and wrong according to God's morals as laid out in His Word. Not those who now try to rationalize or otherwise continue to erase the lines of God's absolutes. At least those who did wrong back in the day knew they were doing wrong and would admit to being wrong, not necessarily changing. Nowadays our jails and prisons are full of people who claim unfair justice for having broken laws that should require punishment.

How long will this country go on this way and how much of God's judgment will man endure before they recall to memory the One who is in control? California has the worst drought in 1200 years, Texas and Oklahoma had been praying for rain six months ago and now they are praying that it will go away as floods send houses down what was once a creek and many towns are under water. A bad winter in the Northeast, fire weather in the Southwest and northern California, tornados tearing up cities here and there. Yet even amongst this we still see God's mercy, few die in these tragedies.

How long before we hear?

"Yet you have forsaken Me and served other gods. Therefore I will deliver you no more. Go and cry out to the gods which you have chosen; let them deliver you in your time of distress." Judges 10:13-14

I ponder, I see, I wonder about these 'zombies'. Are these those who God has given over to a reprobate mind? *(Romans 1)* How many I see whose lives are so shattered, yet when you converse with them, often you will find they had went to some sort of church at some point in their life, in other words they have heard God's Word, which does not return void. They have made their decision.

These 'empty' people who walk about, how much are they given over to the world? I dare say overcome. Could it be the punishment for their sin is being exacted in their life right now by being entrapped in their sin and no longer able to consider the things of God?

How about an America who once believed God's Word? America was never Christian, yet America did follow much of God's laws 50, even 30 years ago. In fact in my lifetime I would dare say that since the onset of the internet, society has finally taken the final plunge. This isn't just an American problem, it is quickly becoming a worldwide problem.

For those who can still hear, all I can think to say to them is:

"Behold, now is the accepted time; behold, now is the day of salvation." 2nd Corinthians 6:2b

The Lord will surely come back and all will be fulfilled! Certainly for those who are out there, NOW is the time. There should be no more fence sitting.

"He who is unjust, let him be unjust still; he who is filthy, let him be filthy still; he who is righteous, let him be righteous still; he who is holy, let him be holy still." Revelation of Jesus Christ 22:11

Looking Up! Come Lord Jesus! Even so, Amen!

Nothing New Under the Sun

"That which has been is that which shall be; and that which has been done is that which shall be done; and there is nothing new under the sun." Ecclesiastes 1:9

Recently on Memorial Day I was pondering what is happening in this country and watching as the evil is seemingly taking over. A friend of mine sent me a reply reminding me that America was never a Christian nation back in the 1950's and older pictures of women in that era have the same sort of inappropriate poses that modern women due, just that they are dressed more. He also threw in how Solomon had already married an Egyptian woman at the time he was dedicating the new Temple to Jehovah. I pondered these things and saw valid points, knowing that America was never a Christian nation, but I thought that surely the world is getting worse.

"But evil men and pretenders will grow worse and worse, leading astray and being led astray." 2nd Timothy 3:13

"But as the days of Noah were, so also will the coming of the Son of Man be." Matthew 24:37

Around America it seems as if this year God is judging the nation more so than in recent past, the weather is quite unusual and even meteorologist are trying to figure out why it is so severe, their main argument points to global warming, a doctrine that I find to be fanciful and imaginative. I ponder the decision from the Supreme Court regarding sodomite marriage. Remember much of the world will take note and follow what the United States does. Are things truly getting worse or are people just being more open and rebellious towards God?

A couple of days after firing off a reply to my friend I was finishing my personal reading in Judges and came across some verses that I have been pondering since then. A realization hit me, think people are bad now? They certainly can be AND HAVE BEEN much worse. These verses that stuck out to me were the following:

"Now as they were making their hearts merry, behold, certain men of the city, sons of wickedness surrounded the house and beat on the door. They spoke to the master of the house, the old man, saying, Bring out the man who has come to your house, that we may know him. And the man, the master of the house, went out to them and said to them, No, my brethren! I beg you, do not act so wickedly! Seeing this man has come into my house, do not do this disgraceful folly. Behold, here is my virgin daughter and his concubine; let me bring them out now. Humble them, and do with them whatever seems good to your eyes; but to this man do not do such a disgraceful thing! But the men would not heed him. So the man took his concubine and brought her out to them. And they knew her and abused her wantonly all night until morning; and when the day began to break, they let her go. Then the woman came as the day was dawning, and fell down at the door of the man's house where her master was, till it was light. And when her master arose in the

morning, and opened the doors of the house and went out to go his way, behold the woman, his concubine, fallen at the door of the house with her hands on the threshold. And he said to her, Get up and let us be going. But there was no answer. So the man lifted her onto the donkey; and the man rose up and went to his place. And when he entered his house he took a knife, laid hold of his concubine, and divided her into twelve pieces with her bones, and sent her throughout all the territory of Israel." Judges 19:22-30*

AND:

"In those days there was no king in Israel. Every man did what was right in his own eyes." Judges 21:25

How many years had passed since Joshua's death? Already you have this city in Israel that is behaving as Sodom and Gomorrah, out of control, literally committing despicable acts AND without excuse as to know why they reside where they do, they are God's people and they know that they had been saved out of Egypt with His strong hand. Yet these people pay no regard to God, but do whatever is right in their own eyes, much like today. What about the Levites, are they not reminding the people to serve Jehovah? Much like pastors out to shepherd Christ's flock to keep them safe and sound.

As bad as things are in this country and yes they are getting worse and worse, if one thinks carefully about Israel's history and how they would go and serve the Baals and other pagan deities, with no regard to their Maker, it just testifies that the hearts of men do not seek after the Most High. They are born in sin, live their life in sin and refuse to heed God due to their sin. Jesus Christ paid the ultimate price for mankind's sin offering them forgiveness, a renewed mind, a personal relationship and eternal life; yet their hearts are stubborn and wicked, refusing to cede from doing evil.

Are you going to be stubborn to the end and not heed God's warning in His Word or are you going to repent of your sins and accept Jesus Christ as your Savior? Time is running out and each man is not guaranteed a breath beyond the one that he is breathing right now. Ponder your path and really consider, it is not too late as you are reading this, you can still accept God's free gift of Salvation.

"For He says: In an acceptable time I have heard you, and in a day of salvation I have helped you. Behold, now is the accepted time; behold, now is the day of salvation." 2nd Corinthians 6:2

"See to it that you do not refuse Him who speaks. For if they did not escape who refused Him who spoke on earth, much more shall we not escape if we turn away from the One speaking from Heaven, whose voice then shook the earth; but now He has promised, saying, Yet once more I shake not only the earth, but also the heavens." Hebrews 12:25-26

Amen!

Fear of God

"The fear of Jehovah is the beginning of wisdom; and the knowledge of the Holy One is understanding." Proverbs 9:10

What is the fear of God?

In order to try and fully comprehend the 'fear of the Lord', let's begin by looking at some definitions of fear.

A.) A painful emotion or passion excited by an expectation of evil, or the apprehension of impending danger. It expresses less apprehension than dread, and is accompanied with a desire to avoid or ward off the expected evil.

B.) Anxiety; solicitude; also, the cause or object which excites apprehension.

C.) In Scripture, reverence for God and his laws, which springs from a just view and love of the divine character. (Jer. 32:40)

D. Reverence; respect; due regard for rightful authority.

(All of this in the 'n.' context; *Webster's University Dictionary Unabridged*, 1942)

Everyone understands the fear of the dark, something that is often learned as a child. When I was young I had watched scary television shows and became afraid of the 'unknown' in the dark of the night. What about the fear of God, certainly we don't have a fear of Him as we would have regarding the supposed evil lurking in the night. In order to get the best understanding of the fear of God, we are going to turn to God's Word and see what the Holy Scriptures says about fear, in respect to God.

"And Abraham said, Because I thought, Surely the fear of God is not in this place; and they will kill me on account of my wife." Genesis 20:11

In regards to this verse, fear is being used in the aspect of lawlessness, a city (society) where it was presumed people would do what they want because they would not fear the consequences of a just God.

"And Joseph said to them the third day, Do this and live, for I fear God:" Genesis 42:18

Here fear is used in the context to verify the word which Joseph is speaking as certain and true, as he then makes a deal with his brothers who are as of yet unbeknown to them. The fear of God is why Joseph would not go back from the deal that he has made.

"Moreover you shall select from all the people able men, who fear God, men of truth, hating unjust gain; and place these over them as rulers of thousands, rulers of hundreds, rulers of fifties, and rulers of tens." Exodus 18:21

When Moses father-in-law is counseling him regarding being overburdened with judging between so many people, he ascertains the characteristics of the people who will judge in the smaller matters. Not only are these people to be honest, not able to be bribed, but they have the fear of God. Would not the fear of God in them help to assure that they do what is right, not simply trying to hide any wrong works from man, but knowing that God would see and know what they are doing, even if man did not figure it out.

"Oh, that this heart of theirs would be fully yielded, to fear Me and to keep all My commandments at all times, that it might be well with them and with their children forever!" Deuteronomy 5:29

What is this biblical fear of God that He desires mankind to hold to? In order to fully understand the definition, a Webster's dictionary will not suffice, nor any dictionary, but we will turn to the Holy Scriptures for the definition.

"You shall fear Jehovah your God and serve Him…" Deuteronomy 6:13a

"Therefore you shall keep the commandments of Jehovah your God, to walk in His ways and to fear Him." Deuteronomy 8:6

"Now therefore, fear Jehovah, serve Him in sincerity and in truth…" Joshua 24:14a

"Then Jehovah said to Satan, Have you set your heart on My servant Job, that there is none like him on the earth, a perfect and upright man, one who fears God and turns away from evil? So Satan answered Jehovah and said, Does Job fear God for nothing?" Job 1:8-9

"And to man He said, Behold, the fear of the Lord, that is wisdom, and to depart from evil is understanding." Job 28:28

The last verse from Job sums it up well. This type of fear is a fear that makes one wise and with that wisdom this fear also produces obedience and obedience to God is following His commandments. In order for a man to get a renewed mind and become a new creature, one must accept God's Son, Jesus the Messiah as their Lord and Savior. This free gift of God allows an individual who comes to understand the fear of the Lord through a repentant heart. When an individual realizes that they are guilty before their Creator and desires to no longer do those things which are displeasing to Him, after accepting Christ, does not a portion of their being have the fear of the Lord?

"And do not be conformed to this world, but be transformed by the renewing of your mind, that you may prove what is that good and acceptable and perfect will of God." Romans 12:2

"Therefore, if anyone is in Christ, he is a new creation; the old things have passed away; behold, all things have become new." 2nd Corinthians 5:17

People speeding on the freeway have the fear of the police. If they are just going over a few miles per hour, they might not fear, or if they are in a crowd of vehicles also speeding, likewise they might feel safe with the masses on the road. Regardless they are guilty and the faster they go on the freeway and the more lone vehicle there are, unless they are truly in the middle of nowhere or on some sort of mind altering chemical or drug, they have the fear of the police. If you ever watch traffic cruising along, when a police officer is seen on the side of the road the whole group of cars slow down immediately. What if one of those in the group still decided to disregard that officer on the side of the road? Likely that officer would burnout, drifting onto the road and quickly come upon the guilty one. That driver, whether or not they chose to accept it, would learn the respect of the law and be given a fine for speeding, they would be in submission to the police officer or the officer would arrest them and take them to jail. How much more righteous fear should an individual have when they walk upon this earth, knowing that the Most High also has rules and laws and He is the Judge of the whole earth. Yet in all of this, how much more should one's heart, with all joy, be in subjection to Jesus, as through Him is the free gift that our Father in Heaven gave to us!

"There is one Lawgiver, who has the power to save and to destroy." Jacob 4:12a

"But God is the Judge; He puts down one and exalts another." Psalms 75:7

"For God so loved the world that He gave His only begotten Son, that everyone believing into Him should not perish but have eternal life." John 3:16

We are both in subjection to our Creator and Christ, not just out of the fear of the Lord, but also from His indescribable gift that He gave to us, sinners who were not worthy to obtain a Heavenly calling.

"Now may the God of hope fill you with all joy and peace in believing, that you may abound in hope by the power of the Holy Spirit." Romans 15:13

If you do not yet fear the Lord, you ought to learn to fear Him who created you and learn quickly. You must realize that indeed God is in control and His plans for the world will not be stopped by your will for your life to be able to be lived with no accountability. Do not look at what your friends and family do, do not justify your sin just because the world embraces it through culture, television, internet, radio and nearly every other venue. For individually, without Christ, you are just as guilty as they. When you stand before the Judge you will be condemned to Hell eternally. Why, why should you die? For what will you give your life?

"For what will it profit a man if he gains the whole world, and loses his own soul? Or what will a man give in exchange for his soul?" Mark 8:36-37

Do you not see that we live in such a late hour, do you not see the dread of Him who Created you beginning to show up on the horizon?

People buy lottery tickets hoping to escape the impoverishment of living. They don't like the paycheck to paycheck, they wish for a bigger house, a better car, fancier clothing and numerous other things that will all rust and rot away, things that we all know will not be able to be taken with us after we die. Yet there is One who gives a ticket to what the soul should be searching for. One who gives a free gift of Salvation, eternal peace and comfort of being with and serving Him who created us. As the clouds darken on the horizon, as things are nearly complete, the time is at hand for those who dwell on this earth to make a final decision, will you accept Jesus as your Savior, will you realize your sin, accept godly repentance, having a truly repentant heart and believe into Christ? God is giving you a one-way first class ticket to escape the judgment that is due to you and the world. Whether you die prior to His judgment on the world or you die during His judgment on the world, you will be eternally judged AS AN INDIVIDUAL (Yes YOU!!!) and the judgment that He casts against you will be just. After all Jesus stands there ready to accept even you, as He did to all of us who have accepted Him as our Savior. If you are still reading this, it is not too late.

"Thanks be to God for His indescribable gift." 2nd Corinthians 9:15

"Jehovah is my strength and my shield; my heart has trusted in Him, and I have been helped; therefore my heart greatly rejoices, and with my song I will praise Him." Psalms 28:7

"Nor is there salvation in any other, for there is no other name under Heaven given among men that is required for us to be saved " Acts 4:12

... "testifying both to Jews, and also to Greeks, repentance toward God and faith toward our Lord Jesus Christ." Acts 20:21

"Behold, I stand at the door and knock. If anyone hears My voice and opens the door, I will come in to him and dine with him, and he with Me." Revelation 3:20

"Seek Jehovah while He may be found; call upon Him while He is near." Isaiah 55:6

"The Lord is not slow concerning His promise, as some count slowness, but is longsuffering toward us, not purposing that any should perish but that all should come to repentance." 2nd Peter 3:9

"Do I delight with pleasure in the death of the wicked? says the Lord Jehovah, and not that he should turn back from his ways and live?" Ezekiel 18:23

... "who desires all men to be saved and to come to a full true knowledge of the truth." 1st Timothy 2:4

"He who is unjust, let him be unjust still; he who is filthy, let him be filthy still; he who is righteous, let him be righteous still; he who is holy, let him be holy still. And behold, I am coming quickly, and My reward is with Me, to give to every one according to what his work shall be. I am the Alpha and the Omega, the Beginning and the Ending, the First and the Last. Blessed are those who do His commandments, that they may have the right to the Tree of Life, and may enter through the gates into the city. But outside are dogs and sorcerers and prostitutes and murderers and idolaters, and whoever loves and produces a lie. I, Jesus, have sent My angel to testify these things to you, to the churches. I am the Root and the Offspring of David, the Bright and Morning Star. And the Spirit and the bride say, Come. And let him who hears say, Come. And let him who thirsts come. Whoever desires, let him take of the Water of Life freely." Revelation of Jesus Christ 22:11-17

Amen!

Will you (or can you?) Wait any Longer?

How long before Jesus comes and takes those who are His out of the world? How long before the world enters the time of Jacob's trouble and receives judgment for man's rejection of the Most High?

For those of you who have been paying attention and even for those of you who don't, there is a lot going on in the world today. The global economy is simply a ruse that is ready to tumble into oblivion. The United States is aligning itself with Iran and other Muslim interests against Israel. China is quickly becoming a superpower, with their money-making scam of an economy and repressive regime. Technology has absolutely exploded and continues to be developed at break-neck speeds. This technology ushers in some very evil gene manipulation (DNA/RNA), as well as very Orwellian goods that take away the anonymous activities of individuals. There are wars and rumors of wars, and have been for many years now.

"And you will hear of wars and rumors of wars. See that you are not troubled; for all these things must come to pass, but the end is not yet." Matthew 24:6

There are major earthquakes happening now and then, here and there. Record temperatures, droughts, fires, floods and other unusual weather is happening in many places.

"And there will be earthquakes in various places, and there will be famines and troubles. These are the beginnings of travail." Mark 13:8b

Yet should you concern yourself with any of these things?

If you are not a true Believer, if you have not accepted Jesus Christ as your Savior, through repentance and faith, then you should be very concerned.

"Then Peter said to them, Repent, and let every one of you be immersed in the name of Jesus Christ to the remission of sins; and you shall receive the gift of the Holy Spirit. For the promise is to you and to your children, and to all who are afar off, as many as the Lord our God will call." Acts 2:38-39

What will you give in exchange for your soul?

"Or what will a man give in exchange for his soul?" Mark 8:37

What holds you back from making that commitment to Christ, for accepting Jesus? Do you seriously want to try and wait until the 'tribulation' begins and then take and seek Him? What if it is too late for you at that point? Likely it will be too late for you.

"The coming of the lawless one is according to the working of Satan, with all power, signs, and lying wonders, and with all unrighteous deception among those who are perishing, because they did not receive the love of the truth, that they might be saved. And for this reason God will send them strong delusion, that they should believe the lie, that they all may be judged who did not believe the truth but had pleasure in unrighteousness." 2nd Thessalonians 2:9-12

Can YOU, who will individually stand before Christ, wait any longer?

"So then each of us shall give account concerning himself to God." Romans 14:12

Is today the day that you make your decision (or not)?

"For He says: In an acceptable time I have heard you, and in a day of salvation I have helped you. Behold, now is the accepted time; behold, now is the day of salvation." 2nd Corinthians 6:2

Dear reader, the time is coming much sooner than later. Even so, you do not know when your last breath will be as an individual.

... *"whereas you do not know what will be tomorrow. For what is your life? It is even a vapor that appears for a little time and then vanishes away."* Jacob 4:14

As I write this, for those who may be aware, it is becoming dangerous to even state online that 'the global economy is…ready to tumble into oblivion'. The thought police in America have determined that even such a simple statement or belief is enough to suspect that a person may be a lone wolf or a domestic terrorist. I write (or try to) behind a wall anonymously. I'm confident that those in power could easily garner my name from this website, yet I put my trust in Him, in His protection. He is my strength and my shield. (Psalms 28:7a) What happens when things really become serious, what happens when the economy finally does come crashing down? *(Revelation 6:6)* What happens when a one-world government finally takes power? *(Revelation chapters 13 & 17, Daniel 2, etc.)* What happens when there is a one global currency? *(Revelation 13)* When the antichrist is seated? *(2nd Thessalonians 2:4)*

What happens when finding a copy of the Bible is nearly impossible?

"Behold, the days are coming, declares the Lord Jehovah, that I will send a famine into the land, not a famine for bread, nor a thirst for water, but rather a famine for hearing the Words of Jehovah." Amos 8:11

What happens when you are beheaded for your faith in Christ? *(Revelation 20:4)* This under the assumption that it isn't too late for you INDIVIDUALLY to accept Jesus Christ as your Savior.

Why do I speak like this? I speak like this because it is my belief that there are individuals out there who will read such an article and God might stir their conscience, that their soul might repent and through faith that they (perhaps you?) might accept Jesus Christ as their Savior…before it is too late. I've come to realize that there seems to be a group of people in the world, right now, who have a sense of dread coming upon them. The Holy Spirit seems to be tugging at their souls, warning them ever so silently that THE TIME IS NOW! These people believe in God, they believe in Jesus, His Son, they know a bit about having to be Saved, but often not the details. These people believe that the world is going to be judged, they are uncertain whether or not there will be a Rapture. They know that there will be a mark of the beast, they have heard of a one-world currency. These are those who have listened to some of the articles, written both by Believers and also those who see the proofs of what is about to happen taking place in legislation and daily news. These are those who have attended church services in their past, perhaps even currently. Often these individuals are confused and hold many doctrines from many different beliefs. Yet these are ALSO those who will not be rescued out of the world prior to these events taking place. These are the lost, they are doomed, they are destined for Hell, they are without Christ, they do not belong to God. They have rejected their Creator and have refused to submit to Christ in repentance and faith.

These are those who hold onto the world. They have their reasons, they have their excuses, they know in their hearts that they must yield to Christ but for various reasons they refuse. If you dear reader are one of these people I urge you to stop right now, drop what you are doing and consider your ways. If God has been pricking your heart, if you feel this sense of dread, now is the time. Now is the time dear reader that you realize that you are a sinner, you are deserving of hell. You realize that there is nothing that you can do (works) to save yourself, you are lost, it is hopeless, you are guilty. Yet now is also the time to realize that Jesus, God's Son, died on the cross for your sins. Yes God sent Jesus to pay the penalty for your sins that you might be forgiven and have life abundantly through Christ.

… "for all have sinned and fall short of the glory of God…" Romans 3:23

"For the wages of sin is death, but the gift of God is eternal life in Christ Jesus our Lord." Romans 6:23

"For by grace you are saved through faith; and that not of yourselves, it is the gift of God; not of works, that no one should boast." Ephesians 2:8-9

"Jesus said to him, I am the Way, the Truth, and the Life. No one comes to the Father except through Me." John 14:6

"For ever since the creation of the world the unseen things of Him are clearly perceived, being understood by the things that are made, even His eternal power and Godhead, so that they are without excuse, because, although they know God, they do not glorify Him as God, nor are thankful, but become vain in their reasonings, and their stupid hearts are darkened." Romans 1:20-21

"For God so loved the world that He gave His only begotten Son, that everyone believing into Him should not perish but have eternal life." John 3:16

... "who Himself bore our sins in His own body on the tree, that we, having died to sins, might live unto righteousness; by whose stripes you were healed." 1st Peter 2:24

"For Christ also suffered for sins once for all, the just for the unjust, that He might bring us to God, being put to death in the flesh but made alive by the Spirit..." 1st Peter 3:18

... "who was delivered up because of our trespasses, and was raised for our justification." Romans 4:25

"...I (Jesus) have come that they may have life, and that they may have it more abundantly." John 10:10b

God gave you a free gift, but you must yield to Him, you must accept it. I can only hope that you will ponder your paths before it is too late and will make the right decision. Do not put it off any longer. Yet understand that accepting Christ as your Savior is not confusing, it is simple, but it does take a willing and repentance heart and faith.

"For the ways of man are before the eyes of Jehovah, and He ponders all his tracks. His own iniquities shall capture the wicked, and he shall be held with the cords of his sin. He shall die without instruction, and in the greatness of his folly he shall go astray." Proverbs 5:21-23

"But I fear, lest somehow, as the serpent deceived Eve by his craftiness, so your minds may be corrupted from the simplicity that is in Christ." 2nd Corinthians 11:3

"For godly sorrow produces repentance leading to salvation, not to be regretted; but the sorrow of the world produces death." 2nd Corinthians 7:10

"The sacrifices of God are a broken spirit; a broken and a contrite heart, O God, You will not despise." Psalms 51:17

Amen!

What is Wisdom?

"The fear of Jehovah is the beginning of wisdom; and the knowledge of the Holy One is understanding." Proverbs 9:10

Having done an article on fear, it only seemed logical to continue in that direction by completing a word study on wisdom. We'll begin by using an old copy of Webster's University Dictionary.

wisdom n.

1.) The quality of being wise; the faculty of making the best use of knowledge; a combination of discernment, judgment, sagacity, and similar powers; understanding

2.) Human learning; erudition; knowledge of arts and sciences; scientific or practical truth.

3.) Quickness of intellect; readiness of apprehension; dexterity in execution; as the wisdom of Bezaleel and Aholiab. – Ex. xxxi. 3,6

4.) Natural instinct and sagacity.

5.) In Scripture, right judgment concerning religious and moral truth; true religion; godliness; piety; the knowledge and fear of God, and sincere and uniform obedience to His commands.

Looking over the definitions it is obvious that the first and fifth most closely represent the type of wisdom described in relation to the fear of God in the Holy Scriptures. Let's take a moment and go over definition three.

"And Jehovah spoke to Moses, saying: Observe that I have called by name Bezalel the son of Uri, the son of Hur, of the tribe of Judah; and I have filled him with the Spirit of God, in wisdom, in understanding, in knowledge, and in all manner of workmanship, to devise designs, to work in gold, in silver, in bronze, in cutting stones to finish them, in carving wood, and to work in all manner of workmanship. And I, behold I, have appointed with him Aholiab the son of Ahisamach, of the tribe of Dan; and I have given wisdom into the hearts of all the wise-hearted, that they may produce all that I have commanded you: the tent of meeting, the ark of the Testimony and the mercy seat that is on it, and all the implements of the tent; the table and its utensils, the pure gold lampstand with all its utensils, the altar of incense, the altar of burnt offering with all its utensils, and the laver and its base; the woven garments, the holy garments for Aaron the priest and the garments of his sons, to serve as priests, and the anointing oil and spiced

incense for the holy place. According to all that I have commanded you they shall do." Exodus 31:1-11

This type of wisdom, though in the above context given by God, is a type of wisdom that men can gain through training, experience and persevering in a certain field. The type of wisdom mentioned in the second definition is more widespread and common.

This type of wisdom is the world's wisdom. We all have certain skills, understanding, training, education, experience in many things that we do each and every day. For those who drive it is experience that helps prevent you from getting into an accident. For those who are careless and don't make sure it is clear before they pull out of a parking lot unto a street, it is often experience from accidents, fines, additional insurance costs and time without a vehicle that creates wisdom.

Young college kids often go off and party hard at college. Some become wise against doing such things through seeing what happens when responsibilities are neglected and consequences happen from not being prepared for the next days studies, others get pregnant out of wedlock, some die, some get arrested, some simply get smart, get wisdom and stop hanging out with those who participate in such debauchery.

There are many other examples that could be given, but each of us with experience and knowledge are wise of some of the world's things. Yet there are all of these experts out there, everywhere if you really look, these are the ones that are considered wise in the world's eyes.

Those who supposedly have all of this wisdom in this world, what sort of things have they purported to us?

The wise tell us that there is climate change, such as Obama's new directives or even the pope's. They tell us that this climate change is caused by man and that man needs to consume less. If you dig into it the real think tanks behind the scenes, those who are the social-psychopathic-engineers of societies, men (and occasionally women) whom most don't even know exist, they also have plans to lower the number of people living on the earth. They claim to know that the earth is being destroyed by man and they are the ones with the wisdom (and positions of power) to do something about it. What these wise ones are, are liars!

Should they have the true wisdom, the wisdom that comes through learning the Holy Scriptures, the wisdom that directs one's soul to their Creator and Salvation into His Son, the wisdom that makes a man's heart repent into dust and ashes before the one and only holy God, then they would also know this:

"But the day of the Lord will come as a thief in the night, in which the heavens will pass away with a loud noise, and the elements will be dissolved with intense burning; both the earth and the works that are in it will be burned up." 2nd Peter 3:10

"And the fourth angel poured out his bowl onto the sun, and it was given to him to scorch men with fire. And men were scorched with great heat, and they blasphemed the name of God who has authority over these plagues; and they did not repent to give Him glory." Revelation 16:8-9

"So I looked, and behold, a pale green horse. And the name of him who sat on it was Death, and Hades followed behind him. And authority was given to them over a fourth of the earth, to kill with sword, with hunger, with death, and by the beasts of the earth." Revelation 6:8

The wise tell us that it is alright to abort babies in the womb. Those who help rip out babies and suck them out with the vacuums, as those poor souls of the yet to breath are sucked into hell, are educated in wisdom, they are doctors, attorneys and the Supreme Court of the United States that does not see the rights of those who have no voice. These people claim to be wise, they purport wisdom to us, they tell us when the fertilized egg supposedly actually becomes a life. Yet what do they know? Who do they think they are? The Most High God gives us wisdom regarding when a soul is alive.

"Where were you when I laid the foundations of the earth? Declare, if you have become acquainted with understanding." Job 38:4

"My frame was not hidden from You when I was made in secret, and skillfully wrought in the lowest parts of the earth." Psalms 139:15

"Before I formed you in the belly I knew you; and before you came forth out of the womb I consecrated you, and I ordained you a prophet to the nations." Jeremiah 1:5

The wise declare to us that we have evolved and that the earth is billions of years old. They search the galaxies ENDLESSLY trying to find earth like planets, not out of simple curiosity, which would not necessarily be wrong, but out of spite, seeking out a planet that appears to be habitable, earthlike, so that they can proclaim to have evidence (of which they have none) about evolution. The wise tell us that dinosaurs went extinct because of an asteroid, they proclaim the ages of rocks, fossils, everything. Even when evidence is found that is contrary they concoct another theory to further propound their supposed educated wisdom. They are fools, declaring that God is a liar. Proclaiming that the works that they see with their eyes, study with their hands were not done by Him who is the Author of Salvation.

Little do these people know that true wisdom, the wisdom that God gives to ALL creation, should they choose to accept it, states the truth in the matter.

"In the beginning God created the heavens and the earth." Genesis 1:1

"For the wrath of God is revealed from Heaven against all ungodliness and unrighteousness of men, who suppress the truth in unrighteousness, because what may be known of God is clearly recognized by them, for God has revealed it to them. For ever

since the creation of the world the unseen things of Him are clearly perceived, being understood by the things that are made, even His eternal power and Godhead, so that they are without excuse, because, although they know God, they do not glorify Him as God, nor are thankful, but become vain in their reasonings, and their stupid hearts are darkened. Professing to be wise, they become foolish, and change the glory of the incorruptible God into an image made like corruptible man, and birds and four-footed animals and creeping things. Therefore God also gives them up to uncleanness, in the lusts of their hearts, to dishonor their bodies among themselves, who change the truth of God into the lie, and fear and serve the created things more than the Creator, who is blessed forever. Amen." Romans 1:18-25

"The fool has said in his heart, There is no God! They are corrupt; they have done abominable works, there is no one who does good." Psalms 14:1

Those with wisdom tell of many different ways to get to Heaven or they speak of an afterlife with rewards that can be obtained through obedience to some sort of vain repetitious act or work. These religious leaders of all sorts direct men on paths, yet they all have a common path. Though the paths seem different there is really only two, one is to Life, the other to death. There once again these people, some such as pope Francis who is the leader of over a billion Catholics, speak things which are seen as wise, but their wisdom goes down to the gates of Hell. These wise leaders refuse to take heed to what the bible states about Salvation, about how a man finds his way Home. They instead are loved by men, telling lies to all who listen to them. God has told man how to find Him, man often seeks to find another way than the Way laid out in the Holy Scriptures.

"Enter by the narrow gate; for wide is the gate and broad is the way that leads to destruction, and there are many entering in through it. Because narrow is the gate and distressing is the way which leads unto life, and there are few who find it." Matthew 7:13-14

"Let them alone. They are blind leaders of the blind. And if the blind leads the blind, both will fall into the ditch." Matthew 15:14

"Jesus said to him, I am the Way, the Truth, and the Life. No one comes to the Father except through Me." John 14:6

Example after example could be given of the world's wisdom. Examples could be given in so-called gay marriage, child-rearing practices, education concepts, life's focuses, etc.. The Bible gives definitions of wisdom also, some of what we will look at.

"Now, my son, may Jehovah be with you; and may you prosper, and build the house of Jehovah your God, as He has spoken concerning you. Only may Jehovah give you wisdom and understanding, and give you charge concerning Israel, to keep the Law of Jehovah your God." 1st Chronicles 22:11-12

Here David is talking to his son Solomon. Note the reasons that David asks for wisdom and understanding: so that he can rule Israel AND keep the Law of Jehovah his God.

"With Him are wisdom and strength, He has counsel and understanding." Job 12:13

God alone is wise, men should seek after his counsel.

"No mention shall be made of coral or crystal, for the acquiring of wisdom is above precious stones." Job 28:18

"From where then does wisdom come? And where is the place of understanding? It is hidden from the eyes of all living, and concealed from the birds of the heavens. Abaddon and Death say, We have heard a report of it with our ears. God understands its way, and He knows its place. For He looks to the ends of the earth, and sees under the whole heavens, to appoint a weight for the wind, and mete out the waters by measure. When He made a decree for the rain, and a path for the thunderbolt, then He saw and declared it; He prepared it, yea, He searched it out. And to man He said, Behold, the fear of the Lord, that is wisdom, and to depart from evil is understanding." Job 28:20-28

"The mouth of the righteous speaks wisdom, and his tongue talks of justice." Psalms 37:30

"The fear of Jehovah is the beginning of wisdom; a good understanding have all those who do His commandments. His praise stands eternally." Psalms 111:10

Man's wisdom is just that, man's. Unless that wisdom is from God, no matter how wise a man might appear to be, no matter how many letters are by his name or his title, no matter the amount of supposed facts that are uttered, that wisdom is worthless. Who do you trust with your eternity? Do you trust man's wisdom or do you trust God? Can you not see the storm clouds on the horizon, do you not worry that it is nearly to late? The time is now to consider and consider with truth and godly wisdom, because through all of this the love of God still abounds, His free gift is still available to all of mankind. Will you consider?

"Then Simon Peter answered Him, Lord, to whom shall we go? You have the Words of eternal life." John 6:68

"But without faith it is impossible to please Him, for he who comes to God must believe that He is, and that He is a rewarder of those who diligently seek Him." Hebrews 11:6

"And you shall seek Me and find Me, when you search for Me with all your heart." Jeremiah 29:13

... *"let it be known to you all, and to all the people of Israel, that in the name of Jesus Christ of Nazareth, whom you crucified, whom God raised from the dead, in Him this man stands here before you whole. This is the Stone which was counted as nothing by you builders, which has become the Head of the Corner. Nor is there salvation in any other, for there is no other name under Heaven given among men that is required for us to be saved." Acts 4:10-12*

Amen!

Separated Unto God

"What shall we say then? Shall we continue in sin that grace may abound? Let it not be! How shall we who died to sin live any longer in it? Or do you not know that as many of us as were immersed into Christ Jesus were immersed into His death? Therefore we were buried with Him through immersion into death, that just as Christ was raised from the dead by the glory of the Father, even so we also should walk in newness of life. For if we have been planted together in the likeness of His death, certainly we also shall be in resurrection, knowing this, that our old man was crucified with Him, that the body of sin might be nullified, that we should no longer serve sin. For he who has died has been justified from sin. Now if we died with Christ, we believe that we shall also live with Him, knowing that Christ, having been raised from the dead, dies no more. Death no longer has dominion over Him. For the death that He died, He died to sin once for all; but the life that He lives, He lives unto God. Likewise you also, reckon yourselves to be dead indeed to sin, but alive to God in Christ Jesus our Lord. Therefore do not let sin reign in your mortal body, that you should obey it in its lusts. And do not present your members as instruments of unrighteousness to sin, but present yourselves to God as being alive from the dead, and your members as instruments of righteousness to God. For sin shall not have dominion over you, for you are not under Law but under grace. What then? Shall we sin because we are not under Law but under grace? Let it not be! Do you not know that to whom you present yourselves slaves to obey, you are that one's slaves whom you obey, whether of sin unto death, or of obedience unto righteousness? But God be thanked that though you were slaves of sin, yet you obeyed from the heart that form of doctrine which was delivered to you. And having been set free from sin, you became slaves to righteousness. I speak in human terms because of the weakness of your flesh. For just as you presented your members as slaves to uncleanness, and to iniquity unto iniquity, so now present your members as slaves to righteousness unto sanctification. For when you were slaves to sin, you were free in regard to righteousness. What fruit did you have then in the things of which you are now ashamed? For the end of those things is death. But now having been set free from sin, and having become slaves to God, you have your fruit unto sanctification, and the end, eternal life. For the wages of sin is death, but the gift of God is eternal life in Christ Jesus our Lord." Romans 6

What does being a Christian entail? What are the attributes of a Christian? What are God's expectations? We are going to take a look at holiness in relation to our behavior towards God and His expectation of those whom are in Christ. We shall see if the world's definition of Christian matches up with God's definition. Let's begin by researching what the word holy means.

Holy (Adjective)

According to *Webster's University Dictionary Unabridged*, 1942

1.) Hallowed; consecrated or set apart to a sacred use; having a sacred character or associations; as, the holy temple; holy vessels; holy words

2.) Free from sin, pure in heart, immaculate in moral character; perfect in a moral sense: exhibiting holiness; righteous; as, a holy man; holy zeal

Here we can see in both definitions characteristics of a true Believer in Christ. In the first, a Believer is set apart unto God through Jesus Christ. In the second, we can see what being holy means in regards to our behavior, actions, thoughts, desires, etc. Now consider this in retrospect to what the world considers to be Christianity.

How many people sitting in a Sunday church service week after week can not wait to 'fellowship' afterwards with a lunch at a local restaurant? Where is their zeal for God or the desire to learn of His Word, growing in Christ. These people spend more time dining for one meal then they will talking about, listening to or reading His Word for the remainder of the week.

How many people even read the bible daily? Weekly? Monthly? How many of those who claim to be Christians have even read the entire Holy Scriptures or are diligently seeking to do so? Yet, how many spend 2, 3, 4 or even 5 or more hours EACH and EVERY day watching television!

"For where your treasure is, there your heart will be also." Matthew 6:21

How many Believers aspire to be pleasing towards God and work towards purifying themselves as He is pure?

"Beloved, now we are children of God; and it has not yet been revealed what we shall be, but we know that when He is revealed, we shall be like Him, for we shall see Him as He is. And everyone who has this hope in Him purifies himself, just as He is pure." 1st John 3:2-3

Really how many of those who call themselves Christians even exhibit fruits of being a Christian? How much different are the mass majority of these supposed christians than that of the rest of the world? With the exception of attending church, a bible study or being involved in some sort of supposed ministry, what is the difference compared to those who claim nothing of the sort and simply live their lives, lost and without Christ?

"Beware of false prophets, who come to you in sheep's clothing, but inwardly they are ravenous wolves. You will know them from their fruits. Do men gather grapes from thornbushes or figs from thistles? Even so, every good tree produces excellent fruit, but a corrupt tree produces evil fruit. A good tree is not able to produce evil fruit, nor is a corrupt tree able to produce excellent fruit. Every tree that does not produce excellent fruit is cut down and thrown into the fire. Therefore from their fruits you will know them." Matthew 7:15-20

How about you, dear reader, are you sure that you are Saved? Are you being separated unto God, are you becoming holy, is your conduct becoming more and more pure, are you abstaining from sin, are you dying to self? What are the attributes laid out in God's Word of a Christian?

"For who has known the mind of the Lord that he may instruct Him? But we have the mind of Christ." 1st Corinthians 2:16

"Therefore gird up the loins of your mind, be sober, and rest your hope fully upon the grace that is to be brought to you at the revelation of Jesus Christ; as obedient children, not conforming yourselves to the former lusts in your ignorance; but as He who called you is holy, you also become holy in all conduct, because it is written, Be holy, because I am holy." 1st Peter 1:13-16

"For the love of Christ holds us, because we judge thus: that if One died for all, then all died; and He died for all, that those who live should no longer live unto themselves, but unto Him who died for them and rose again. Therefore, from now on, we regard no one according to the flesh. Even though we have known Christ according to the flesh, yet now we know Him thus no longer. Therefore, if anyone is in Christ, he is a new creation; the old things have passed away; behold, all things have become new." 2nd Corinthians 5:14-15

"I have been crucified with Christ; it is no longer I who live, but Christ lives in me; and the life which I now live in the flesh I live by the faith of the Son of God, who loved me and gave Himself for me." Galatians 2:20

As Believers in Christ we are to become holy as He is holy. We are servants of God, no longer self-seeking, but rather servants of the Most High God.

"For he who is called in the Lord while a slave is the Lord's freedman. Likewise he who is called while free is Christ's slave." 1st Corinthians 7:22

We need to become more and more separated from the world in our Christian lives, those of us who are actually in Christ. However, for those who are unsure or those who simply know that they are not truly born-again Christians, but have simply been going through the motions.

Do you not see that the time is at hand, that it is near, at the doors?

"For He says: In an acceptable time I have heard you, and in a day of salvation I have helped you. Behold, now is the accepted time; behold, now is the day of salvation." 2nd Corinthians 6:2

Time is nearly out, will you answer His call?

"And to the angel of the church of the Laodiceans write, These things says the Amen, the Faithful and True Witness, the Beginning of the creation of God: I know your works, that you are neither cold nor hot. I would that you were cold or hot. So then, because you are

lukewarm, and neither cold nor hot, I will vomit you out of My mouth. Because you say, I am rich, have become wealthy, and have need of nothing; and do not know that you are wretched and miserable and poor and blind and naked; I counsel you to buy from Me gold refined in the fire, that you may be rich; and white garments, that you may be clothed, that the shame of your nakedness may not be revealed; and anoint your eyes with eye salve, that you may see. As many as I love, I rebuke and chasten. Therefore be zealous and repent. Behold, I stand at the door and knock. If anyone hears My voice and opens the door, I will come in to him and dine with him, and he with Me. To him who overcomes I will grant to sit with Me on My throne, as I also overcame and sat down with My Father on His throne. He who has an ear, let him hear what the Spirit says to the churches." Revelation of Jesus Christ 3:14-22

"He who is unjust, let him be unjust still; he who is filthy, let him be filthy still; he who is righteous, let him be righteous still; he who is holy, let him be holy still." Revelation of Jesus Christ 22:11

If Jesus is knocking on the door of your heart, you best answer it while you still can.

Amen!

Heaven or Hell?

If I were to take a walk down main street and asked 100 passers-by how many of them believed in Heaven, I do believe I would get an overwhelming majority. While there would be some that would scoff at such an idea, the vast masses of people believe in Heaven.

Now if I were to take the same walk and ask 100 passers-by how many of them believe in Hell, I believe I would get an entirely different response. Here I would probably dare say that I would be closer to 50%, perhaps even only a third of people believing in Hell. For the sake of argument, let's assume 50%.

If I posed a second question to these same people, how do you think they would respond?

How would you respond?

If I were to ask these people who believe in Heaven whether or not they were going there, I would assume nearly all of them, but not all of them, would tell me that they would go there or think they would go there when they died. Likewise if I were to ask these same people that believe in Hell whether or not they would go there, I would assume most would say no, probably a few would say that they hoped not.

Now the problem herein lies with this. If I were to ask those who believe they were going to Heaven if they believed in a Hell, I believe that it would quickly dive down to the 50% ratio. Now if I were to ask these same people how I would get to Heaven, assuming 85 out of 100 believed in Heaven, I would probably get at least 50 different answers.

How many different answers do you think I would get out of the following questions?

1.) How do you get to Heaven?

2.) What type of people/who goes to Hell?

3.) How many different ways are there to get to Heaven?

4.) What religions would be excluded from the Pearly Gates?

5.) Is Hell eternal?

From experience, I would get several, several different answers. However it is possible to know PRECIOUSLY the answer to ALL of these questions. How? Through God's Word, the bible, the Holy Scriptures.
Is not Heaven where God lives? Would He not be the Authority to give us the map to get there? Who created Heaven? God, right? The only sensible way to get these answers, THAT WILL MATTER TO EACH PERSON, is through the bible. Let's take a look...

How do you get to Heaven?

In order to get to Heaven, an individual must go before God in repentance and believe into Jesus Christ as their Lord and Savior, plainly put THERE IS NO OTHER WAY.

A.) Repentance

"Repent therefore and be converted, that your sins may be blotted out, so that times of refreshing may come from the presence of the Lord..." Acts 3:19

"Truly, these times of ignorance God overlooked, but now commands all men everywhere to repent..." Acts 17:30

"I tell you, no; but unless you repent you will all likewise perish." Luke 13:3

B.) Believing that Jesus was God in the flesh, died on the cross for our sins and rose from the dead.

... "that if you confess with your mouth the Lord Jesus and believe in your heart that God has raised Him from the dead, you will be saved. For with the heart one believes unto righteousness, and with the mouth confession is made unto salvation." Romans 10:9-10

"For I delivered to you first of all that which I also received: that Christ died for our sins according to the Scriptures, and that He was buried, and that He was raised the third day according to the Scriptures" 1st Corinthians 15:3-4

"Now it was not written for his sake alone, that it was accounted to him, but also for us, to whom it shall be accounted, believing in Him who raised up Jesus our Lord from the dead, who was delivered up because of our trespasses, and was raised for our justification." Romans 4:23-25

C.) Accepting Jesus as your Savior

"For everyone, whoever calls on the name of the Lord shall be saved." Romans 10:13

"For God so loved the world that He gave His only begotten Son, that everyone believing into Him should not perish but have eternal life." John 3:16

"In the beginning was the Word, and the Word was with God, and the Word was God." John 1:1

Here in lies one of the BIGGEST misconceptions and problems in our societies. Everyone thinks they are going to Heaven, but really the vast majority are wrong. In my opinion this is one of the biggest, if not biggest deception that Satan has placed upon the earth. Instead of an individual finding out the truth and simply deciding for themselves of whether or not to accept Jesus as their Savior, following the true method laid out in the bible verses above, the deception is that the person believes they are saved, continues on with their life, dies and goes to Hell.

"Not everyone who says to Me, Lord, Lord, will enter the kingdom of Heaven, but he who does the will of My Father in Heaven. Many will say to Me in that day, Lord, Lord, have we not prophesied in Your name, cast out demons in Your name, and done many works of power in Your name? And then I will declare to them, I never knew you; depart from Me, you who work out lawlessness!" Matthew 7:21-23

What type of people/who goes to hell?

Many people will proclaim that those who are the most evil, those who do the worst crimes or those who simply follow satanism are the ones who end up in Hell, however this could not be further from the truth.

"Behold, I was brought forth in iniquity, and in sin did my mother conceive me." Psalms 51:5

... " for all have sinned and fall short of the glory of God..." Romans 3:23

"For the wages of sin is death, but the gift of God is eternal life in Christ Jesus our Lord." Romans 6:23

The truth is that EVERYONE has sinned and ALL are doomed to Hell UNLESS that individual repents and accepts Jesus Christ as their Savior. Too many times people assume that the 'good' people would have a place in Heaven. Getting to Heaven is NOT works based, no matter how much good someone would appear to do, unless they have become rectified with their Creator, they will go to Hell, no if's, and's or but's.

So yes, that old woman who knitted hats for every newborn baby in the local hospital, the elderly man who donated much money to the local city and provided a food pantry and housing for the poor and desolate will likewise go to Hell when he dies. No matter how much good an individual does or appears to do, it makes NO DIFFERENCE. Unless that individual repents and believes into Jesus, there is NO HOPE, NO CHANCE. Hell is the future destination for that person.

How many different ways are there to get to Heaven?

As addressed above, there is only ONE WAY.

"Jesus said to him, I am the Way, the Truth, and the Life. No one comes to the Father except through Me." John 14:6

What religions would be excluded from the Pearly Gates?

Rather the question would be which religions would go to Heaven. Herein is a tough question with a difficult answer for most to bear, nonetheless the truth shall be told.

Our societies are pluck full of churches on many corners of our cities around the globe. The United States of America has many different kinds of churches, whereas if one traveled to the European Union you would find predominately Roman Catholic churches. The deception is two-sided. Clearly, and not the purpose of this article (See either of the following books: *The Two Babylons*, Hislop; *A Woman Rides the Beast*, Hunt) the Roman Catholic church is a gigantic false religion. However, the vast majority (and I mean vast) of the churches on the corners of our cities in the USA are also false. They are the opposite sides of the same coin or rather just a newer form of deception that never had but an inkling of truth from their inception.

There is a true Church and that is the true body of Jesus Christ.

"Now you are the body of Christ, and members individually." 1st Corinthians 12:27

This church might go by different names, could be called a Baptist Church, a Bible Church or it might be a group of people meeting in someone's home with no name.

"For where two or three are gathered together in My name, I am there in the midst of them." Matthew 18:20

Would you rather know the truth now, research, pray, read the Holy Scriptures to see whether or not these things are so OR stand before God as He rightfully judges you and sends you to Hell for eternity? The choice is yours.

Is Hell eternal?

Yes Hell is eternal, in fact it will eventually be cast into the Lake of Fire where those souls who were disobedient to God, those who refused to repent of their sins, those who would not truly believe in Christ will go. There they will spend eternity.

"And the devil, who led them astray, was cast into the Lake of Fire and brimstone where the beast and the false prophet are. And they will be tormented day and night forever and ever." Revelation 20:10

"And the sea gave up the dead who were in it, and Death and Hades delivered up the dead who were in them. And they were judged, each one, according to their works. And Death and Hades were cast into the Lake of Fire. This is the second death. And anyone not found written in the Book of Life was cast into the Lake of Fire." Revelation 20:13-15

"And many of those sleeping in the earth's dust shall awake, some to everlasting life, and some to reproach and everlasting abhorrence." Daniel 12:2

Summary:

Dear Reader,

These things may appear harsh, but how harsh would it be for a Christian to not warn you and present you with the truth? How harsh would it be for you to go through life, die and stand before your Creator, without the truth being presented to you. These are not my truths, but the Truth that is found only in the Holy Scriptures. This is God's Truth and He gave us His Son to provide an escape from our judgment that is just and due to everyone.

"For God so loved the world that He gave His only begotten Son, that everyone believing into Him should not perish but have eternal life." John 3:16

Unfortunately men have manipulated God's Word, for MANY years and continue to do so.

"For the time will come when they will not endure sound doctrine, but according to their own lusts, desiring to hear pleasant things, they will heap up for themselves teachers; and they will turn their ears away from the truth, and be turned aside to myths." 2nd Timothy 4:3-4

Recall though that God is merciful. Will you come before Him in repentance and accept Jesus Christ as your Savior before it is too late? Eventually, perhaps soon, perhaps today or even at this very moment, time will run out.

Amen!

Who Will Remember You? – Vanity

"For there is a man whose labor is in wisdom, and in knowledge, and with success; yet he shall leave it as inheritance to a man who has not labored in it. This also is vanity and a great evil." Ecclesiastes 2:21

"For the living know that they shall die; but the dead do not know anything, nor do they have any more a reward; for the memory of them is forgotten. Also their love, and their hatred, and their envy, have now perished; nor do they ever any longer have a part in anything that is done under the sun." Ecclesiastes 9:5-6

The American Dream, for many it has become the American Nightmare in the past several years. The idea is simple.

After high school, go to college or get a good hard-working American job. Either way, once your career choice is established, meet the woman of your dreams, buy a house, have a family. From there take vacations to great places throughout your life, all while saving for retirement. Retire at a decently 'young' age and enjoy your later years without having to worry about money. Die.

While the exact definition of the American dream may vary a bit, none of the versions include the last word, die. There is a reality behind it, nobody likes to think about it, but we all know that eventually death will come to find us. We will all die. So what has happened in the past several decades in America to help alleviate this uncomfortable truth?

The churches in America have grown in unison with the 'trust us' mentality. There are different variations used in their methodology. Some churches simply use a repeat-after-me prayer and then 'resolve' the problem, others have a works based methodology. Still others simply convince their converts to not be worried about dying, things will work out in the end. Death, dying, the dead, this is something that man seeks to be comforted over.

Sometimes this comforting is not even about oneself at the moment, at times it is in regarding a loved one. When a parent, a spouse, a child, a loved friend or family member or in many cases for many people, a celebrity dies, what does everyone proclaim? The proclamations are generally that the person is now 'in a better place' or 'they are in heaven'. People are comforted that they are now 'looking down on them'. What if there was such a great evil purported, what if a grand scheme that was SO HORRIBLE had taken place?

The American Dream, it now includes the fact that one not only has what they desire BUT that they also have eternal rest. The real question is this, does it really include your eternal soul? To further the deception, for whom does one really put their trust in when it comes to God's eternal Word?

The world has churches with stages, fancy lighting, coffee shops or the other extreme–the conservative Baptist church on the corner that proclaims 'just repeat after me' or easy-believerism. God has laid out in His Word how man can be Saved.

In the past several years the American Dream has turned into a nightmare for many. Their mortgage is underwater, they are cash strapped, they have lost their homes, too much debt, not enough decent paying jobs, etc. Yet for those whom have in the past and still do continue to live the American Dream, what has become of them, what will become of those once they die?

Even with all of the luxuries in the world, the comforts, delectable food, warm and fine imported linens, sports cars (or huge SUV's), a dolled-up wife (for the man) or a loaded husband (for the woman), vacations that present pictures that create envy and jealously on Facebook, Instagram and other social media outlets and finally that tenure from the career that one chose, what then? What is the conclusion? What is the value of these things? In the end, what is it all worth without Christ? Have you considered! This is important, stop and think!

Those of you who have acquired such things know that it is not enough! Do not say it is not so, I have been there. Tossing money here and there buying what one wants does NOT satisfy the soul, except for a brief moment. As soon as the newness wears off the mind immediately affixes itself on something different, something else.

"I made my works great; I built houses for myself; I planted vineyards for myself. I made gardens and orchards for myself, and I planted trees in them, of all kinds of fruit. I made pools of water for myself, to water the forest springing up with trees. I have bought slaves and maids, and had servants born in my house; I also had more livestock, herds and flocks, than all who were before me in Jerusalem. I also gathered silver and gold to myself, and the treasure of kings and of the provinces. I got men singers and women singers for myself, and the delights of the sons of men, wives and concubines. I was great and increased more than all that were before me in Jerusalem; also my wisdom remained with me. And whatever my eyes desired I did not keep from them; I did not withhold my heart from any joy; for my heart rejoiced in all my labor, and this was my share from all my labor. Then I looked on all the works that my hands had done, and on the labor that I had labored to do; and, behold, all was vanity and striving of spirit; and there was no profit under the sun. And I turned myself to consider wisdom and madness and folly; for what can the man do who comes after the king, when it has already been done? Then I saw that wisdom excels folly, as far as light excels darkness. The wise man's eyes are in his head; but the fool walks in darkness; and I also considered that one event happens to them all. Then I said in my heart, As it happens to the fool, so it happens even to me; and why was I then more wise? And I said in my heart that this also is vanity. For there is no remembrance of the wise more than of the fool forever, since that which is now shall all be forgotten in the days to come. And how does the wise man die? Same as the fool! Therefore I hated life; because the work that is done under the sun is evil to me; for all is vanity and striving of spirit." Ecclesiastes 2:4-17

Recently there was a website that was hacked. This site is designed for married people only and for finding another married person to commit infidelity with, adultery! Clearly this practice is forbidden, but yet nearly 37 million people, mostly Americans, were on this website! 37 MILLION! This is just ONE website, there are MANY more. Apparently most people are not content with their spouse, it is never enough!

Rest assured that if you don't figure it out sooner than later, realize that it will never be enough. The increase of goods never satisfies the soul. Yet man tries to include a sense of security, a thought or promise from those WHO CANNOT PROMISE SUCH THINGS that their soul is secure, that they are going to Heaven when they die or to paradise, or perhaps floating around in space or commandeering a planet as a little god. Yet the Creator, the Most High, the One who lives in Heaven, the One who sent His Son to die for your sins, should you accept that, has told man how to get to heaven. This is serious stuff.

Time is nearly out, the time to continue on with this charade, these distractions of life, these vain things are passing away. You will pass away, you will die, yet the Lord God Almighty proclaims that there is an accountability before Him. Will you not at least consider what God has told you regarding Salvation, Himself, Jesus, Creation, how to live, repentance, sin, life and death? Will you not hear from Him how to get to Heaven?

Many people put their trust in things, I know first hand. Despite trusting God, I also trusted in preparations made by myself should bad times come. Yet in all of these issues, nearly none of the preparations made were of any value. When a time came to utilize such backup or emergency preparation, the trouble that came was not what was expected. There had been no plan for such an emergency. Trusting in anything except God is vanity and a large lack of faith.

What happens when the world starts to fall apart? What happens when the 'end' that everyone has dreaded becomes a reality? What plan could you possibly have to survive the entirety of such a scenario? Are you rich? What if your riches can't buy food. Are you secluded? What prevents the USSA or a foreign entity from traveling to your driveway? Are you prepared with food and extra supplies? How are you going to carry such things should your planned location not work? You have no clue.

Without Christ all is lost, without Christ your life is a breath of air, without Christ you are not only on your way to Hell when you die, your life is vanity…all is vanity. To gain Christ is to gain the world. To have Jesus as your Savior, to follow Him to TRULY accept Him through repentance and believing into Him is life.

"For to me, to live is Christ, and to die is gain." Philippians 1:21

"But what things were gain to me, these I have counted loss because of Christ. But no, rather, I also count all things loss for the excellence of the knowledge of Christ Jesus my Lord, for whom I have suffered the loss of all things, and count them as refuse, that I may

gain Christ and be found in Him, not having my own righteousness, which is from the Law, but that which is through the faith of Christ, the righteousness which is from God by faith; that I may know Him and the power of His resurrection, and the fellowship of His sufferings, being conformed to His death, if, by any means, I may attain to the resurrection from the dead. Not that I have already attained, or am already perfected; but I press on, that I may lay hold, since Christ Jesus has also laid hold of me. Brethren, I do not count myself to have laid hold; but one thing I do, forgetting those things which are behind and stretching forward to those things which are ahead, I press toward the goal for the prize of the upward call of God in Christ Jesus. Therefore let us, as many as are complete, be of this mind; and if in anything you think differently, God will reveal even this to you. Nevertheless, to the degree that we have already attained, let us walk by the same rule, let us be of the same mind. Brethren, join in being imitators of me, and note those who so walk, as you have us for a pattern. For many conduct themselves, of whom I have told you often, and now tell you even weeping, that they are enemies of the cross of Christ: whose end is destruction, whose god is their belly, and who glory in their shame; who set their mind on earthly things. For our citizenship is in Heaven, from which we also eagerly wait for the Savior, the Lord Jesus Christ, who will transform our lowly body that it may be conformed to His glorious body, according to the working by which He is able even to subject all things to Himself." Philippians 3:17-21

You are dead without Jesus. Enough with the vanity, drop what you are doing and consider your ways!

"Let us hear the conclusion of the whole matter: Fear God, and keep His commandments; for this is for every man. For God will bring every work into judgment, including every secret thing, whether good or evil." Ecclesiastes 12:3-4

Amen!

If Today were the Last Day?

What if today was the last day? What if you knew that there would be no tomorrow, that sudden death and destruction were upon you? What if it was just your last day, as you sit in a hospital bed, knowing that death is about to come?

How many people go through out life knowing that they have to be right before God, but not ever spending the time to figure out exactly how to do that? Many people believe that there is a God, yet why will they not give Him the time of day to figure out what He requires of them?

"For man does not see as He sees; for man looks at the outward appearance, but Jehovah looks at the heart." 1st Samuel 16:7b

Man's logic is backwards. How many hours will be spent not only watching television, but watching a rerun that you have already seen, yet not picking up God's Word and seeking Him? Do you not realize that the nagging feeling that you have about getting right with God is His warning to you that you ought to seek Him and find Salvation through His Son before it is too late?

"The Lord is not slow concerning His promise, as some count slowness, but is longsuffering toward us, not purposing that any should perish but that all should come to repentance." 2nd Peter 3:9

"The heart is deceitful above all things, and desperately wicked; who can know it? I Jehovah search the heart, I examine the soul, even to give to each man according to his ways, according to the fruit of his doings." Jeremiah 17:9-10

... "if you say, Behold, we did not know it; does not He who ponders the heart consider it? And the Keeper of your soul, does He not know it? And shall He not repay to a man according to his deeds?" Proverbs 24:12

So what would men do knowing that they are nearly out of time? There is a consensus out there nowadays where many people think we are in the last days and that some sort of destruction is going to come upon the Earth. In fact, many people even believe that it will be well deserved, yet they themselves think to be able to skirt such destruction. In the face of these theories do they lay prostrate on the ground before the Almighty in repentance, seeking to do His will or do they continue on with their lives, living in sin and refusing to repent before their Maker?

"And in that day Jehovah of Hosts called for weeping and mourning, and for baldness, and for girding with sackcloth. But behold, joy and gladness, slaying oxen and killing sheep, eating flesh and drinking wine, saying, Let us eat and drink, for tomorrow we die!" Isaiah 22:12-13

"Let us eat and drink, for tomorrow we die!" 1st Corinthians 15:32b

If today were the last day and men knew it, violence would unfold. Probably more crime would take place today then would have happened in all of history until that point. People would finally get their big screen television. The neighbor's wife that the man next door had been lusting over for years, would be forcefully taken. The ongoing feud between two people would finally end up with one of them lying dead on the ground. Stores would quickly run out of alcohol. People would spend all of their money at a casino and not even care. There would yet be another group also.

Those who consider themselves religious would run to their churches and spend time in prayer, works and idolatry, trying to ensure that they would go to Heaven. Suddenly the pagan statues of Mary would be surrounded with many pointless trinkets, valuable items and prayers written on notes as people would scramble to do all they think they could do prior to destruction. Other churches would have special meetings and get spirit-filled, supposedly in the name of Jesus, only in reality calling on demons to further manifest their deception as the members babble endlessly in demonic tongues. Pastors at larger churches would be pushing their deception to the max about how God desires their members to give all that they have to the church. The pastors would be groveling over the amount of wealth that they were acquiring, secretly hoping that the Lord would not come back and they might be able to spend all of their gain on their lusts. Despite God's just judgment coming, they would not listen.

"They struck me, but I was not hurt; they beat me, but I did not feel it. When I awake, I will ask for more; to do it again." Proverbs 23:35

Indeed the world would scramble to make mends with some of their family members and friends, where the relationships had gone sour, but in the end the world would still refuse to acknowledge the Most High and would continue on with their sins, demanding that a just God eradicate them from the Earth and commence judgment. Men would party like there is no tomorrow, doing all of their lusts, evil would abound and scarcely would there be a man who would be on the ground before Jehovah God begging for His mercy, knowing that the coming destruction was just and deserving.

"And men were scorched with great heat, and they blasphemed the name of God who has authority over these plagues; and they did not repent to give Him glory." Revelation 16:9

"And they blasphemed the God of Heaven because of their pains and their sores, and did not repent of their deeds." Revelation 16:11

"But the rest of mankind, who were not killed by these plagues, did not repent of the works of their hands, that they should not do homage to demons, and idols of gold, silver, brass, stone, and wood, which are not able to see nor hear nor walk. And they did not repent of their murders nor their sorceries nor their sexual perversions nor their thefts." Revelation 9:20-21

The future has already been prophesied by God. Most men will not repent of their sins and accept Jesus Christ as their Savior.

So what about you? Are you going to continue to put off that nagging or are you going to listen to His voice and seek Him while He can still be found.

"Seek Jehovah while He may be found; call upon Him while He is near. Let the wicked forsake his way, and the unrighteous man his thoughts; and let him return to Jehovah, and He will have mercy on him; and to our God, for He will abundantly pardon. For My thoughts are not your thoughts, nor are your ways My ways, says Jehovah. For as the heavens are higher than the earth, so are My ways higher than your ways, and My thoughts than your thoughts." Isaiah 55:6-9

"Every way of a man is right in his own eyes, but Jehovah ponders the hearts." Proverbs 21:2

"The soul who sins shall die. The son shall not bear the guilt of the father, nor the father bear the guilt of the son. The righteousness of the righteous shall be upon himself, and the wickedness of the wicked shall be upon himself. But if a wicked man turns from all his sins which he has done, keeps all My statutes, and does what is lawful and right, he shall live life; he shall not die. None of the transgressions which he has done shall be remembered against him; because of the righteousness which he has done, he shall live. Do I delight with pleasure in the death of the wicked? says the Lord Jehovah, and not that he should turn back from his ways and live? But when a righteous man turns away from his righteousness and commits iniquity, and does according to all the abominations that the wicked man does, shall he live? All the righteousness which he has done shall not be remembered; because of the treachery of his unfaithfulness, and the sin which he has sinned, in them he shall die. Yet you say, The way of the Lord is not fair. Hear now, O house of Israel, is it not My way which is fair, and your ways which are not fair. When a righteous man turns away from his righteousness, commits iniquity, and dies in it, it is for the iniquity which he has done that he dies. Again, when a wicked man turns away from the wickedness which he has done, and does what is lawful and right, he preserves himself alive. Because he considers and turns away from all the transgressions which he has done, he shall live life; he shall not die." Ezekiel 18:20-28

Amen!

Don't Join Us!!!

Quite a long time ago I was working in a dairy cooler training a younger employee to unload milk pallets. Watching carefully for milk crates to come crashing down, that would send a deluge of milk toward us, our discussion went into Christianity. We had talked before, but this time I didn't bring up Salvation, he did.

Answering question after question I was fully explaining the Gospel and he was seemingly understanding it. I thought perhaps he would make a decision for God. Then the look came in his eyes, I knew he understood it, he knew...suddenly there was a large backlash.

"You mean to tell me that my family and friends who have died are in Hell!!!!", followed by a bleepitly-bleep. He had not asked about his friends or family, but when the sudden realization that without Jesus Christ as your Savior, without accepting Him, without repenting to God Almighty, one is deservingly condemned to Hell, became known to him, he had concluded such a fact. Such a fact is hard for many to swallow, yet in it is truth, those without Christ, yes even those whom you loved, yet have died, are in Hell. I stood there for a moment, a loss of words as he then stormed out of the walk-in cooler, slamming the door.

The remainder of the time I would work in that grocery store we would never again have a conversation. While we would pass a few words between us, as necessary to complete our assigned tasks, there would be no conversation. To my former friend I had become odious. I had told him the truth as laid out in the Gospel, yet he refused to repent and accept Christ, he did believe. The truth was so horrible that he continued on his way to Hell, to join them.

For years this would trouble me, what could I have said? I had talked to others, a few had mentioned such things, usually simply stating that 'someone would only be in Heaven if they accepted Jesus' was suffice. In America the argument about numerous people being in Hell is one that is often not considered. There is SO MUCH false Christianity that most people assume the masses are going to Heaven. Therefore if a loved one who passed away had believed in Jesus or went to church or professed to be 'saved' at any point in their life, there is hope left to those who are still on this earth.

I am not the judge, so I do not know where an individual goes when they die. Yet I can boldly proclaim that if they haven't accepted Jesus Christ as their Savior, they are in Hell...THERE IS NO OTHER PLACE FOR THEM! Yet therein lies the delusion. Many people proclaim salvation, yet they do not understand:

"They have not known nor understood; for He has shut their eyes so that they cannot see; and their hearts so that they cannot understand." Isaiah 44:18

After so many years since the incidence with the young man, now I am sure in his thirties, probably with a family of his own, suddenly I realize the answer to such a response. If those whom he knew, his family and friends, who without Christ are indeed in Hell, could speak to him they would cry out with a loud voice:

DON'T JOIN US!!!

Those who have died have seen the afterlife, they have realized their way was wrong, there is no hope. Those without Christ will spend an eternity in Hell, they will never have an appeals court, their sentence with never be exonerated, nor completed. The Holy Scriptures gives us an example of such:

"There was a certain rich man who was clothed in purple and fine linen and fared sumptuously every day. And there was a certain beggar named Lazarus, full of sores, who was laid at his gate, desiring to be fed with the crumbs which fell from the rich man's table. Moreover the dogs came and licked his sores. So it happened that the beggar died, and was carried by the angels into Abraham's bosom. The rich man also died and was buried. And being in torments in Hades, he lifted up his eyes and saw Abraham afar off, and Lazarus in his bosom. Then he cried and said, Father Abraham, have mercy on me, and send Lazarus that he may dip the tip of his finger in water and cool my tongue; for I am tormented in this flame. But Abraham said, Son, remember that in your lifetime you received your good things, and likewise Lazarus evil things; but now he is comforted and you are tormented. And besides all this, between us and you there is a great chasm fixed, so that those who want to pass from here to you are not able, nor can those from there pass to us. Then he said, I beg you therefore, father, that you would send him to my father's house, for I have five brothers, that he may testify to them, that they not also come to this place of torment. Abraham said to him, They have Moses and the Prophets; let them hear them. And he said, No, father Abraham; but if one goes to them from the dead, they will repent. But he said to him, If they do not hear Moses and the Prophets, neither will they be persuaded though one should rise from the dead." Luke 16:19-31

You are responsible for yourself. God has not hidden Himself, nor has He made the Way of Salvation difficult to find. No vain religion is going to save you, nor is attendance at church. No belief that there is a God is going to help you, nor the acknowledgement of Jesus. You must be Saved, you must be born again.

"I am Jehovah, and there is none other, no God besides Me; I embraced you, though you have not known Me; that they may know from the rising of the sun, to its setting, that there is none besides Me. I am Jehovah, and there is no other; forming the light and creating darkness; making peace and creating evil. I, Jehovah, do all these things. Rain down from above, O heavens, and let the clouds pour down righteousness. Let the earth open, and let salvation bear fruit; and let righteousness spring up together. I, Jehovah, have created it. Woe to him who strives with the One who formed him, a potsherd among the potsherds of the earth! Shall the clay say to the one who forms it, What are you making? Or your work, He has no hands?" Isaiah 45:5-9

"Declare and approach; yea, let them take counsel together. Who has declared this from antiquity? Who has told it since then? Is it not I, Jehovah. And there is no other God besides Me; a just Mighty God and a Savior; there is no one besides Me. Turn to Me, and be saved, all the ends of the earth; for I am the Mighty God, and there is no other. I have sworn by Myself, the word has gone out of My mouth in righteousness, and shall not return, that to Me every knee shall bow, every tongue shall swear." Isaiah 45:21-23

"Jesus answered and said to him, Truly, truly, I say to you, unless one is born from above, he is not able to see the kingdom of God." John 3:3

The choice truly is yours and yours alone. No one can make a decision for you, nor will anyone ultimately be responsible for the choice that you decide to make. You will be held accountable for your sins and without repenting and believing into Jesus Christ, accepting Him as your Savior, you will also join those whom you know and knew in Hell, for eternity. You too will be one who would cry out to those who are still alive and walking under the sun to not join you. You will then see the errors of your ways and know in horror that those whom you loved have the same destiny without Jesus Christ.

Jesus Christ is the ONLY way.

"Jesus said to him, I am the Way, the Truth, and the Life. No one comes to the Father except through Me." John 14:6

Amen!

What is Truth?

truth, n.

1.) The quality or state of being true; trueness, as (a) conformity to facts or reality, as of statements to facts, words, to thoughts, motives or actions to professions; exact accordance with what is, has been, or shall be; (b) the quality or state of being made or constructed true or exact; exact adherence to a model; accuracy of adjustment, exactness; (c) in the fine arts, the proper and correct representation of any object in nature, or of whatever subject may be under treatment; (d) habitual disposition to speak only what is true; veracity; freedom from falsehood; (e) honesty; sincerity; virtue; uprightness; (f) disposition to be faithful to one's engagements; fidelity; constancy; (g) genuineness; purity.

2.) That which is true, as (a) a fact; a reality; a verity; the opposite of falsehood; (b) that which conforms to fact or reality; the real or true state of things; (c) a verified fact; a true statement or proposition; an established principle, a fixed law, or the like; (d) divine command; the doctrines of the gospel.

Webster's Universities Dictionary Unabridged, Webster, 1942

I'm in my mid-to-late thirties, my father was many years older than my mother, he died at age 87 nearly 7 years ago. I've seen those of the hippy generation, I know my generation, I work with the younger generation and because of my father's age, when I was young, I spent much time with the senior senior-citizens. I spent much of my late childhood talking to some of my neighbors who were much older than I. I have worked nearly 50 different jobs and owned several businesses. I have been self employed from those in poverty to those who were very wealthy. I have associated with many different people from many different walks of life.

I have been friends with those who are very book smart, nearly genius, I have been acquainted with those who were off of the streets, gang-banging. I have lived in small charming towns and I have lived in cities where gunfire erupts at night, just up the block. I've spoken with people who are homeless, desolate and even crazy. I've talked with people who truly seek after God and try to put together the pieces of the puzzle. I've been poor and walked to work, I've been wealthy and able to buy whatever small trinkets I desired. I've known people who follow after evil, seeking it diligently and I know people who are true disciples of Christ and follow Him as they should. After having observed all of these things throughout my life, I can say that everyone claims to know some truth.

Most people will never lay hold of truth, they refuse to hear it. Though they seek it, they avoid it. They search all day long for truth to support their lies.

"For the time will come when they will not endure sound doctrine, but according to their own lusts, desiring to hear pleasant things, they will heap up for themselves teachers; and they will turn their ears away from the truth, and be turned aside to myths." 2nd Timothy 4:3-4

Scientists will avoid the truth of paleontology, instead they seek to find truth to back up their claims that dinosaurs evolved and died millions and millions of years ago. When confronted with real truth, facts that sway from their truth, they harden their hearts, block their minds and continue on with diligence that is rarely seen. These men run full force towards Hell, barrowing down to Hades, these men can not get there quick enough. Yet they are not satisfied with going alone, but desire a great wicked company to join them.

"Sheol and Abaddon are never full; so the eyes of man are never satisfied." Proverbs 27:20

Those who are rich and live at ease put truth in the supposed truth of their wealth. Attorneys, managers, business partners, financial advisors are their saviors who proclaim to them the steps to take to produce more wealth, manage all of their possessions and protect their assets from being taken. With smoothness they walk around with a spirit of satisfaction, yet if their mind is taken for just a moment off of their treasure, away from their family, friends or others who constantly praise them and stick closely to them, then a fear strikes their soul. Yet a phone call to their banker, their stock broker, their attorney and the praise from such people once again lifts their spirit and they continue on. Should they realize that their friends are only there because of their wealth, a quick trip and a business lunch where they can pursue pride by establishing their wealth before those who dine and they have once again forgotten their misery, continuing on. As with a heavy drug, they become drunk with their wealth, able to forget truth and pursue their own vain truth, one that will not stand.

"Wealth makes many friends…" Proverbs 19:4a

"It is easier for a camel to go through the eye of a needle than for a rich man to enter into the kingdom of God." Mark 10:25

Hard faces are amongst the boys in the hood. They have their truths and they have there facts. Moral relativism prevails as truth, an eye for an eye in the ghetto. Catch one of these men alone and speak to them and you will find that they seek a better life. You will find that they use their background as facts for why they roll. Truth for the street thug is belief, simply belief. They believe in God and when one of their family and friends gather around the coffin holding the bullet-ridden body, they assume that God will prevail and the soul of their loved one is now in Heaven, this truth is taught by the local churches who proclaim that it is God's truth. These hoodlum pastors cater to the whims of society instead of declaring the facts and God's truth against a wicked generation that seeks to continuously murder and gang bang, dealing and stealing for a living.

These men surrounded by evil, use the truth of their micro world to ignore the real truth. Their street smarts are their bible and their wanton lust for riches and fame, to be the next 50 Cent or boss around the corner who has the local fear based respect. These men engulf themselves in truths of rivalry that never has enough blood, of the supposed Robin Hood mentality, ready to take a life in an instant. Though created in God's image, these men as a group ignore fearing the Almighty, as the hardness of their faces proclaim their truth to fear no one. Their truth leads to Hell and most of them get their sooner than later, with some who are lucky enough to end up in prison, giving them time to consider their ways. Yet even behind those bars there are truths and rules that must be followed. The status quo still works to ensure their soul is prepared for eternal damnation.

... "for their feet run to evil and they make haste to shed blood." Proverbs 1:16

"The heart of the righteous studies how to answer, but the mouth of the wicked pours forth evil." Proverbs 15:28

Truth for many extends to their trust of their church. Many people attend church on a semi regular basis. Yet these pastors who do not shepherd their flocks, ensuring that they are taught the right ways of God, the truth of God, instead they shepherd them to Hell. They corral them like cattle, closing the gate as they are lead away to the slaughter. These pastors use trickery, stage shows, lighting, enticement of the eyes and the ears to gather them into their traps. The church which is supposed to be for the good of God, often become the place where those who are damned meet on a weekly basis.

"Let them alone. They are blind leaders of the blind. And if the blind leads the blind, both will fall into the ditch." Matthew 15:14

"Now the Spirit expressly says that in latter times some will depart from the faith, being devoted to corrupting spirits and doctrines of demons..." 1st Timothy 4:1

Those pastors out there who shepherd flocks, utilizing most of God's truth, still hold back some. Their compromise to Truth results in blurring the lines, signs that should point to God's Way are not as clear as they should be. Rare is the man who declares boldly 'thus saith the Lord' and will not compromise to His Truth. Rare is the pastor who against all odds stands up to the apostasy. Where or where is the men who will do as Christ commanded and fulfill the Great Commission? Where or where are those who will drop the lies of this world and follow not after self, but after the Truth?

Every day graves are dug and every day souls enter an eternal damnation. That is truth. Those who are truly workers of Christ are out there on the battlefield trying to proclaim God's Truth, the real Truth that men everywhere might hear, repent and be Saved through the precious blood of Christ, God's gift to mankind. Yet with an equal vengeance are those who are worker's of Satan, great numbers of men who go about pushing humanity into the flames!

Men can study facts and get truth, men can observe God's Creation and get truth, men can read the Holy Scriptures and get His Truth, or men can simply succumb to their true sinful state and remain there. That truth, that without repenting from a most pathetic state, one that is full of sins, one that is displeasing to the Most High God, one that without Christ all is lost, that Truth is the only one that matters.

How long must those who are in Christ, those who are born again watch as humanity marches toward death. The truth is that people are heavily mistaken and laden with sins. Their heads are in a cloud of deceit and surrounded by entertainment, material items, the lust of the eyes, the sin of the soul. Whether they are a scientist who tries to disprove God, a wealthy man who focuses on material items, a gang banger who is stuck in their training and society, a poor person who refuses to repent or what appears to be the average family who goes around keeping busy, busy, busy, promoting large corporations to become bigger and bigger, breaking the backs of those whom they stand upon, while everyone appears to become more and more united watching television, engaging socially upon the internet, connecting with the music and media, they are doomed! This generation cannot hasten to the gates of Hell quick enough. They run full force, they nearly beg God to punish them for their sins as their wickedness knows no end!

As we near the end, these people are uniting against God's truth. They refuse to wake out of the slumber that their enemy has put them into and by doing so have become an enemy to the very God who created them. They would rather put their trust in culture, they would rather trust in the truths of falsehood, they do not want to know the truth, they do not want to seek after God. Their gods are themselves, they have become little gods, yet it is in their power to do nothing great, nothing out of the ordinary of which is common to mankind. These people continue on blaspheming Him by calling upon His name, by pretending to worship Him. They speak of God but do not know Him. They lie, there is no truth in them. There is a truth and for those who will hear, God provided a way out from the curse. For those who can hear, for those who are willing to unplug themselves for a moment from the world and listen to His voice, there is Truth.

One of the definitions of truth is freedom from falsehood. The things of this world are falsehood. What we do under the sun, what we see, our interactions are false, unless they are for Christ. Unless we become partakers of the good things of God, unless our sins are forgiven and we die from our lives, living for Jesus, we are not free from sin. That sin will lead to Hell, that is truth. What Jesus offers is freedom from that reality, the true state of our souls.

For a Believer there are many truths. They live for Christ, they are a new creature, they have the mind of Christ, their sins are forgiven, their citizenship is in Heaven, they will eternally be joyful. For the rest of mankind there are also many truths, they are of the devil, they are in a sinful nature, they are doomed, they will spend eternity in Hell and they will be a witness to God's truth.

"I have been crucified with Christ; it is no longer I who live, but Christ lives in me; and the life which I now live in the flesh I live by the faith of the Son of God, who loved me and gave Himself for me." Galatians 2:20

"Therefore, if anyone is in Christ, he is a new creation; the old things have passed away; behold, all things have become new." 2nd Corinthians 5:17

"For who has known the mind of the Lord that he may instruct Him? But we have the mind of Christ." 1st Corinthians 2:16

"If we confess our sins, He is faithful and just to forgive us our sins and to cleanse us from all unrighteousness." 1st John 1:9

"For our citizenship is in Heaven, from which we also eagerly wait for the Savior, the Lord Jesus Christ, who will transform our lowly body that it may be conformed to His glorious body, according to the working by which He is able even to subject all things to Himself." Philippians 3:20-21

"Therefore the redeemed of Jehovah shall return and come with singing into Zion; and everlasting joy shall be on their head. Gladness and joy shall overtake them; sorrow and mourning shall flee away." Isaiah 51:11

"You are of the devil as your father, and the lusts of your father you purpose to do. He was a murderer from the beginning, and does not stand in the truth, because there is no truth in him. When he speaks a lie, he speaks from his own, for he is a liar and the father of it." John 8:44

"Therefore, just as through one man sin entered the world, and death through sin, and thus death spread to every person, because everyone sinned." Romans 5:12

"But the cowardly, unbelieving, abominable, murderers, prostitutes, sorcerers, idolaters, and all liars shall have their part in the lake which burns with fire and brimstone, which is the second death." Revelation 21:8

"And they shall go out and observe the dead corpses of the men who have rebelled against Me. For their worm does not die, nor is their fire quenched; and they shall be an abhorrence to all flesh." Isaiah 66:24

What is truth? Truth is that without Jesus Christ as your Lord and Savior there is no point. Without the grace and mercy of God, the forgiveness of sins through repentance, all is lost. The truth is that ALL will stand before God Almighty.

Amen!

All to Stand

An individual accepts the gift of Salvation from their Creator, through repentance and believing into Jesus Christ their Savior, they now have become followers of Christ, they have become Christians. Yet now the battle has just begun.

What is required of a Christian? What characteristic attributes should be found in those who are in Christ? What works are befitting those who are Saved? Is it simply that an individual gets Saved and then goes on with their life as they did before, with the exception of now keeping the commands of God?

How does a Believer know what God desires? How does one in Christ know what commands to keep? Is it even possible for one who is Saved to continue on with little change in their life permanently? Should not the one who was pardoned now spring forth into life, rejoicing at their liberty in Jesus, proclaiming that Salvation is through no other name?

A young boy is a regular amongst the elderly in Bucharest, Romania. This lad helps old women with taking out their rubbish on a weekly basis. He does well in school and as he grows up is known to be a 'good boy'. Yet he is now a man and as a man who gets into partying with the other people his age. In less than a year he is sitting in a smashed BMW awaiting the police to put handcuffs on him. He is drunk, has made a girl who wants nothing to do with him pregnant, now is covered in tattoos and has just ran over two young children who lay in the street dead. His 'fun' going to parties is over. In a drunken stupor he hopes that when he 'awakes' he will have had a horrible nightmare, he wishes that he had simply kept going to the youth group, knowing that somewhere there was truth, yet his other friends were so persistent. A month later he is before the judge and with the families of the slain children hollering and crying for justice, he sobs as the judge renders his life for theirs.

The gallows are prepared and the man is marched outside to the city square behind the courthouse. There a black hood is placed over his head, the noose around his neck. As the magistrate reads off the judge's decision and the executor prepares to unleash the trap door beneath his feet, there is suddenly a ruckus amongst the crowd. A man has walked up on the stage of the doomed and managed to quiet the crowd, beginning to speak. He desires to take the place of the man whom is about to be hanged. He wants to offer life to the man who has committed the crimes and instead be the one who will be hanged. The judge begins to intercede that not such a thing is possible, but because of the persistence of his words allows the noose to be placed around his neck. The trap door is opened and the man who was sentenced to death walks away bewildered and perplexed. A man whom he did not know has given his life for him.

Later the guilty searches out who this man was and finds that he ran an orphanage near the city center. Those children had lived at that orphanage, as their families did not want them. Now the orphanage is about ready to close its doors. The man who was hung had not asked for wages, but was given a room and board, with a few dollars per month, in exchange for managing the orphanage. No one else is willing to take the job without pay. Without hesitation the man who was doomed goes before the workers and accepts the job, working diligently all the years of his life at the orphanage, until he dies at a good old age.

You were dead in your sins, you were doomed to Hell for eternity. God sent His only Son Jesus Christ to die for your sins. He died for your sins on the Cross and it pleased God to crush Him. He took your place and now o' man what will you do? Will you continue on as if nothing had happened, will you not die to yourself and live for Christ Jesus your Lord and Savior. The One who you have eternal life through!

Will you not declare His Salvation to the ends of the earth? Will you not do all to stand before the God whom all will stand? This world is exceedingly evil and wicked. In America, and indeed many nations, it is so easy to get distracted, to get 'off track', to become burdened with the cares of this world so that our testimony as Christians become watered down more and more, until there is scarcely an inkling left that we are Saved.

Why must we watch as the Jehovah Witness and Mormon cults go two by two throughout our communities preaching and proclaiming lies, gathering the ignorant to ensure they are fuel for the fire that never consumes and those who are in Christ are more apt to simply toss a twenty dollar bill in the offering plate, supposedly having done enough to further the Gospel. The here is some money, go do the work mentality.

These damned individuals who walk about with their perverse scriptures in hand, go door to door proclaiming lies and many of those who proclaim to be a Christian do nothing, even bidding them well! Shall a man bid his murderer well before he pulls the trigger? Then how do supposed Christians bid well those who go around seeking to ensure the soul is doomed to eternal Hell!

What about the testimony of Christ, even that which is not spoken of with words. Do our coworkers see the difference between us and them or do we also laugh at the crude and perverse jokes that are made at the workplace? What about the responsibilities that God has given a man towards his wife and children or the responsibilities that a wife has towards her husband?

The Bible in many homes of proclaimed Christians gathers dust, indeed being an object that requires occasional dusting, as it is often left out to give a false testimony to guests who come over. The assumption is that the owner reads the Word of God and grows in knowledge of Him. Yet a quick swipe of the finger across the cover reveals the dust that man will return to.

Does God not see? Does He who Created the heavens and the earth not take notice? We might be able to skirt doing the work of Him, whether in deed or testimony, before man, but I assure you that you will not slight God. God is not a man that He can be tricked, take heed you who do such things.

"And it came to pass in the sixth year, in the sixth month, on the fifth day of the month, as I sat in my house, with the elders of Judah sitting before me, that the hand of the Lord Jehovah fell upon me there. Then I looked, and there was a likeness, like the appearance of fire; from the appearance of His waist and downward, fire; and from His waist and upward, like the appearance of brightness, like the color of amber. And He stretched out the form of a hand, and took me by a lock of my head; and the Spirit lifted me up between earth and the heavens, and brought me in the visions of God to Jerusalem, to the door of the north gate of the inner court, where the seat of the image of jealousy was, which provokes to jealousy. And behold, the glory of the God of Israel was there, like the vision that I saw in the plain. Then He said to me, Son of man, lift up your eyes now toward the north. So I lifted up my eyes toward the north, and behold, toward the north at the gate of the altar, was this image of jealousy at the entrance. Furthermore He said to me, Son of man, do you see what they are doing, the great abominations that the house of Israel commits here, to make Me go far away from My sanctuary? Now turn again, you will see greater abominations. So He brought me to the door of the court; and when I looked, behold, a hole in the wall. Then He said to me, Son of man, dig into the wall; and when I dug into the wall, there was an opening. And He said to me, Go in, and see the evil abominations which they do there. So I went in and saw; and behold, every sort of creeping thing, abominable beasts, and all the idols of the house of Israel, carved all around on the wall. And there stood before them seventy men of the elders of the house of Israel, and in their midst stood Jaazaniah the son of Shaphan. Each man had a censer in his hand, and a thick cloud of incense went up. Then He said to me, Son of man, have you seen what the elders of the house of Israel do in the dark, every man in the room of his idols? For they say, Jehovah does not see us, Jehovah has forsaken the land. And He said to me, Turn again, and you will see greater abominations that they are doing. So He brought me to the door of the north gate of the house of Jehovah; and behold, women were sitting there weeping for Tammuz. Then He said to me, Have you seen this, O son of man? Turn again, you will see greater abominations than these. So He brought me into the inner court of the house of Jehovah; and behold, at the door of the temple of Jehovah, between the porch and the altar, were about twenty-five men with their backs toward the temple of Jehovah and their faces toward the east, and they were bowing down to the sun toward the east. And He said to me, Have you seen this, O son of man? Is it a trivial thing to the house of Judah to commit the abominations which they commit here? For they have filled the land with violence; then they have returned to provoke Me to anger. Indeed they put the branch to their nose. Therefore I also will act in fury. My eye will not spare nor will I have pity; and though they cry in My ears with a loud voice, I will not hear them." Ezekiel 8

What is required of a Christian?

"I have been crucified with Christ; it is no longer I who live, but Christ lives in me; and the life which I now live in the flesh I live by the faith of the Son of God, who loved me and gave Himself for me." Galatians 2:20

"But you have not so learned Christ, if indeed you have heard Him and have been taught by Him, as the truth is in Jesus: that you put off, concerning your former conduct, the old man which is corrupted according to the deceitful lusts, and be renewed in the spirit of your mind, and that you put on the new man which was created according to God, in true righteousness and holiness. Therefore, putting away lying, let each one of you speak truth with his neighbor, for we are members of one another. Be angry, but do not sin: do not let the sun go down on your wrath, nor give place to the devil. Let him who stole steal no longer, but rather let him labor, working with his hands what is good, that he may have something to give to him who has need. Let no corrupt word proceed out of your mouth, but what is good for the business of building up, that it may impart grace to the hearers. And do not grieve the Holy Spirit of God, by whom you were sealed for the day of redemption. Let all bitterness, wrath, anger, clamor, and evil speaking be put away from you, with all wickedness. And be kind to one another, tenderhearted, forgiving one another, just as God in Christ forgave you." Ephesians 4:20-32

What characteristic attributes should be found in those who are in Christ?

"I beseech you therefore, brethren, by the mercies of God, that you present your bodies a living sacrifice, holy, acceptable to God, which is your reasonable service. And do not be conformed to this world, but be transformed by the renewing of your mind, that you may prove what is that good and acceptable and perfect will of God." Romans 12:1-2

"Finally then, brethren, we urge and exhort in the Lord Jesus that you should abound more and more, just as you received from us how you ought to walk and to please God; for you know what commandments we gave you through the Lord Jesus." 1st Thessalonians 4:1-2

"If then you are raised with Christ, seek those things which are above, where Christ is, sitting at the right hand of God. Set your mind on things above, not on the things of the earth; for you died, and your life is hidden with Christ in God. When Christ who is our life is revealed, then you also will be revealed with Him in glory. Therefore put to death your members which are on the earth: sexual perversion, uncleanness, passion, evil lusts, and covetousness, which is idolatry. Because of these things the wrath of God is coming upon the sons of disobedience; in which you yourselves once walked when you lived in them. But now you yourselves are to put off all these: anger, wrath, malice, blasphemy, filthy language out of your mouth. Do not lie to one another, since you have put off the old man with his practices, and have put on the new man who is renewed in full true knowledge according to the image of the One who created him, where there is neither Greek nor Jew, circumcised nor uncircumcised, barbarian, Scythian, slave nor free, but Christ is all things and in all. Therefore, as the elect of God, holy and beloved, put on a heart of compassion, kindness, humility, meekness, longsuffering; bearing with one another, and forgiving one another, if anyone has a complaint against another; even as

Christ forgave you, so you also do. And above all these things put on love, which is the bond of perfectness. And let the peace of God rule in your hearts, to which also you were called in one body; and be thankful. Let the Word of Christ dwell in you richly in all wisdom, teaching and admonishing one another in psalms and hymns and spiritual songs, singing with grace in your hearts to the Lord. And whatever you do in word or deed, do all in the name of the Lord Jesus, giving thanks to God, even the Father, through Him. Wives, submit to your own husbands, as is fitting in the Lord. Husbands, love your wives and do not be bitter towards them. Children, obey your parents in all things, for this is pleasing to the Lord. Fathers, do not provoke your children, that they may not become discouraged. Bondservants, obey in all things your masters according to the flesh, not with eyeservice, as men-pleasers, but in sincerity of heart, fearing God. And whatever you do, do it from the soul, as to the Lord and not to men, knowing that from the Lord you will receive the reward of the inheritance; for you serve the Lord Christ. But he who does wrong will be repaid for what he has done, and there is no partiality." Colossians 3

What works are befitting those who are Saved?

... "but declared first to those in Damascus and in Jerusalem, and throughout all the region of Judea, and then to the Gentiles, that they should repent, turn to God, and do works befitting repentance." Acts 26:20

"What does it profit, my brethren, if someone says he has faith but does not have works? Is faith able to save him? If a brother or sister is naked and destitute of daily food, and one of you says to them, Depart in peace, be warmed and filled, but you do not give them the things which are needed for the body, what does it profit? Thus also faith, if it does not have works, being alone, is dead. But someone will say, You have faith, and I have works. Show me your faith without your works, and I will show you my faith from my works." Jacob (James) 2:14-18

"Now it happened as He went to Jerusalem that He passed through the midst of Samaria and Galilee. And as He entered a certain village, there met Him ten men who were lepers, who stood afar off. And they lifted up their voices and said, Jesus, Master, have mercy on us! So when He saw them, He said to them, Go, show yourselves to the priests. And so it was that as they went, they were cleansed. And one of them, when he saw that he was healed, returned, and with a loud voice glorified God, and fell down on his face at His feet, giving Him thanks. And he was a Samaritan. So Jesus answered and said, Were there not ten cleansed? But where are the nine? Were there not any found who returned to give glory to God except this foreigner? And He said to him, Arise, go your way. Your faith has made you well." Luke 17:11-19

How does a Believer know what God desires?

"And so we also have a more sure Word of prophecy, which you do well to heed as to a light that shines in a dark place, until the day dawns and the morning star rises in your hearts; knowing this first, that not any of the prophecies of Scripture came into being

from personal exposition, for prophecy was not formerly brought forth by man's choice, but holy men of God spoke as they were propelled along by the Holy Spirit." 2nd Peter 1:19-21

"All Scripture is breathed by God, and is profitable for doctrine, for reproof, for correction, for instruction in righteousness, that the man of God may be complete, thoroughly equipped for every good work." 2nd Timothy 3:16-17

"But Jesus answered him, saying, It is written, Man shall not live by bread alone, but by every Word of God." Luke 4:4

How does one in Christ know what commands to keep?

"So he answered and said, You shall love the Lord your God with all your heart, with all your soul, with all your strength, and with all your mind, and your neighbor as yourself." Luke 10:27

Finally…

"Finally, my brethren, be strong in the Lord and in the power of His might. Put on all the armor of God, that you may be able to stand against the wiles of the devil. For we do not wrestle against flesh and blood, but against rulers, against authorities, against the world's rulers of the darkness of this age, against spiritual wickedness in the heavenlies. Therefore take up all the armor of God, that you may be able to resist in the evil day, and having done all, to stand. Stand firm therefore, having girded your waist with truth, having put on the breastplate of righteousness, and having shod your feet with the preparation of the gospel of peace; above all, taking the shield of faith with which you will be able to quench all the fiery darts of the wicked one. And take the helmet of salvation, and the sword of the Spirit, which is the Word of God; praying always with all prayer and supplication in the Spirit, being watchful to this end with all perseverance and supplication for all the saints;"… Ephesians 6:10-18

Amen!

Lies

Perhaps to become a student of history, one would really be a student of historical lies. Many people have quoted that the winners write history and indeed it is true, but also the conquerors control the writings of men. What happens when all of the books that someone reads are approved by the 'winners' or 'conquerors'.

"If you tell a lie big enough and keep repeating it, people will eventually come to believe it. The lie can be maintained only for such time as the State can shield the people from the political, economic and/or military consequences of the lie. It thus becomes vitally important for the State to use all of its powers to repress dissent, for the truth is the mortal enemy of the lie, and thus by extension, the truth is the greatest enemy of the State." Joseph Goebbels, Propaganda Minister for the Nazi Regime

People are easily manipulated, easily swayed. Oftentimes people do not think for themselves, but go on with the 'flow' of things. Yet if they would stop and look around, considering for a moment, then maybe their eyes would be open to the fact that much of what they consider truth is actually lies.

The debate rages on about so-called gun control. Yet who is really behind this debate? The big media? The New York Times with their front page story about gun control and violence. Who runs the New York Times or these other vain talking mouths that people watch day in and day out? Our media is controlled, it is full of lies and nobody seems to notice. The lie, the falsehood couldn't possible be that big could it? Guns don't kill people, people kill people. Did you hear about the murderers who stabbed to death 31 people at a train station in China last year?

So where is this global warming? Why are there maps with Antarctica drawn with no ice? These maps are hundreds of years old. Ever heard of clean coal? How about Climate Gate, where scientists from around the world were found to be collaborating and deliberately lying about temperatures to supposedly prove global warming? Finally to be politically correct I should note that these same experts started with global cooling, then global warming and finally settled on climate change as their coined phrase. At least with climate change they can blame ANY weather problems on mankind to further reign them in and control them.

Three building fell on 9/11, straight down, only two of them got hit by a plane. It just so happens that the third building held every spook agency's office, probably removing the evidence of their complacency in the inside job. There are so many lies regarding the official story of 9/11 and so many dead people who can no longer tell the public about the deception put out by the United States government. These scientists, many working for large academic institutions are now six feet under. Then there are the lists of witnesses, whose story interfered with the lies promoted by the government, they too are dead. As Goebbels said, the lie is certainly big enough. You can still view clips of WTC Building 7 being reported as having collapsed with it still visible in the background of the news clip. The media control is mind-boggling.

What about the red blood cells found inside dinosaur bones, to say nothing about the skin that has been found on some fossils. A well-known scientist lost her job for daring to expose the lies and looking carefully under the microscope at these fossilized bones that she was examining. Not even proclaiming to be a Christian or believing in Creation, intelligent design, etc., she simply reported on the truth of what she had seen. She had noticed some sticky material that could be reconstituted, and upon further inspection found red blood cells still existing inside the fossilized bones. After reporting this major discovery she quickly was without a job. Yet there were others who were intrigued and they also checked the museums and dusted off the old crates of bones they had collected. Indeed there were red blood cells to be found everywhere…impossible to go along with the dating scheme of these evil and perverse men. With so many scientist now seeing the truth that had been there ALL ALONG, the evolutionist, those God hating men, were forced to come up with an explanation as to how it was possible that there were still blood cells. Originally impossible, then possible, their lies about evolution constantly having to be changed BECAUSE IT IS NOT THE TRUTH!

From restaurants that claim to have food straight from the farm, yet put ingredients in their food to PURPOSELY promote the eugenic dream of elitists who promote lies based on evolution and climate change, to cities that add fluoride to their water to help keep a subversive population that is more apt to believe the lies.

From social media websites that are a backdoor for information collecting on dissidents for Homeland Security and the FBI, to the endless amounts of horrific sexual depravation online that breaks the God created union of a man and a woman to become one.

From the lies of the government regarding the war on drugs, to the lies purported to continue skirmishes and battles in the Middle East and elsewhere. From the poppy fields controlled by the US in Afghanistan (to create heroin and other opiate based drugs), to the proxy war that is beginning with Russia.

From the lies of the war on terror, to the truth of the war on Americans freedom and from the ineligible President Obama, to the controlled congressional House and Senate, lies are abounding.

The books and magazines we read, the education that our child are put through in the public school system, the inert ingredients in the vaccinations and the truth about the medical monopoly are all covered up and lies are taught and promoted. Yet there is a truth amongst that.

People, our fellow citizens, would rather believe these lies than believe the true condition of this country and indeed the world! There is a lie so big and a lie so bad that it makes every other lie small in comparison. That lie is that there is more than one way to get to Heaven and it is pushed in so many different ways that one can hardly keep track of them. David Cloud, wayoflife.org, may have the best understanding of these lies and agendas that are destroying what is left of the church worldwide.

Most all lies can be attributed to promoting greed, control, agendas or some other self centered philosophy held by a person or group of leaders. Yet HEREIN LIES GREAT DANGER!

When lies are told about the Gospel, God's Word, Jesus Christ, how to be Saved, what His truth is, etc., these lies affect your eternal destiny, not your earthly life. While a man can only avoid and protect his family so much against the crushing tyranny, Jesus Christ can set you free, truly free, even among a world full of lies.

"And you shall know the truth, and the truth shall set you free." John 8:32

Remember, who is the father of lies?

"You are of the devil as your father, and the lusts of your father you purpose to do. He was a murderer from the beginning, and does not stand in the truth, because there is no truth in him. When he speaks a lie, he speaks from his own, for he is a liar and the father of it." John 8:44

The time will coming and indeed is coming rapidly where there will be several more lies spread by these same people. They will lie about who and why Christians were taken away by Jesus at the start of the *"time of Jacobs trouble" (Jeremiah 30:7)* or the Great Tribulation as it is more commonly known. There is even evidence through leaks about Project Blue Beam that the deception will be very great.

"And for this reason God will send them strong delusion, that they should believe the lie, that they all may be judged who did not believe the truth but had pleasure in unrighteousness." 2nd Thessalonians 2:11-12

Keep that verse in mind for those of you who know the truth, yet refuse to submit to God. Do not think that this will not apply to you, God is great and His Truth will stand!

The lies will be promoted to push a global currency, a unified one world religion, the mark of the beast and many other things. Yet know this and know this well. God has provided the Holy Scriptures, His Word for us. Unless you have a perverted text, you can very plainly read the Truth.

The Truth from the Creation of mankind, to the Flood, to Israel's history, to Jesus is found in the Bible. From learning about who God is, to who His Son is, to how to become Saved and what will take place in the end times is at your fingertips. Do not let the deceptions of man's imagination through the endless avenues of entertainment grab your soul and not give you rest to find the real Truth in His Word. Do not be entertained to death.

God's truth is very simple and indeed Salvation is offered to ALL who seek it. Yet you must understand that MANY churches do not abide by His Truth, rather they twist His Words to their own destruction.

"Therefore, beloved, looking forward to these things, be diligent to be found by Him in peace, spotless and without blemish; and consider that the longsuffering of our Lord is salvation; as also our beloved brother Paul, according to the wisdom given to him, has written to you, as also in all his epistles, speaking in them of these things, in which are some things hard to understand, which the unlearned and unstable twist, as they do also the rest of the Scriptures, to their own destruction." 2nd Peter 3:14-16

"For the time will come when they will not endure sound doctrine, but according to their own lusts, desiring to hear pleasant things, they will heap up for themselves teachers; and they will turn their ears away from the truth, and be turned aside to myths." 2nd Timothy 4:3-4

Yet if a man is truly seeking after God, they will find Him.

"And you shall seek Me and find Me, when you search for Me with all your heart." Jeremiah 29:13

Even in these last days, Truth can still be found. Truth is still there and the only thing we can know for absolute certain is what God told us in the Bible. This is why man spends so much energy telling lies and trying to make God's Word false, yet it will stand.

"The grass withers, the flower fades; but the Word of our God stands forever." Isaiah 40:8

"Since you have purified your souls in obeying the truth through the Spirit unto sincere love of the brethren, love one another fervently out of a pure heart, having been born again, not of corruptible seed but incorruptible, through the Word of God which lives and abides forever, because All flesh is as grass, and all the glory of man as the flower of the grass. The grass withers, and its flower falls away, but the Word of the Lord endures forever. Now this is the Word which by the gospel was preached to you." 2nd Peter 1:22-25

"Heaven and earth will pass away, but My Words will by no means pass away." Matthew 24:35

"LAMED: Forever, O Jehovah, Your Word stands firm in the heavens." Psalms 119:89

The truth of the matter is this, we will each stand before God Almighty and give an account. Most of the world will go to Hell for eternity, yet you AS AN INDIVIDUAL have a choice, you have a freewill, you are able to assert and see if these things are so. You have a choice to accept Jesus as your Savior and follow Him until the end OR continue down the path that you are currently on, one that will certainly lead to destruction.

The choice is yours and yours alone, consider it carefully, your soul is at stake!

"For He says: In an acceptable time I have heard you, and in a day of salvation I have helped you. Behold, now is the accepted time; behold, now is the day of salvation." 2nd Corinthians 6:2

"And if it seems evil to you to serve Jehovah, choose for yourselves this day whom you will serve, whether the gods which your fathers have served that were on the other side of the River, or the gods of the Amorites, in whose land you are living. But as for me and my house, we will serve Jehovah." Joshua 24:15

"Man is like a breath; his days are like a shadow that vanishes." Psalms 144:4

Amen!

Trappings!

"But take heed to yourselves, lest your hearts be weighed down with giddiness, drunkenness, and cares of this life, and that Day come upon you unexpectedly. For it will come as a snare on all those who dwell on the face of the whole earth." Luke 21:34-35

"For man also does not know his time; as the fish that are taken in an evil net, and as the birds that are caught in the snare; so are the sons of men snared in an evil time, when it falls suddenly upon them." Ecclesiastes 9:12

"For he is cast into a net by his own feet, and he walks into a netting. The snare takes him by the heel, and the noose takes hold of him. A rope is hidden for him on the ground, and a trap for him in the path." Job 18:8-10

There are trappings everywhere, yet as this discussion begins, understand that without Jesus as your Lord and Savior you are already trapped, doomed and on your way to Hell. Without Christ, all is lost, nothing is gain.

"But what things were gain to me, these I have counted loss because of Christ." Philippians 3:7

There is a prevalence in society of drunkenness, drug abuse and a partying lifestyle associated with all sorts of sexual immorality and debauchery. Even in small town America, hardly a week goes by without a high speed police chase, a stabbing, a shooting, a murder, armed robbery or some off the wall crime that is usually committed by someone who is on drugs, most commonly meth.

If one pays attention you can notice the trappings that have caught the souls of men all around you.

If you were to visit the bar on a late Friday night you would hear music that is full of men's rage and lusts blasting as those who remain are so intoxicated they probably wouldn't even notice you observing them. There the souls of people partaking in drunkenness, debauchery and other fleshly lusts would continue on with their night. Indeed if state laws didn't prohibit buying drinks after 2am, certainly there would likely be deaths every weekend from those who wouldn't stop drinking.

If one was curious as to what took place at a gas station on any given night, receiving a job at a local gas station hot spot would certainly provide an insight into the lives of men. As evening came and men got done with work, the lines would start to form and the souls of men would purchase quantities of beer, man after man. Mixed in would be those who would lean on the counter, scratching their lottery tickets, hoping for a break and those who would purchase the regular lottery tickets, hoping that the god of mammon would be on their side. Pack after pack of cigarettes would be sold to those whose lives seemingly required the drug to manage.

Each layer of obvious sins could be looked at and peeled away, layer after layer, like an onion. Should one peel away to the core, sin would reel its ugly head, a lost soul, someone without Christ, damned and doomed to Hell without the grace and mercy of an Almighty God who is willing to forgive them and grant them eternal life through Jesus, should they chose to consider their ways and repent from their wickedness.

Yet sometimes sin is not so obvious as those 'sinners' who are at the bars, buying the booze, outside the local strip joints, gambling houses or slinging rocks on the street corners. The devil is very crafty in his presentation of sin and oftentimes what should be very obvious is not at all readily seen for what it is.

The staggering divorce rate in America suggests that marriages are not honored as God has commanded they be.

"For this, a man shall leave his father and mother and cleave to his wife, and the two shall be one flesh." Ephesians 5:31

The arguings of families who have an appearance of being well-dressed, well-groomed and successful according to the vehicles they drive and the home they live in, is astonishing. Their family unit that should be honoring to the Most High, their Creator, is broken. Time spent as a family doing something that everyone is enjoying is rare as the children are stuck playing video games, the mother is scrambling to retrieve her phone to send off a quick text that she has just realized needed to be done and the father looks at the product of his household, the demeanor of his wife, and realizes his place is simply to pay the bill for the unthankful family that has just ordered their food. With a slight smile he looks to his wife, whom simply gives him the eye that he has done what was required of him so far today.

"For men will be lovers of themselves, lovers of money, boasters, proud, blasphemers, disobedient to parents, unthankful, unholy, without natural affection, unyielding, slanderers, without self-control, savage, despisers of good, traitors, headstrong, haughty, lovers of pleasure rather than lovers of God, having a form of godliness but denying its power. And from such people turn away." 2nd Timothy 2:3-5

"As for My people, children are their oppressors, and women rule over them. O My people, those leading you cause you to go astray, and they swallow the way of your paths." Isaiah 3:12

Still someone who wanted to observe men, an outside, a citizen from another country who wanted to see whether or not those who at least claimed to serve Jesus were of a different attitude, character and spirit, might visit a restaurant on Sunday afternoon, after the main church service is over.

"For our citizenship is in Heaven, from which we also eagerly wait for the Savior, the Lord Jesus Christ, who will transform our lowly body that it may be conformed to His glorious body, according to the working by which He is able even to subject all things to Himself." Philippians 3:20-21

If a person were to in advance get a table in such a restaurant, eating a meal, just prior to the onset of the rush, what they would see would not be those who had just learned the teachings of Christ, those who had just humbled themselves before the Lord in worshipping Him and in prayer, knowing that without Jesus as their High Priest they could not make supplication to their Creator. What they would see is a loud, proud and boisterous crowd enter in.

"The expression of their faces witnesses against them; they have declared their sin like Sodom; they do not hide it. Woe to their soul! For they have recompensed evil upon themselves. Say to the righteous that it is well; for they shall eat of the fruit of their doings. Woe to the wicked! For the evil, the recompense of his hand, shall be done unto him. As for My people, children are their oppressors, and women rule over them. O My people, those leading you cause you to go astray, and they swallow the way of your paths. Jehovah stands up to plead His case, and stands up to judge the peoples. Jehovah will enter into judgment with the elders of His people, and their rulers. For you have eaten up the vineyard, the plunder of the poor is in your houses. What do you mean that you crush My people, and grind the faces of the poor? says the Lord Jehovah of Hosts. Furthermore Jehovah says, Because the daughters of Zion are haughty, and walk with stretched out necks and wanton eyes, walking and mincing as they go, and make a tinkling with their feet; therefore Jehovah will attach scabs to the top of the head of the daughters of Zion; and Jehovah will lay bare their secret parts. In that day the Lord will take away the beauty of their anklets, and their headbands, and their crescents of the moon, the pendants, and the bracelets, and the veils; the turbans, and the leg ornaments, and the sashes, and the perfume boxes, and the amulets; the rings and nose jewels; the festal apparel and the outer garments; and the mantles, and the purses; the mirrors and the fine linen; and the turbans and the veils. And it shall be, instead of a smell of perfume, there shall be an odor of decay. And instead of a belt, a rope. And instead of well set hair, baldness. And instead of a rich robe, a girding of sackcloth; and branding instead of beauty. Your men shall fall by the sword, and your mighty in the war." Isaiah 3:9-25

Should this person also eat at this restaurant on other days they would notice a difference with this crowd. The percent of scantily-clad women would be notably higher. After all their Sunday dress is not at all glorifying the Lord, but rather a spectacle more prone to a night club. Rather their dress would become a distraction, a trapping in their church, as they would do the work of their father, navigating the minds of men away from any Truth that may be spoken from the pulpit and instead full of the lusts of the flesh.

"But these, like natural brute beasts made to be caught and destroyed, speak evil of the things they do not understand, and will utterly perish in their own corruption, and will receive the wages of unrighteousness, as those who consider it pleasure to carouse in the

daytime. They are spots and blemishes, delighting in their own deceptions while they feast with you, having eyes full of adultery and that cannot cease from sin, enticing unstable souls; having a heart exercised in covetousness; accursed children." 2nd Peter 2:12-14

"You are of the devil as your father, and the lusts of your father you purpose to do. He was a murderer from the beginning, and does not stand in the truth, because there is no truth in him. When he speaks a lie, he speaks from his own, for he is a liar and the father of it." John 8:44

The observer might also note that this crowd of people were particularly demanding, rude and despite their constant smiles, jesting and friendly gestures to those who had come into the restaurant with them, a certain herd mentality amongst all of the now patrons would demand that their needs be met and even what was right be exceeded. They would want for free, what should be of cost.

If the man observing needed any further evidence of the naughtiness of those who had just pretended to be disciples of Christ, they could get a job at that restaurant. Their they would hear the cries of the poor workers noting that on Sunday's they would have to work very hard for an hour or two when the church people came, yet their tips would be very petty compared to most day. Apparently they would surmise that they had given all in the 'tip jar' to the church they attended and were therefore impoverished at the moment. The generosity of the people could only be obtained once during the day.

"For the time will come when they will not endure sound doctrine, but according to their own lusts, desiring to hear pleasant things, they will heap up for themselves teachers;" 2nd Timothy 4:3

Sin is obvious when someone is gambling away their livelihood, while there are hungry mouths to feed at home. Yet it is not as obvious for those who proclaim to be Christians, yet go on their once in a lifetime trip to the strip on Las Vegas. One can see evil when children are beaten, yet the man who neglects his children due to the cares of this world, neglecting the Word of God, that is one that is not seen as frequently.

"Train up a child in the way he should go; and when he is old, he will not depart from it." Proverbs 22:6

Dear reader, the list of trappings could involve many volumes of books, even then there would be more that one wouldn't even consider or acknowledge. Yet without Christ ALL ARE TRAPPED and on there way to Hell. Without the forgiveness of sins, without accepting the free gift given by your Creator, without Christ having died on the Cross for YOUR sins and repenting plus believing into Him, ALL is lost. Without Christ you are trapped, the devil has you right where he wants you. All you have to do is die and the trap is sealed around your soul, without any hope for you whatsoever.

"For by grace you are saved through faith; and that not of yourselves, it is the gift of God;" Ephesians 2:8

"For God so loved the world that He gave His only begotten Son, that everyone believing into Him should not perish but have eternal life. For God did not send His Son into the world to judge the world, but that the world through Him might be saved. The one believing into Him is not judged; but the one not believing is judged already, because he has not believed in the name of the only begotten Son of God. And this is the judgment, that the Light has come into the world, and men loved darkness rather than the Light, for their deeds were evil. For everyone practicing evil hates the Light and does not come to the Light, lest his deeds should be reproved. But the one doing the truth comes to the Light, that his deeds may be clearly seen, that they have been worked in God." John 3:16-21

"...The time is fulfilled, and the kingdom of God is at hand. Repent, and believe in the gospel." Mark 1:15

"There will be weeping and gnashing of teeth, when you see Abraham and Isaac and Jacob and all the prophets in the kingdom of God, and yourselves being thrust outside." Luke 13:28

If you are reading this, you can still cry out to God Almighty, you can still seek Him who Created you, you can still accept the gift of Salvation. You can not break free from the trappings of men yourself, only through Jesus Christ can you be set free.

"And you shall know the truth, and the truth shall set you free. They answered Him, We are Abraham's seed, and have been in slavery to no one at any time. How can You say, You will be made free? Jesus answered them, Truly, truly, I say to you, Everyone practicing sin is a slave of sin. And a slave does not remain in the house forever, but the son remains forever. Therefore if the Son sets you free, you shall truly be free." John 8:32-36

"Keep me from the snares they have laid for me, and from the traps of the workers of iniquity." Psalms 141:9

"Be sober, be vigilant; because your adversary the devil walks about like a roaring lion, seeking whom he may devour." 1st Peter 5:8

Amen!

The Path is Narrow

"Enter by the narrow gate; for wide is the gate and broad is the way that leads to destruction, and there are many entering in through it. Because narrow is the gate and distressing is the way which leads unto life, and there are few who find it." Matthew 7:13-14

"Then one said to Him, Lord, are there few who are saved? And He said to them, Strive to enter through the narrow gate, for many, I say to you, will seek to enter and will not be able." Luke 13:23-24

When I was a child I attended a Nazarene church on a regular basis. If my parents didn't attend on Sunday the church bus would come and pick me and my sister up. There I met some really great people growing up and attended Sunday school. For what it is worth, more biblically sound doctrine was probably taught at that church then what is at many Baptist churches nowadays.

It was at this same church that I would give my life to the Lord. At 9 years old during an alter call I would go forward and accept Jesus Christ as my Lord and Savior. Eventually my parents divorced and we moved a few miles away. Here my family began to attend a Pentecostal church. With rock instruments up on stage, a pastor would preach his sermon and some well-to-do people who were given authority as Sunday school teachers, etc., we would go there for a couple of years.

This was my first instance of seeing speaking in tongues. I never believed it and thought that those who would speak out during church were not only rude, but lying. Then an acquaintance of whom I also went to school with one day spoke in tongues, I believed him. Though I believed that he spoke in tongues, I never had the urge to do so myself. Despite the best effort of the entertainers to keep our attention, I eventually migrated to the sound booth as an assistant, due to my lack of participation. For whatever reason my family began to attend a missionary church.

For the entirety of my high school years this would be the church that I would attend until I graduated. Here I made friends with the youth pastor's and the pastor's son, participated in many outings and listened to the sermons week after week. It was also at this church that I began to listen to 'christian' rock and I also attended a Youth for Christ ministry on a weekly basis. YFC is run by Campus Crusade, the youth pastor was also the director of this organization locally.

Years would go by and I began to consider that everything that called itself Christian could not be so. I had always wondered why there were so many different sects, but assumed that they were small disagreements, not knowing that one was necessary more wrong than the other, with the exception of the Jehovah Witnesses and Mormons. I became friends with a former Bob Jones University student at work and we started studying the bible.

We also considered starting a 'christian' rock radio station, something which the local area did not yet have. We both would listen to popular bands, include rap artist DC Talk. There seemed to be a lot of good that could come out of getting people's interest in Christ through music. As I was truly seeking what was correct and right in the eyes of the Lord, I prayed that he would help me find the truth. After an internet search, way back in 1999, I came across a website called A Voice in the Wilderness (www.a-voice.org).

"And you shall seek Me and find Me, when you search for Me with all your heart." Jeremiah 29:13

"However, when He, the Spirit of Truth, has come, He will guide you into all Truth; for He will not speak things originating from Himself, but whatever He hears He will speak; and He will make known to you things to come." John 16:13

I wanted truth, God's truth and there on that website was many of the answers to questions that I had been seeking out. Confused, as I was pondering, I began to debate with the caretaker of that website about 'christian' rock and how it was not wrong. My debate was based on feelings, emotions and what I was used to, his was based on the word of God. Of course, I had my verses to throw back towards him as we went back and forth. Finally, he won.

"But the Helper, the Holy Spirit, whom the Father will send in My name, He will teach you all things, and bring to your remembrance all things that I said to you." John 14:26

Now I wasn't sure what to think, here was this man on some strange website who appeared to be a Christian and had proven what I thought was certain to be wrong. There was a catch though, I had to continue on, I had to go down the path that now appeared to indeed be very narrow.

Many of my friends, my family, my pastor and youth pastor all listened to 'christian' rock. Now was I suddenly smarter or 'better' than they? How couldn't they see it, especially those who had taught me? How could it be so obvious, yet hidden to those people?

Regardless of what people might think, I chose to be obedient to God. I destroyed all of my 'christian' rock albums. As time went on there were many other things that would be discovered. I had a hunger for the Truth and sought very hard to find it. Suddenly my life began to quickly change and I marched down the narrow path, but as I went down something was happening.

"And you will be hated by everyone on account of My name. But he who endures to the end will be kept safe." Matthew 10:22

"And everyone who has left houses or brothers or sisters or father or mother or wife or children or lands, for My name, shall receive a hundredfold, and inherit eternal life." Matthew 19:29

"I have been crucified with Christ; it is no longer I who live, but Christ lives in me; and the life which I now live in the flesh I live by the faith of the Son of God, who loved me and gave Himself for me." Galatians 2:20

The narrow path is indeed the way Home, but in the meantime people were not so considerate to some of these new 'ideas' that my wife and I had. Decisions had to be made and those decisions were made for Christ, to follow Him.

"Adulterers and adulteresses, do you not know that friendship with the world is enmity with God? Whoever therefore purposes to be a friend of the world is shown to be opposing God." Jacob (James) 4:4

Take a look around at the world. Take a better and closer look at the world's so-called Christianity. Salvation is simple, there is not much too it, repent to God and believe into Christ, yet somehow the world has changed it to talking about how God accepts you as you are. If that is the case then why did Christ have to suffer and die on the Cross for our sins? Why then did sin enter the world through Adam? Why is there the 'time of Jacob's trouble' or the end times as an overwhelming amount of people believe?

"Even so you also outwardly appear righteous to men, but inside you are full of hypocrisy and lawlessness." Matthew 23:28

"If the world hates you, you know that it has hated Me before you. If you were of the world, the world would love its own. Yet because you are not of the world, but I chose you out of the world, therefore the world hates you." John 15:18-19

The harsh reality is that most people are on the straight and wide path that leads to destruction. Pay attention!

"The wicked shall be turned away into Sheol, all the nations that forget God." Psalm 9:17

"But the cowardly, unbelieving, abominable, murderers, prostitutes, sorcerers, idolaters, and all liars shall have their part in the lake which burns with fire and brimstone, which is the second death." Revelation 21:8

"Now the works of the flesh are evident, which are: adultery, sexual perversion, uncleanness, licentiousness, idolatry, sorcery, hatred, contentions, jealousies, outbursts of wrath, selfish ambitions, dissensions, heresies, envy, murders, drunkenness, revelries, and the like; of which I tell you beforehand, just as I also told you in time past, that those who practice such things will not inherit the kingdom of God." Galatians 5:19-21

"Do you not know that the unrighteous will not inherit the kingdom of God? Do not be led astray. Neither prostitutes, nor idolaters, nor adulterers, nor effeminate, nor sodomites, nor thieves, nor covetous, nor drunkards, nor revilers, nor extortioners will inherit the kingdom of God." 1st Corinthians 6:9-10

Most churches do not worship the true God. Most pastors are leading their flock astray and on the path straight to Hell.

"And He spoke a parable to them: Is the blind able to lead the blind? Will they not both fall into the ditch?" Luke 6:39

If a man really wants to find out the truth, the real Truth then he needs to seek God, because Jesus is the Truth that every individual needs to find. Through the Holy Scriptures, God's Word to mankind, are the words of life. This is how someone measures what is right and wrong and what God expects out of all of us. The bible holds the keys to life, read it!

... "holding fast the Word of Life, so that I may rejoice in the day of Christ that I have not run in vain or labored in vain." Philippians 2:16

"Then Simon Peter answered Him, Lord, to whom shall we go? You have the Words of eternal life." John 6:68

"Be diligent to present yourself approved to God, a worker who does not need to be ashamed, rightly dividing the Word of Truth." 2nd Timothy 2:15

"Sanctify them in Your Truth. Your Word is Truth." John 17:17

Dear reader, are you on the narrow path?

"Jesus answered and said to him, If anyone loves Me, he will keep My Word; and My Father will love him, and We will come to him and make Our abode with him. He who does not love Me does not keep My words; and the Word which you hear is not Mine but the Father's who sent Me." John 14:23-24

"Jesus said to him, I am the Way, the Truth, and the Life. No one comes to the Father except through Me." John 14:6

Amen!

Tragedies

By now most people have heard about the earthquake in Taiwan. As of this writing there are still people who are trapped alive underneath the debris of buildings and rescue workers are trying hard to get them out. A lot of tragedies never make but a brief mention in national or international news.

Take a house fire that kills a family, a tornado that rips through part of a town or a car accident that renders people dead. In all of our local communities there are tragedies on nearly a weekly, if not daily basis. The bigger the city one lives in, the more common the tragedies become. On occasion we hear of really big tragedies.

Take the 2004 tsunami in the Indian ocean that killed over 200,000 people. Throughout history there have been some very big disasters that have killed scores of people. Take the Black Plague for instance and the staggering number of lives that the disease claimed, estimated from 75 million upward to 200 million. In America the biggest tragedies ever recorded was that of the Galveston hurricane in 1900. It is estimated that between 6,000 – 12,000 people died as a result of that storm.

As I watched some videos of the devastation in Taiwan and the rescue workers working hard to get to people, I couldn't help but to get saddened at the need for the world to understand the necessity of accepting the Lord Jesus Christ as their Savior. Even as these men and women are pulled out of these buildings, with little life left in them, though eventually vibrant and healed once more, these same people are on the highway to Hell, with no hope, no rescue once they enter their eternal punishment.

All around the world there are people just like that, indeed all around America. How many people die in the world each year? Yet the soul does not die. How many of those who are dead awaken to life and how many of those awaken to a tragic ending that could have been avoided, if they had just STOPPED and considered their way. If they had understood their deserving punishment and cried out to God Almighty for mercy, believing into His Son who paid the price for their sins and going forth following Him. If only!

Rather what is happening and will continue to happen, is that man goes on living his life, determining to do what he will, refusing to acknowledge his sin and that he is guilty. Shall a man who has a severed limb pretend that he does not? Shall a blind man pretend that he can see? Shall a deaf man pretend that he can hear or a mute man pretend that he can speak? If not, then why do those who are on their way to Hell, pretend that they are not?!

You who read this and say "one more day, one more day", will there be one more day? Will your heart be receptive to repent before an Almighty God? Do not be deceived, if God is speaking to your heart, then now is the time to go before Him.

"For He says: In an acceptable time I have heard you, and in a day of salvation I have helped you. Behold, now is the accepted time; behold, now is the day of salvation." 2nd Corinthians 6:2

"For godly sorrow produces repentance leading to salvation, not to be regretted; but the sorrow of the world produces death." 2nd Corinthians 7:10

"And as it is appointed for men to die once, and after this the judgment..." Hebrews 9:27

"Behold, I stand at the door and knock. If anyone hears My voice and opens the door, I will come in to him and dine with him, and he with Me." Revelation 3:20

"Jesus said to him, I am the Way, the Truth, and the Life. No one comes to the Father except through Me." John 14:6

"And this is His commandment: that we should believe on the name of His Son, Jesus Christ, and love one another, as He gave us commandment." 1st John 3:23

Amen!

Evidence Around Us

Nearly every day while reading the news I spot an article headline that depicts some sort of 'evolutionary' evidence portrayed to the reader as fact. The most recent headline that I spotted was that *"humans and neanderthals had breed as recently as 50,000 years ago"*. I quickly scuff off such nonsense, continuing to scan the headlines for an article that perks my interest.

The problem is that these sorts of articles are written for those who are uneducated in the Truth of God's Word. The average person will view the headline or read the article and thus have one more excuse not to believe God's Word, one more reason to not consider their Salvation, one more thought as to why they can continue on as they are.

A long time ago in Sunday school I listened as the teacher used an argument that evolution made about as much sense as a chair appearing out of nowhere in the room. A ridiculous argument you say? Have you ever checked into the 'evidence' that the evolutionist have? I assure you if you do some digging, you will find that a chair appearing in a room on its own would take less faith to believe in then the assumptions that evolutionists and our supposed scientific community makes.

I'm sure many readers would consider me an unscientific ignorant person, who believes in fairy-tales and old out-dated religious views, but I ask that you bear with me for yet another moment. I will wholly admit that I am not very scientific, I have not studied with the scholars at universities, I scoffed at my high school science books and I have not taken and read endless amounts of supposed documentation against Creation.

"For since, in the wisdom of God, the world through wisdom did not know God, it pleased God through the foolishness of the message preached to save those who are believing." 1st Corinthians 1:21

Rather I believe God and His Word to humanity, I believe that God Created the heavens and the earth, I believe that God sent His only begotten Son, Jesus, to die on the Cross for my sins that I might through Christ be rectified before Him. I believe that God will judge the world and believe that all will stand before the Almighty. I believe that God will open the Book of Life and whoever's name is not written in that Book will be cast into Hell. I believe that those of us who are Christians will endure until it is our time to go Home to be with our Savior. I believe God.

The arguments against many of the evolutionist's foundational hypothesis could fill the volumes of many books. For those who are curious I recommend David Cloud's, *Seeing the Non-Existent* book on such a topic. That book is the best I have ever read, using basic logic and going over the now covered-up and seldom mentioned evolutionary arguments that have been long ago debunked. Charles Darwin did not know about DNA/RNA when he came up with his argument against God. Nor until recently did any scientist realize just how non-simple a human cell really is.

The evidence is all around us, I see evidence of God's Creation on a daily basis. Something as simple as a box elder and its uncanny behavior is enough to prove to me that God's Word is true.

"Let it not be! Indeed, let God be true but every man a liar. As it is written: That You may be found just in Your words, and may win the case when You are judged." Romans 3:4

I look at the mountains and see His hand, I look at the stars and see His Almighty work. The communion between the land and His Creation speak volumes. A blade of grass tells of His wonders, a dragonfly shows His creativity and then there are us, men Created in the image of God.

Will those who attend church on a regular basis argue that there is a God and pretend to worship Him, yet refuse to believe Him? It simply doesn't make sense. Consider to understand that many of those who oppose Him are in the scientific world for just that purpose. Understand that many of the leading scientists are contrary to Him. Look around and wake up, the evidence is all around us.

"For ever since the creation of the world the unseen things of Him are clearly perceived, being understood by the things that are made, even His eternal power and Godhead, so that they are without excuse, because, although they know God, they do not glorify Him as God, nor are thankful, but become vain in their reasonings, and their stupid hearts are darkened. Professing to be wise, they become foolish, and change the glory of the incorruptible God into an image made like corruptible man, and birds and four-footed animals and creeping things. Therefore God also gives them up to uncleanness, in the lusts of their hearts, to dishonor their bodies among themselves, who change the truth of God into the lie, and fear and serve the created things more than the Creator, who is blessed forever. Amen." Romans 1:20-25

Amen!

Trendy

The cultural of the world constantly changes and that of those who live in the United States of America see new trends on a constant basis. One who is trendy tends to be one who follows the current trend or influence, fashion and ideologies.

For years I have tried to figure out how society can be so wrong and the collective, hive-mind mentality that goes behind that. Ask anyone nowadays and they will tell you that families have fallen apart, lives are being destroyed, people are more alienated from normal forms of conversation and have become more distanced in terms of relationships, despite new forms of communication that allow for constant status updating, connecting to one another through social media and an onslaught of instant notification through text messaging, email, cellular phones and other venues.

Yet with all of these options at our fingertips, a true Believer can see these things and also see the amount of sin that society engages in as a whole. They willingly seem to love things that are contrary to God and furthermore purport through their trendy actions that nothing is wrong with the way they behave. They are without God, not only do their actions prove it, but by their actions they prove that they are brute beasts. Harsh? There are two passages of Scripture that has long spoke to my heart about today's society.

"But know this, that in the last days perilous times will come: For men will be lovers of themselves, lovers of money, boasters, proud, blasphemers, disobedient to parents, unthankful, unholy, without natural affection, unyielding, slanderers, without self-control, savage, despisers of good, traitors, headstrong, haughty, lovers of pleasure rather than lovers of God, having a form of godliness but denying its power. And from such people turn away." 2nd Timothy 3:1-5

And…

"Preach the Word. Be ready in season and out of season. Convict, rebuke, exhort, with all longsuffering and teaching. For the time will come when they will not endure sound doctrine, but according to their own lusts, desiring to hear pleasant things, they will heap up for themselves teachers; and they will turn their ears away from the truth, and be turned aside to myths." 2nd Timothy 4:2-4

Just because 'everyone is doing it' doesn't make it right. There is no justification of sin through the collective of sinners.

"Do not be led astray, God is not mocked; for whatever a man sows, that he will also reap. For he who sows to his flesh will of the flesh reap corruption, but he who sows to the Spirit will of the Spirit reap eternal life." Galatians 6:7-8

"There is a way which seems right to a man, but the end of it is the ways of death." Proverbs 14:12

Certainly it was never trendy to follow God, the masses have always followed Satan and that path leads to Hell. Will you go along with the masses and be trendy unto death, not seeking His Son, not repenting of your sins or will you stop and consider that the ways of the world are not His way?

"Enter by the narrow gate; for wide is the gate and broad is the way that leads to destruction, and there are many entering in through it. Because narrow is the gate and distressing is the way which leads unto life, and there are few who find it." Matthew 7:13-14

"And I saw the dead, small and great, standing before God. And books were opened. And another book was opened, which is the Book of Life. And the dead were judged according to their works, out of the things which were written in the books. And the sea gave up the dead who were in it, and Death and Hades delivered up the dead who were in them. And they were judged, each one, according to their works. And Death and Hades were cast into the Lake of Fire. This is the second death. And anyone not found written in the Book of Life was cast into the Lake of Fire." Revelation 20:12-15

Amen!

A Perishing World

"For we are to God the fragrance of Christ among those who are being saved and among those who are perishing. To the one we are the aroma of death leading to death, and to the other the aroma of life leading to life. And who is sufficient for these things?" 2nd Corinthians 2:15-16

Have we as a society become so complex, so manipulated, so burdened by our own prisons that most can not possibly see the simplicity that is in Christ? I would equate the situation of America like that of an apartment complex meeting trying to solve how to fix the darkness in the hallway.

As the meeting is ongoing there is much debate back and forth on how to solve the problem. The meeting drags out days with finally it being decided that the light bulb is burnt out and needs to be tended to. One man suggests that he has some welding tools and perhaps if another can put a small incision into the side of the bulb he can fix the broken filament. Another suggests that the bulb be carefully opened and tritium gas be put inside, perhaps the glow will provide enough light to get by. One resident suggests pointing a flashlight towards the bulb to give it the appearance of operating and casting light, then they can continue on with there business. After much debate, finally the newest member of the apartment community provides an extra night light for the hallway. The light is red, but the residents are now able to function and begin to build their community strong once again, no longer debating over the darkness in the hallway.

There is one voice that is not heard though, a young child, meek and quiet, approaches the group several times during the meetings with an extra light bulb that their parents, who didn't attend, had in their cupboard. The residents are troubled by this little rascal whose behavior often troubles them. The child is different, causing all of their children to get angry at his anti-social behavior. While the parents are used to yelling at their children to be quiet, the fact that this one youngster is quiet becomes quite the annoyance to them. The child tries many times to interject that the problem with the dark hallway is simply that a new light bulb is needed, but no one will listen. Instead they bid the troublemaker to continue on his way, they do not have time to waste dealing with childish nonsense.

Have you ever wished that people would simply listen to the Gospel message? Rather as you try to explain it to supposedly desiring ears, how many times can you count that instead of being able to explain the Gospel in its simplicity that you are now spending time refuting false doctrine after false doctrine, usually to no avail! Who or what is to blame largely for such things?

"But I fear, lest somehow, as the serpent deceived Eve by his craftiness, so your minds may be corrupted from the simplicity that is in Christ." 2nd Corinthians 11:3

How many hoops must a Roman Catholic church member jump through in order to be supposedly affirmed by the priest? How many steps does it take for one to be 'secure' while attending a Jehovah Witness church? How much effort and learning of false doctrine does it take for someone to become a 'good' Mormon? Rather how much positivism must be preached from the pulpit of so-called churches for someone to convince themselves of the 'good' that is in them and that they are part of the body of Christ? Where are the simple Churches that preach the whole Gospel, that makes a man consider his ways, that creates godly sorrow and points the soon-to-be Believer to their Savior Jesus Christ, that the person might simply come to God in repentance, believing into His Son? It is a free gift from God, Jesus Christ paid the price for our sins on the Cross.

"For godly sorrow produces repentance leading to salvation, not to be regretted; but the sorrow of the world produces death." 2nd Corinthians 7:10

"For the wages of sin is death, but the gift of God is eternal life in Christ Jesus our Lord." Romans 6:23

"But God demonstrates His own love toward us, in that while we were yet sinners, Christ died for us." Romans 5:8

"Then Peter said to them, Repent, and let every one of you be immersed in the name of Jesus Christ to the remission of sins; and you shall receive the gift of the Holy Spirit." Acts 2:38

"Now it was not written for his sake alone, that it was accounted to him, but also for us, to whom it shall be accounted, believing in Him who raised up Jesus our Lord from the dead, who was delivered up because of our trespasses, and was raised for our justification." Romans 4:23-25

"For to this you were called, because Christ also suffered for us, leaving us an example, that you should follow His steps: Who committed no sin, nor was deceit found in His mouth; who, when He was reviled, did not revile in return; when He suffered, He did not threaten, but gave Himself over to Him who judges righteously; who Himself bore our sins in His own body on the tree, that we, having died to sins, might live unto righteousness; by whose stripes you were healed." 1st Peter 2:21-24

... *"for all have sinned and fall short of the glory of God..." Romans 3:23*

"For God so loved the world that He gave His only begotten Son, that everyone believing into Him should not perish but have eternal life. For God did not send His Son into the world to judge the world, but that the world through Him might be saved. The one believing into Him is not judged; but the one not believing is judged already, because he has not believed in the name of the only begotten Son of God. And this is the judgment, that the Light has come into the world, and men loved darkness rather than the Light, for their deeds were evil. For everyone practicing evil hates the Light and does not come to the Light, lest his deeds should be reproved. But the one doing the truth comes to the

Light, that his deeds may be clearly seen, that they have been worked in God." John 3:16-21

Man tries to create their own ways to become supposedly justified before Almighty God, yet it is God who created the Way for man to become reconciled to Him. Will you, dear reader, realize the simplicity that is in Christ, understand that you are guilty of your sins before your Creator and accept the gift of Salvation before it is too late? Will you consider for a moment?

"For the message of the cross is foolishness to those who are perishing, but to us who are being saved it is the power of God." 1st Corinthians 1:18

"Jesus said to him, I am the Way, the Truth, and the Life. No one comes to the Father except through Me." John 14:6

"Behold, I stand at the door and knock. If anyone hears My voice and opens the door, I will come in to him and dine with him, and he with Me. To him who overcomes I will grant to sit with Me on My throne, as I also overcame and sat down with My Father on His throne." Revelation 3:20-21

Amen!

Take a Moment

"Come now, you who say, Today or tomorrow we will go to this city, spend a year there, do business, and make a profit; whereas you do not know what will be tomorrow. For what is your life? It is even a vapor that appears for a little time and then vanishes away." Jacob (James) 4:13-14

Plans…plans…plans, most Americans have some sort of plan, goal or objective. Yet take a moment to realize that without Jesus as your Savior, it doesn't matter whether you succeed at any such plans.

America is a busy place, one that is fueled by endless consumer spending, often time that spending is directly related to being busy. Having been in restaurant management off and on for years, busyness results in jobs. Handing out food on the other side of the counter to endless people could not be done if they all had the time to make a lunch or dinner at home. Coffee shops would not be on every block corner if there was time for people to enjoy a cup in the morning.

Children take up time or at least should. As they get older parents often consider activities that they would like their children to participate in and things that they would like their children to learn, such as instruments. While there is nothing necessarily wrong with participating in such activities, just as there is nothing wrong with grabbing a bite to eat, which oftentimes can be very affordable if chosen wisely, there is once again the aspect of whether or not parents take the time to ensure that their children know about Jesus Christ and Salvation.

Yet any plans that an individual or family makes, no matter the ultimate outcome, whether successful or a failure, are part of the *"vapor that appears for a little time and then vanishes away."* What is our life without Christ? What is the objective to living if we do not honor God who Created us? What is the point of parenting and trying to avoid the trappings of evil if we do not instill in our children the precepts of His Word?

"Therefore you shall fix these words of mine in your hearts and in your souls, and shall bind them as a sign on your hands, and they shall be as frontlets between your eyes. You shall teach them to your children, speaking of them when you sit in your house, when you walk by the way, when you lie down, and when you rise up. And you shall write them on the doorposts of your house and on your gates, that your days and the days of your children may be multiplied in the land of which Jehovah has sworn to your fathers to give to them, like the days of the heavens above the earth." Deuteronomy 11:18-21

"Train up a child in the way he should go; and when he is old, he will not depart from it." Proverbs 22:6

Jesus is not something that we add to our daily lives, but He is the center of our daily lives with everything else on the outside. Every decision that must be made should be centered around a Believer's life in Christ, yet for those who are unsaved, the entire point of existence is being lost.

Those who save for retirement, save so that they have enough money to be able to live what they consider comfortably until their death. A man may gather much and hit those goals, but what has he stored up for eternity?

Many times people will work for a company for years and years, eventually taking advantage of retiring from them. Yet should not our lives be spent serving the Lord Jesus Christ and entering into eternal retirement? Has not God called those who are Believers to also be stewards to do His work?

"Go therefore and instruct all the nations, immersing them into the name of the Father and of the Son and of the Holy Spirit, teaching them to observe all things whatever I have commanded you; and lo, I am with you always, even to the end of the age. Amen." Matthew 28:19-20

"Preach the Word. Be ready in season and out of season. Convict, rebuke, exhort, with all longsuffering and teaching." 2nd Timothy 4:2

What about those who haven't accepted the free gift of Salvation? Would you take a moment to consider the vanity of your life and understand that there is more to it then simply living, whether it is just making ends meet, being 'successful' or even affluent.

Every single person will stand before God Almighty, this is a fact, this includes you.

"And I saw a great white throne and Him who sat on it, from whose face the earth and the heavens fled away. And there was found no place for them. And I saw the dead, small and great, standing before God. And books were opened. And another book was opened, which is the Book of Life. And the dead were judged according to their works, out of the things which were written in the books. And the sea gave up the dead who were in it, and Death and Hades delivered up the dead who were in them. And they were judged, each one, according to their works. And Death and Hades were cast into the Lake of Fire. This is the second death. And anyone not found written in the Book of Life was cast into the Lake of Fire." Revelation 20:11-15

When that time comes you will no longer have an option to rectify yourself or to change what it is you had done while on this earth. While there might be great remorse and sorrow as you stand before your Creator, He is a just Judge who will do as He says. A list of excuses will not be able to save you on that day, whether or not you consider them justifiable.

"God judges the righteous, and the Mighty God is angry with the wicked every day." Psalms 7:11

"O Jehovah, Mighty God, to whom vengeance belongs; O Mighty God, to whom vengeance belongs, shine forth! Be exalted, O Judge of the earth; restore recompense to the proud. Jehovah, how long will the wicked, how long will the wicked triumph? They belch forth, and speak arrogant things; all the workers of iniquity boast in themselves. They crush Your people, O Jehovah, and afflict Your heritage. They slay the widow and the sojourner, and murder the fatherless. Yet they say, YAH does not see, nor does the God of Jacob perceive it. Understand, you stupid ones among the people; and you fools, when will you be wise? He who planted the ear, shall He not hear? He who formed the eye, shall He not see? He who chastens the nations, shall He not correct, He who teaches man knowledge? Jehovah knows the thoughts of man, that they are vanity." Psalms 94:1-11

The lives of men focus on pleasing themselves, on doing what they decide they want to do. Despite what the naysayers out there might say about the existence of God, understand that He does exist and He has given His Holy Scriptures as the source to learn about Him, what is expected and containing the words of life that you might find Salvation through His Son who died on the Cross for your sins and rose again nearly two thousand years ago.

Without Jesus as your Savior, what is your life? What is the point of gathering up treasures or spending endless time enduring vanities? Without Jesus there is nothing, no point, no hope, all is lost. Jesus paid the penalty for your sins on the Cross and every man can freely partake of the gift from God, should he take a moment to consider his ways and understand that he is lost.

What Jesus did two thousand years ago still stands today. Even in a society that is filled with techno-marvels, understand that the reality of our existence is still that *"for all have sinned and fall short of the glory of God". (Romans 3:23)* Really it is quite simple, so simple a young child can understand it.

Man sinned, man is guilty. You must realize that you are also guilty and that the wages of your sin is death. With godly sorrow you come to repentance before your Creator, no longer wanting to do those things and realizing that Jesus paid the penalty for your sins on the Cross. Understanding that God sent His own Son to die for your sins and through believing into Him you become a new Creature who is born-again, Saved. Salvation is only through the Son of God who died and rose again, from Jesus, the only way.

"Therefore, just as through one man sin entered the world, and death through sin, and thus death spread to every person, because everyone sinned." Romans 5:12

"For the wages of sin is death, but the gift of God is eternal life in Christ Jesus our Lord." Romans 6:23

"Now it was not written for his sake alone, that it was accounted to him, but also for us, to whom it shall be accounted, believing in Him who raised up Jesus our Lord from the

dead, who was delivered up because of our trespasses, and was raised for our justification." Romans 4:23-25

"For godly sorrow produces repentance leading to salvation, not to be regretted; but the sorrow of the world produces death." 2nd Corinthians 7:10

"Therefore, if anyone is in Christ, he is a new creation; the old things have passed away; behold, all things have become new." 2nd Corinthians 5:17

"For God so loved the world that He gave His only begotten Son, that everyone believing into Him should not perish but have eternal life. For God did not send His Son into the world to judge the world, but that the world through Him might be saved." John 3:16-17

"But what does it say? The Word is near you, in your mouth and in your heart (that is, the Word of Faith which we preach): that if you confess with your mouth the Lord Jesus and believe in your heart that God has raised Him from the dead, you will be saved." Romans 10:8-9

"But as many as received Him, to them He gave the authority to become children of God, to those believing into His name: who were born, not of blood, nor of the will of the flesh, nor of the will of man, but of God." John 1:12-13

"For the love of Christ holds us, because we judge thus: that if One died for all, then all died; and He died for all, that those who live should no longer live unto themselves, but unto Him who died for them and rose again." 2nd Corinthians 5:14-15

"He is not here; for He is risen, as He said. Come, see the place where the Lord was lying." Matthew 28:6

"Jesus said to him, I am the Way, the Truth, and the Life. No one comes to the Father except through Me." John 14:6

Take a moment, consider.

Amen!

In a Twinkling of an Eye

"Behold, I tell you a mystery: We shall not all sleep, but we shall all be changed; in a moment, in the twinkling of an eye, at the last trumpet. For the trumpet will sound, and the dead will be raised incorruptible, and we shall be changed." 1st Corinthians 15:51-52

The other day as I got up in the morning, I heard a sound, a clamor that turned out to be a hole being punched into the ground, likely for electrical lighting for a future light pole. For a moment I pondered what the noise might be, but upon a brief investigation its source became apparent, simply men working.

The thought then occurred to me about how the Rapture of God's people and the judgment against mankind will come in a moment. The *"time of Jacob's trouble" (Jer. 30:7)* will begin and those of us who are Saved will from that moment be with the Lord forever. There is certainly rejoicing in this for the Believer, but my heart is saddened at the fact that so many chase after falsehood or refuse to submit, let alone acknowledge their Maker.

Life comes and is given by the Creator, He wielded each one of us, irregardless of racism throughout the world, it is God who made each man. Yet as I stared out the window from work I could see the billowing black clouds of smoke coming from the funeral home across the street. A body was being cremated, the former occupant of the body now either asleep awaiting the Trumpet or in Hell. Whatever choice they had made regarding Salvation in their lifetime was settled, there was no more time, no more chance, either rejoicing that they had counted the things of God worthy to be wholeheartedly followed, having accepted Jesus Christ as their Savior or else regret and eternal remorse, destitute, without hope and forever apart from their Creator, being justly punished by the Almighty for what is a fitting judgment for those who refuse to be obedient to the Most High.

A few days later I am at work and the power flashes ever so briefly that no one seemed to take note. My heart pondered this once more as I considered the end of those who stand around me, those that fill the restaurant and realize that it is not a joke, but a VERY serious matter. In the twinkling of an eye, in a moment, things will change. The line will have been drawn in the sand and while there is still hope for many men, the consequences for having been part of the rebellion against God is at that moment in full swing…too late.

Finally I had to take a special order to a local nursing home. As I entered the doors to track down the nurse, whom I had just spoken to minutes ago, I saw the eyes of the forgotten, those who paced back and forth or sat quietly with blank stares on their face. If I could guess, the regrets of life, the sorrow of no longer being able to run about, the feelings of depression from the sole lifestyle that produces great loneliness seemed heavy upon many of the residents mind. They seemed to scream, if only I could walk, if only I could once again work, if only I could live. Yet do they realize that they can walk, they can live, they can serve, if only they belonged to Christ, if only they were sealed unto their redemption through Jesus, IF ONLY!!

The horrors of this life and the horrors that man bring upon his own soul. Why or why would man chose death instead of being with a God who loved them and provided Salvation through His Son? What could possibly have advantaged them or any other person walking the face of the earth today that is more valuable than their eternal soul? Would they give both eyes for a million dollars? Then why would they give up serving a holy and righteous God for the vanities of sin?

Dear reader, at the moment it is not too late. Will you consider, will you ponder, will you realize that the path you are on, without Jesus as your Savior, is one that leads to doom! Jesus is willing to pardon your sins if only you come to Him with a repentant heart and believe into Him. God has made the way of Salvation very simple that even a young child can Believe, yet what holds you back? I will tell you what holds you back, sin.

Consider your ways and realize that it is not too late, the path without Christ is the path that leads to Hell.

Amen!

The Night is Far Spent

"And do this, knowing the time, that now it is high time to awake out of sleep; for now our salvation is nearer than when we first believed. The night is far spent, the day is at hand. Therefore let us cast off the works of darkness, and let us put on the armor of light. Let us walk decently, as in the day, not in carousings and drunkenness, not in cohabitation and licentiousness, not in strife and envy. But put on the Lord Jesus Christ, and make no provision for the flesh, to fulfill its lusts." Romans 13:11-14

There will be a time, a moment, in this world when the day is at hand and the night is over. That time is when Jesus comes to receive us Believers to Himself and the world enters the *"time of Jacob's trouble." (Jer. 30:7)*

For those who are not Saved, not born-again, not in Christ, it is a time of judgment that the world will face. For those of us who are Believers, *"...the Lord Himself will descend from Heaven with a shouted command, with the voice of the archangel, and with the trumpet of God. And the dead in Christ will rise first. Then we who are alive and remain shall be caught up together at the same time with them in the clouds to meet the Lord in the air. And thus we shall always be with the Lord." 1st Thessalonians 4:16b-17*

As it stands at this very moment, as each individual reads this, understand what has been done in your past is what has been done, there is no undoing anything. For those who are Believers there may be many regrets about what could have been done for God, where one should be in terms of growing in the knowledge of Him through His Word. Where some might be able to be 'scholars' they are yet just taking solid food, or even milk. For some perhaps they could rattle off the things that they should've done for Christ, how they could've lived differently, regrets, sorrow and guilt. For those who are unsaved, the matter is different.

Not only could there be personal regrets from their choices in life, but perhaps a long time ago they heard a pastor preach a sermon, believed, but just refused to yield their life to Christ. Perhaps they simply know that they need to seek God, that they must find the Way, but they just continuously put it off. Well for both parties the consequences are certainly different, but the solution is the same.

Are you alive now, are you willing to straighten up and go where He leads, to do what He wants, to yield and repent from those things that you know are not pleasing to God. If you are not yet Saved, are you willing to truly put aside whatever trappings you might find your self in and seek God. Are you willing to realize that it is as if you are dying at the very moment, as if your home is on fire, as if you car is sliding off a cliff, you must acknowledge Jesus Christ, believing into Him and repent of your sins! At some point it will be too late, that time could be now, you never know. You must realize that without God you are in the middle of a full fledge emergency and Jesus Christ stands at the Door, willing to help you, willing to breath life into you and rescue you, you are the one resisting.

Would a dying man resist the ambulance as he is nearly dead from an automobile accident? Would someone in a house that is burning not try to escape out a window? Will not a sinner come to Jesus Christ when there soul is headed straight to Hell and He is the only One who can Save them?

As for Believers, is there not still today? Has He said to stop working, have you been told to 'never mind' with those 'sin' issues in your life? The night might be far spent and the day at hand, but it really is time to awake up out of sleep.

Wake up! Do what your supposed to do.

"I know your works, that you are neither cold nor hot. I would that you were cold or hot. So then, because you are lukewarm, and neither cold nor hot, I will vomit you out of My mouth." Revelation 3:15-16

"Then Jesus said to them again, Truly, truly, I say to you, I am the door of the sheep." John 10:7

"As many as I love, I rebuke and chasten. Therefore be zealous and repent. Behold, I stand at the door and knock. If anyone hears My voice and opens the door, I will come in to him and dine with him, and he with Me." Revelation 3:19-20

"For He says: In an acceptable time I have heard you, and in a day of salvation I have helped you. Behold, now is the accepted time; behold, now is the day of salvation." 2nd Corinthians 6:2

"The harvest is past, the summer is ended, and we are not saved." Jeremiah 8:20

"And I saw the dead, small and great, standing before God. And books were opened. And another book was opened, which is the Book of Life. And the dead were judged according to their works, out of the things which were written in the books. And the sea gave up the dead who were in it, and Death and Hades delivered up the dead who were in them. And they were judged, each one, according to their works. And Death and Hades were cast into the Lake of Fire. This is the second death. And anyone not found written in the Book of Life was cast into the Lake of Fire." Revelation 20:12-15

"There is a way that seems right to a man, but the end of it is the ways of death." Proverbs 16:25

Amen!

The Collective

"But as the days of Noah were, so also will the coming of the Son of Man be. For as in the days before the flood, they were eating and drinking, marrying and giving in marriage, until the day that Noah entered into the ark, and did not realize until the flood came and took them all away, so also will the coming of the Son of Man be. Then two will be in the field: one is taken and the other is left. Two will be grinding at the mill: one is taken and the other is left. Watch therefore, for you do not know what hour your Lord comes. But know this, that if the master of the house had known what hour the thief comes, he would have watched and not allowed his house to be dug through. Therefore you also be ready, for the Son of Man comes at an hour you do not expect." Matthew 24:37-44

"And Jehovah saw that the evil of man was great on the earth, and that every imagination of the thoughts of his heart was only evil all day long." Genesis 6:5

"But evil men and pretenders will grow worse and worse, leading astray and being led astray." 2nd Timothy 3:13

There is a collective mindset amongst most people nowadays. While the degrees of evil vary on whether or not one has a 'conservative' or a 'liberal' mindset, nonetheless the collective as a whole is very evil and against their Creator.

Tons of psycho-babble has been pushed on the masses. The media industry via entertainment constantly fights for the minds of men and introduces ideologies that are contrary to the Most High. The education system pushes for a humanistic approach, helping to ensure that the young ones are trained fully in accepting evil and denying their Creator. We live in a time where news from a corner of the globe can suddenly appear on our screens, be it phones, television or internet.

Yet these paths that the collective travel down are paths that lead straight to Hell. If one inside the collective decides to think for themselves, to ponder their ways, then those who support these ideas quickly try to put these thoughts to rest, trying to ensure them that nothing is wrong. Yet something is VERY wrong.

"My son, if sinners entice you, do not consent." Proverbs 1:10

"My son, do not walk in the way with them! Withhold your foot from their path; for their feet run to evil and they make haste to shed blood." Proverbs 1:15-16

"Because they hated knowledge and chose not the fear of Jehovah. They did not desire my counsel; they despised all my reproof. Therefore they shall eat of the fruit of their own way and be filled with their own devices." Proverbs 1:29-31

The standards that man are to live by are laid out in God's Word. God has given His Word so that man may know about Him, further God sent His Son to die for our sins that man may find Salvation through repentance and believing into Jesus Christ. Yet the world tells us otherwise.

"Then Simon Peter answered Him, Lord, to whom shall we go? You have the Words of eternal life. And we have believed and understood that You are the Christ, the Son of the living God." John 6:68-69

"Now it was not written for his sake alone, that it was accounted to him, but also for us, to whom it shall be accounted, believing in Him who raised up Jesus our Lord from the dead, who was delivered up because of our trespasses, and was raised for our justification." Romans 3:23-25

"But what does it say? The Word is near you, in your mouth and in your heart (that is, the Word of Faith which we preach): that if you confess with your mouth the Lord Jesus and believe in your heart that God has raised Him from the dead, you will be saved. For with the heart one believes unto righteousness, and with the mouth confession is made unto salvation." Romans 10:8-10

"For godly sorrow produces repentance leading to salvation, not to be regretted; but the sorrow of the world produces death." 2nd Corinthians 7:10

"But those things which God foretold through the mouth of all His prophets, that the Christ would suffer, He has thus fulfilled. Repent therefore and be converted, that your sins may be blotted out, so that times of refreshing may come from the presence of the Lord, and that He may send Jesus Christ, who was preached to you before, whom Heaven must receive until the times of restoration of all things, of which God has spoken through the mouth of all His holy prophets since the past ages." Acts 3:18-21

... *"testifying both to Jews, and also to Greeks, repentance toward God and faith toward our Lord Jesus Christ." Acts 20:21*

"For God so loved the world that He gave His only begotten Son, that everyone believing into Him should not perish but have eternal life. For God did not send His Son into the world to judge the world, but that the world through Him might be saved. The one believing into Him is not judged; but the one not believing is judged already, because he has not believed in the name of the only begotten Son of God. And this is the judgment, that the Light has come into the world, and men loved darkness rather than the Light, for their deeds were evil. For everyone practicing evil hates the Light and does not come to the Light, lest his deeds should be reproved. But the one doing the truth comes to the Light, that his deeds may be clearly seen, that they have been worked in God." John 3:16-21

The collective would have you believe that it is a worthwhile conversation to engage with the 'social justice warriors' and declare that those who refuse to repent, those who refuse to believe God, those evil and reprehensible individuals who push to use the bathroom of their choice are worthy of their path and should be heeded to.

"For ever since the creation of the world the unseen things of Him are clearly perceived, being understood by the things that are made, even His eternal power and Godhead, so that they are without excuse, because, although they know God, they do not glorify Him as God, nor are thankful, but become vain in their reasonings, and their stupid hearts are darkened. Professing to be wise, they become foolish, and change the glory of the incorruptible God into an image made like corruptible man, and birds and four-footed animals and creeping things. Therefore God also gives them up to uncleanness, in the lusts of their hearts, to dishonor their bodies among themselves, who change the truth of God into the lie, and fear and serve the created things more than the Creator, who is blessed forever. Amen. For this reason God gives them up to vile passions. For even their women change the natural use for what is contrary to nature. Likewise also the men, abandoning the natural use of the woman, burned in their lust toward one another, men with men performing what is shameful, and receiving the retribution within themselves, the penalty which is fitting for their error. And even as they do not like to have God in their full true knowledge, God gives them over to a reprobate mind, to do those things which are not fitting; being filled with every unrighteousness, sexual perversion, wickedness, covetousness, maliciousness; full of envy, murder, strife, deceit, depravity; whisperers, defamers, haters of God, insolent, proud, boasters, inventors of evil things, disobedient to parents, without understanding, untrustworthy, without natural affection, unforgiving, unmerciful; who, knowing the righteous judgment of God, that those who practice such things are deserving of death, not only do them, but also approve of those who practice them." Romans 1:20-32

"But from the beginning of the creation, God made them male and female." Mark 10:6

The collective would have you believe that the marriage between two men or two women is alright, that our society is finally turning to a point of accepting everyone in the giant melting pot of not only people from different countries, but also the melting and molding of ideas into the great collective.

"You shall not lie with a male as with a female. It is an abomination." Leviticus 18:22

"Do you not know that the unrighteous will not inherit the kingdom of God? Do not be led astray. Neither prostitutes, nor idolaters, nor adulterers, nor effeminate, nor sodomites, nor thieves, nor covetous, nor drunkards, nor revilers, nor extortioners will inherit the kingdom of God." 1st Corinthians 6:9-10

"And the angels who did not keep their proper domain, but left their own abode, He has reserved in everlasting bonds under darkness for the judgment of the Great Day; as Sodom and Gomorrah, and the cities around them in a similar manner to these, having

given themselves over to sexual immorality and gone after other flesh, are set forth as an example, suffering the vengeance of eternal fire." Judas 1:6-7

The collective would have you believe that what you view for entertainment is acceptable, proper and without consequences. Likewise they live to entertain you all the way to Hell.

"As righteousness leads to life, so the one pursuing evil does so to his own death. Those who are of a perverse heart are an abomination to Jehovah, but the perfect in their way are His delight." Proverbs 11:19-20

"The way of the wicked is an abomination to Jehovah, but He loves him who pursues righteousness." Proverbs 15:9

"The thoughts of the wicked are an abomination to Jehovah, but the words of the pure are pleasant." Proverbs 15:26

The time will come when the collective will also declare the Antichrist to be followed, the collective will also declare to accept the mark of the beast, the collective will continue to declare that the Most High is not who He says He is. The collective will continue on the broad path that leads to destruction. There the collective will be given the recompense that God will rightly cast judgment on them, there they will be repaid for their sins and receive the fruit from their activities, there they will join Satan and his demons in the Lake of Fire.

"Enter by the narrow gate; for wide is the gate and broad is the way that leads to destruction, and there are many entering in through it." Matthew 7:13

"And the devil, who led them astray, was cast into the Lake of Fire and brimstone where the beast and the false prophet are. And they will be tormented day and night forever and ever. And I saw a great white throne and Him who sat on it, from whose face the earth and the heavens fled away. And there was found no place for them. And I saw the dead, small and great, standing before God. And books were opened. And another book was opened, which is the Book of Life. And the dead were judged according to their works, out of the things which were written in the books. And the sea gave up the dead who were in it, and Death and Hades delivered up the dead who were in them. And they were judged, each one, according to their works. And Death and Hades were cast into the Lake of Fire. This is the second death. And anyone not found written in the Book of Life was cast into the Lake of Fire." Revelation 20:10-15

"No one is able to serve two masters; for either he will hate the one and love the other, or else he will hold to the one and despise the other. It is not possible to serve God and mammon." Matthew 6:24

Are you part of the collective, do you know how to even consider things for yourself? Do you realize that you are on your way to Hell without Jesus? Do you even understand that what God says is what He says and His Word will stand, man's will not.

"For truly I say to you, till heaven and earth pass away, one jot or one tittle will by no means pass from the Law till all is fulfilled. Whoever therefore relaxes one of the least of these commandments, and teaches men so, shall be called least in the kingdom of Heaven; but whoever does and teaches them, he shall be called great in the kingdom of Heaven." Matthew 5:18-19

"The counsel of Jehovah stands forever, the thoughts of His heart from generation to generation." Psalms 33:11

God is not mocked, nor will any ideology or belief system at the fullness of its fruit save you from His just judgment. God Almighty, the Most High does not change. He has set the standards, the Creator will do as He pleases and He has offered you, yes you, a chance to change, to come to repentance, to understand His will and accept Jesus Christ as your Savior by believing into Him.

"Do not be led astray, God is not mocked; for whatever a man sows, that he will also reap. For he who sows to his flesh will of the flesh reap corruption, but he who sows to the Spirit will of the Spirit reap eternal life." Galatians 6:7-8

"For I, Jehovah, change not." Malachi 3:6a

"Jesus Christ the same yesterday, today, and forever." Hebrews 13:8

Do not listen to the masses, think for yourself. If you are a Believer reading this, understand that as the apostasy thickens, as things wax worse and worse, our job as Christians is simply to be obedient to Christ, living righteously and holy, purifying ourselves. We must simply stand firm and wait to meet our Redeemer, whether through the exit of these bodies or in the clouds.

"All Scripture is breathed by God, and is profitable for doctrine, for reproof, for correction, for instruction in righteousness, that the man of God may be complete, thoroughly equipped for every good work." 2nd Timothy 3:16-17

"Therefore, having these promises, beloved, let us cleanse ourselves from all defilements of the flesh and spirit, perfecting holiness in the fear of God." 2nd Corinthians 7:1

"And everyone who has this hope in Him purifies himself, just as He is pure." 1st John 3:3

"Therefore gird up the loins of your mind, be sober, and rest your hope fully upon the grace that is to be brought to you at the revelation of Jesus Christ; as obedient children, not conforming yourselves to the former lusts in your ignorance; but as He who called

you is holy, you also become holy in all conduct, because it is written, Be holy, because I am holy." 1st Peter 1:13-16

"And if it seems evil to you to serve Jehovah, choose for yourselves this day whom you will serve, whether the gods which your fathers have served that were on the other side of the River, or the gods of the Amorites, in whose land you are living. But as for me and my house, we will serve Jehovah." Joshua 24:15

"Watch, stand fast in the faith, be like men, be strong." 1st Corinthians 16:13

"The wicked shall see and be indignant; he shall gnash his teeth and melt away; the desire of the wicked shall perish." Psalms 112:10

Amen!

As He Says

"For ever since the creation of the world the unseen things of Him are clearly perceived, being understood by the things that are made, even His eternal power and Godhead, so that they are without excuse..." Romans 1:20

The other day in a mailing I received the author had CLEARLY PERCEIVED and emphasized how true that is. As I watched a robin out in the yard this morning gathering up pieces of dead grass to make a nest, common sense suggests that there is a Creator.

How did the robin learn to make a nest, did she go to school? Did her parents hold class to show her how to do so? Silly you say, well it also is silly to assume that evolution preprogrammed this nest making process.

Prior to going outside I had seen an article making national news headlines that North Carolina was suing the federal government over its attempt to force them to have bathrooms for so-called transgenders. North Carolina was filing suit on the premise that the federal government doesn't have mandate over such actions and that their law (which requires you to use the bathroom that matches the sex listed on your birth certificate) doesn't discriminate against anyone, simply the same rules apply for everyone.

I'm not sure what has caused North Carolina to take a stand, but they are. In the article I saw there was a picture of what appeared to be protestors trying to assert their 'rights' to be perverse in the public. Looking at the photo of people dressed in drag and what I can only call circus outfits, I noted the stares of hatred toward whomever they were protesting against. The though quickly came to mind about Jeremiah and what God told him.

"Do not be afraid of their faces, for I am with you to deliver you, says Jehovah." Jeremiah 1:8

Ezekiel was also told:

"And you, son of man, do not be afraid of them nor be afraid of their words, though briers and thorns are with you and you dwell among scorpions; do not be afraid of their words or dismayed by their looks, though they are a rebellious house." Ezekiel 2:6

What God says is what He says, He does not change, nor do His Words.

"For I, Jehovah, change not." Malachi 3:6a

"The grass withers, the flower fades; but the Word of our God stands forever." Isaiah 40:8

"Forever, O Jehovah, Your Word stands firm in the heavens." Psalms 119:89b

"but the Word of the Lord endures forever." 1st Peter 1:25a

The more I consider these things, the more I begin to understand the basis for how come things seem to be getting so bad in the world. What man needs is truth, absolute truth. Things have to be measured against truth to see whether they are true or not. If I purchase a ruler and assuming it was manufactured correctly I would be able to correctly measure something. In a jam, I might use a finger to measure up inches, but that is not a true measurement, where it would matter I would need a true measurement.

Does not your soul matter? Does not ensuring you are Saved make a difference to you? In today's evil and fallen world things need to be lined up with Truth. The only way we can measure things correctly is by weighing them against the Word of God, the Holy Scriptures. Then when pitted against God's Word we are able to see what the truth of any matter might be, whether or not it is a new movement going across the United States, or even an older accepted religion or belief system. And finally even the churches that many attend across the land. God has already told us all we need to know, it is as He says and will always be.

"Your Word is truth since the beginning, and every one of Your righteous judgments is everlasting." Psalms 119:60

"Sanctify them in Your Truth. Your Word is Truth." John 17:17

"These were more noble than those in Thessalonica, in that they received the Word with all readiness, and searched the Scriptures daily, to see whether these things are so." Acts 17:11

So when it comes down to it, a response from a Believer is simply that this is what God says and that is all to the matter. It is not our opinion, but it is a fact, a fact discerned from the Truth, God's Word.

Amen!

God Sees You

"For the Word of God is living and active, and sharper than any two-edged sword, piercing even to the division of soul and spirit, and of joints and marrow, and is a discerner of the thoughts and intents of the heart. And there is no creature that is not revealed in His presence, but all things are naked and laid bare to the eyes of Him to whom we must give answer." Hebrews 4:12-13

In the midst of my young son and I playing with my homemade Lego 'Chicago', one of the bad guys has a cannon is about ready to shoot cannon Lego balls towards his version of Lego 'Chicago'. As the bad guys lets out a hardy laugh, suddenly the Lego cat comes over to try and talk sense into them from annihilating cat's Lego 'Chicago'.

Cat says, *"Don't you know that God sees you?"*

"Really, but I will hide underneath this building!", proclaims the green bad guy.

Cat responds, *"God still sees you and if you don't stop choosing evil and choose the good, you are going to go to Hell."*

Adding, *"Don't you want to go to Heaven? You need to talk to Lego Dad about what you are doing."*

The Lego bad guys consider whether or not to choose the good or the bad as they hear reasoning from Lego Dada about why they need to be Saved. In the end all is well, they choose the good and become the factory guys, producing various sorts of Lego goods.

The simplicity in a young child's heart is amazing. Yet really how simple is it for the world. Is not the answer the same? Perhaps we use a bit of a different wording, but Salvation is still the same, through repentance and believing into Jesus Christ. For those of you who scoff, do you not realize that God sees you? For those of you who choose sin, who choose the bad, don't you realize that God also sees you?

Where will you go to hide from your Maker? What evil can you do that the Judge will not render judgment to you in the day you stand before Him? Can you pretend that He doesn't exist and try to ignore all thoughts or reasonings that enter your mind otherwise? Even if you do not believe or do not want to believe, God still sees you!

"For the ways of man are before the eyes of Jehovah, and He ponders all his tracks. His own iniquities shall capture the wicked, and he shall be held with the cords of his sin. He shall die without instruction, and in the greatness of his folly he shall go astray." Proverbs 5:21-23

"O Jehovah, You have searched me and known me. You know my sitting down and my rising up; You understand my thoughts afar off. You have sifted through my way of life and my lying down, and are familiar with all my ways. For there is not a word on my tongue, but behold, O Jehovah, You know it altogether. You have hedged me behind and before, and laid Your hand upon me. Such knowledge is incomprehensible to me; it is high, I am not able to reach it. Where can I go from Your Spirit? Or where can I flee from Your presence? If I ascend into the heavens, You are there; if I make my bed in Sheol, behold, You are there. If I take the wings of the dawn, and dwell in the uttermost parts of the sea, even there Your hand shall lead me, and Your right hand shall take hold of me. If I say, Surely the darkness shall fall upon me, even the night shall be light round about me; yea, the darkness shall not hide from You, but the night shines as the day; the darkness and the light are both alike to You." Psalms 139:1-12

Amen!

Lone Wolves?

"Then they will deliver you up to affliction and kill you, and you will be hated by all nations because of My name." Matthew 24:19

True Christians have always been the focus of derision throughout the ages, certainly it is nothing new. In America there has always been tolerance and aside from some name calling, usually there is no true violence against Believers. This of course is not the case in other countries, such as Iran, Syria, India, China or historically in place like Russia. The Roman Catholic church persecuted and killed millions of Believers throughout the middle ages, even into the 1800's.

"Behold, I send you out as sheep in the midst of wolves. Therefore be wise as serpents and harmless as doves. But beware of men, for they will deliver you up to councils and scourge you in their synagogues." Matthew 10:16-17

The government has coined the term 'lone wolves', but in reality those who truly know Christ are His sheep. As our society continues to become more and more degraded, the threat from the actual wolves out there increases. What is a Believer to do?

"Therefore, my beloved brethren, be steadfast, immovable, always abounding in the work of the Lord, knowing that your labor is not in vain in the Lord." 1st Corinthians 15:58

Persecution comes with our Citizenship *(Philippians 3:20)*. While we might live in a region of the world where the persecution is light, nonetheless, if we lived in a region where the persecution is severe, including the threat of being killed, we must remember the words that Jesus spoke to us.

"If the world hates you, you know that it has hated Me before you. If you were of the world, the world would love its own. Yet because you are not of the world, but I chose you out of the world, therefore the world hates you. Remember the Word that I said to you, A servant is not greater than his master. If they persecuted Me, they will also persecute you. If they kept My Word, they will keep yours also." John 15:18-20

The tide in America is turning. The threat of true Believers being persecuted by fellow citizens or even our own government is growing exponentially day by day. In the name of tolerance, people are beginning to determine that there is one group of people they can not tolerate, that is conservative Christians.

In the wake of the Orlando massacre, there have been liberal writers, some who are very well known and followed, blaming the shooting not on Islamic radicalism, but rather on the ideologies that conservative Christians hold and promote. They say that it was the baseline hate that some Christians have put into the fabric of this nation that allows for people like the Orlando shooter to become radicalized off of. The list of these people purporting such ideas include popular think tank writers, university professors, lawyers and even elected leaders.

Already in America we had a society where even pastors who recognized the difference between right and wrong, as laid out in the Holy Scriptures, would not publicly speak out against such sin, for fear of backlash from their congregation or their community. Now how much more so will those who know withhold their voice from proclaiming God's truth?

Around the world there have been calls for tolerance, to end the hate, to just get along with everyone and a renewed call for not only acceptance of the LGBTQ community, but embracing their ideologies and supporting their perversity. Yet in the wake of the shooting comes forth a dangerous idea by our leaders and those who are in charge of intelligence departments of the United States.

Omar Mateen, the shooter at the Pulse nightclub in Orlando, had been on the terrorist watchlist maintained by the FBI. Apparently his name was removed from the watchlist, the investigation we are told had been closed. Mateen had been one of 800,000 people on the watchlist. There are just over 204 million working age Americans in the United States. That means that 1 out of every 255 Americans are on the terrorist watchlist maintained by the FBI.

There has always been a debate going back and forth about where the line is drawn between civil liberties and the government surveilling supposed dissidents. In the case of Mateen, the FBI is under fire for having stopped their investigation and there are renewed calls for the FBI to tighten up its grip on watching dissidents. Their definition of a lone wolf is *"people who may be inspired to commit an attack from their consumption of online content without receiving any material or logistical support from groups."* President Obama stated, *"it is increasingly clear"* that the killer, a U.S. citizen, became *"radicalized"* by *"extremist information and propaganda over the internet"* — noting that such lone-wolf attacks are *"the hardest to detect."*

Will true Believers find themselves in the crosshairs of the Federal government? Will the Lord come and gather His own before things get that bad? The public is now susceptible to scrutinization of people whose views differ from their own, or rather people who hold viewpoints that are called 'extreme'.

The problem is that true Believers viewpoints are not their own ideas, but rather God's firm word on the matter. The fact that a Believer is labeled homophobic, a hater, or now deemed as a threat for holding such truth that those who are gay will be judged by God and have a need for Jesus Christ to save them, is now extreme. If you do not believe that our society is on that path, I challenge you to use your Facebook account or other social media and intercede with one of the remember Orlando postings or rehashes by simply telling your friends that God calls all to repentance *(Acts 17:30)*. If you do not believe that the turning of the tide is now alive and well towards evil, the responses you receive from your family and friends should be a quick awakening.

Unfortunately since the massacre in Orlando there has been much renewed discussion about how the FBI should deal with those on the terrorist watchlist, as well as protocols for ensuring lone wolves be tracked down, investigated relentlessly. Hillary Clinton said the following in a recent speech:

"The Orlando terrorist may be dead, but the virus that poisoned his mind remains very much alive. And we must attack it with clear eyes, steady hands, unwavering determination and pride in our country and our values." Adding, "we have to be just as adaptable and versatile as our enemies. As president, I will make identifying and stopping lone wolves a top priority." Finally she states, "I will put a team together from across our government, the entire government, as well as the private sector and communities to get on top of this urgent challenge."

Obama stated, *"That's something that the LGBT community is subject to not just by ISIL but by a lot of groups that purport to speak on behalf of God around the world."*

True Believers would never resort to violence, nor should such thoughts even enter the mind.

"Vengeance is Mine, and recompense; their foot shall slip in due time; for the day of their calamity is near, and the things prepared have made haste upon them." Deuteronomy 32:35

"For though we walk in the flesh, we do not war according to the flesh. For the weapons of our warfare are not carnal but mighty through God for pulling down strongholds, casting down arguments and every high thing that exalts itself against the knowledge of God, bringing every thought into captivity unto the obedience of Christ, and being ready to avenge all disobedience when your obedience is fulfilled." 2nd Corinthians 10:3-6

Yet in the minds of the politicians who represent us, there is little difference to them whether or not one has claims to ISIS, but whether those ideas that supposedly rot the brain and create a potential for violence are present. A Christian, when appropriate to do so, must not shy away from proclaiming God's truth. Should a situation occur where the Holy Spirit directs a Believer's heart to proclaim His truth, do so. If being a true Christian in today's society lands a Believer on the terrorist watchlist, so be it! God will investigate their doings.

"Therefore do not fear them. For there is nothing covered that will not be uncovered, and hidden that will not be known. Whatever I tell you in the dark, speak in the light; and what you hear in the ear, proclaim on the housetops. And do not fear those who kill the body but are not able to kill the soul. But rather fear Him who has power to destroy both soul and body in Gehenna." Matthew 10:26-28

"For He is coming, for He is coming to judge the earth. He shall judge the world with righteousness, and the peoples with His truth." Psalms 96:13

Amen!

They Forgot About God

"I will praise You, O Jehovah, with my whole heart; I will tell of all Your marvelous works. I will be glad and rejoice in You; I will sing praise to Your name, O Most High. When my enemies have turned back, they shall fall and perish at Your presence. For You have maintained my right and my cause; You sat on the throne judging in righteousness. You have rebuked the nations, You have destroyed the wicked, You have blotted out their name forever and ever. The desolations of the enemy have come to an end forever, and You have destroyed the cities; the remembrance of them has perished with them. But Jehovah shall endure forever; He has prepared His throne for justice. And He shall judge the world in righteousness; He shall execute judgment to the people with equity. Jehovah also will be a refuge for the oppressed, a refuge in times of distress. And those who know Your name will put their trust in You; for You, Jehovah, have not forsaken those who seek You. Sing praises to Jehovah, who dwells in Zion; declare His deeds among the nations. When He investigates bloodshed, He forgets not the cry of the lowly. Have mercy upon me, O Jehovah; look upon my affliction from those who hate me, You who lift me up from the gates of death, so that I may declare all Your praise in the gates of the daughter of Zion. I will rejoice in Your salvation. The nations have sunk down in the pit that they made; their own foot is caught in the net which they hid. Jehovah is known. He has executed judgment; the wicked is snared in the work of his own hands. Higgaion. Selah. The wicked shall be turned away into Sheol, all the nations that forget God. For the needy shall not always be forgotten; the expectation of the poor shall not perish forever. Arise, O Jehovah; let not man prevail. Let the nations be judged before Your face. Put them in fear, O Jehovah; let the nations know that they are but men. Selah." Psalms 9:1-20

If you are paying attention to the news nowadays, there seems to be an engulf of tragedies, violence, movements, oppression and troubles worldwide. As a friend mentioned recently, such things as the gay movement is not isolated to the United States.

"And because lawlessness will abound, the love of many will grow cold." Matthew 24:12

Troubles increase upon troubles and we are all awakened to the news of yet another shooting, rioting and violence in Venezuela, problems with worldwide financial markets, disputes over who controls the South China sea, aggressions between Russia and the

United States, as well as America's upcoming election. To top it off, supposedly Osama Bin Laden's son has issued a warning to Americans that he is going to take revenge with a *"we are all Osama"* threat.

Behind a lot of these issues there are political ideologies and motives. The shooting in Orlando was from an Islamist extremist who was bent on using violence to make a statement. The Dallas shooting was motivated by the Black Lives Matter movement and he was also bent on using violence to make a statement. Then the *"we are all Osama"* issued by Bin Laden's son is yet another statement that could induce many followers, just as ISIS has.

The world is a very troubling place and in these last days events are becoming more and more disturbing. While there has always been violence, a lot of what is being done now is based upon individuals who follow very loose connections to ideologies. Most of these people who are involved in circles listed above are Generation Y and Z, also known as the Millennials (1975-1995) and iGeneration (1995-2015).

By time 1981 came and went, the Millennials had begun being born and the Churches in America were beginning to cease. Generation X (1961-1981) and the Baby Boomer Generation (1945-1964) had rode the wave of rebellion and pushed the hippy movement throughout the United States (and world) causing new flows of ideas that wrecked havoc on many true Churches throughout the country, as pastors who stood firm to the Word of God were politicked out of their own congregations for refusing to bend to the people. Instead they placed teachers who went along with the masses, changing the Truth of God, into watered down teachings and lies.

"For the time will come when they will not endure sound doctrine, but according to their own lusts, desiring to hear pleasant things, they will heap up for themselves teachers; and they will turn their ears away from the truth, and be turned aside to myths." 2nd Timothy 4:3-4

In the meantime the Government took over education and science dropped bombshell after bombshell on darkening the Truth and purporting lies. Hollywood rolled out film after film that helped push our degradation of society into even lower levels of morality, the rock bands and hip hop/rap industry continued to play music that dishonored their Creator and promoted hysterical fans who came in droves to indulge in their fleshly lusts. Then came the internet…

"Professing to be wise, they become foolish, and change the glory of the incorruptible God into an image made like corruptible man, and birds and four-footed animals and creeping things." Romans 1:22-23

"Do not be led astray: Evil company corrupts good character." 1st Corinthians 15:33

Suddenly the world had a link to each other, at first there was little information out on the internet. As the world wide web grew, so did it's influence upon mankind. Suddenly information, both good and bad, became available at our fingertips with a simple search. As technology increased the ease of access became better and now people around the world have smart phones which allow for access to the net with minimal technical knowledge. In the meantime, most of the world forgot about God.

"But you, O Daniel, shut up the words and seal the book, to the time of the end. Many shall run to and fro, and knowledge shall be increased." Daniel 12:4

If they had remembered God and His words to mankind, then they would have realized that much of what the world participates in is contrary to His Word. Yet those who warn are so far and few, the amount who listen to them are but a drop in the bucket of humanity. For many the internet opened up information that had been kept secret and hidden. We realized that there is a web of influence that motivates our leaders, education system and religions around the world. We realized that there is a vast conspiracy against We The People and also the world population as a whole. This caused ripples in the fabric of how society behaved, causing ideologies to turn into mass movements. Never before in the history of America would an unnecessary death cause something like Black Lives Matter to ignite and spread from corner to corner of the country. I use the LA riots as an example.

"For we do not wrestle against flesh and blood, but against rulers, against authorities, against the world's rulers of the darkness of this age, against spiritual wickedness in the heavenlies." Ephesians 6:12

There the violence was for the most part kept in LA, others who might have agreed had no way, nor reason to protest, whether peacefully or otherwise, in their cities across the country. Now with a few tweets, posts and other links via social media, a mob frenzy can appear almost instantaneously in any large city in America. The problem is their direction is off, they are looking for immediate change when they should consider that black lives matter to a holy and righteous God. While only a small percentage of them will be killed unjustifiably by police, the vast majority will end up in Hell because they forgot about God.

"So then each of us shall give account concerning himself to God." Romans 14:12

"And I saw the dead, small and great, standing before God. And books were opened. And another book was opened, which is the Book of Life. And the dead were judged according to their works, out of the things which were written in the books." Revelation 20:12

"And these will go away into everlasting punishment, but the righteous into eternal life." Matthew 25:46

"Because narrow is the gate and distressing is the way which leads unto life, and there are few who find it." Matthew 7:14

"You shall not follow the majority in doing evil"... Exodus 23:2a

Then you have what is termed the 'conspiracy theorist'. Much information has made itself available and there are many different writers, alternative news outlets and vendors who pump out information to the masses in endless droves. Yet while their information might often times be spot-on, they have forgotten about God also. Their solutions are to prep, prepare and to try to educate their fellow citizens, whilst saving the Republic, yet they miss the mark.

While there are many who name the name of Jesus or God on occasion, there are none that I know of that actually tell people the real solution, which is Salvation through Jesus Christ, our Lord and Savior. So you have all of these people who are prepared for endless disasters and scenarios that can and will unfold, yet rarely are one of them prepared to meet their Maker. Their preparations fall short.

"But know this, that in the last days perilous times will come: For men will be lovers of themselves, lovers of money, boasters, proud, blasphemers, disobedient to parents, unthankful, unholy, without natural affection, unyielding, slanderers, without self-control, savage, despisers of good, traitors, headstrong, haughty, lovers of pleasure rather than lovers of God, having a form of godliness but denying its power. And from such people turn away." 2nd Timothy 3:1-5

Nations are their people whom make them. We are the ones who elect our leaders, who push for legislation to be passed and who cause movements across the country to pursue 'change'. Indeed America has forgotten about God, all nations have forgotten about God.

Legislation is passed around the world that defy the Almighty. Countries around the world allow and even participate in state-sanctioned martyrdom against Christians, the Bible and true Churches. Furthermore the people love to have it that way and continue to pursue evil, even imagining more and more devious plots.

"The prophets prophesy falsely, and the priests bear rule by their own power; and my people love to have it so, and what will you do in the end?" Jeremiah 5:31

"These six things Jehovah hates; yea, seven are an abomination to his soul: Haughty eyes, a lying tongue, and hands that shed innocent blood, a heart that devises evil plans, feet hurrying to run to evil, a false witness who breathes lies, and he who spreads strife among brothers." Proverbs 6:16-19

"Woe to those who devise wickedness and do evil on their beds! In the morning light they practice it, because it is in the power of their hand. And they covet and seize fields and houses, and carry them away. And they oppress a man and his household, even a man and his inheritance." Micah 2:1-2

I am part of a movement, that movement is being a true Christian. This movement was started by Jesus Christ, my Lord and Savior, and that movement means making available the Truth to those who will hear it. The hour is late, the days are numbered, but where are those with the real answers?

"Now you are the body of Christ, and members individually." 1st Corinthians 12:27

"And He Himself gave some to be apostles, some prophets, some evangelists, and some pastors and teachers, for the equipping of the saints for the work of ministry, for the building up of the body of Christ, till we all come to the unity of the faith and of the full true knowledge of the Son of God, to a complete man, to the measure of the stature of the fullness of Christ; that we should no longer be children, tossed to and fro and carried about with every wind of doctrine, by the trickery of men, in the cunning craftiness of deceitful plotting, but, speaking the truth in love, may grow up in all things into Him who is the head, Christ, from whom the whole body, joined and knit together by what every joint supplies, according to the effective working by which every individual does its part, causes growth of the body for the building up of itself in love." Ephesians 4:11-16

"Truly, truly, I say to you, he who hears My Word and believes Him who sent Me has eternal life, and does not come into judgment, but has passed from death unto life." John 5:24

Understand that as the world seems to be falling apart around us, as another election comes upon this land, as the wealthy continually builds bunkers, as the masses protest, prep or chose to ignore the facts, there is an answer.

Jesus Christ is the answer and the only real solution. You must repent and believe into Him, before it is too late. The world isn't going to join in a mass movement to repent and come to Christ, but you must consider -your- ways and understand that in the end, all that will really matter is whether or not you chose to accept Christ as your Savior or refused and rebelled against God.

Heaven or Hell, the choice is really that simple. No matter what type of change is hoisted upon us, understand that God is the One who causes change in an individual's heart. Things are eventually going to get a lot worse in this country and the world. Eventually the nations will fight against God Almighty and be quickly brought to an end. Most of the world's population will die during that time and those who become Saved will most likely give their lives for doing so. Calamity upon calamity will eventually hit the Earth, but the solution, even then, will remain the same…you need to accept Jesus Christ as your Savior, before it is too late to do so.

"Create in me a clean heart, O God, and renew a steadfast spirit within me." Psalms 51:10

"God is our refuge and strength, a very present help in trouble. Therefore we will not fear when the earth changes, when mountains are slipping into the midst of the seas. Let its waters roar and foam; let the mountains shake with the swelling of it. Selah. There is a river whose streams cause rejoicing in the city of God, the consecrated place of the tabernacle of the Most High. God is in the midst of her; she shall not be moved; God shall help her at the break of day. The nations raged, the kingdoms were shaken; He uttered His voice, the earth melted. Jehovah of Hosts is with us; the God of Jacob is our refuge. Selah. Come, behold the works of Jehovah, who has made desolations on the earth; who makes wars to cease to the ends of the earth; He breaks the bow and cuts the spear in two; He burns the chariots in the fire. Be still, and know that I am God! I will be exalted among the nations, I will be exalted in the earth! Jehovah of Hosts is with us; the God of Jacob is our refuge. Selah." Psalms 46:1-11

Do not forget about God, because He will not forget about you! For in the end all will stand before the Most High individually and God will make Himself known to the nations. They will remember and you will know.

Amen!

What's Next?

"And because lawlessness will abound, the love of many will grow cold. But he who endures to the end shall be kept safe. And this gospel of the kingdom will be preached in all the world as a testimony to all the nations, and then the end will come." Matthew 24:12-14

An act of extraordinary evil happened in Nice, France. Numerous deaths occurred as a man driving a truck purposely drove through crowds of people during the Bastille Day celebration in France. As I saw the news while at work, I was dismayed and saddened that things of such nature continue to plaque the world. Then another attack on police in Baton Rogue, though I am not convinced that there is sufficient evidence to prove that this was indeed a purposely planned ambush. As a Christian I understand that not only will things get worse, but eventually the reality of the world will become so desperate that what happened in Nice will be relatively minor in comparison.

"Woe to those who desire the day of Jehovah! Of what good is this to you? The day of Jehovah is darkness, and not light. It is as if a man fled before a lion, and a bear met him. Or he goes into the house and leans his hand against the wall, and a snake bites him. Is not the day of Jehovah darkness, and not light; even very dark, and not any brightness in it?" Amos 5:18-20

As we get into this article, let it be known that no man knows the day or the hour. The Lord Jesus Christ has made that quite clear! I am no exception, yet there are things that can be declared that are clear from the Holy Scriptures that will take place.

"But of that day and hour no one knows, not the angels in Heaven, nor the Son, except the Father." Mark 13:32

In the article titled *Lone Wolves?*, the question was presented as to whether or not a Believer could soon come underneath condemnation for expressing the Truth regarding the Holy Scriptures. With the ordeal in Nice, France, there was talk about whether or not America should declare war on ISIS. President Roosevelt was the last President to actually declare war the correct and Constitutional way. While a lot people proclaim that it is unlikely that the United States would do so, understand the potential exists and the consequences for Believers could be of an extreme nature.

Donald Trump has stated that, if elected, he would ask Congress to declare war. The big media outlets state that such a measure is unlikely, but I point the reader to our current state of affairs and ask them to consider how quickly things have been changing and ponder what would happen if they continue to quickly erode.

Fighting ISIS is not an easy task. Many of their fighters are based only loosely on the ideology of ISIS, not actually directly connected. Essentially their fighters agree with ISIS, carry out an attack while proclaiming it is done on behalf of ISIS. Consider the current affairs with the Department of Justice (DOJ), their Federal Bureau of Investigation (FBI) and the Department of Homeland Security (DHS).

Together they have collected a dossier of over a million citizens whom they deem to be potential terrorists. While they have been able to keep a renewing of the unpatriotic Patriot Act, their power is still limited, due to restrictions regarding Constitutional rights afforded to the American people. What would happen if suddenly several attacks happened in the United States in comparison to what has recently happened in Nice, France and Brussels, Belgium?

With war powers permitted by Congress and an enemy whom is not defined in one country or region of the world, this would cause intelligence sources to be at the forefront of the battle. This not only including the Central Intelligence Agency (CIA) and the Office of the Director of National Intelligence (ODNI) with foreign intelligence duties, but would push to the forefront the DOJ, including the FBI, and DHS. Quickly what is left of Americans freedom would disappear and under the National Defense Authorization Act (NDAA) any citizen could be declared an enemy combatant and hauled off to some sort of secret rendition prison, without any of their Constitutional rights remaining. This is dangerous stuff! Let us not forget what happened to American citizens of Japanese descent during World War 2.

What formulates ISIS is an ideology that is based on religion and their determination to wage jihad (war) to further that ideology. When you read into what the federal government guidelines are for adding a name to the already over-bloated terrorist watchlist, you see that someone who not only engages in behavior and actions that is unacceptable to the list-makers, but further has strong religious beliefs, immediately becomes a larger security threat than the neighbor down the street who just received a one year supply of freeze-dried food. The Government firmly believes that those who hold extreme religious views are many times more likely to commit an act of terror than those who do not. Is there a distinguishing between Islamic jihad and true Believers telling others about the gospel of peace? *(Eph. 6:15)*

Regardless of what is next, the Bible offers some insight regarding future events and ultimately the solution to all of the woes that an individual might eventually face. At some point in the future the world is going to enter the *"time of Jacob's trouble" (Jer. 30:7)* or what is commonly referred to as the Great Tribulation. Immediately prior Christ will come to take those who are His out of this world, as the dead in Him also rise.

(It is beyond the scope of this article to debate the numerous modern arguments against the Rapture. I point readers to an article on the website entitled *His Glorious Appearing*, which has already put to rest every argument against a pre-Tribulation Rapture.)

If you, dear reader, are -left behind- what you are seeing unfold in this modern era of troubles, uncertainties and hopelessness, is but a drop in the bucket of what will eventually come into reality. Just to give you a few glimpses of what the future holds from the Word of God, let me interject the follow bible verses.

"And there were noises and thunderings and lightnings; and there was a great earthquake, such a mighty and great earthquake as had not occurred since men came to be on the earth. And the great city was divided into three parts, and the cities of the nations fell. And Babylon the great was remembered before God, to give her the cup of the wine of the anger of His wrath. And every island fled away, and the mountains were not found." Revelation 16:18-20

"For in My jealousy and in the fire of My wrath I have spoken. Surely in that day there shall be a great earthquake in the land of Israel, so that the fish of the sea, the birds of the heavens, the beasts of the field, all creeping things that creep on the earth, and all men who are on the face of the earth shall quake at My presence. The mountains shall be thrown down, the steep places shall fall, and every wall shall fall to the ground." Ezekiel 38:19-20

"And I heard the angel of the waters saying: You are righteous, O Lord, the One who is and who was and who is to be, because You have judged these things, for they have shed the blood of saints and prophets, and You have given them blood to drink, for they are deserving. And I heard another out of the altar saying, Even so, Lord God Almighty, true and righteous are Your judgments. And the fourth angel poured out his bowl onto the sun, and it was given to him to scorch men with fire. And men were scorched with great heat, and they blasphemed the name of God who has authority over these plagues; and they did not repent to give Him glory." Revelation 16: 5-9

"And the light of the moon shall be as the light of the sun, and the light of the sun shall be sevenfold, as the light of seven days, in the day that Jehovah binds up the breach of His people and heals the stroke of their wound." Isaiah 30:26

"And another horse, fiery red, went out. And it was granted to the one who sat on it to take peace from the earth, and that people should kill one another; and there was given to him a great sword." Revelation 6:4

"So I looked, and behold, a pale green horse. And the name of him who sat on it was Death, and Hades followed behind him. And authority was given to them over a fourth of

the earth, to kill with sword, with hunger, with death, and by the beasts of the earth." Revelation 6:8

"So the four angels, who had been prepared for the hour and day and month and year, were released to kill a third of mankind." Revelation 9:15

This is just an inkling of what will take place during the *"time of Jacob's trouble" (Jer. 30:7)* where the world will be judged by God Almighty. The vast majority of the world's population is going to enter this time period unprepared and it will come to them as a shock and horror. Why or why do you who do not know Christ refuse to repent of your sins and believe into Him who is the author and finisher of our Salvation? Why do you choose death rather than life? *(Duet. 30:15)*

... "looking unto Jesus, the author and finisher of our faith, who for the joy that was set before Him endured the cross, despising the shame, and has sat down at the right hand of the throne of God." Hebrew 12:2

Many people, not just in America, but around the world are concerned with the way the world is going, as event after event unfolds. This is to say nothing about the threats of war with China and Russia, as a dispute is engaged regarding the South China Sea with China and NATO with Russia. There is also the house of cards of the world financial markets that could come crashing down at any moment. Yet in these situations the Believer can take comfort in knowing that our departing will not be caused from the actions of man, but will happen when God has predetermined it would happen.

"And now you know what is restraining, that he may be unveiled in his own time. For the mystery of lawlessness is already at work; only He is now restraining, until it is raised from out of the midst. And then the lawless one will be unveiled, whom the Lord will consume with the breath of His mouth and destroy with the brightness of His coming." 2nd Thessalonians 2:6-8

What is next is to be determined and until Jesus receives us unto Himself, your guess might be as good as mine, but the time will come when Believers, those who were not Saved unto AFTER the 'Great Tribulation' began, will become enemies of the state or rather world government.

"And it was given to him to give spirit to the image of the beast, that the image of the beast should both speak and cause as many as would not do homage to the image of the beast to be killed. And he causes all, both small and great, rich and poor, free and slave, to receive a mark on their right hand or on their foreheads, so that no one may buy or sell except one who has the mark or the name of the beast, or the number of his name. Here is wisdom. Let him who has understanding calculate the number of the beast, for it is the number of a man, and his number is 666." Revelation 13:15-18

"And when He opened the fifth seal, I saw under the altar the souls of those who had been slain because of the Word of God and because of the testimony which they held.

And they cried with a loud voice, saying, How long, O Lord, holy and true, until You judge and avenge our blood on those who dwell on the earth? And a white robe was given to each one of them; and it was said to them that they should rest a little while longer, until both the number of their fellow servants and their brethren, who were about to be killed as they were, was filled up." Revelation 6:9-11

One thing to understand is that any of us could suddenly die today and where would you go? Without Christ as your Savior, you will go to Hell for eternity. As things progress worse and worse in this world, what exactly prevents you from repenting of your sins and believing into Jesus? What roadblocks have you placed from hearing the Word of God? What issues do you think you must resolve before you are ready to accept Jesus? Do you not understand that this is a SERIOUS matter that should require immediate attention.

If your home suddenly had smoke pouring out from one of the walls, would you not immediately call the fire department and try to rectify the situation, ensuring that everyone in the household was safe? If your home is that valuable in your eyes and the safety our family is of utmost importance, than how much more your soul? Understand that this world is not going to get better, things are going to get worse. What is next, is not known to man, but what I do know is that those who die without Christ as their Savior will spend eternity in Hell. What I do know is that this is not the wish of your Creator, He made Salvation available to all men that they should repent and accept His free gift. Please take a moment to consider your priorities.

"For he does not know what shall be; so who can tell him when it shall be?" Ecclesiastes 8:7

"Abide in Me, and I in you. As the branch cannot bear fruit of itself, unless it abides in the vine, so neither can you, unless you abide in Me. I am the Vine, you are the branches. He who abides in Me, and I in him, bears much fruit; for apart from Me there is not a thing you are able to do. If anyone does not abide in Me, he is cast out as a branch and is dried up; and they gather them and throw them into the fire, and they are burned." John 15:4-6

"The Lord is not slow concerning His promise, as some count slowness, but is longsuffering toward us, not purposing that any should perish but that all should come to repentance. But the day of the Lord will come as a thief in the night, in which the heavens will pass away with a loud noise, and the elements will be dissolved with intense burning; both the earth and the works that are in it will be burned up. Therefore, since all these things will be dissolved, of what sort ought you to be in holy behavior and godliness, looking for and earnestly hastening unto the coming of the Day of God, through which the heavens will be dissolved, being set on fire, and the elements will melt with intense burning? Nevertheless we, according to His promise, look for new heavens and a new earth in which righteousness dwells. Therefore, beloved, looking forward to these things, be diligent to be found by Him in peace, spotless and without blemish; and consider that the longsuffering of our Lord is salvation; as also our beloved brother Paul, according to the wisdom given to him, has written to you, as also in all his epistles, *speaking in them of these things, in which are some things hard to understand, which the unlearned and unstable twist, as they do also the rest of the Scriptures, to their own destruction. You therefore, beloved, since you know this beforehand, beware also that you not be led away with the error of the wicked, and fall from your own steadfastness. But grow in the grace and knowledge of our Lord and Savior Jesus Christ. To Him be the glory both now and forever. Amen."* 2nd Peter 3:9-18

"For God so loved the world that He gave His only begotten Son, that everyone believing into Him should not perish but have eternal life. For God did not send His Son into the world to judge the world, but that the world through Him might be saved." John 3:16-17

Amen!

The Deception is Great!

"So the great dragon was cast out, that serpent of old, called the Devil and Satan, who leads the whole world astray; he was cast out onto the earth, and his angels were cast out with him." Revelation 12:9

The deceptions in the world are great, the trappings are many and if one considers, all around there are roadblocks put in place by the world that help ensure that it is lead astray. Satan has been deceiving mankind since Adam and Eve partook of the forbidden fruit. That act right there caused all to be born into sin and all to have a need of a Savior to rescue them.

"for all have sinned and fall short of the glory of God"…. Romans 3:23

"Behold, I was brought forth in iniquity, and in sin did my mother conceive me." Psalms 51:5

"But God demonstrates His own love toward us, in that while we were yet sinners, Christ died for us. Much more then, having now been justified by His blood, we shall be saved from wrath through Him. For if when we were enemies we were reconciled to God through the death of His Son, much more, being reconciled, we shall be saved by His life. And not only that, but we also rejoice in God through our Lord Jesus Christ, through whom we have now received the reconciliation. Therefore, just as through one man sin entered the world, and death through sin, and thus death spread to every person, because everyone sinned." Romans 5:8-12

We live in a time where things seem to be continuously getting more and more precarious on a weekly basis. There are attempted attacks and terror acts taking place in Europe on a regular basis, shootings across the United States on almost a daily basis and an increasing in troubles throughout the world.

While many are alarmed at the ongoing events there are another group who seems to quickly adapt to these changes and continue on, almost in an ignorant bliss, unaware of the aroma of death that fills the air of those without Christ, who are at current the walking dead.

"For we are to God the fragrance of Christ among those who are being saved and among those who are perishing. To the one we are the aroma of death leading to death, and to the other the aroma of life leading to life. And who is sufficient for these things? For we are not, as so many, peddling the Word of God; but as of sincerity, but as from God, we speak in Christ, in the sight of God." 2nd Corinthians 2:15-17

By now most have seen the Pokemon Go hunters wandering around on street corners, their phones lit up as they scour to find these pocket monsters, but where is the man who is seeking and searching out God?

"And you shall seek Me and find Me, when you search for Me with all your heart." Jeremiah 29:13

"Therefore, having obtained help from God, to this day I stand, witnessing both to small and great, saying no other things than those which the prophets and Moses said would come to be; that the Christ would suffer, that He would be the first to rise from the dead, and would proclaim light to the Jewish people and to the Gentiles. Now as he thus made his defense, Festus said with a loud voice, Paul, you are beside yourself! Much learning is driving you mad! But he said, I am not mad, most noble Festus, but speak the words of truth and sobriety. For the king, before whom I also speak freely, knows these things; for I am convinced that none of these things are hidden from him, since this thing was not done in a corner." Acts 26:22-26

The Way of Life *(John 14:6)* is not hidden that a man cannot find it, but indeed the deception is great. There are so many different avenues of distraction that in a person's life they might seek to know the truth about their eternal destiny, they might ponder whether or not there is a God, whether or not there is a Heaven or Hell, whether or not Jesus really died on the Cross for their sins, whether or not there is Truth to the matter of Christianity that they hear about, but at the very second there is an opportune time, those thoughts quickly erode and they are once again entangled in their sin, unwilling to truly seek the Most High God whom they will stand before. They need to accept Salvation through repentance and believing into Jesus Christ who paid the price for their sins and it is through Him, the only way to rectify these wretched bodies before a Holy and Almighty God!

"When anyone hears the Word of the kingdom, and does not understand it, then the wicked one comes and snatches away what was sown in his heart. This is that which was sown by the wayside." Matthew 13:19

The other day I was driving home late at night from having worked and the police are parked in the middle of the highway, a man, looking lifeless, is laying in the road. I followed up on the police blotter a few days later and read that he was taken to the hospital, having been drunk and fallen out of his friend's truck, who had left him behind, because he had a warrant. Then scarcely a week later I observe a young woman walking through the alley, unable to stand up without holding on to objects.

A friend comes to her rescue and tries to assist her to get to their vehicle, but while doing so she falls and hits her head on a dumpster, laying there on the ground, passed out, with more friends coming along to drag her off, trying to comfort her. Who is going to comfort these people when the wages of sin are due? Who is going to comfort those without Christ as these souls stand before God Almighty at the Great White Throne judgment? Indeed there will be weeping and gnashing of teeth as the hopelessness and despair of an eternal punishment are realized. Not only they themselves, but those who observe them who they loved while walking under the sun, be also condemned to the Lake of Fire.

"For the wages of sin is death, but the gift of God is eternal life in Christ Jesus our Lord." Romans 6:23

"And I saw a great white throne and Him who sat on it, from whose face the earth and the heavens fled away. And there was found no place for them. And I saw the dead, small and great, standing before God. And books were opened. And another book was opened, which is the Book of Life. And the dead were judged according to their works, out of the things which were written in the books. And the sea gave up the dead who were in it, and Death and Hades delivered up the dead who were in them. And they were judged, each one, according to their works. And Death and Hades were cast into the Lake of Fire. This is the second death. And anyone not found written in the Book of Life was cast into the Lake of Fire." Revelation 20:11-15

"There will be weeping and gnashing of teeth, when you see Abraham and Isaac and Jacob and all the prophets in the kingdom of God, and yourselves being thrust outside." Luke 13:28

"And these will go away into everlasting punishment, but the righteous into eternal life." Matthew 25:46

I wish that I could reason with everyone of them. I wish I could tell them all about a Savior who loves them and a God who provided a solution to sin. I wish I could tell them how greatly they are deceived, how everything is working against them, how they must forsake all, repent of their doings and follow Christ. With tears I would cry out and beg them, plead with them not to continue on the path to destruction, but rather repent. Repent! Seek God while He may be found! Stop the madness, why or why will you die? Yet as I open my mouth they laugh, they argue, they consider me to be mad to live such a 'shallow' life. Others taunt me that things are not as I say, that they are not that bad, that all ways lead to Heaven or this pastor says so-n-so.

"But there were also false prophets among the people, even as there will be false teachers among you, who will secretly bring in destructive heresies, even denying the Lord who bought them, and bring on themselves swift destruction. And many will follow their destructive ways, through whom the way of truth will be blasphemed. By covetousness they will exploit you with well-turned words; whose judgment of old is not idle, and their destruction does not slumber. For if God did not spare the angels who

sinned, but cast them down to Tartarus and delivered them into chains of darkness, to be reserved for judgment; and did not spare the ancient world, but saved Noah, one of eight people, a preacher of righteousness, bringing the flood on the world of the ungodly; and turning the cities of Sodom and Gomorrah into ashes, condemned them to destruction, making them an example to those intending to live ungodly; and delivered righteous Lot, who was oppressed by the lustful behavior of the wicked (for that righteous man, dwelling among them, his righteous soul was tormented from day to day by seeing and hearing their lawless deeds); then the Lord knows how to deliver the godly out of temptations and to reserve the unjust for the day of judgment, to be punished, and especially those who walk according to the flesh in the lust of defilement and despise authority. They are presumptuous, self-willed. They are not afraid to speak evil of dignitaries." 2nd Peter 2:1-10*

Yet should I consider these things and stop? Should I not warn them that there is trouble around the corner, that their souls are at stake? I press on, I continue for the sake of those who might listen. For to me if even one person somewhere down the road repents and believes the Gospel, that is a job well done. I once was a sinner in desperate need of Christ and I am thankful that someone took the time to point me in the right direction, to point me towards Jesus, my Lord and Savior.

"Nevertheless if you warn the wicked to turn from his way, and he does not turn from his way, he shall die in his iniquity; but you have delivered your soul." Ezekiel 33:9

Consider the times, realize the vanities that fill your day and understand that the deception is great. Satan is going to continue his battle for the souls of men and he is going to try to ensure that he can get as many people to go to Hell as possible. Realize that you are being deceived, seek God before it is too late!

"For the living know that they shall die; but the dead do not know anything, nor do they have any more a reward; for the memory of them is forgotten. Also their love, and their hatred, and their envy, have now perished; nor do they ever any longer have a part in anything that is done under the sun." Ecclesiastes 9:5-6

"Say to them: As I live, declares the Lord Jehovah, I take no delight in the death of the wicked, but that the wicked turn from his way and live. Turn! Turn from your evil ways! For why will you die..." Ezekiel 33:11a

Amen!

What is Your Soul Worth?

"For what will it profit a man if he gains the whole world, and loses his own soul? Or what will a man give in exchange for his soul?" Mark 8:36-37

A simple question, really, yet how serious of a question. This question is so serious that it pertains to EACH PERSON. What is Jesus saying here that a man could lose his own soul or exchange his soul for something?

I heard a pastor say once that he heard of a very rich man who was old in years, near the end of his life. Someone asked the rich man, if he could have anything else, what would it be? The rich man's reply was a little bit more money. No one is going to gain the whole world, if one could, there would be nothing else to get, no extra money, no extra toys, no islands, no private jets, the list could go on into infinity. For that reason, it is not possible to gain the whole world. Yet men do try to gain numerous positions of power and wealth, to which there is no end to their acquiring.

This same pastor went on further, breaking down the discussion of the rich man. He spoke about how kings, those who would have plenty of power and wealth, would give it all in exchange for an extension of their life, for just a few weeks. Think about that for a moment.

As those who have presumably 'gained it all' are near the end of their lives, would not most give it all up to just extend their life for just a brief time? Most of us will never be in positions to have such power or wealth, but this is relevant to EACH PERSON. Imagine if a rich man were to come up to you.

This rich man is nearly blind and only has a small field of vision in one eye. The one whom the rich man speaks to, is but a poor worker, just making ends meet. The rich man invites the poor man for a dinner at a fabulous restaurant. Presented before the poor man is the finest food and wine, this just after having been picked up by a limo for the ride to the restaurant. Around the rich man are beautiful women, some who seem to know the proposition that is at had, wondering if the poor man might consider their well-keeping. As the poor man is overwhelmed with the choices of fine food before him, the rich man begins his conversation, at hand is an offer.

The rich man tells the poor man how he might have everything, but he is unable to enjoy it because his eye sight is so very bad. He offers to bestow 90% of his wealth to the poor man, in exchange for his eyes. The deal is simple, the poor man becomes wildly rich and able to buy whatever he desires, but he takes upon himself the handicap of the rich man, blindness. The rich man gets back his vision and is able to once again see, but will have just enough money to live a very modest life the remainder of his years. The poor man only has until the end of their dessert to decide what to do, and if he chooses to trade his eyes for the rich man's wealth, it will be done immediately, there are surgeons and doctors waiting for his phone call.

Such an unlikely scenario, though I know there are some who would actually trade their eyesight for power and wealth. Yet how much more is the soul worth? These bodies die, but the soul lives forever! We all know that you 'can't take it with you.'

"Then Job arose, tore his robe, and shaved his head; and he fell down upon the ground and prostrated himself; and he said: Naked I have come from my mother's womb, and naked shall I return there. Jehovah has given, and Jehovah has taken away; blessed is the name of Jehovah." Job 1:20-21

Most people will scoff at the idea that they are exchanging their souls for anything. Yet understand that, *"There is a way which seems right to a man, but the end of it is the ways of death." Proverbs 14:12*

Remember, each person will stand before God Almighty INDIVIDUALLY and be held accountable. The reality is quite simple, either your name is written in the Book of Life, you have repented of your sins and believed into Jesus Christ, His Son, OR you have not. You are either exchanging your soul for your refusal to repent and believe OR you are His bondservant *(Rom. 1:1)*, a Christian, a true Believer.

"And I saw a great white throne and Him who sat on it, from whose face the earth and the heavens fled away. And there was found no place for them. And I saw the dead, small and great, standing before God. And books were opened. And another book was opened, which is the Book of Life. And the dead were judged according to their works, out of the things which were written in the books. And the sea gave up the dead who were in it, and Death and Hades delivered up the dead who were in them. And they were judged, each one, according to their works. And Death and Hades were cast into the Lake of Fire. This is the second death. And anyone not found written in the Book of Life was cast into the Lake of Fire." Revelation 20:11-15

"Jesus said to him, I am the Way, the Truth, and the Life. No one comes to the Father except through Me." John 14:6

"For with the heart one believes unto righteousness, and with the mouth confession is made unto salvation." Romans 10:10

Will your soul go to Heaven or Hell? Will you rather the praise of men and deny your Creator? Would you refuse to repent of your sin and believe into a loving Savior? Would you rather focus on 'your life' and not die to yourself, picking up your cross daily and following the ONE who CREATED your soul? God has made in quite clear in His Word what the results of refusing to accept Salvation are.

"for they loved the praise of men more than the praise of God." John 12:43

"For God so loved the world that He gave His only begotten Son, that everyone believing into Him should not perish but have eternal life. For God did not send His Son into the world to judge the world, but that the world through Him might be saved. The one believing into Him is not judged; but the one not believing is judged already, because he has not believed in the name of the only begotten Son of God. And this is the judgment, that the Light has come into the world, and men loved darkness rather than the Light, for their deeds were evil. For everyone practicing evil hates the Light and does not come to the Light, lest his deeds should be reproved." John 3:16-20

"Then He said to them all, If anyone desires to come after Me, let him deny himself, and take up his cross daily, and follow Me. For whoever desires to save his life will lose it, but whoever loses his life on account of Me will save it." Luke 9:23-24

"So God created man in His own image; in the image of God He created him; male and female He created them." Genesis 1:27

For most people they will not even come close to gaining the whole world. Most will not be rich, nor powerful. Most in fact will have a life that is riddled with troubles and problems. Many will spend that life on alcohol, medication or drugs, to deal with their 'issues'. They will refuse to consider the real issue: sin. What will most people give in exchange for their soul: DISBELIEF.

"Then He said to Thomas, Bring your finger here, and look at My hands; and bring your hand here, and put it into My side. Do not be unbelieving, but believing. And Thomas answered and said to Him, My Lord and my God! Jesus said to him, Thomas, because you have seen Me, you have believed. Blessed are those not seeing and yet believing. And truly Jesus did many other signs before His disciples, which are not written in this book; but these are written that you may believe that Jesus is the Christ, the Son of God, and that believing you may have life in His name." John 20:27-31

Amen!

Ineffective Christianity

"And these are the ones sown among thorns; they are the ones who hear the Word, and the cares of this world, the deceitfulness of riches, and the lusts for other things entering in choke the Word, and it becomes unfruitful." Mark 4:18-19

Recently it was discussed about roadblocks and trappings. The possibilities are endless for the things that can become a barrier between someone repenting and believing into Christ. My thoughts recently turned to the word: justification.

According to *Webster's University Dictionary Unabridged*, 1942, one meaning of justify is:

1.) To declare free from guilt or blame, to absolve; to clear.
2.) In theology the definition listed is the following:
3.) In theology, to pardon and clear from guilt; to treat as just, though guilty and deserving punishment; to pardon.

A synonym of justify is excuse. Let's turn our attention to the first given definition of justify.

How many Believers, unfortunately we are talking about Believers, have created a justification argument for their sin? We often take the time to look at the lost, those who are without Christ, those whom have not had the justification of God, through Jesus Christ our Lord and Savior. Those to whom do not have a pardon, through repentance and belief into Jesus Christ. What does the world do?

Does not the drunkard that lives next door justify his drunken behavior due to the bad circumstances of his life, the memories, regret, remorse of the past and the outcome of decisions that perhaps could've and should've been avoided? The man who lives on the sidewalk that people walk past, does not a great deal of excuses or personal justification equate a situation that would've been unimaginable at it's inception? The broken families, those who sought eye for eye, those who justified their sinful behavior and now regret it, everywhere around you. Clearly a Believer sees the unsaved and knows that they need a Savior.

The Believer, the Christian, understands much of the world's trappings, as they were once entangled in the same system of sin, but Jesus Christ set them free and through Salvation they were changed. Yet consider for a moment if you will that the battle is not over, even Believer's can become entangled in sin. Satan would like nothing more than to render each Christian an ineffective Christian, if not even go as far as having a true Believer disbelieve and turn their back on the Most High.

"For if, after they have escaped the defilements of the world through the full true knowledge of the Lord and Savior Jesus Christ, they are again entangled in them and overcome, the end is worse for them than the beginning. For it would have been better for them not to have known the way of righteousness, than having known it, to turn from the holy commandment delivered to them. But it has happened to them according to the true proverb: A dog returns to his own vomit, and, a sow, having been washed, to her wallowing in the mire." 2nd Peter 2:20-22

"Be sober, be vigilant; because your adversary the devil walks about like a roaring lion, seeking whom he may devour." 1st Peter 5:8

When we hear of a pastor whose life become national news due to an affair that he had, do we automatically assume that this pastor is certainly not a true Christian? What if he is, but has been rendered ineffective? I once read of this black Baptist pastor in the Deep South of the United States who had been having several affairs with women in the church. On a Sunday morning he stood up in front of his congregation and declared to them that he had HIV and had been having affairs with women who were amongst them. Yet instead of coming out with an apology because the matter had been made widely known by media, which it had not been, he repented publicly and ended his pastoral duties because God had chastised his behavior. He was now HIV positive and his sin was found out, for God made in known. The media then had a frenzy descending on the church.

Let it be known, if you are a Believer and you are sinning, the Lord God Almighty will chastise you. If you are without chastisement, living in sin, then are you even a true Christian?

"And you have forgotten the exhortation which speaks to you as to sons: My son, do not despise the chastening of the Lord, nor faint when you are rebuked by Him. For whom the Lord loves He disciplines, and whips every son whom He receives. If you endure chastening, God deals with you as with sons; for what son is there whom a father does not discipline? But if you are without chastening, of which all have become partakers, then you are illegitimate and not sons." Hebrews 12:5-8

The commands are given by Jesus Christ, our Lord and Savior:

"Jesus said to him, You shall love the Lord your God with all your heart, with all your soul, and with all your mind. This is the first and great commandment. And the second

is like it: You shall love your neighbor as yourself. On these two commandments hang all the Law and the Prophets." Matthew 22:37-40

When we allow sin into our lives we are forsaking these commandments. At that point we are loving sin more than loving God.

"If then you are raised with Christ, seek those things which are above, where Christ is, sitting at the right hand of God. Set your mind on things above, not on the things of the earth; for you died, and your life is hidden with Christ in God. When Christ who is our life is revealed, then you also will be revealed with Him in glory. Therefore put to death your members which are on the earth: sexual perversion, uncleanness, passion, evil lusts, and covetousness, which is idolatry. Because of these things the wrath of God is coming upon the sons of disobedience; in which you yourselves once walked when you lived in them. But now you yourselves are to put off all these: anger, wrath, malice, blasphemy, filthy language out of your mouth. Do not lie to one another, since you have put off the old man with his practices, and have put on the new man who is renewed in full true knowledge according to the image of the One who created him, where there is neither Greek nor Jew, circumcised nor uncircumcised, barbarian, Scythian, slave nor free, but Christ is all things and in all. Therefore, as the elect of God, holy and beloved, put on a heart of compassion, kindness, humility, meekness, longsuffering; bearing with one another, and forgiving one another, if anyone has a complaint against another; even as Christ forgave you, so you also do. And above all these things put on love, which is the bond of perfectness. And let the peace of God rule in your hearts, to which also you were called in one body; and be thankful. Let the Word of Christ dwell in you richly in all wisdom, teaching and admonishing one another in psalms and hymns and spiritual songs, singing with grace in your hearts to the Lord. And whatever you do in word or deed, do all in the name of the Lord Jesus, giving thanks to God, even the Father, through Him." Colossians 3:1-17

If you are justifying your sinful behavior with whatever excuses that you might have, no matter how 'well sounding' the argument might be, understand that there is NO excuse before God Almighty.

"For we must all appear before the judgment seat of Christ, that each one may receive the things done in the body, according to what he has done, whether good or bad." 2nd Corinthians 5:10

So what happens when a Believer gets entangled in sin, receives not only the chastisement of God, but perhaps in the process also receives the consequences for their actions? What happens if a Believer's spouse leaves due to their behavior, the children are not raised right and are of the world, the finances are totally out of order, the body is damaged due to abuse, the emotions, depression and regret weigh heavily on the soul, despite a repentant part on the guilty one, whom Jesus has forgiven?

"If we confess our sins, He is faithful and just to forgive us our sins and to cleanse us from all unrighteousness." 1st John 1:9

Perhaps the one is no longer qualified to be a pastor? Perhaps a child has been locked up in prison for life, partially due to the neglecting of teaching them God's Word? Maybe the person is now on an oxygen tank for having smoked so many years? Or depression weighs so heavily due to regret of one's actions that they feel beat down and unable to stand back up and press on. Yet that is EXACTLY what a true Christian needs to do is press on, get back in the race, get back on your feet and do your duty, follow Christ and walk as you should've been walking all along, knowing that if you have repented of your sin, Christ has forgiven you and you MUST press on.

"Not that I have already attained, or am already perfected; but I press on, that I may lay hold, since Christ Jesus has also laid hold of me. Brethren, I do not count myself to have laid hold; but one thing I do, forgetting those things which are behind and stretching forward to those things which are ahead, I press toward the goal for the prize of the upward call of God in Christ Jesus. Therefore let us, as many as are complete, be of this mind; and if in anything you think differently, God will reveal even this to you. Nevertheless, to the degree that we have already attained, let us walk by the same rule, let us be of the same mind. Brethren, join in being imitators of me, and note those who so walk, as you have us for a pattern. For many conduct themselves, of whom I have told you often, and now tell you even weeping, that they are enemies of the cross of Christ: whose end is destruction, whose god is their belly, and who glory in their shame; who set their mind on earthly things. For our citizenship is in Heaven, from which we also eagerly wait for the Savior, the Lord Jesus Christ, who will transform our lowly body that it may be conformed to His glorious body, according to the working by which He is able even to subject all things to Himself." Philippians 3:12-21

"Therefore we also, since we are surrounded by so great a cloud of witnesses, let us lay aside every weight, and the sin which so persistently harasses us, and let us run with perseverance the race that is set before us, looking unto Jesus, the author and finisher of our faith, who for the joy that was set before Him endured the cross, despising the shame, and has sat down at the right hand of the throne of God. For consider Him who endured such opposition from sinners against Himself, that you not become weary and faint in your souls." Hebrews 12:1-3

Get back into the race, pick yourself up, go on…!

"Do you not know that those who run in a race all run, but one receives the prize? Run in such a way that you may obtain it. And everyone who competes for the prize controls himself in all things. Now they do it to obtain a perishable crown, but we an imperishable. Therefore I run in this manner: not with uncertainty. Thus I fight: not as one who beats the air. But I discipline my body and bring it into subjection, lest, when I have preached to others, I myself should become disqualified." 1st Corinthians 9:24-27

"Finally, my brethren, be strong in the Lord and in the power of His might. Put on all the armor of God, that you may be able to stand against the wiles of the devil. For we do not wrestle against flesh and blood, but against rulers, against authorities, against the

world's rulers of the darkness of this age, against spiritual wickedness in the heavenlies. Therefore take up all the armor of God, that you may be able to resist in the evil day, and having done all, to stand. Stand firm therefore, having girded your waist with truth, having put on the breastplate of righteousness, and having shod your feet with the preparation of the gospel of peace; above all, taking the shield of faith with which you will be able to quench all the fiery darts of the wicked one. And take the helmet of salvation, and the sword of the Spirit, which is the Word of God; praying always with all prayer and supplication in the Spirit, being watchful to this end with all perseverance and supplication for all the saints;" Ephesians 6:10-18

Amen!

At Any Moment

"Behold, I tell you a mystery: We shall not all sleep, but we shall all be changed; in a moment, in the twinkling of an eye, at the last trumpet. For the trumpet will sound, and the dead will be raised incorruptible, and we shall be changed." 1st Corinthians 15:51-52

"But of that day and hour no one knows, not even the angels of Heaven, but My Father only. But as the days of Noah were, so also will the coming of the Son of Man be. For as in the days before the flood, they were eating and drinking, marrying and giving in marriage, until the day that Noah entered into the ark, and did not realize until the flood came and took them all away, so also will the coming of the Son of Man be. Then two will be in the field: one is taken and the other is left. Two will be grinding at the mill: one is taken and the other is left. Watch therefore, for you do not know what hour your Lord comes. But know this, that if the master of the house had known what hour the thief comes, he would have watched and not allowed his house to be dug through. Therefore you also be ready, for the Son of Man comes at an hour you do not expect." Matthew 24:36-44

How many people really understand that at some time, time itself is simply going to run out? Those who are Saved will go to be with the Lord, those who are not will be left behind on this earth. How many people sit on the fence in regards to Salvation? They realize that they need to change (repent) and believe into Jesus Christ, yet the cares of this world have so far overcome that necessity?

The other day I am with my son who suddenly looks right at me and says, "Dad, the Trumpet could go off right now, at this moment." Though only four years old, I wish more people hand the same understanding. At any moment the Rapture could happen, the *"time of Jacob's trouble" (Jer. 30:7)* could start and if you are without Christ, you will be left behind.

On the other hand, we do not know how much longer we shall live. There is no guarantee of another breath beyond the one you are breathing right now. Being apathetic about your soul is not a wise choice when the decision is eternal. There are numerous reasons that people hold to as to why they are not going to repent and believe, but for many simply not truly believing in Jesus, the necessity of Salvation, that they are a guilty sinner, that there is a Creator, that they will be held accountable are some of the many reasons.

Regardless of what is holding you back, dear reader, please understand that at any moment it could simply be too late! There will come a time when there simply is no more time left for you.

If you consider all of the effort that you put into living into this life on earth, the cares, the concerns, the plans, the relationships, goals, problems, etc., how much more thought should be put into your eternity?!

"But the cowardly, unbelieving, abominable, murderers, prostitutes, sorcerers, idolaters, and all liars shall have their part in the lake which burns with fire and brimstone, which is the second death." Revelation 21:8

"From that time Jesus began to preach and to say, Repent, for the kingdom of Heaven has drawn near." Matthew 4:17

"He who finds his life will lose it, and he who loses his life on account of Me will find it." Matthew 10:39

At what point are you really going to take time to consider these things? When will you understand that you are lost, in need of a Savior?

"For He says: In an acceptable time I have heard you, and in a day of salvation I have helped you. Behold, now is the accepted time; behold, now is the day of salvation." 2nd Corinthians 6:2

"For to me, to live is Christ, and to die is gain." Philippians 1:21

Amen!

They Took the Bait

"But know this, that in the last days perilous times will come: For men will be lovers of themselves, lovers of money, boasters, proud, blasphemers, disobedient to parents, unthankful, unholy, without natural affection, unyielding, slanderers, without self-control, savage, despisers of good, traitors, headstrong, haughty, lovers of pleasure rather than lovers of God, having a form of godliness but denying its power. And from such people turn away." 2nd Timothy 3:1-5

"So the great dragon was cast out, that serpent of old, called the Devil and Satan, who leads the whole world astray; he was cast out onto the earth, and his angels were cast out with him." Revelation 12:9

It's high noon in any city in America, lunch is being served at restaurants throughout the town. Walk into any hip joint and you will observe a vast majority of occupants, whether alone at a table or with others, staring at a phone with a blank expression on their face. Most, if you were to approach, are keeping up with their social media contacts throughout the day.

Walk into nearly any American home and observe the television flickering as programming is displayed on the large screen. Whether there are actively people watching the shows or the television is just being used for background noise, it is on, in most homes over 40 hours per week.

Drive on the highway, particularly on a hot summer day with your window down and at a stop light you can hear the noise of the radios blaring with a variety of tunes, many coming off of a connected phone.

Stop in a your local Walmart, Target, Kmart, mall or other major retailer and you can see the rush of people picking up some of the latest fashion or some other trinkets to make their home or themselves more lovely.

On Sunday morning the social rush begins for a percentage of Americans who are conversing, while dressed as if prepared to walk a runway, getting ready to attend their obligatory church service, part of their social status. Afterwards whatever the preacher may have taught, they continue to the social meeting at the predetermined restaurant, the beginning of another work week.

At home the children are actively pursuing video games, social media and other activities. All over people are pursuing pleasure, rather it is what the eyes see, the ears hear, the mouth tastes or the body feels, they are focused on it. Yet do they stop and ponder about their Creator, their eternal future, truly walking with the Lord, willing to do so, even at a great expense to their social, economic and political lives?

"For the time will come when they will not endure sound doctrine, but according to their own lusts, desiring to hear pleasant things, they will heap up for themselves teachers; and they will turn their ears away from the truth, and be turned aside to myths." 2nd Timothy 4:3-4

"Let them alone. They are blind leaders of the blind. And if the blind leads the blind, both will fall into the ditch." Matthew 15:14

They may ponder, but our so-called churches are telling them what they desire to hear. What will come of this, what will the end be for these people?

"He who loves father or mother more than Me is not worthy of Me. And he who loves son or daughter more than Me is not worthy of Me. And he who does not take his cross and follow after Me is not worthy of Me. He who finds his life will lose it, and he who loses his life on account of Me will find it." Matthew 10:37-38

"Enter by the narrow gate; for wide is the gate and broad is the way that leads to destruction, and there are many entering in through it. Because narrow is the gate and distressing is the way which leads unto life, and there are few who find it. Beware of false prophets, who come to you in sheep's clothing, but inwardly they are ravenous wolves. You will know them from their fruits. Do men gather grapes from thornbushes or figs from thistles? Even so, every good tree produces excellent fruit, but a corrupt tree produces evil fruit. A good tree is not able to produce evil fruit, nor is a corrupt tree able to produce excellent fruit. Every tree that does not produce excellent fruit is cut down and thrown into the fire. Therefore from their fruits you will know them. Not everyone who says to Me, Lord, Lord, will enter the kingdom of Heaven, but he who does the will of My Father in Heaven. Many will say to Me in that day, Lord, Lord, have we not prophesied in Your name, cast out demons in Your name, and done many works of power in Your name? And then I will declare to them, I never knew you; depart from Me, you who work out lawlessness!" Matthew 7:13-23

"But the cowardly, unbelieving, abominable, murderers, prostitutes, sorcerers, idolaters, and all liars shall have their part in the lake which burns with fire and brimstone, which is the second death." Revelation 21:8

"I know your works, that you are neither cold nor hot. I would that you were cold or hot. So then, because you are lukewarm, and neither cold nor hot, I will vomit you out of My

mouth. Because you say, I am rich, have become wealthy, and have need of nothing; and do not know that you are wretched and miserable and poor and blind and naked; I counsel you to buy from Me gold refined in the fire, that you may be rich; and white garments, that you may be clothed, that the shame of your nakedness may not be revealed; and anoint your eyes with eye salve, that you may see. As many as I love, I rebuke and chasten. Therefore be zealous and repent. Behold, I stand at the door and knock. If anyone hears My voice and opens the door, I will come in to him and dine with him, and he with Me. To him who overcomes I will grant to sit with Me on My throne, as I also overcame and sat down with My Father on His throne." Revelation 3:15-21*

Take heed! It is no joke that without Jesus Christ as your Savior, you will spend eternity in Hell. Without repenting and believing into Jesus Christ, there is NO HOPE WHATSOEVER! Do not be deceived!

"Nevertheless, when the Son of Man comes, will He find faith on the earth?" Luke 18:8b

You can not look to the majority to determine what is correct, but most look towards God and do what is correct.

"You shall not follow the majority in doing evil..." Exodus 23:2a

If you fill your life with all of these distractions, if you try hard to keep up on the trends, social media, the latest entertainment, where is your time for God? If you only go to church to be socially acceptable with your family and friends or refuse to attend a pulpit that preaches God's truth because it is no longer trendy or old-fashioned, what will you do when you stand before the Almighty God?

"For I, Jehovah, change not." Malachi 3:6a

There are no excuses at that point, you will either have your name written in the Book of Life or not, you will either have repented and believed into Jesus or be doomed to the Lake of Fire for eternity *(Rev. 20:15)*, there is NO gray area, it is cut and dry, the Holy Scriptures provides God's truth to all of mankind.

If your reading this, there is still time to consider these truths. Please do so.

"For He says: In an acceptable time I have heard you, and in a day of salvation I have helped you. Behold, now is the accepted time; behold, now is the day of salvation." 2nd Corinthians 6:2

Amen!

Intolerant

"And they said, There is no hope; but we will walk after our own thoughts, and we will each one do according to the stubbornness of his evil heart." Jeremiah 18:12

"For the wrath of God is revealed from Heaven against all ungodliness and unrighteousness of men, who suppress the truth in unrighteousness, because what may be known of God is clearly recognized by them, for God has revealed it to them. For ever since the creation of the world the unseen things of Him are clearly perceived, being understood by the things that are made, even His eternal power and Godhead, so that they are without excuse, because, although they know God, they do not glorify Him as God, nor are thankful, but become vain in their reasonings, and their stupid hearts are darkened. Professing to be wise, they become foolish, and change the glory of the incorruptible God into an image made like corruptible man, and birds and four-footed animals and creeping things. Therefore God also gives them up to uncleanness, in the lusts of their hearts, to dishonor their bodies among themselves, who change the truth of God into the lie, and fear and serve the created things more than the Creator, who is blessed forever. Amen. For this reason God gives them up to vile passions. For even their women change the natural use for what is contrary to nature. Likewise also the men, abandoning the natural use of the woman, burned in their lust toward one another, men with men performing what is shameful, and receiving the retribution within themselves, the penalty which is fitting for their error. And even as they do not like to have God in their full true knowledge, God gives them over to a reprobate mind, to do those things which are not fitting; being filled with every unrighteousness, sexual perversion, wickedness, covetousness, maliciousness; full of envy, murder, strife, deceit, depravity; whisperers, defamers, haters of God, insolent, proud, boasters, inventors of evil things, disobedient to parents, without understanding, untrustworthy, without natural affection, unforgiving, unmerciful; who, knowing the righteous judgment of God, that those who practice such things are deserving of death, not only do them, but also approve of those who practice them." Romans 1:18-32

A recent survey suggested that the amount of adults who believe in God is on a decline, one, that if time allowed, is expected to continue in that trend. In Europe atheism is on the rise, with more atheists in Norway than those who even believe in God. Yet it should be pointed out that despite now 89% of Americans claim to believe in God, down from 98% in the early 60's, would it even matter?

Nearly every article out there suggests to the reading public that eventually less and less people will believe in God. Many supposed christian websites push out articles pointing to the decline as a sign of the times. Perhaps, but taking a different spin on the numbers the question must be presented.

If 89% of Americans still believe in God, is it the God of the bible or 'a god' that they believe in? If 89% of Americans believe in God, why do the vast majority live as if there is no God?

"You believe that God is One. You do well. Even the demons believe, and shudder." Jacob (James) 2:19

If the far vast majority of Americans believe in God, then why do they not follow the Holy Scriptures?

Is God silent on His take regarding the LGBT movement?

Did God not declare how mankind should treat one another?

Is God not able to be found and known by mankind?

Did God not give warnings regarding sexual perversity and adultery?

Has God been silent about abortion?

Has not God warned about the coming Judgment and given mankind time to repent and believe in His Son Jesus Christ?

As these movements continue to spread across this country and the world, does not mankind see that the just judgment of God will eventually come upon them? Do they not realize that there will be a 'starting gun', the Rapture of the Church, that will hoist upon the world *"the time of Jacob's trouble"* (Jer. 30:7) or the Great Tribulation? How much time is left before such events begin to unfold, how much time is left, before there is simply no time left.

If a warning could be given to the entire world that they must repent and believe into Jesus Christ, how many of those would simply say that they will 'do according to the stubbornness' of their evil hearts. Yet out of the mercies of God, some indeed would listen, some would yield to their Creator and be Saved. You, dear reader, if you have been thinking about these things for some time, if you have been uncertain or unwilling to yield, to repent, to believe into Jesus Christ and be Saved, how much longer do you have or how much longer will you wait? Can you wait much longer?!

For those who are of the 89% who believe in God, which god do you believe in? The God of the bible, the Most High God, your Creator or a god that caters to you liberal beliefs, a god that has a preacher who teaches your intolerant hearts what you want to hear, a god that allows you to live your life as you want, not having a repentant heart, one that follows a formula of some words or actions, or a god is in 'everything' or 'all religions lead to god' philosophy. If that is you, if your god is tolerant to sodomy, abortion, sexual immorality, adultery, every kind of wickedness, which is contrary to the Holy Scriptures, than the god that you serve is not a god at all, but a figment of your imagination. For God Almighty has declared Himself, He has sent His Son who died on the Cross for the sins of mankind, for all who would receive, His prophets have testified, and His Word is true, He is not tolerant of man's wickedness and will not always be patient and merciful with them, if that is you, then you are intolerant to the ways of the Mighty God, you are walking contrary to Him, unto your own destruction.

"Let no one deceive you by any means; for that Day will not come unless the falling away comes first, and the man of sin is unveiled, the son of perdition, who opposes and exalts himself above all that is called God or that is honored, so that he sits as God in the temple of God, declaring of himself that he is God. Do you not remember that when I was still with you I told you these things? And now you know what is restraining, that he may be unveiled in his own time. For the mystery of lawlessness is already at work; only He is now restraining, until it is raised from out of the midst. And then the lawless one will be unveiled, whom the Lord will consume with the breath of His mouth and destroy with the brightness of His coming. The coming of the lawless one is according to the working of Satan, with all power, signs, and lying wonders, and with all unrighteous deception among those who are perishing, because they did not receive the love of the truth, that they might be saved. And for this reason God will send them strong delusion, that they should believe the lie, that they all may be judged who did not believe the truth but had pleasure in unrighteousness." 2nd Thessalonians 2:3-12

"For He says: In an acceptable time I have heard you, and in a day of salvation I have helped you. Behold, now is the accepted time; behold, now is the day of salvation." 2nd Corinthians 6:2

"And he said to me, Do not seal the Words of the Prophecy of this Book, for the time is at hand. He who is unjust, let him be unjust still; he who is filthy, let him be filthy still; he who is righteous, let him be righteous still; he who is holy, let him be holy still. And behold, I am coming quickly, and My reward is with Me, to give to every one according to what his work shall be. I am the Alpha and the Omega, the Beginning and the Ending, the First and the Last. Blessed are those who do His commandments, that they may have the right to the Tree of Life, and may enter through the gates into the city. But outside are dogs and sorcerers and prostitutes and murderers and idolaters, and whoever loves and produces a lie." Revelation 22:10-15

"Now after John was put in prison, Jesus came into Galilee, preaching the gospel of the kingdom of God, and saying, The time is fulfilled, and the kingdom of God is at hand. Repent, and believe in the gospel." Mark 1:14-15

Amen!

Enslavement

"The prophets who have been before me and before you of old prophesied against many lands and against great kingdoms; of war, and of evil, and of pestilence. As for the prophet who prophesies of peace, when the word of the prophet shall come to pass, then the prophet shall be known, that Jehovah has truly sent him." Jeremiah 28:8-9

"Jehovah stands up to plead His case, and stands up to judge the peoples. Jehovah will enter into judgment with the elders of His people, and their rulers. For you have eaten up the vineyard, the plunder of the poor is in your houses. What do you mean that you crush My people, and grind the faces of the poor? says the Lord Jehovah of Hosts. Furthermore Jehovah says, Because the daughters of Zion are haughty, and walk with stretched out necks and wanton eyes, walking and mincing as they go, and make a tinkling with their feet; therefore Jehovah will attach scabs to the top of the head of the daughters of Zion; and Jehovah will lay bare their secret parts. In that day the Lord will take away the beauty of their anklets, and their headbands, and their crescents of the moon, the pendants, and the bracelets, and the veils; the turbans, and the leg ornaments, and the sashes, and the perfume boxes, and the amulets; the rings and nose jewels; the festal apparel and the outer garments; and the mantles, and the purses; the mirrors and the fine linen; and the turbans and the veils. And it shall be, instead of a smell of perfume, there shall be an odor of decay. And instead of a belt, a rope. And instead of well set hair, baldness. And instead of a rich robe, a girding of sackcloth; and branding instead of beauty. Your men shall fall by the sword, and your mighty in the war." Isaiah 3:13-25

The entire world is facing problems that are unprecedented in scale. There are revolts against the powers-that-be in many countries going on right now. People are divided on their beliefs regarding how to fix the many ails facing their nations, but how many times are those divisions in various places firmly affixed to whether or not a group of people believe in God or deny their Creator?

All over the world there are countries failing, economic problems — a literal worldwide time bomb waiting to implode the established financial norms, wars regarding religious beliefs, rumors of wars regarding ideologies and geopolitical statuses and numerous other ills. In America it is not much different, we now stand at over $20,000,000,000,000 for our National Debt with MUCH more owed on all of the future obligations, like Social Security and government pensions. Our infrastructure of the nation is in need of

TRILLIONS of dollars in repair, our health care system is broken with prices skyrocketing for services at our local hospitals, the price of needed goods, such as utilities, food, home and car maintenance continue to climb, all as wages continue to fall to the battle of inflation. America is debt-ridden and so far gone all Americans can do is hope that something will change that will fix these and many other ails. Yet consider for a moment, take the wool out of your eyes and look around.

America is the land of enslavement…

A lot could be said about our rates of cancer, compared to other industrialized first world nations or the fact that we spend more on healthcare than any other country. I could add the fact that our privacy is all but eroded, a secretive police state surrounds Americans that live inside a virtual prison without walls. Our food is tainted containing ingredients and chemicals that are banned in many other countries, all while being irradiated, mixed with genetically modified foods, nanotechnology and a whole host of other issues, in essence, if you will, poisoned. The same would go with our water treatment processes in most places around the country, the spraying of who-knows-what chemicals in the skies around the globe and now our hackable televisions that are recording when turned off and sending the information to unknown government agencies.

Our emails our watched, our phone data collected, our driving patterns and plans recorded, our faces scanned and our beliefs recorded. All around us is a tightening of a noose around our necks as the country continues down a path to destruction, enslaved, yet still insistent on refusing to repent to our Creator. The trap has been set, the plans have been laid out and all around us there are the dead walking around while alive. They cannot see, nor comprehend the evil that has been planned for them. Instead of realizing the peril that they and our society are in, they rather plead to the very keepers of the prison to continue to build the walls stronger, to ensure that there be no escape, that all of those who dissent in any form be quarantined from their supposed utopia.

Do you not see the Babylonian corporate system all around you? Does one who works in a corporate industry not hear the plans laid out to continue the conquering through deceit and treachery and not perceive that ultimately that will include them? The enticement is great, the deception is huge, the very enemy that is praised, the one that makes society tick, the one where countless women scramble from shop to shop and spend many meals divulging on their delicacies of deceit and men are engulfed in a culture that has been laid out for them, are part of the same financial arm of those who seek to do you harm, those who have created a plan to deny their Creator and swallow up as many souls with their doomed dominating scheme.

All around us there are individuals who are trapped in this grand diabolical scheme of whose depths should not be searched out. Yet we can clearly see the enslavement of the souls of men all around us and the lie has not just spread throughout the secular ills of our society, but has enwrapped the church as well.

The other day it came out that much of the chicken purchased at fast food restaurants is not all chicken. As in times past, this shouldn't have been a shock, but one of the companies had a rate of around 50% of real chicken, with the rest mixed with textured soy protein to give it the look and mouth feel of chicken, of which I think it would be better termed, 'picken'. Flavored to taste like chicken, designed to look like chicken, priced to be chicken, yet it by definition is not chicken, simply contains chicken.

There were also other well known companies who were not as bad, theirs contained up to 85% chicken, a more notable percent. In comparison with the well known company that contained only 50% or less of chicken, the others seemed to be able to be brushed off as being 'good enough' and not so bad. Yet consider for a moment the partial truths being handed to people all over the world.

If churches were only preaching half of the truth of God's Word, would not the other half be lies out of their mouth? When eternity is at stake, would they not be placing the souls of every hearer at risk of never coming to repentance and believing into God's Son, Jesus Christ, who died on the Cross for their sins and rose again from the dead? What if 85% of the truth was told in churches, would it then be any different? Still the truth wouldn't be fully told, perhaps some churches might even preach 98% truth? What then, what if the Truth they left out was regarding the Salvation of your soul?

What if they told people that 'God accepts them just as they are' or what if they promised them wealth and prosperity? What if they told them repentance wasn't necessary or had them simply repeat a prayer after them and proclaimed them to be children of God, Christians, without even delivering the full gospel message that they might not even know themselves? What if they refused to believe and preach in a literal Hell, or refused to believe that Jesus Christ was truly the Son of God, born of a virgin, who became a Man, suffered and died on the Cross for our sins, rose again, conquering death, to sit at the right hand of God, even though we were not worthy to receive such a free gift from our Creator? What if they took something so easy, such as the simplicity that is found in Jesus Christ and made it so complex that it became so confusing as to what the truth surrounding such a message as the Gospel even was?

"But I fear, lest somehow, as the serpent deceived Eve by his craftiness, so your minds may be corrupted from the simplicity that is in Christ." 2nd Corinthians 11:3

"Then Peter said to them, Repent, and let every one of you be immersed in the name of Jesus Christ to the remission of sins; and you shall receive the gift of the Holy Spirit. For the promise is to you and to your children, and to all who are afar off, as many as the Lord our God will call." Acts 2:38-39

... *"testifying both to Jews, and also to Greeks, repentance toward God and faith toward our Lord Jesus Christ."* Acts 20:21

"For He made Him who knew no sin to be sin for us, that we might become the righteousness of God in Him." 2nd Corinthians 5:21

"Now after John was put in prison, Jesus came into Galilee, preaching the gospel of the kingdom of God, and saying, The time is fulfilled, and the kingdom of God is at hand. Repent, and believe in the gospel." Mark 1:14-15

"And you being dead in trespasses and sins, in which you formerly walked according to the course of this world, according to the ruler of the authority of the air, the spirit who now works in the sons of disobedience, among whom also we all formerly conducted ourselves in the lusts of our flesh, fulfilling the desires of the flesh and of the mind, and were by nature children of wrath, just as the others; but God, who is rich in mercy, because of His great love with which He loved us, even when we were dead in trespasses, made us alive together with Christ (by grace you are saved), and raised us up together, and made us sit together in the heavenlies in Christ Jesus, that in the ages to come He might display the exceeding riches of His grace in His kindness toward us in Christ Jesus. For by grace you are saved through faith; and that not of yourselves, it is the gift of God; not of works, that no one should boast." Ephesians 2:1-9

"No one has ascended to Heaven but He who came down from Heaven, that is, the Son of Man who is in Heaven. And as Moses lifted up the serpent in the wilderness, even so must the Son of Man be lifted up, that everyone believing into Him should not perish but have eternal life. For God so loved the world that He gave His only begotten Son, that everyone believing into Him should not perish but have eternal life. For God did not send His Son into the world to judge the world, but that the world through Him might be saved. The one believing into Him is not judged; but the one not believing is judged already, because he has not believed in the name of the only begotten Son of God. And this is the judgment, that the Light has come into the world, and men loved darkness rather than the Light, for their deeds were evil. For everyone practicing evil hates the Light and does not come to the Light, lest his deeds should be reproved. But the one doing the truth comes to the Light, that his deeds may be clearly seen, that they have been worked in God." John 3:13-21

"Behold, I stand at the door and knock. If anyone hears My voice and opens the door, I will come in to him and dine with him, and he with Me. To him who overcomes I will grant to sit with Me on My throne, as I also overcame and sat down with My Father on His throne." Revelation 3:20-21

Indeed! They have done it and they will continue to do so. The remaining Churches that still refuse to fall to the whelms of society are surrounded and under constant attack. They know in Whom to trust and have acted wisely in trusting in Him who is able to deliver, no matter the odds against them. Outside, the wall is being built to ensure that the enslavement if permanent, from within those whom themselves are enslaved are acting in the gulag as guards and pressing against those who have refused to be overcome by the powers of darkness. Those who put their trust in something more than material items or a god of the imagination of their wicked hearts are wise for they put their trust, their faith, their lives in the hands of the Almighty, the Most High, the One who will never forsake them or let them down, their King is a mighty King who will indeed deliver and avenge. Though they live among those who are perishing they are free, they are not enslaved though they see those being led away.

"For we do not wrestle against flesh and blood, but against rulers, against authorities, against the world's rulers of the darkness of this age, against spiritual wickedness in the heavenlies." Ephesians 6:12

"Trust in Jehovah with all your heart, and lean not unto your own understanding. In all your ways acknowledge Him, and He shall direct your paths. Do not be wise in your own eyes; fear Jehovah and depart from evil. It shall be healing to your navel and refreshment to your bones." Proverbs 3:5-8

"Do not fret yourself over evil doers, nor be envious of the workers of iniquity. For they shall soon be cut down like the grass; and wither as the green herb. Trust in Jehovah, and do good; dwell in the land, and feed on faithfulness. Delight yourself also in Jehovah, and He shall give you the desires of your heart. Roll your ways upon Jehovah; trust also in Him, and He will bring it to pass. And He will bring forth your righteousness like the light, and your justice like the noonday. Rest in Jehovah, and wait patiently for Him; do not fret over him who prospers in his way, because of him who works out wicked devices. Cease from anger, and forsake wrath; do not fret; it only leads to evil. For evildoers shall be cut off; but those who wait upon Jehovah, they shall inherit the earth. For yet a little while, and the wicked shall be no more; indeed, you shall diligently consider his place, and it shall be no more. But the lowly shall inherit the earth, and shall delight themselves in the abundance of peace. The wicked plots against the just, and gnashes at him with his teeth. Jehovah laughs at him, for He sees that his day is coming. The wicked have drawn out the sword and have bent their bow, to cast down the poor and needy, to slaughter those who walk uprightly. Their sword shall enter into their own heart, and their bows shall be broken. A little that the righteous has is better than the riches of many wicked. For the arms of the wicked shall be broken, but Jehovah upholds the righteous. Jehovah knows the days of the upright, and their inheritance shall be forever. They shall not be ashamed in the evil time, and in the days of famine they shall be satisfied. But the wicked shall perish, and the enemies of Jehovah shall be as prized lambs; they are consumed; like smoke they vanish. The wicked borrows and does not repay, but the righteous shows mercy and gives. For those blessed by Him shall inherit the earth, and those cursed by Him shall be cut off. The steps of a good man are ordered by Jehovah, and he delights in His way. Though he fall, he shall not be cast down, for Jehovah upholds his hand." Psalms 37:1-24

"Fear not, for I am with you; be not dismayed, for I am your God. I will make you strong; yes, I will help you; yes, I will uphold you with the right hand of My righteousness. Behold, all those who were enraged against you shall be ashamed and disgraced; they shall be as nothing. And those who strive with you shall perish. You shall seek them, and shall not find them; the men striving against you shall be as nothing; at an end. For I, Jehovah your God, will hold your right hand, saying to you, Fear not; I will help you." Isaiah 41:10-13

"The earth is Jehovah's, and the fullness of it; the world, and those who dwell in it. For He has founded it upon the seas, and established it upon the rivers. Who shall go up into the hill of Jehovah? Or who shall stand in His holy place? He who has clean hands and a pure heart; who has not lifted up his soul to vanity, nor sworn deceitfully. He shall receive the blessing from Jehovah, and righteousness from the God of his salvation. This is the generation of Jacob of those who seek Him, who seek Your face. Selah. Lift up your heads, O you gates! And be lifted up, you everlasting doors! And the King of Glory shall come in. Who is this King of Glory? Jehovah strong and mighty, Jehovah mighty in battle. Lift up your heads, O you gates! Lift up, you everlasting doors! And the King of Glory shall come in. Who is this King of Glory? Jehovah of Hosts, He is the King of Glory. Selah." Psalms 24

"For You have delivered my soul from death, my eyes from tears, and my feet from stumbling." Psalms 116:8

"Therefore thus says Jehovah: Behold, I will plead your case and take vengeance for you; and I will dry up her sea and make her springs dry. And Babylon shall become heaps, a dwelling place for dragons, a horror and a hissing, without inhabitant. They shall roar together like lions; they shall growl like lions' cubs. In their heat I will make their feasts, and I will make them drunk so that they may rejoice and sleep a never-ending sleep, and not wake up, says Jehovah. I will bring them down like lambs to the slaughter, like rams with the male goats. How Sheshach is captured! And how the praise of the whole earth is seized! How Babylon has become a waste among the nations! The sea has come up over Babylon; she is covered with the multitude of its waves. Her cities are desolate, a dry land and a wilderness, a land in which no man dwells, nor does any son of man pass by it. And I will punish Bel in Babylon, and I will bring forth out of his mouth that which he has swallowed up. And the nations shall not flow together to him any more; yea, the wall of Babylon shall fall. My people, go out of her midst; and let each man deliver his soul from the fierce anger of Jehovah." Jeremiah 51:36-45

"For Christ did not send me to immerse, but to preach the gospel, not with wisdom of words, lest the cross of Christ should be made of no effect. For the message of the cross is foolishness to those who are perishing, but to us who are being saved it is the power of God. For it is written: I will destroy the wisdom of the wise, and bring to nothing the understanding of the intelligent. Where is the wise? Where is the scribe? Where is the disputer of this age? Has not God made foolish the wisdom of this world? For since, in the wisdom of God, the world through wisdom did not know God, it pleased God through the foolishness of the message preached to save those who are believing. For Jews request a sign, and Greeks seek after wisdom; but we preach Christ crucified, truly to the Jews a stumbling block and to the Greeks foolishness, but to those who are called, both Jews and Greeks, Christ the power of God and the wisdom of God. Because the foolishness of God is wiser than men, and the weakness of God is stronger than men." 1st Corinthians 1:17-25

"For we are to God the fragrance of Christ among those who are being saved and among those who are perishing. To the one we are the aroma of death leading to death,

and to the other the aroma of life leading to life. And who is sufficient for these things? For we are not, as so many, peddling the Word of God; but as of sincerity, but as from God, we speak in Christ, in the sight of God." 2nd Corinthians 2:15-17

"Then Jesus said to those Jews who had believed in Him, If you continue to abide in My Word, you are truly My disciples. And you shall know the truth, and the truth shall set you free. They answered Him, We are Abraham's seed, and have been in slavery to no one at any time. How can You say, You will be made free? Jesus answered them, Truly, truly, I say to you, Everyone practicing sin is a slave of sin. And a slave does not remain in the house forever, but the son remains forever. Therefore if the Son sets you free, you shall truly be free." John 8:31-36

"Then Simon Peter answered Him, Lord, to whom shall we go? You have the Words of eternal life. And we have believed and understood that You are the Christ, the Son of the living God." John 6:68-69

"Now hear this, O foolish people, without understanding; who have eyes and see not; who have ears and hear not. Do you not fear Me? says Jehovah. Will you not tremble at My presence, I who have placed the sand for the boundary of the sea by a perpetual decree, so that it cannot pass it? And though its waves toss to and fro, yet they cannot prevail; though they roar, yet they cannot pass over it? But this people has a stubborn and rebellious heart; they have turned aside and departed. Neither do they say in their heart, Let us now fear Jehovah our God, who gives both the former and the latter rain in its season; He reserves unto us the appointed weeks of the harvest. Your iniquities have turned away these things, and your sins have withheld good from you. For among My people are found wicked ones; they lie in wait, as one who sets snares; they set a trap, they catch men. Like a cage full of birds, so their houses are full of deceit; therefore they have become great and grown rich. They have grown fat, they gleam. Yes, they surpass the deeds of the wicked; they do not plead the cause, the cause of the fatherless, that they may get rich; and they do not judge the right of the needy. Shall I not punish for these things? says Jehovah. Shall not My soul be avenged on such a nation as this? An appalling and horrible thing has happened in the land. The prophets prophesy falsely, and the priests bear rule by their own power; and my people love to have it so, and what will you do in the end?" Jeremiah 5:21-31

Dear Reader, it is not too late to break free from the enslavement of sin, from the ills of society. Why continue to march along with those who are dead in their sins, those whom the Curse is devouring? They will be punished for their wickedness, but God is merciful and kind, willing to pardon, to remove your sins and make you white as snow. His Son Jesus Christ has already paid the price, repent and believe into Jesus, let the bonds that secure you be broken, take hold of the free gift, change from your wicked ways, be set free and set your mind on things above.

"Now if we died with Christ, we believe that we shall also live with Him, knowing that Christ, having been raised from the dead, dies no more. Death no longer has dominion over Him. For the death that He died, He died to sin once for all; but the life that He

lives, He lives unto God. Likewise you also, reckon yourselves to be dead indeed to sin, but alive to God in Christ Jesus our Lord. Therefore do not let sin reign in your mortal body, that you should obey it in its lusts. And do not present your members as instruments of unrighteousness to sin, but present yourselves to God as being alive from the dead, and your members as instruments of righteousness to God. For sin shall not have dominion over you, for you are not under Law but under grace. What then? Shall we sin because we are not under Law but under grace? Let it not be! Do you not know that to whom you present yourselves slaves to obey, you are that one's slaves whom you obey, whether of sin unto death, or of obedience unto righteousness? But God be thanked that though you were slaves of sin, yet you obeyed from the heart that form of doctrine which was delivered to you. And having been set free from sin, you became slaves to righteousness. I speak in human terms because of the weakness of your flesh. For just as you presented your members as slaves to uncleanness, and to iniquity unto iniquity, so now present your members as slaves to righteousness unto sanctification. For when you were slaves to sin, you were free in regard to righteousness. What fruit did you have then in the things of which you are now ashamed? For the end of those things is death. But now having been set free from sin, and having become slaves to God, you have your fruit unto sanctification, and the end, eternal life. For the wages of sin is death, but the gift of God is eternal life in Christ Jesus our Lord." Romans 6:8-23

"The earth mourns and fades away; the world droops and fades away; the haughty people of the earth grow feeble. The earth is also defiled under its inhabitants; because they have transgressed the laws, changed the ordinance, and have broken the perpetual covenant. Therefore the curse has devoured the earth, and those who dwell in it are held guilty; therefore the inhabitants of the earth are burned, and few men are left." Isaiah 24:4-6

"He who is unjust, let him be unjust still; he who is filthy, let him be filthy still; he who is righteous, let him be righteous still; he who is holy, let him be holy still. And behold, I am coming quickly, and My reward is with Me, to give to every one according to what his work shall be. I am the Alpha and the Omega, the Beginning and the Ending, the First and the Last. Blessed are those who do His commandments, that they may have the right to the Tree of Life, and may enter through the gates into the city. But outside are dogs and sorcerers and prostitutes and murderers and idolaters, and whoever loves and produces a lie. I, Jesus, have sent My angel to testify these things to you, to the churches. I am the Root and the Offspring of David, the Bright and Morning Star. And the Spirit and the bride say, Come. And let him who hears say, Come. And let him who thirsts come. Whoever desires, let him take of the Water of Life freely." Revelation 22:11-17

"And the devil, who led them astray, was cast into the Lake of Fire and brimstone where the beast and the false prophet are. And they will be tormented day and night forever and ever. And I saw a great white throne and Him who sat on it, from whose face the earth and the heavens fled away. And there was found no place for them. And I saw the dead, small and great, standing before God. And books were opened. And another book was opened, which is the Book of Life. And the dead were judged according to their works, out of the things which were written in the books. And the sea gave up the dead who were in it, and Death and Hades delivered up the dead who were in them. And they were judged, each one, according to their works. And Death and Hades were cast into the Lake of Fire. This is the second death. And anyone not found written in the Book of Life was cast into the Lake of Fire." Revelation 20:10-15

"Truly, these times of ignorance God overlooked, but now commands all men everywhere to repent, because He has established a day on which He will judge the world in righteousness by the Man whom He has appointed. He has given assurance of this to everyone by raising Him from the dead." Acts 17:30-31

"Come now and let us reason together, says Jehovah: Though your sins are as scarlet, they shall be as white as snow; though they are red like crimson, they shall be as wool." Isaiah 1:18

"Christ has redeemed us from the curse of the Law, having become a curse for us (for it is written, Cursed is everyone who hangs on a tree), that the blessing of Abraham might come upon the Gentiles in Christ Jesus, that we might receive the promise of the Spirit through faith." Galatians 3:13-14

"Those who sat in darkness and in the shadow of death, prisoners in affliction and irons; because they rebelled against the Words of the Mighty God, and despised the counsel of the Most High; therefore He humbled their heart with labor; they fell down, and there was no one to help. Then they cried out unto Jehovah in their adversity, and He delivered them out of their distresses. He brought them out of darkness and the shadow of death, and broke and tore their bonds apart. Oh, that men would give thanks unto Jehovah for His goodness, and for His wonderful works to the sons of men!" Psalms 107:10-15

"For I have no pleasure in the death of one who dies, declares the Lord Jehovah. Therefore turn and live!" Ezekiel 18:32

"If then you are raised with Christ, seek those things which are above, where Christ is, sitting at the right hand of God. Set your mind on things above, not on the things of the earth; for you died, and your life is hidden with Christ in God. When Christ who is our life is revealed, then you also will be revealed with Him in glory. Therefore put to death your members which are on the earth: sexual perversion, uncleanness, passion, evil lusts, and covetousness, which is idolatry. Because of these things the wrath of God is coming upon the sons of disobedience; in which you yourselves once walked when you lived in them. But now you yourselves are to put off all these: anger, wrath, malice, blasphemy, filthy language out of your mouth." Colossians 3:1-8

Then you will be truly free, then liberty will have come to you. Irregardless of the situation you might find yourself in, as numerous people are in many troubles, God is a kind, merciful and loving God to those who are His, yet He will repay for those who refuse to repent of their sins and believe into His Son. What will you do if it is too late?

"But as many as received Him, to them He gave the authority to become children of God, to those believing into His name: who were born, not of blood, nor of the will of the flesh, nor of the will of man, but of God." John 1:12-13

"After these things I saw another angel coming down from Heaven, having great power, and the earth was illuminated with his glory. And he cried mightily with a loud voice, saying, Babylon the great is fallen, is fallen, and has become a dwelling place of demons, a prison for every unclean spirit, and a cage for every unclean and hated bird! For all the nations have drunk of the wine of the wrath of her sexual perversities, the kings of the earth have prostituted themselves with her, and the merchants of the earth have become rich through the power of her luxury. And I heard another voice from Heaven saying, Come out of her, my people, so that you not share in her sins, and so that you not receive of her plagues. For her sins have reached to Heaven, and God has remembered her iniquities. Render to her just as she rendered to you, and repay her double according to her works; in the cup which she has mixed, mix double for her. By however much she has glorified herself and lived luxuriously, by the same amount give her torment and sorrow; for she says in her heart, I sit as queen, and am no widow, and will not see sorrow. Therefore her plagues will come in one day; death and mourning and famine. And she will be consumed with fire, for strong is the Lord God who judges her. The kings of the earth who prostituted themselves and lived luxuriously with her will weep and lament for her, when they see the smoke of her burning, standing at a distance because of the terror of her torment, saying, Alas, alas, that great city Babylon, that mighty city! For in one hour your judgment has come. And the merchants of the earth will weep and mourn over her, for no one buys their merchandise anymore: merchandise of gold and silver, precious stones and pearls, fine linen and purple, silk and scarlet, every kind of thyine wood, every kind of object of ivory, every kind of object of most precious wood, bronze, iron, and marble; and cinnamon and incense, ointment and frankincense, wine and oil, fine flour and wheat, beasts and sheep, horses and chariots, and bodies and souls of men. And the fruit that your soul lusted for has gone from you, and all the things which are rich and splendid have gone from you, and you shall find them no more at all. The merchants of these things, who became rich by her, will stand at a distance because of the terror of her torment, weeping and wailing, and saying, Alas, alas, that great city that was clothed in fine linen, purple, and scarlet, and adorned with gold and precious stones and pearls! For in one hour such great riches is come to nothing. Every shipmaster, all who travel by ship, sailors, and as many as trade on the sea, stood at a distance and cried out when they saw the smoke of her burning, saying, What is like this great city? And they threw dust on their heads and cried out, weeping and wailing, and saying, Alas, alas, that great city, in which all who had ships on the sea became rich by her wealth! For in one hour she is made desolate. Rejoice over her, O Heaven, and you holy apostles and prophets, for God has avenged you on her! Then a mighty angel took up a stone like a great millstone and threw it into the sea, saying, Thus with violence the great city Babylon shall be thrown down, and shall by no means be found anymore. The sound of harpists, musicians, flutists, and trumpeters shall by no means be heard in you anymore. No craftsman of any craft shall ever be found in you anymore, and the sound of a millstone shall by no means be heard in you anymore. And

the light of a lamp shall not ever shine in you anymore, and the voice of bridegroom and bride shall not ever be heard in you anymore. For your merchants were the great men of the earth, for by your sorcery all the nations were led astray. And in her was found the blood of prophets and saints, and of all who were slain on the earth." Revelation 18

There would be nothing you could do, there is nowhere to hide from His presence, there is no case to be made against your Creator. You might have a haughty argument prepared in your mind, but as you drop as if dead standing before Him in judgment, your mouth will be shut and you will be doomed for eternity in Hell. Do you laugh at such a notion, such a statement? I would rather you would not laugh, but mourn in realization that it is true and you are deserving of such, but God is not mocked.

"Am I a God near by, says Jehovah, and not a God afar off? Can anyone hide himself in secret places so that I shall not see him? says Jehovah. Do I not fill the heavens and earth? says Jehovah." Jeremiah 23:23-24

"And when I saw Him, I fell at His feet as dead. And He laid His right hand on me, saying to me, Do not be terrified; I am the First and the Last. I am He who lives, and was dead, and behold, I am alive forevermore. Amen. And I have the keys of Hades and of Death." Revelation 1:17-18

"Turn to Me, and be saved, all the ends of the earth; for I am the Mighty God, and there is no other. I have sworn by Myself, the word has gone out of My mouth in righteousness, and shall not return, that to Me every knee shall bow, every tongue shall swear." Isaiah 45:22-23

"And these will go away into everlasting punishment, but the righteous into eternal life." Matthew 25:46

"And at that time, Michael shall stand up, the great ruler who stands for the sons of your people. And there shall be a time of distress, such as has not been since there was a nation until that time. And at that time, your people shall be delivered, everyone that shall be found written in the Book. And many of those sleeping in the earth's dust shall awake, some to everlasting life, and some to reproach and everlasting abhorrence." Daniel 12:1-2

"Do not marvel at this; for the hour is coming in which all who are in the graves will hear His voice and come forth; those who have done good, unto the resurrection of life, and those who have practiced evil, unto the resurrection of judgment." John 5:28-29

"And they shall go out and observe the dead corpses of the men who have rebelled against Me. For their worm does not die, nor is their fire quenched; and they shall be an abhorrence to all flesh." Isaiah 66:24

"Do not be led astray, God is not mocked; for whatever a man sows, that he will also reap. For he who sows to his flesh will of the flesh reap corruption, but he who sows to the Spirit will of the Spirit reap eternal life." Galatians 6:7-8

Do you fear walking down a dark alley late at night in a bad neighborhood? Well you would be better off spending your nights walking the alleys of Chicago, awaiting your day of death, than not fearing Him who has power not only over your body, but your soul.

"And do not fear those who kill the body but are not able to kill the soul. But rather fear Him who has power to destroy both soul and body in Gehenna." Matthew 10:28

Wake up and look around, this is not a joke, this is serious!

Amen!

P.S. To those who watch these writing from afar, God sees you and the same message applies to you. Repent and seek Him before it is too late, you too are in the same trap, though you might think you are exempt, I challenge you to see how far your 'exemption' goes. In the very moment of discovery you will find yourself also underneath condemnation by the very wicked system that will also devour you. Take a look at those who opened the window of exposure into your schemes and the plots against them. Your safety only rests in your enslavement to the very evil scheme that will also seal your soul to an eternity in a literal Hell for those who have refused their Creator.

"Jehovah has sworn and will not regret it: You are a priest forever according to the order of Melchizedek. The Lord at Your right hand shall shatter kings in the day of His wrath. He shall judge among the nations, He shall fill them with dead bodies; He shall greatly shatter the heads over the earth." Psalms 110:4-6

As Little Children

"At that time the disciples came to Jesus, saying, Who then is greater in the kingdom of Heaven? And Jesus called a little child to Him, set him in the midst of them, and said, Truly, I say to you, unless you are converted and become as little children, you will by no means enter the kingdom of Heaven. Therefore whoever humbles himself as this little child is greater in the kingdom of Heaven." Matthew 18:1-4

I awoke today with a thought of just how simple it should be for people to believe the Gospel. Irregardless of what might be taught by the 'professionals' throughout the world, I wondered why no one questions the fact that the world is not yet overpopulated.

A quick Google search and I found that supposedly mankind is six million years old, the current evolved form of mankind (I guess that would be us) is around 200,000 years old, civilization as we know it is around 6,000 years old and the industrial revolution started in the 1800's. In and of itself that evolutionary statement of disbelief aligns itself with the Word of God in that the world is around 6,000 years old, so I agree with the civilization portion, any book would quickly verify the industrial revolution. But according to mankind, the current form of humans is 200,000 years old, why isn't the population of the world too many people?

In 2000 years, according to those who do such research, the population has went from somewhere between 170 – 400 million, increasing steadily to around 7.5 billion people today. If mankind were as old as those who deny our Creator state, than our population would have vast exceeded the ability of the planet to contain us. I've read somewhere that the world could contain around 50 billion people, if evolution were true we would have far exceeded that number long, long ago and been likely on our way towards 500 billion people or more.

I remember a debate that I had years ago while working in the dish tank shortly after high school at a busy restaurant. I don't recall how it was brought up, but this girl I was working with proclaimed that she did not believe in God, but she did believe in demons. I looked at her and made a simple argument: if there are demons then there are angels, if there are demons than there is a devil, if there is a devil than there is a God, if there is a God then there is a Heaven, if there is a Heaven, then there is a Hell and unless you become Saved you are heading straight there. Her mouth was shut.

When I was in high school there was no debate that a person named Jesus actually lived. Even the non-believing teachers would acknowledge that. The problem was that they didn't believe that Jesus was the Christ, that He was the Son of God who died on the Cross for our sins. The argument is an old one, one that goes all the way back to when Jesus was preaching the Gospel in Israel. Yet the question remains, why did God have His Son Jesus die on the Cross, the answer is so simple. He died for your sins.

"And Jesus and His disciples went out to the towns of Caesarea Philippi; and on the road He asked His disciples, saying to them, Who do men say that I am? So they answered, John the Immerser; but some say, Elijah; and others, one of the prophets. He said to them, But who do you say that I am? Peter answered and said to Him, You are the Christ." Mark 8:27-29

"And the Scripture was fulfilled which says, And He was numbered with the transgressors. And those who passed by blasphemed Him, wagging their heads and saying, Aha! You who destroy the temple and build it in three days, save Yourself, and come down from the cross! Likewise the chief priests also, mocking among themselves with the scribes, said, He saved others, but He is not able to save Himself. Let the Christ, the King of Israel, descend now from the cross, that we may see and believe. Even those who were crucified with Him reviled Him. And when the sixth hour had come, there was darkness over the whole land until the ninth hour. And at the ninth hour Jesus cried out with a loud voice, saying, Eloi, Eloi, lama sabachthani? which is translated, My God, My God, why have You forsaken Me? And some of those who stood by, when they heard that, said, Behold, He is calling for Elijah. And someone ran and filled a sponge full of vinegar, put it on a reed, and gave it to Him to drink, saying, Let Him alone; let us see if Elijah will come to take Him down. And Jesus cried out with a loud voice, and breathed His last. And the veil of the temple was torn in two from top to bottom. And when the centurion, who stood opposite Him, saw that He cried out like this and breathed His last, he said, Truly this Man was the Son of God!" Mark 15:28-39

"Now it was not written for his sake alone, that it was accounted to him, but also for us, to whom it shall be accounted, believing in Him who raised up Jesus our Lord from the dead, who was delivered up because of our trespasses, and was raised for our justification." Romans 4:23-25

"And He Himself is the propitiation for our sins, and not for ours only but also for the whole world." 1st John 2:2

The Gospel is that simple, yes you were Created, yes sin entered the world through Adam, yes all are born in sin. Each person, each soul who God has wrought *(Psalms 139:15)* needs a Savior, the only way to Salvation is through Jesus Christ, there is NO OTHER WAY. Once a person comes to realize that they are lost, that they are on their way to Hell, then as they also believe in God, they must believe in Jesus, the author of our Salvation. Only as they come to the point of godly repentance, knowing that their sinful deeds are worthy of God's eternal judgment, then realizing the magnitude of the free gift of Salvation through Jesus Christ, they come to Him with not only a repentant heart, but one who believes into Jesus Christ. As soon as that happens they are a new creation, no longer under the same condemnation, but are now children of the Most High in Christ Jesus our Lord.

"Therefore, just as through one man sin entered the world, and death through sin, and thus death spread to every person, because everyone sinned." Romans 5:12

"For since through man came death, through Man also came the resurrection of the dead. For as in Adam everyone dies, even so in Christ everyone shall be made alive." 1st Corinthians 15:21-22

"for all have sinned and fall short of the glory of God"... Romans 3:23

"Jesus said to him, I am the Way, the Truth, and the Life. No one comes to the Father except through Me." John 14:6

"And having been found perfect, He became the author of eternal salvation to all who obey Him"... Hebrews 5:9

"And you being dead in trespasses and sins, in which you formerly walked according to the course of this world, according to the ruler of the authority of the air, the spirit who now works in the sons of disobedience, among whom also we all formerly conducted ourselves in the lusts of our flesh, fulfilling the desires of the flesh and of the mind, and were by nature children of wrath, just as the others; but God, who is rich in mercy, because of His great love with which He loved us, even when we were dead in trespasses, made us alive together with Christ (by grace you are saved), and raised us up together, and made us sit together in the heavenlies in Christ Jesus, that in the ages to come He might display the exceeding riches of His grace in His kindness toward us in Christ Jesus. For by grace you are saved through faith; and that not of yourselves, it is the gift of God; not of works, that no one should boast. For we are His workmanship, created in Christ Jesus unto good works, which God prepared beforehand that we should walk in them. Therefore remember that you, being Gentiles in the flesh; who are called uncircumcision by what is called the circumcision made in the flesh by hands; that at that time you were without Christ, being aliens from the commonwealth of Israel and strangers from the covenants of promise, having no hope and without God in the world. But now in Christ Jesus you who once were far off have been made near by the blood of Christ. For He Himself is our peace, who has made both one, and has broken down the middle wall of separation, having abolished in His flesh the enmity, that is, the Law of commandments contained in ordinances, that He might create in Himself one new man from the two, thus making peace, and that He might reconcile them both to God in one body through the cross, thereby putting to death the enmity. And He came and preached peace to you who were afar off and to those who were near. For through Him we both have access by one Spirit to the Father. Now, therefore, you are no longer strangers and foreigners, but fellow citizens with the saints and members of the household of God, having been built on the foundation of the apostles and prophets, Jesus Christ Himself being the chief corner stone, in whom the whole building, being joined together, grows

into a holy temple in the Lord, in whom you also are being built together into a dwelling place of God in the Spirit." Ephesians 2

Jesus said, *"I tell you, no; but unless you repent you will all likewise perish."* Luke 13:3

"Therefore, if anyone is in Christ, he is a new creation; the old things have passed away; behold, all things have become new." 2nd Corinthians 5:17

How long will you go on believing the lies of the devil? How long before you wake out of the slumber and finally realize just how simple it is? Then when you realize that you are wrong will you continue on refusing to repent and yield to your Creator? The reason that so many people go along with the lies that have been created by men is quite simple, they do not want to change, they want things to remain the way they are. Fine, one can hold to such a viewpoint, but it is wrong and in the end it leads to death, eternity in Hell, without hope.

"You are of the devil as your father, and the lusts of your father you purpose to do. He was a murderer from the beginning, and does not stand in the truth, because there is no truth in him. When he speaks a lie, he speaks from his own, for he is a liar and the father of it." John 8:44

"And I saw a great white throne and Him who sat on it, from whose face the earth and the heavens fled away. And there was found no place for them. And I saw the dead, small and great, standing before God. And books were opened. And another book was opened, which is the Book of Life. And the dead were judged according to their works, out of the things which were written in the books. And the sea gave up the dead who were in it, and Death and Hades delivered up the dead who were in them. And they were judged, each one, according to their works. And Death and Hades were cast into the Lake of Fire. This is the second death. And anyone not found written in the Book of Life was cast into the Lake of Fire." Revelation 20:11-15

Why would anyone do that?

Amen!

Following Who?

There is a very dangerous trend that has happened in the past and will surely happen in the future. Man looking for man to solve man's problems. While societies could look at their ills that need to be addressed, such as jobs, infrastructure, health care, etc., often times for many people, not only in the United States, but around the world, the are truly focused on their own household.

While there are certainly things that leaders, whether elected, celebrities with their foundations, political movement figures, etc., can certainly do, such as donate a large amount of food or clothing, give money, help create jobs, the bottom line is people are looking towards man to not only fix the ills of society, but those of their own household.

There certainly can be merit in some of the efforts that man does to provide help, but too often the problems they intend to fix create other problems or their public intentions are not their private intentions. Even if man was able to begin to provide some sort of utopia, what would be a utopia for one segment of society would be a dystopia to another segment.

Families around the world are concerned about a job to make enough income to provide the necessities of life. Then those who have such an amount of income are often focused on making more to provide for the desires and pleasures of life. A healthy family who supposedly remains so through access to proper medical care, is another focus, then there are the concerns that some focus on regarding their imagined rights, as well as the rights of the earth. However in all of this there is great error, who are they following?

If they turned to their Creator and saw their medical condition, they would realize they are on life support. Should their last breath be breathed, their condition would be eternally fatal as they would then be lost and without a Savior, their sinful condition would mean they are destined for eternity in the Lake of Fire.

... "for all have sinned and fall short of the glory of God"... Romans 3:23

"For the wages of sin is death, but the gift of God is eternal life in Christ Jesus our Lord." Romans 6:23

"And anyone not found written in the Book of Life was cast into the Lake of Fire." Revelation 20:15

If they turned to their Creator and realized the great Gift that He has bestowed to those who will accept it, then they would realize that Jesus Christ, the Son of God, came to save that which was lost. He came to pay the penalty for their sins and died on the Cross for them. He rose from the dead three days later, having conquered death. Would they then realize that they have been looking to a man for help, instead of God? If they thought they needed help in the necessities of this life, who would they turn to in regards to their home for eternity? A man or Jesus?

"For God so loved the world that He gave His only begotten Son, that everyone believing into Him should not perish but have eternal life. For God did not send His Son into the world to judge the world, but that the world through Him might be saved. The one believing into Him is not judged; but the one not believing is judged already, because he has not believed in the name of the only begotten Son of God. And this is the judgment, that the Light has come into the world, and men loved darkness rather than the Light, for their deeds were evil. For everyone practicing evil hates the Light and does not come to the Light, lest his deeds should be reproved. But the one doing the truth comes to the Light, that his deeds may be clearly seen, that they have been worked in God." John 3:16-21

... *" for the Son of Man has come to seek and to save that which was lost." Luke 19:10*

... *" believing in Him who raised up Jesus our Lord from the dead, who was delivered up because of our trespasses, and was raised for our justification. Therefore, having been justified by faith, we have peace with God through our Lord Jesus Christ, through whom also we have access by faith into this grace in which we stand, and rejoice on the hope of the glory of God." Romans 4:24b – 5:2*

"Now on the first day of the week, very early in the morning, they, and certain other women with them, came to the tomb bringing the spices which they had prepared. But they found the stone having been rolled away from the tomb. And they went in and did not find the body of the Lord Jesus. And it happened, as they were greatly perplexed about this, that behold, two men stood by them in shining garments. And, as they were terrified and bowed their faces to the earth, they said to them, Why do you seek the living among the dead? He is not here, but is risen! Remember how He spoke to you when He was still in Galilee, saying, The Son of Man must be delivered into the hands of sinful men, and be crucified, and the third day rise again. And they remembered His words." Luke 24:1-8

Truly there are many poor people throughout the world. While America has its fair share, we have all seen the images that are on television asking for money for poor starving African children, this is not a joke or to be taken lightly. While Americans scramble to figure out ways to scam the government for more money for food, others would be very happy to eat rice and beans, with a few vegetables on a daily basis, foods that most people stick their nose up to. Meat on every plate has been a battle cry for some politicians, yet where is their daily meat from hearing the Word of God? Those who have trusted in Him, know that they can safely rest assured that He will provide their basic necessities.

"But He answered and said, It is written, Man shall not live by bread alone, but by every Word that comes forth from the mouth of God." Matthew 4:4

"Your Words were found, and I ate them; and Your Word was to me the joy and rejoicing of my heart; for I am called by Your name, O Jehovah the God of Hosts." Jeremiah 15:16

"I have been young, and now am old; yet I have not seen the righteous forsaken, nor his seed begging bread. All day long he is gracious and lends, and his seed is blessed. Depart from evil and do good, and live forevermore. For Jehovah loves justice and does not forsake His Godly ones; they are preserved forever; but the seed of the wicked shall be cut off. The righteous shall inherit the earth, and dwell in it forever." Pslams 37:25-29

Jobs are always a large battle cry to create a movement of followers looking towards a future leader or a current leader regarding the ultimate saving mechanism. A good job with benefits is a well-rounded wish that would seemingly provide for all of one's earthly desires. Yet it is self that they are after, not anything else. For they desire the good jobs with great benefits, but themselves vote to continue to enslave people around the world in sweat-shop conditions producing cheap goods. The overwhelming abundance of foreign manufactured goods testifies that the few bucks saved for self was the ultimate vote that took away these jobs in the first place. It is the same selfish mindset of seeking one's own pleasure, rather than the things of God, that will cause the vast majority of those to continue on the broad path to destruction.

"No one is able to serve two masters; for either he will hate the one and love the other, or else he will hold to the one and despise the other. It is not possible to serve God and mammon. Therefore I say to you, do not be anxious about your life, what you will eat or what you will drink; nor about your body, what you will put on. Is not life more than food and the body more than clothing? Observe the birds of the air, for they neither sow nor reap nor gather into barns; yet your Heavenly Father feeds them. Are you not of more value than they? Which of you by being anxious is able to add one cubit to his stature? So why are you anxious about clothing? Consider the lilies of the field, how they grow: they neither toil nor spin; and yet I say to you that even Solomon in all his glory was not arrayed like one of these. Now if God so clothes the grass of the field, which today is, and tomorrow is thrown into the furnace, will He not much more clothe you, O you of little faith? Therefore do not be anxious, saying, What shall we eat? or What shall we drink? or What shall we wear? For after all these things the Gentiles seek. For your Heavenly Father knows that you need all these things. But seek first the kingdom of God and His righteousness, and all these things shall be added to you. Therefore do not be anxious about tomorrow, for tomorrow will worry about its own things. Sufficient for the day is its own trouble." Matthew 6:24-34

"Do not lay up for yourselves treasures on earth, where moth and rust destroy and where thieves dig through and steal; but lay up for yourselves treasures in Heaven, where

neither moth nor rust destroys and where thieves do not dig through and steal. For where your treasure is, there your heart will be also." Matthew 6:19-21

"Enter by the narrow gate; for wide is the gate and broad is the way that leads to destruction, and there are many entering in through it. Because narrow is the gate and distressing is the way which leads unto life, and there are few who find it." Matthew 7:13-14

Rather than realize the lack of self-worth, the utter helpless and despicable condition of their sin before their Creator, they will continue on trying to figure out how to get the things in life that will best fit themselves. In their end, due to their refusal to acknowledge their sin, repent and cry out to God Almighty, believing into Jesus Christ as their Savior, they will continue to vehemently search out for someone to follow who will promise to provide them with the pleasures of this life. God has a promise to those who truly become born-again Believers also, Him should you follow, Him alone, for there is equally a promise to those who refuse to repent and seek Him and I assure you that all of the words of God will stand, irregardless of what a man might otherwise tell you.

"For godly sorrow produces repentance leading to salvation, not to be regretted; but the sorrow of the world produces death." 2nd Corinthians 7:10

"And he brought them out and said, Sirs, what must I do to be saved? So they said, Believe on the Lord Jesus Christ, and you will be saved, you and your household." Acts 16:30-31

"Behold, I stand at the door and knock. If anyone hears My voice and opens the door, I will come in to him and dine with him, and he with Me. To him who overcomes I will grant to sit with Me on My throne, as I also overcame and sat down with My Father on His throne." Revelation 3:20-21

Amen!

First in Line

The other day I had to pick up something at the post office. As I entered the main lobby, I took my place in line waiting patiently as there were several people in front of me, mailing and picking up packages. Soon the line behind me stretched all the way to the door and as more people started to approach some became frustrated and stated that they would have to come back later.

That day the line was long and slow. It seemed to take nearly 20 minutes for me to finally get to the counter to conduct business, but alas it happened. On my way home I was pondering how many of those who were waiting would have liked to have been able to cut to the front, to be first in line. I thought of this in regards to the final Judgment where each individual man and woman will stand before God Almighty, one at a time, waiting for their turn.

"And I saw a great white throne and Him who sat on it, from whose face the earth and the heavens fled away. And there was found no place for them. And I saw the dead, small and great, standing before God. And books were opened. And another book was opened, which is the Book of Life. And the dead were judged according to their works, out of the things which were written in the books. And the sea gave up the dead who were in it, and Death and Hades delivered up the dead who were in them. And they were judged, each one, according to their works. And Death and Hades were cast into the Lake of Fire. This is the second death. And anyone not found written in the Book of Life was cast into the Lake of Fire." Revelation 20:11-15

"So then each of us shall give account concerning himself to God." Romans 14:12

"And as it is appointed for men to die once, and after this the judgment, so Christ was offered once to bear the sins of many. To those who eagerly wait for Him He will appear a second time, without sin, unto salvation." Hebrews 9:27-28

"Though hand join to hand, the wicked shall not be held innocent, but the seed of the righteous shall be delivered." Proverbs 11:21

"Therefore you are without excuse, O man, whoever you are who judges, for in whatever you judge another you condemn yourself; for you who judge practice the same things. But we know that the judgment of God is according to truth upon those who practice such things. And do you think this, O man, you who judges those practicing such things,

and doing the same, that you will escape the judgment of God? Or do you despise the riches of His kindness, forbearance, and longsuffering, not knowing that the kindness of God leads you to repentance? But according to your hardness and impenitent heart you are treasuring up for yourself wrath in the day of wrath and revelation of the righteous judgment of God, who will render to each one according to his works: eternal life to those who steadfastly doing good, seek for glory, honor, and incorruptibility; but to those who are self-seeking and do not obey the truth, but obey unrighteousness; anger and wrath, trouble and anguish, on every soul of man who produces evil, of the Jew first and also of the Greek; but glory, honor, and peace to everyone who works what is good, to the Jew first and also to the Greek. For there is no partiality with God." Romans 2:1-11

This is serious stuff, while it might not be popular amongst those who are your friends, family or acquaintances, when a man dies without having repented of his sins and believed into Jesus Christ, they will undoubtedly be waiting at the Great White Throne Judgment and who then will want to be first in line. For once, the eagerness of people to be pleasant and allow others to go first before them would be unprecedented. What man would want to be next, knowing their fate?

At that time there will be no more debate about whether or not there is a God. The debate will be well done and over with. There will be no more debate on whether or not repentance is necessary or if Jesus is the only Way *(John 14:6)*. When that time comes there will only be sorrow, no hope, for it is too late. There is no more time to go back, there is no more time to warn, there is no more time to rethink, there is no more time period. Then and at that time if it took a million years to wait until you stood before the Most High, you would gladly do so, for the realization of an eternity in Hell, a lifetime blown by sin and refusal to repent of sin and accept God's gift of Salvation through Jesus Christ, our Lord and Savior, will be far spent. At that time only sadness, guilt, regret and hopelessness will be felt as your time to meet God, whom you rejected, will be at hand.

If only you would stop, just stop and consider for a moment the goodness of God Almighty who has provided a clear process to rectify yourself before Him through His Son. Will you continue on a stubborn path to destruction? Will you continue to make up excuses? Will you continue to refuse to repent or will you consider before such a scenario becomes reality, for surely as God created the heavens and the earth, it will happen. I plead for you to reconsider before it is too late, to simply ask yourself why you refuse to repent, why you refuse to accept Salvation. For what are you trying to gain by rebelling against your Creator?

"The harvest is past, the summer is ended, and we are not saved." Jeremiah 8:20

"The night is far spent, the day is at hand. Therefore let us cast off the works of darkness, and let us put on the armor of light." Romans 13:12

"For He says: In an acceptable time I have heard you, and in a day of salvation I have helped you. Behold, now is the accepted time; behold, now is the day of salvation." 2nd Corinthians 6:2

"For what will it profit a man if he gains the whole world, and loses his own soul? Or what will a man give in exchange for his soul?" Mark 8:36-37

"And he showed me a pure river of Water of Life, clear as crystal, going forth out of the throne of God and of the Lamb. In the middle of its street, and on either side of the river, was the Tree of Life, which bore twelve fruits, each tree yielding its fruit every month. The leaves of the tree were for the healing of the nations. And there shall be no more curse, but the throne of God and of the Lamb shall be in it, and His servants shall serve Him. And they shall see His face, and His name shall be on their foreheads. And there shall be no night there: They need no lamp nor light of the sun, for the Lord God gives them light. And they shall reign forever and ever. And he said to me, These Words are faithful and true. And the Lord God of the holy prophets sent His angel to show His servants the things which must quickly come to pass. Behold, I am coming quickly. Blessed is he who keeps the Words of the Prophecy of this Book. Now I, John, saw and heard these things. And when I heard and saw, I fell down to do homage before the feet of the angel who showed me these things. And he said to me, Now see here! No! For I am your fellow servant, and of your brethren the prophets, and of those who keep the Words of this Book. Do homage to God. And he said to me, Do not seal the Words of the Prophecy of this Book, for the time is at hand. He who is unjust, let him be unjust still; he who is filthy, let him be filthy still; he who is righteous, let him be righteous still; he who is holy, let him be holy still. And behold, I am coming quickly, and My reward is with Me, to give to every one according to what his work shall be. I am the Alpha and the Omega, the Beginning and the Ending, the First and the Last. Blessed are those who do His commandments, that they may have the right to the Tree of Life, and may enter through the gates into the city. But outside are dogs and sorcerers and prostitutes and murderers and idolaters, and whoever loves and produces a lie. I, Jesus, have sent My angel to testify these things to you, to the churches. I am the Root and the Offspring of David, the Bright and Morning Star. And the Spirit and the bride say, Come. And let him who hears say, Come. And let him who thirsts come. Whoever desires, let him take of the Water of Life freely." Revelation 22:1-17

Amen!

No Place for Them

"And I saw a great white throne and Him who sat on it, from whose face the earth and the heavens fled away. And there was found no place for them. And I saw the dead, small and great, standing before God. And books were opened. And another book was opened, which is the Book of Life. And the dead were judged according to their works, out of the things which were written in the books. And the sea gave up the dead who were in it, and Death and Hades delivered up the dead who were in them. And they were judged, each one, according to their works. And Death and Hades were cast into the Lake of Fire. This is the second death. And anyone not found written in the Book of Life was cast into the Lake of Fire." Revelation 20:11-15

Eventually time is going to run out. With the way things are looking it could be soon, perhaps even before this article becomes published. Yet no one knows the day nor the hour. One thing that man often does is kick the can down the road on things they know they ought to do.

"But of that day and hour no one knows, not even the angels of Heaven, but My Father only. But as the days of Noah were, so also will the coming of the Son of Man be. For as in the days before the flood, they were eating and drinking, marrying and giving in marriage, until the day that Noah entered into the ark, and did not realize until the flood came and took them all away, so also will the coming of the Son of Man be. Then two will be in the field: one is taken and the other is left. Two will be grinding at the mill: one is taken and the other is left. Watch therefore, for you do not know what hour your Lord comes. But know this, that if the master of the house had known what hour the thief comes, he would have watched and not allowed his house to be dug through. Therefore you also be ready, for the Son of Man comes at an hour you do not expect." Matthew 24:36-44

Unlike putting that garage project off to the next weekend, your soul is at stake. What if you plan on eventually accepting Jesus Christ as your Lord and Savior, but decide to put it off and your life ends before doing so? What man would see his house on fire and decide to put off calling the fire department for a few minutes? Who would see their little child, who cannot swim, fall into a pool and not immediately jump in to save them? Who would watch as a loved one is in immediate peril and not do whatever they can to help them? Why would you not see clearly the imminent danger of refusing to repent and believe into Jesus Christ, to accept the free gift of Salvation? Do you not realize that what happens to the body on this earth is only a one-time ordeal and afterwards we will all stand before God Almighty. Those who are Saved at the Judgment Seat of Christ *(2nd Corinthians 5:10)* and everyone else at the Great White Throne Judgment.

"For whoever desires to save his life will lose it, but whoever loses his life for My sake and the gospel's will save it. For what will it profit a man if he gains the whole world, and loses his own soul? Or what will a man give in exchange for his soul?" Mark 8:35-37

"Now if the righteous one is scarcely saved, where will the ungodly and the sinner appear?" 1st Peter 4:18

"But why do you judge your brother? Or why do you treat your brother as being of no account? For everyone shall appear before the judgment seat of Christ. For it is written: As I live, says the Lord, Every knee shall bow to Me, and every tongue shall confess to God. So then each of us shall give account concerning himself to God." Romans 14:10-12

Nonetheless most refuse to repent of their sin, they refuse to believe in God Almighty, they refuse to accept Jesus Christ, there will be no place for them. Do you suppose that your good works will allow you a place in Heaven? Do you rather believe the accounts of men who talk about having a near death experience and how their family and friends who have died were living with God in perfect harmony, not realizing that this goes against the Holy Scriptures, not realizing that there would have been no reason for Christ to have to die on the Cross for your sins, if you could simply be a 'good' person and get to Heaven through works or simply believing that God exists.

"Be sober, be vigilant; because your adversary the devil walks about like a roaring lion, seeking whom he may devour." 1st Peter 5:8

"Enter by the narrow gate; for wide is the gate and broad is the way that leads to destruction, and there are many entering in through it. Because narrow is the gate and distressing is the way which leads unto life, and there are few who find it. Beware of false prophets, who come to you in sheep's clothing, but inwardly they are ravenous wolves. You will know them from their fruits. Do men gather grapes from thornbushes or figs from thistles? Even so, every good tree produces excellent fruit, but a corrupt tree produces evil fruit. A good tree is not able to produce evil fruit, nor is a corrupt tree able to produce excellent fruit. Every tree that does not produce excellent fruit is cut down and thrown into the fire. Therefore from their fruits you will know them. Not everyone who says to Me, Lord, Lord, will enter the kingdom of Heaven, but he who does the will of My Father in Heaven." Matthew 7:13-21

"You believe that God is One. You do well. Even the demons believe, and shudder." Jacob (James) 2:19

"For to this you were called, because Christ also suffered for us, leaving us an example, that you should follow His steps: Who committed no sin, nor was deceit found in His

mouth; who, when He was reviled, did not revile in return; when He suffered, He did not threaten, but gave Himself over to Him who judges righteously; who Himself bore our sins in His own body on the tree, that we, having died to sins, might live unto righteousness; by whose stripes you were healed. For you were like sheep going astray, but have now returned to the Shepherd and Overseer of your souls." 1st Peter 2:21-25*

"Jesus said to him, I am the Way, the Truth, and the Life. No one comes to the Father except through Me." John 14:6*

Rather what an individual is to do is repent and believe into Jesus Christ, believe the Gospel. You can only ponder Salvation for so long, you can only sit on the fence regarding your soul for so long. Either Jesus will have prepared a place for you or else there will be no place for you. Do you trust what God's Word says about Salvation or do you put your trust in men who tell you what you want to hear, so that you can assume to live life as you want and add 'Jesus' to the equation, presumably on your way to Heaven. Do you get warm and fuzzy when you hear an account of the afterlife and instead of the teller speaking about repentance, rather just 'do the best you can' and listen to such accounts as evidence that indeed you are correct? Well for those of you who refuse to acknowledge, repent and believe into the One and only true Savior, Jesus Christ, for you there will be no place.

"Truly, these times of ignorance God overlooked, but now commands all men everywhere to repent, because He has established a day on which He will judge the world in righteousness by the Man whom He has appointed. He has given assurance of this to everyone by raising Him from the dead." Acts 17:30-31*

"In My Father's house are many mansions; if it were not so, I would have told you. I go to prepare a place for you. And if I go and prepare a place for you, I will come again and receive you to Myself; that where I am, there you may be also." John 14:2-3*

No place for them!

"Do you not know that the unrighteous will not inherit the kingdom of God? Do not be led astray. Neither prostitutes, nor idolaters, nor adulterers, nor effeminate, nor sodomites, nor thieves, nor covetous, nor drunkards, nor revilers, nor extortioners will inherit the kingdom of God. And such were some of you. But you were washed, but you were sanctified, but you were justified in the name of the Lord Jesus and by the Spirit of our God." 1st Corinthians 6:9-11*

"But the cowardly, unbelieving, abominable, murderers, prostitutes, sorcerers, idolaters, and all liars shall have their part in the lake which burns with fire and brimstone, which is the second death." Revelation 21:8*

"But there were also false prophets among the people, even as there will be false teachers among you, who will secretly bring in destructive heresies, even denying the Lord who bought them, and bring on themselves swift destruction. And many will follow *their destructive ways, through whom the way of truth will be blasphemed. By covetousness they will exploit you with well-turned words; whose judgment of old is not idle, and their destruction does not slumber. For if God did not spare the angels who sinned, but cast them down to Tartarus and delivered them into chains of darkness, to be reserved for judgment; and did not spare the ancient world, but saved Noah, one of eight people, a preacher of righteousness, bringing the flood on the world of the ungodly; and turning the cities of Sodom and Gomorrah into ashes, condemned them to destruction, making them an example to those intending to live ungodly; and delivered righteous Lot, who was oppressed by the lustful behavior of the wicked (for that righteous man, dwelling among them, his righteous soul was tormented from day to day by seeing and hearing their lawless deeds); then the Lord knows how to deliver the godly out of temptations and to reserve the unjust for the day of judgment, to be punished, and especially those who walk according to the flesh in the lust of defilement and despise authority. They are presumptuous, self-willed. They are not afraid to speak evil of dignitaries. Whereas angels, who are greater in power and might, do not bring a reviling accusation against them before the Lord. But these, like natural brute beasts made to be caught and destroyed, speak evil of the things they do not understand, and will utterly perish in their own corruption, and will receive the wages of unrighteousness, as those who consider it pleasure to carouse in the daytime. They are spots and blemishes, delighting in their own deceptions while they feast with you, having eyes full of adultery and that cannot cease from sin, enticing unstable souls; having a heart exercised in covetousness; accursed children. They have forsaken the right way and gone astray, following the way of Balaam the son of Beor, who loved the wages of unrighteousness; but he was rebuked for his iniquity: a dumb donkey speaking with a man's voice restrained the madness of the prophet. These are wells without water, clouds being driven by a tempest, for whom is reserved the blackness of darkness forever. For when they speak great swelling words of vanity, they allure through the lusts of the flesh, through wantonness, the ones who have actually escaped from those living in error. While they promise them liberty, they themselves are slaves of corruption; for by whom a person is overcome, by him also he is brought into bondage. For if, after they have escaped the defilements of the world through the full true knowledge of the Lord and Savior Jesus Christ, they are again entangled in them and overcome, the end is worse for them than the beginning. For it would have been better for them not to have known the way of righteousness, than having known it, to turn from the holy commandment delivered to them. But it has happened to them according to the true proverb: A dog returns to his own vomit, and, a sow, having been washed, to her wallowing in the mire." 2nd Peter 2*

"Now if the righteous one is scarcely saved, where will the ungodly and the sinner appear?" 1st Peter 4:18

Jesus invites, will you accept His invitation or will you refuse and hear His Words.

"Behold, I stand at the door and knock. If anyone hears My voice and opens the door, I will come in to him and dine with him, and he with Me. To him who overcomes I will

grant to sit with Me on My throne, as I also overcame and sat down with My Father on His throne." Revelation 3:20-21

"Many will say to Me in that day, Lord, Lord, have we not prophesied in Your name, cast out demons in Your name, and done many works of power in Your name? And then I will declare to them, I never knew you; depart from Me, you who work out lawlessness!" Matthew 7:22-23

Amen!

They Didn't Make It

"Now it came to pass, when men began to multiply on the face of the earth, and daughters were born to them, that the sons of God saw the daughters of men, that they were pleasing; and they took wives for themselves of all whom they chose. And Jehovah said, My Spirit shall not continually strive with man, for indeed it is in flesh to sin; yet his days shall be one hundred and twenty years. There were giants on the earth in those days. And also afterward, when the sons of God came in to the daughters of men and they bore children to them, these were the mighty men from antiquity, men of renown. And Jehovah saw that the evil of man was great on the earth, and that every imagination of the thoughts of his heart was only evil all day long. And Jehovah regretted that He had made man on the earth, and He was grieved to His heart. And Jehovah said, I will obliterate man whom I have created from off the face of the earth, both man and beast, creeping thing and flying creatures of the heavens, for I regret having made them. But Noah found favor in the eyes of Jehovah. These are the generations of Noah. Noah was a just man, perfect in his generation. Noah walked with God. And Noah begot three sons: Shem, Ham, and Japheth. The earth also was corrupt before God, and the earth was filled with violence. And God looked upon the earth, and behold it was corrupt; for all flesh had corrupted their way upon the earth. And God said to Noah, The end of all flesh has come before Me, for the earth is filled with violence through them; and behold, I will destroy them along with the earth. Make yourself an ark of gopherwood; make rooms in the ark, and cover it inside and out with pitch. And this is how you shall make it: The length of the ark shall be three hundred cubits, its width fifty cubits, and its height thirty cubits. You shall make a window for the ark, and you shall finish it to a cubit from above; and set the door of the ark in its side. You shall make it with lower, second, and third levels. And behold I, even I, am bringing a flood of waters upon the earth, to destroy from under the heavens all flesh in which is the breath of life; everything that is on the earth shall die. And I will establish My covenant with you; and you shall go into the ark; you, your sons, your wife, and your sons' wives with you. And of every living thing of all flesh you shall bring two of every kind into the ark, to keep them alive with you; they shall be male and female. Of flying creatures after their kind, of animals after their kind, and of every creeping thing of the earth after its kind, two of every kind will come in to you, to keep them alive. And take for yourself of all food that is eaten, and gather it to yourself; and it shall be food for you and for them. Thus Noah did; according to all that God commanded him, so he did.

And Jehovah said to Noah, Come into the ark, you and all your house, for I have seen you as being righteous before Me in this generation. You shall take unto you of every clean animal seven and seven, a male and his female; and two each of animals that are not clean, a male and his female; also seven and seven of the flying creatures of the heavens, male and female, to keep seed alive on the face of all the earth. For after seven more days I will cause it to rain on the earth forty days and forty nights, and I will obliterate from off the face of the earth all living substance that I have made. And Noah did according to all that Jehovah commanded him. Noah was six hundred years old when the flood of waters was upon the earth. So Noah, with his sons, his wife, and his sons' wives, went into the ark because of the waters of the flood. Of clean animals, of animals that are not clean, of flying creatures, and of everything that moves upon the earth, two by two they went into the ark to Noah, male and female, as God had commanded Noah. And it came to pass after seven days that the waters of the flood were upon the earth. In the six hundredth year of Noah's life, in the second month, the seventeenth day of the month, on that day all the fountains of the great deep were broken up, and the windows of the heavens were opened. And the rain was upon the earth forty days and forty nights. On the very same day Noah and Noah's sons, Shem, Ham, and Japheth, and Noah's wife and the three wives of his sons with them, entered the ark; they and every living thing after its kind, all animals after their kind, every creeping thing that moves on the earth after its kind, and every flying creature after its kind, every bird of every wing. And they went into the ark to Noah, two by two, of all flesh in which is the breath of life. So those that entered, male and female of all flesh, went in as God had commanded him. And Jehovah shut him in. And the flood was on the earth forty days. The waters increased and lifted up the ark, and it was high above the earth. The waters prevailed and greatly increased upon the earth, and the ark moved about upon the surface of the waters. And the waters prevailed with abundant force upon the earth, and all the high hills under the heavens were covered. The waters prevailed fifteen cubits upward, and the mountains were covered. And all flesh died that moved on the earth: flying creatures and animals and living things and every creeping thing that moves on the earth, and every man. All in whose nostrils was the breath of the spirit of life, all that was on the dry land, died. So He obliterated all living substance which was on the face of the ground: both man and animal, creeping thing and flying creatures of the heavens. They were obliterated from off the earth. Only Noah and those who were with him in the ark were left alive. And the waters prevailed upon the earth one hundred and fifty days." Genesis 6-7

Normally we would not start off with quoting two full chapters from the Bible. Most people have heard of the Flood, Noah's Ark and God's judgment regarding mankind, but there are many who will never once read the actually account. The silly toys that are sold that have a little ark with big animals on top for children to play with do not accurately portray what actually took place.

The problem with mankind during those days was sin, a lot of it. In fact so much that only Noah found favor in God's eyes and God saved him and his family from the Flood that destroyed mankind. Just how many people were on the earth prior to the Flood? That answer is not recorded for us, therefore it is only a guess. I've seen estimates from hundreds of millions to billions, some even suggesting more people prior to the Flood than our current population of the world. Either way would it matter?

Over 4,000 years ago the Flood occurred and now our world is once again built up. Most consider themselves to be far more advanced than the 'cave men' of old, but it should not be put outside the realm of possibility that portions of the world prior to the Flood had advanced technology, perhaps even technology that is suppressed today, but was possibly not suppressed back then. Either way you look at it, the question is where are those ancestors of old? They didn't make it.

There is a war that has been going on for years between the religion of evolution and God's Truth. In all of that there is a great deal of misinformation purposely put forth from those who claim to be scientist, many cover-ups of finds that provide evidence of the Holy Scriptures account of our history, as well as those who flat out refuse to accept that they were Created, no matter the overwhelming evidence in front of them. With some diligent research and the onset of the digital age, one can quickly see evidence that is contrary to the lies pushed by mainstream science.

Did you know that there are tons of human fossils found, many mixed right in the fossil beds of dinosaurs? Human fossils are found in rocks that would be impossible, due to the age listed for evolution. These hard rocks are supposedly much older than the evolved humans. So what happens to these records? In times past there were hidden deep within warehouses of the Smithsonian. There they were either never to be heard of again or they would be relabeled as not having been human fossils, but rather that of a mammoth or another animal. There is even a rumor that a barge full of giant bones that did not have a place, as no answer could be given, except a biblical one, to their origins, were put in a barge and dumped into the ocean. These policies continue, not just with human fossilized remains, but with anything that is out of place and found. Sometimes the 'cat gets out of the bag' and it is too late for the find to be catalogued and never talked about again, lest it ends up like the hoofs of fossilized animals found near and on display in a small town museum like the one in Choteau, Montana.

No one will talk about the camels, horses, rhinoceros, elephants and zebra fossils found throughout the United States and the world. Bits of information, like a local news article from Montana were a man found a fossilized camel in an irrigation channel, will surface because of it simply being news, but you won't see this being promoted from the scientist directly, too much effort is needed to answer these oddities that don't fit in. So when I stumbled across this news article from Taiwan, I knew if it weren't for the media, this is one of those things that are never to see the light of day. So when fossils like this are found, they are dated quite closely to the time of the Flood, but labeled to be a 'stone age' death.

Please do tell, who is telling the truth? God and His Word that is provided to mankind or the accepted scientific interpretation that is ever changing to explain away finds like this that they wish had just been hauled away and put in a warehouse before being made public? Researching this I found that scientist have stated that there was strong evidence of a flood in China and blame it on the Yellow river. Using this article as just one of many examples, I pondered many things regarding it.

A woman is clutching her baby, sudden death comes upon them and both of them are fossilized. To be fossilized while still holding the baby seems even the more amazing, something had to happen instantly.

At Egg Mountain in Montana where the there have been found fossilized nests, complete with eggs, the sign states that scientists believe it to be either a volcano or a hurricane. Well if it was a volcano you would know for CERTAIN as there would be a layer of volcanic ash mixed in with the fossils and above them. A hurricane? Chasing and watching storms is a favorite past time, I could only imagine the awesomeness of being able to view a hurricane that powerful! A hurricane that could not only kill everything in its path, destroying as the winds prevailed, the rains poured, the tornados turned and maybe even giant hail stones falling with lightning fireballs flying through the sky! Such a hurricane that powerful that not only killed all life, but provided the conditions to instantly create a fossil records, yet gentle enough to leave all of the eggs lying in a nest, sitting above ground fossilized for someone to find eons later. What an event that must have been, the best place to view that would have been with rain gear, sitting right next to the dinosaur nest! The same is true with this fossilized woman and baby.

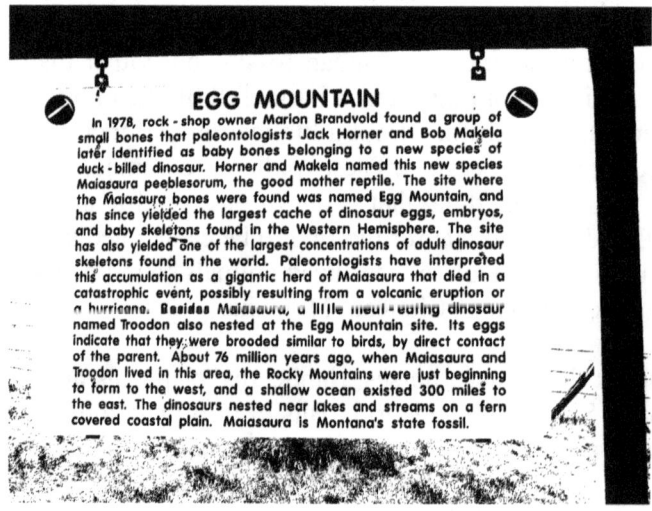

Of course scientists are going to give us a reason of the woman and child's death, an earthquake, they think. Can we go back the past 1,000 years of all historical recorded powerful earthquakes and start finding the fossils from then? You will NEVER see one example of a historically recorded earthquake, no matter how powerful, were scientists are digging up fossils, complete with tools, writings and other things from a civilization that has recorded history…NEVER. Mummies are found in pyramid tombs, bones of men are found from ancient societies, but human fossils from recorded history are not found EVER! With that said, neither are fossilized nests.

I imagine that the woman watched in horror as the Flood waters began to come up quickly. People scurrying around, nowhere to go, seeing death right in front of them. Clutching her baby she would have been overcome by the waters with force and turned into the earth due to the violence of the waters, becoming entombed instantly and providing a fossilized record thousands of year later. With the exception of Noah and his family, his wife, three sons and their wives, everyone was killed by the Flood, no exceptions.

"For Christ also suffered for sins once for all, the just for the unjust, that He might bring us to God, being put to death in the flesh but made alive by the Spirit, by whom also He went and preached to the spirits in prison, who formerly were disobedient, when once the Divine longsuffering waited in the days of Noah, while the ark was being prepared, in which a few, that is, eight souls, were saved through water." 1st Peter 3:18-20

What about our future as a society? Has God spoken about what will come eventually?

"But as the days of Noah were, so also will the coming of the Son of Man be. For as in the days before the flood, they were eating and drinking, marrying and giving in marriage, until the day that Noah entered into the ark, and did not realize until the flood came and took them all away, so also will the coming of the Son of Man be." Matthew 24:37-39

"But evil men and pretenders will grow worse and worse, leading astray and being led astray." 2nd Timothy 3:13

"And this gospel of the kingdom will be preached in all the world as a testimony to all the nations, and then the end will come." Matthew 24:14

"Therefore God also gives them up to uncleanness, in the lusts of their hearts, to dishonor their bodies among themselves, who change the truth of God into the lie, and fear and serve the created things more than the Creator, who is blessed forever. Amen." Romans 1:24-25

Understand that there were people who died prior to the Flood from natural causes. Then there was the Flood that wiped out everyone at once, except Noah and his family. For those who are Believers that are still alive at the appearing of Christ, they can rest assured knowing that our Savior will take us out of here prior to God's judgment.

Do you think any of those who saw the Flood waters rising pondered their sin and regretted it?

"For this let everyone who is godly pray unto You, in a time when You may be found; surely in the floods of great waters they shall not come near him." Psalms 32:6

Jesus Christ has provided Salvation for all of those who desire it. Those who realize and forsake their sin, who change their minds, repent, and through faith accept Jesus Christ as their Lord and Savior have a sure 'ark' against the troubled times that will eventually happen. Just as Lot was saved, so too those who are in Christ will eventually be at Home with the Lord. Do not be found guilty when standing before God, but ensure that you become rectified with your Creator, through Jesus Christ, having ensured that your name is written in His Book.

"For by grace you are saved through faith; and that not of yourselves, it is the gift of God; not of works, that no one should boast." Ephesians 2:8-9

"Now when they heard this, they were pierced to the heart, and said to Peter and the rest of the apostles, Men and brethren, what shall we do? Then Peter said to them, Repent, and let every one of you be immersed in the name of Jesus Christ to the remission of sins; and you shall receive the gift of the Holy Spirit." Acts 2:37-38

"Now it was not written for his sake alone, that it was accounted to him, but also for us, to whom it shall be accounted, believing in Him who raised up Jesus our Lord from the dead, who was delivered up because of our trespasses, and was raised for our justification." Romans 4:23-25

"I tell you, no; but unless you repent you will all likewise perish." Luke 13:5

"For God so loved the world that He gave His only begotten Son, that everyone believing into Him should not perish but have eternal life. For God did not send His Son into the world to judge the world, but that the world through Him might be saved. The one believing into Him is not judged; but the one not believing is judged already, because he has not believed in the name of the only begotten Son of God. And this is the judgment, that the Light has come into the world, and men loved darkness rather than the Light, for their deeds were evil. For everyone practicing evil hates the Light and does not come to the Light, lest his deeds should be reproved. But the one doing the truth comes to the Light, that his deeds may be clearly seen, that they have been worked in God." John 3:16-21

Amen!

Freedom

Recently I was reminded of the struggles of people during the Soviet Union. The oppression of those who wished to actually serve God according to the Holy Scriptures and preach what the Holy Spirit had led them to preach was quite staggering. In the Soviet Union each sermon had to be approved by the state, any swaying from that could lead to immediate trouble.

The Soviet Union was not alone in this regard, even with the fall of the Soviet Union, now Vladimir Putin has reinstated laws that require a Christian to be licensed in order to hand out religious literature or witness to another person. Everything must be within the organized religions setup within Russia. However, China is much more repressive than Russia is, with a strong underground Church movement.

"We ought to obey God rather than men." Acts 5:29b

In any country where there is oppression against Believers, understand that many people are carted off to prisons, camps or put into mental institutions, some will die, others will be maimed or permanently damaged. Those who are arrested for such offenses know that it is worthy to be in trouble for the cause of following the Lord. They realize that suffering persecution is part of being a Believer.

"If the world hates you, you know that it has hated Me before you. If you were of the world, the world would love its own. Yet because you are not of the world, but I chose you out of the world, therefore the world hates you. Remember the Word that I said to you, A servant is not greater than his master. If they persecuted Me, they will also persecute you. If they kept My Word, they will keep yours also." John 15:18-20

"But before all these things, they will lay their hands on you and persecute you, delivering you up to the synagogues and prisons. You will be brought before kings and rulers on account of My name." Luke 21:12

"And what more shall I say? For the time would fail me to tell of Gideon and Barak and Samson and Jephthah, also of David and Samuel and the prophets: who through faith subdued kingdoms, worked righteousness, obtained promises, stopped the mouths of lions, quenched the power of fire, escaped the edge of the sword, out of weakness were made strong, became mighty in battle, turned to flight the armies of foreigners. Women received their dead raised to life again. And others were tortured, not accepting deliverance, that they might obtain a better resurrection. Still others had trial of mockings and floggings, yes, and of bonds and imprisonment. They were stoned, they were sawn in two, were tried, were slain with the sword. They wandered about in

sheepskins and goatskins, being destitute, afflicted, oppressed; of whom the world was not worthy. They wandered in deserts and mountains, in dens and caves of the earth. And all these, having borne witness through faith, did not obtain the promise, God having provided something better for us, that they should not be made complete apart from us." Hebrews 11:32-40

These things are nothing new. Men and women who look toward their Lord and Savior Jesus Christ, witnessing to others, telling others about Jesus. Pastors who hold underground Churches so they can freely speak that which they have been led to preach. Those who smuggle Bibles and tracts, trying to get the Gospel to the lost, so they too might be Saved. Believers who put their life on the line to serve Him who Saved them.

"For he who has died has been justified from sin. Now if we died with Christ, we believe that we shall also live with Him, knowing that Christ, having been raised from the dead, dies no more. Death no longer has dominion over Him. For the death that He died, He died to sin once for all; but the life that He lives, He lives unto God. Likewise you also, reckon yourselves to be dead indeed to sin, but alive to God in Christ Jesus our Lord." Romans 6:7-11

"Therefore, if anyone is in Christ, he is a new creation; the old things have passed away; behold, all things have become new." 2nd Corinthians 5:17

Around the country many churches would become stirred up emotionally watching a movie, hearing from a missionary or a history lesson from a traveling evangelist regarding those who have been or are a martyr for the sake of the Gospel. For most though these stories are something that others do, while they will agree that they are noteworthy, there is no necessity seen in the United States.

Here in the land of the free and home of the brave, each Christian has the opportunity to freely speak about the Gospel with very little threat of oppression or persecution, aside from the name calling. Imagine those who are suffering in a Chinese prison for the Gospel, if they realized that Americans could go door to door or freely talk to their neighbor about Jesus, but they won't. In America we have the freedom to spread the Gospel or simply to just be a witness through our conversation, unfortunately this rarely happens.

How long before our window of opportunity is closed in this country too? Do you not think that would ever happen? Well the days are coming and perhaps those of us who are actually Believers will be taken Home prior, but you can see the writing on the wall, eventually it will not be safe to preach the Gospel in America either. When that time comes perhaps instead of sorrow there will actually be rejoicing.

How you say? Looking at the history of those who have suffered for the sake of the Gospel, generally freedom and prosperity equates to what you see in our society and oppression and persecution yields the fruits of the Believers in a country where there is an iron grid against such things. In persecuted countries sinners get Saved, in free countries often times the focus is on the world.

"Set your mind on things above, not on the things of the earth; for you died, and your life is hidden with Christ in God." Colossians 3:2-3

For those of you who are Believers, are you doing as the Lord leads? Are you living a life that is a testimony to those who are lost and on their way to Hell? Do your neighbors know you are a Christian, how about your coworkers or even your family? Have you ever shared the Gospel with anyone? If you are ashamed to tell others about your Salvation, imagine those who do it under the threat of being secretly whisked away in the middle of the night. For you, someone might say something mean or they might not like you, for others it might be their life.

"You are the light of the world. A city that is set on a hill cannot be hidden. Nor do they light a lamp and put it under a grain measure, but on a lampstand, and it shines for all who are in the house. Let your light so shine before men, so that they may see your good works and glorify your Father in Heaven." Matthew 5:14-16

"Therefore whoever shall confess Me before men, I will also confess him before My Father in Heaven. But whoever denies Me before men, I will also deny him before My Father in Heaven. Do not think that I came to bring peace on earth. I did not come to bring peace but a sword. For I have come to set a man against his father, a daughter against her mother, and a daughter-in-law against her mother-in-law; and a man's enemies will be those of his own household. He who loves father or mother more than Me is not worthy of Me. And he who loves son or daughter more than Me is not worthy of Me. And he who does not take his cross and follow after Me is not worthy of Me. He who finds his life will lose it, and he who loses his life on account of Me will find it. He who receives you receives Me, and he who receives Me receives Him who sent Me." Matthew 10:32-40

Amen!

What Will You Do?

The nation awoke last week to a devastating hurricane that literally ended up zeroing in on Houston with huge amounts of rainfalls. I downloaded a rain map that showed Houston as ground zero for the rain. Then, the now tropical storm, backed up into the Gulf of Mexico and landed in southeast Texas, dropping 25 more inches of rain in a day, totally flooding cities.

When that happened there were a bunch of headlines on the news, but the one that really caught my eye was how the rain was called punishing and there was a quote from a resident begging God to have it stop raining. The event was terrible and now people are more cautiously eyeing the other storms that are heading towards the United States. The amount of rain that was dropped in Houston set a record for rainfall in the contiguous United States, never had that much been recorded out of one event…never.

Who is to blame? Is it simply chance, after all Houston had those reservoirs for a reason, they had been flooded before, in fact a different storm years ago had dropped just a couple of inches less rain. Was it God's judgment? Some speculate so. What about utilizing HAARP or other technology to weaponize the storm, to cause President Trump a crisis? There are those who are pushing this theory also. Around the same time 1,200 people died in a flood in Asia, but we as Americans simply brush that off.

"You have heard that it was said, You shall love your neighbor and hate your enemy. But I say to you, Love your enemies, bless those who curse you, do good to those who hate you, and pray for those who abuse you and persecute you, that you may become sons of your Father in Heaven; for He makes His sun rise on the evil and on the good, and sends rain on the just and on the unjust." Matthew 5:43-45

Did people forget about the great earthquake in San Francisco? How about the Chicago fire? What about the 200,000 people who died in a Tsunami? What about the large amounts of death and destruction from the Japanese tsunami? Things do happen, but a country that has swayed so far away from their Creator would be wise to question their actions against the Almighty.

If a country diligently sought after God, a country that put God first and upheld His holy standards were to have a natural disaster, would they then question if it was God's judgment? I don't have the answer for why it happened, but in all reality it could have been much worse, the death toll could have been higher. A lot of material items are destroyed, but our minds should not be set on these things. Those things can be replaced, but a soul who is cast into the Lake of Fire is an undoable ordeal.

"And you shall seek Me and find Me, when you search for Me with all your heart." Jeremiah 29:13

"Yea, before the day was, I am He; and no one can deliver out of My hand; I work, and who will reverse it?" Isaiah 43:15

"But seek first the kingdom of God and His righteousness, and all these things shall be added to you." Matthew 6:33

"But the cowardly, unbelieving, abominable, murderers, prostitutes, sorcerers, idolaters, and all liars shall have their part in the lake which burns with fire and brimstone, which is the second death." Revelation 21:8

This country continues on a trajectory that is contrary to the Most High. We continue on, as a people, promoting sexual deviance, perversities, as well as a culture whose ideologies are contrary to their Creator. There is no repentance, there is no awakening to their error, in fact there is only an invite for those who are on the outside to come and join them in their wickedness. Do you not think that God takes notice?

"Jehovah, how long will the wicked, how long will the wicked triumph? They belch forth, and speak arrogant things; all the workers of iniquity boast in themselves. They crush Your people, O Jehovah, and afflict Your heritage. They slay the widow and the sojourner, and murder the fatherless. Yet they say, YAH does not see, nor does the God of Jacob perceive it. Understand, you stupid ones among the people; and you fools, when will you be wise? He who planted the ear, shall He not hear? He who formed the eye, shall He not see? He who chastens the nations, shall He not correct, He who teaches man knowledge? Jehovah knows the thoughts of man, that they are vanity. Blessed is the man whom You correct, O YAH, and teach out of Your Law, that You may give him rest from the evil days, until the pit is dug for the wicked." Psalms 94:3-13

Who ponders the fact that at least 45,000,000 residents in the United States live in poor air quality due to mold issues in their homes? The number of people who work in such environments is equally as staggering. Who ponders that our wealth as a nation is gone and people continue on pretending it is still there, by utilizing credit to continue the 'dream'? Who ponders that the rapidly growing income inequality creates slave-like conditions for the majority of regular workers? Who ponders that America has the sickest population out of all industrialized nations? Who ponders that America has the highest rates of cancer?

Why do our people allow the bureaucracy to continue to poison our food system with chemicals and processes banned throughout Europe? Why do people no longer have natural affection, but relationships via social media or texting? Why is there so much violence that every city in America knows it? Why has our government created a prison grid around us, seemingly preparing to come after Americans who hadn't joined the masses of distracted individuals? Why do we have so many people with mental illnesses, without acknowledging demon possessed individuals all around us? Why are a good percentage of the youth so wicked?

What will you do when you are Left Behind, the Rapture having occurred and God's judgment is truly poured out on the inhabitants of the earth? Do you not realize that in harsher conditions, accepting how horrific our situation as a whole society is, and repenting, would be a wondrous thing? Sometimes in what seems like horrible conditions, like what will happen during the *"time of Jacob's trouble (Jer. 30:7)"* will actually be merciful as many will come to know the Lord during that time period.

I recall reading a book where people were imprisoned, forced on medications, all for smuggling bibles into the Soviet Union. Finally a large group of them escaped to another European country, only to see the results of that escape. Where they had no freedom, were heavily repressed, yet they had focused on Christ, had a strong Church that met in the woods and people prepared to lay down their lives for Him; yet in this new country their children were being lost to vanities. While they now had the freedom to worship as they pleased, in the open, the children became swallowed up by sin and the pleasures of this world, rather than the riches in Christ.

"And my God shall supply all your need according to His riches in glory in Christ Jesus." Philippians 4:19

The time is coming when it will be too late, will you wait until then? Most people like to deny the Gospel and a large percent of them who claim they don't, purposely do not put the biblical doctrine of Salvation into their messages. Just the other day, while watching television, I saw a man on a stage trick a large amount of people, leading them through what is known as the 'sinner's prayer', while a band played soothing music to stir up the emotions. Then he had them lift their hands up, saying they are now God's people. Salvation is simple, it is not complex, but what stands in the way for most people?

For most people, their hearts are what make it complex, they refuse to surrender, they refuse to repent and change from their wicked ways, while believing into Jesus Christ, who died on the Cross and rose again. They want Salvation, but they don't want to change to get it.

"The heart is deceitful above all things, and desperately wicked; who can know it? I Jehovah search the heart, I examine the soul, even to give to each man according to his ways, according to the fruit of his doings." Jeremiah 17:9-10

You can't wait for the masses of people to repent, each INDIVIDUAL stands before God Almighty, that includes you. You will be responsible for yourself and if your name is not written in the Book of Life, then you can know your future, your end is eternity in the Lake of Fire.

"So then each of us shall give account concerning himself to God." Romans 14:12

"And anyone not found written in the Book of Life was cast into the Lake of Fire." Revelation 20:15

Yet God does not desire this, what He desires is that people repent and seek Him. After all, why else did He send His Son to die on the Cross for our sins?

"Do I delight with pleasure in the death of the wicked? says the Lord Jehovah, and not that he should turn back from his ways and live?" Ezekiel 18:23

Amen!

Atrocities

This is being written as hurricane Irma is churning out in the Atlantic, with hurricane Harvey in people's minds, the perceived threat as to what will occur is yet unknown. Historically hurricanes on that path often hit Florida OR turn and go to the North Atlantic, hitting no one. Yet as this is also being written, smoke continues to fill the skies in Kalispell, Montana on a daily basis.

The Los Angeles area has the La Tuna wildfire, which is the biggest ever recorded in the area. With Montana's 'flash drought' we continue to get very little rain and still unseasonable warm weather. Just a little spark and another wildfire will appear somewhere, this with thunderstorms forecast in a few days. As the flood waters from Houston are drying up, people are starting to speculate that this is either God's judgment or considering that somehow this is pointing to a major end times event. Of course these who ponder the later, are in every case I see, those who also purport that there will be no Rapture or it will be at the end of the Tribulation *("time of Jacob's trouble" Jer. 30:7)*.

Well I can't speak on behalf of God and neither can they, unless God has truly given them some insight. Sure these are interesting times that we live in, but these are times where instead of people looking and presuming that God is going to come in and 'fix' all of man's woes, they should be looking at fixing their hearts before our Creator, before it is too late. As I watch these things unfold, and ponder the outcome regarding North Korea, I must admit it is not welcoming to see all of these things, yet I know that if it is God's judgment, it is just. America can't seem to get enough evil in, committing atrocity after atrocity.

There are some that claim that the KGB developed a plan that went into full motion, still continuing to this day, to destroy America through subversion, slowly over time. The very first step of this was to create an increase in demoralization, which was expected to take nearly a generation. Indeed the amount of younger adults who deny that God even exits is nearly 50/50, verses the older generations where it is often close to 90% who do believe in Him. Yet belief in God is not enough, one must repent and believe into Jesus Christ as their Lord and Savior.

"You believe that God is One. You do well. Even the demons believe, and shudder." Jacob (James) 2:19

Certainly we have elected officials who seem bent on putting Marxism as a way of our society and by all means they do appear to have accomplished much in that regard. The recent explosion of Antifa, shows how a 'tolerant' so-called group can actually become a backbone of a movement that during tough times would be equal to the Bolsheviks of

Russia or the brown shirts of Nazi Germany. Given the right circumstances, chaos could easily ensue and our country could be swallowed up, the lock down finished, the prison grid fully in place and those who refuse to bow to such an evil regime, hunted down and placed in concentration camps and prisons.

Shall I list off the most recent atrocities from my local area, Montana or even the United States? Indeed not! Rather let me point out that a nation or a world that forgets just who God is, what He requires and that simply sinners need to repent, is a nation or a world that is in big trouble. The Holy Scriptures clearly lays out that a time will come when God will judge the nations and certainly it should be obvious as to why.

"And He shall judge among the nations and shall rebuke many people. And they shall beat their swords into plowshares, and their spears into pruning hooks. Nation shall not lift up sword against nation, nor shall they learn war anymore." Isaiah 2:4

"All the kings of the nations, even all of them, lie in glory, every one in his own house. But you are cast out of your grave like an abhorred branch, and like the apparel of those who are slain, thrust through with a sword, that go down to the stones of the pit; like a carcass trampled under foot. You shall not be joined with them in burial, because you destroyed your land and killed your people; the seed of evildoers shall never be renowned. Prepare slaughter for his children because of the iniquity of their fathers, so that they may not rise nor possess the land, nor fill the face of the world with cities. For I will rise up against them, says Jehovah of Hosts, and cut off from Babylon the name and remnant, and offspring, and posterity, says Jehovah. I will also make it a possession for the hedgehog, and marshes of muddy water; and I will sweep it with the broom of destruction, says Jehovah of Hosts. Jehovah of Hosts has sworn, saying, Surely as I have thought, so it shall come to pass; and as I have purposed, so it shall stand; to break Assyria in My land, and on My mountains to trample him under foot. Then his yoke shall be removed from them, and his burden shall be taken from off their shoulders. This is the purpose that is purposed upon all the earth; and this is the hand that is stretched out upon all the nations. For Jehovah of Hosts has purposed, and who shall annul it? And His hand is stretched out, and who shall turn it back?" Isaiah 14:18-27

"All the nations before Him are as nothing; and to Him they are accounted as less than nothing, and vanity. To whom then will you compare the Mighty God? Or what likeness will you compare to Him?" Isaiah 40:17-18

To those who can hear, to those who can see, to those who can understand, please consider for a moment that the nations of the world are not going to repent, that eventually what has been prophesied in the Bible is certain, as certain as the sun coming up tomorrow, it's going to happen. So that is why we always try to persuade the individual to come to God, to repent and accept His free gift, Salvation through Jesus Christ.

Jesus Christ paid the penalty on the Cross for your sins. He died and rose again from the dead, all you have to do is simply repent and believe into Him.

"Therefore, just as through one man sin entered the world, and death through sin, and thus death spread to every person, because everyone sinned." Romans 5:12

"For the wages of sin is death, but the gift of God is eternal life in Christ Jesus our Lord." Romans 6:23

"Now it was not written for his sake alone, that it was accounted to him, but also for us, to whom it shall be accounted, believing in Him who raised up Jesus our Lord from the dead, who was delivered up because of our trespasses, and was raised for our justification." Romans 4:23-25

"For godly sorrow produces repentance leading to salvation, not to be regretted; but the sorrow of the world produces death." 2nd Corinthians 7:10

"Therefore, if anyone is in Christ, he is a new creation; the old things have passed away; behold, all things have become new." 2nd Corinthians 5:17

"For God so loved the world that He gave His only begotten Son, that everyone believing into Him should not perish but have eternal life. For God did not send His Son into the world to judge the world, but that the world through Him might be saved." John 3:16-17

"But what does it say? The Word is near you, in your mouth and in your heart (that is, the Word of Faith which we preach): that if you confess with your mouth the Lord Jesus and believe in your heart that God has raised Him from the dead, you will be saved." Romans 10:8-9

"But as many as received Him, to them He gave the authority to become children of God, to those believing into His name: who were born, not of blood, nor of the will of the flesh, nor of the will of man, but of God." John 1:12-13

"For the love of Christ holds us, because we judge thus: that if One died for all, then all died; and He died for all, that those who live should no longer live unto themselves, but unto Him who died for them and rose again." 2nd Corinthians 5:14-15

"He is not here; for He is risen, as He said. Come, see the place where the Lord was lying." Matthew 28:6

"Jesus said to him, I am the Way, the Truth, and the Life. No one comes to the Father except through Me." John 14:6

Do you ponder what is going on in the world? Do you wonder if we are living in the end times? Do you wait to see what is going to happen? Please understand that most of those who write these things WILL NOT tell you the full Gospel message. Most of those will tell you there is not a pretribulation Rapture, a flat out lie. Those who are waiting for Jesus Christ to come and gather us to Himself, are watching and ready, waiting to hear the Trumpet and be Home with the Lord forever. Will you join us before it is too late? Will you change your ways or will you be part of the deserving judgment of the nation you live in, just one more reason for God to invoke just justice.

Time is running out, I urge you to consider.

"But of that day and hour no one knows, not even the angels of Heaven, but My Father only." Matthew 24:36

"Watch therefore, for you do not know what hour your Lord comes." Matthew 24:42

Amen!

Is it Finally the End?

Numerous news reports about the devastating fires in California had quotes from first hand accounts of people involved who thought that perhaps the end had come or that Armageddon was ongoing. There were people who took photos that made their rounds across the globe in the media regarding how California's Disneyland looked liked a scene from Hell.

There were those who were thinking and saying the same thing when Harvey hit Texas, when Irma hit tropical islands, etc. They thought perhaps the end was upon them, as devastation appeared on all sides around them, as far as they could see. In one case there were people begging for God to make the rain stop from Harvey, as the nonstop rain became the biggest rain event in the continental United States recorded history.

All of these terrible disasters the United States has been experiencing are just a drop in the bucket of similar events that have been taking place around the world. Unfortunately many in America hold an attitude of such self worth that they care little about floods in Asia or terrifying events in India. A point-in-case would be an attitude regarding a potential North Korean & United States war, where the talking point of many is sacrificing Seoul in South Korea is better than it coming to our homeland. In other words, millions dying 'over there' is a small price to pay.

Our country is being destroyed slowly by disasters that are costing tens of billions of dollars in damage EACH. While we have the advantage of holding the world reserve currency that is backed off of nations having had to (largely still doing so) purchase oil in Federal Reserve notes, eventually the time will come where the debt will be too obvious to the world. The United States will be bankrupt, as it technically already is. Just how much more money will we continue to put into our national debt in order to offset these disasters?

How about the insurance companies, how many people are going to see an increase in their premiums, simply because these insurance companies can not have these sort of losses over and over again, they were not designed for that many dollars of catastrophic events? The following graph illustrates the complexity of these issues, regarding just one type of emergency event.

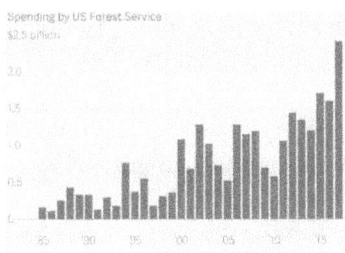

Nearly every year since my family moved out to Kalispell, Montana, we have had a smoky August. This year was particularly bad, as the smoke hit very toxic levels in Flathead Valley. In fact there was an area south of us in Seeley Lake, Montana, where the toxic air levels exceeded the ability of the air quality gauges, promoting some to suggest that a new level of threat, beyond hazardous needed to be thought of. How about catastrophic?

The orange groves in Florida, where much of our orange juice comes from, has its lowest yield since World War 2. Now much of the nations well-known wine groves are under serious threat, as several people have been killed and scores more are missing in the devastating northern California wildfires. As of this writing there were 3,500 homes and businesses lost in that area of California with a threat of winds to cause even more damage. Truly as one news reporter put it, the firescape simply looked as if entire neighborhoods in the Santa Rosa area had been bombed out. Historically when a city was bombed, like as the world saw throughout Europe in World War 2, there were at least the remnants of standing structures, rather than totally burned to the ground neighborhoods, the prospect of finding some items of value leftover were much greater.

FEMA is nearly fully activated with 95% of their employees on the ground at disaster sites right now. The California wildfires might just be what requires them to go above their perceived need to get more boots on the ground to help out. What if we have yet another disaster in the upcoming weeks or months in the United States? Just how much more can we handle?

Unfortunately there are always those who lurk in the shadows, who in but a moment are ready to take advantage of such disasters and purport evil upon a community. Such was the case with hurricane Harvey and Irma, such is the case with the wildfires in California. Scarcely have people evacuated from their homes, running for their lives that the criminals start breaking into homes and looting as much as they can. Yet most Americans are willing to open up their wallets, lend a hand and help each other out, despite the constant media badgering about racial divide in the United States. Truly one American helping another, irregardless of race, is often the images that those who would rather promote a divide and conquer worldview prefer not to play on our televisions.

Certainly disasters happen in this country and around the world from time to time. This has always been the case and until the end of the age, this will be the case. However it is certain that America has seen an increase in disasters over the past couple of decades and this year we have been hit particularly hard. Some of these disasters have been harsher than others that we have seen in a long time, thus prompting people to ponder whether or not the end has come or Armageddon is upon us.

Surely those who know the Holy Scriptures, understand that what America is experiencing would not even be measurable in comparison to what God has foretold will happen during the *"time of Jacob's trouble" (Jer. 30:7)* or what is coming known as the Great Tribulation or Tribulation amongst many people. So to liken these current events to such scenarios is modest to say in comparison to what events are prophesied to unfold during that time. Truly comparing Houston or Santa Rosa, even Barbuda, to Armageddon shows a large lack of knowledge amongst the inhabitants of this once great land regarding biblical truth. Even more so, comparing a smoky sky with an ominous backdrop outside California's Disneyland to Hell is even more folly. There is a large lack of knowledge amongst people regarding what the Word of God teaches in all regards.

"My people are destroyed for lack of knowledge." Hosea 4:6a

So what of those who think such things? What about America as a whole reflecting upon these disasters that are played endlessly by the big media outlets? Do we look at our hearts towards our Creator and consider our way? Rather do we band together to 'do good' to help out those who have need after such a disaster, but refuse to contemplate whether our sinful actions as a society need to be corrected?

Indeed! What we are seeing is but a drop in the bucket of what will take place upon the inhabitants of the Earth. Those who truly know the Lord, whom have repented and believed into Jesus Christ as their Savior, accepted the free gift of Salvation will be Raptured out of this world to be with Jesus prior to the Tribulation beginning, despite the naysayers. For those who are 'left behind' they truly don't understand the Bible, they truly don't understand the seriousness of the situation as a comparison of such events as we have currently seen would offer absolutely no comparison to what will take place. The bodies of the wicked will lie upon the ground all over the planet, with no one to bury them during that time. A situation will unfold that is truly catastrophic and one that should gather the attention of all the inhabitants of the Earth.

"A roaring noise shall come to the ends of the earth; for Jehovah has a controversy with the nations; He will enter into judgment with all flesh. He will give those who are wicked to the sword, says Jehovah. Thus says Jehovah of Hosts, Behold, evil shall go forth from nation to nation, and a great tempest shall be roused up from the recesses of the earth. And in that day the slain of Jehovah shall be from one end of the earth even to the other end of the earth. They shall not be mourned, nor gathered, nor buried. They shall be as dung on the ground." Jeremiah 25:31-33

Yet even in that time the vast majority of people will refuse to repent of their wickedness before their Creator.

"And they did not repent of their murders nor their sorceries nor their sexual perversions nor their thefts." Revelation 9:21

The ignorance of humanity's understanding of God's Word isn't going to go away anytime soon. For those same people who refuse to acknowledge their Creator and repent of their sins, accepting the free gift of Salvation through His Son Jesus Christ, will continue to do so. How is it that the inhabitants of the world marvel that the Two Witnesses rise again after three and a half days? Clearly God's Word teaches that this event will take place, yet the world will marvel.

"And after three and a half days the spirit of life from God entered into them, and they stood on their feet, and great terror fell on those who saw them." Revelation 11:11

There will be those who do repent and become martyrs for Jesus Christ during that time.

"Then one of the elders answered, saying to me, Who are these arrayed in white robes, and where did they come from? And I said to him, Sir, you know. So he said to me, These are the ones coming out of great affliction, and have washed their robes and made them white in the blood of the Lamb." Revelation 7:13-14

So while the world as a whole will not repent, those individuals who do will have secured their eternity in Heaven, a far cry from those who will inevitably end up in the Lake of Fire, of which there is no comparison to a smoky Disneyland sky. Even now, those who hear, those who are willing to understand, as this is written the Rapture has yet to occur and God's mercy is still extended to those who are willing to seek Him. Will you seek the Lord before it is too late?

"Seek Jehovah while He may be found; call upon Him while He is near. Let the wicked forsake his way, and the unrighteous man his thoughts; and let him return to Jehovah, and He will have mercy on him; and to our God, for He will abundantly pardon. For My thoughts are not your thoughts, nor are your ways My ways, says Jehovah. For as the heavens are higher than the earth, so are My ways higher than your ways, and My thoughts than your thoughts." Isaiah 55:6-9

"The harvest is past, the summer is ended, and we are not saved." Jeremiah 8:20

Do not be of the later crowd! For all will stand before God Almighty!

"So then each of us shall give account concerning himself to God." Romans 14:12

"And the devil, who led them astray, was cast into the Lake of Fire and brimstone where the beast and the false prophet are. And they will be tormented day and night forever and ever. And I saw a great white throne and Him who sat on it, from whose face the earth and the heavens fled away. And there was found no place for them. And I saw the dead, small and great, standing before God. And books were opened. And another book was opened, which is the Book of Life. And the dead were judged according to their works,

out of the things which were written in the books. And the sea gave up the dead who were in it, and Death and Hades delivered up the dead who were in them. And they were judged, each one, according to their works. And Death and Hades were cast into the Lake of Fire. This is the second death. And anyone not found written in the Book of Life was cast into the Lake of Fire." Revelation 20:10-15

Amen!

Willfully Ignorant

"This I say, therefore, and testify in the Lord, that you no longer walk as the rest of the Gentiles walk, in the emptiness of their mind, having their understanding darkened, being alienated from the life of God, because of the ignorance that is in them, because of the hardness of their heart; who, being past feeling, have given themselves over to licentiousness, to work all uncleanness with greediness." Ephesians 4:17-19

There are some who like to use the term 'entertained to death' and there is truth to such a notion. All around the world, not just in the United States, there are large problems that have formed. The cracks of our world governmental systems are starting to show their weaknesses, the ugly truth is starting to rear it's head. In America we have a society where information is at our fingertips.

Never before in the history of the world has the access to knowledge been so readily available to the average citizen. While there are still the things that go on in backrooms of corporations and our governments, that have yet to see the light of day, we can easily see the writing on the wall that not all is well. The assumption for most is that somehow our ails of our societies will fix these issues eventually. Yet, do we not consider that the only person who might offer the ultimate solution would be the Antichrist?

Hour after hour Americans sideswipe their responsibility as citizens to ensure the government is adhering to its constitutional boundaries. Day after day many around the world in civilized countries would rather watch television, do drugs or engage in sinful behavior, rather than clearly look into the whims of our society and the problems that are being hoisted upon them. As motion picture after motion picture is actively pursued, the real picture of what is going on in the world becomes less and less clear to those who are willfully ignorant, to which there is no excuse.

While on the surface this would seem to be a major problem as governments prepare for war, corporations decide to exert more control over society, pricing of stocks, home, autos, health insurance and the basic necessities continue to increase, essentially we become more and more ingrained in our enslavement to a system that seems determined to inevitably declare us to be wards of the state – to their bidding- by stripping us of our basic freedoms engrained by the founders of this country.

In our self centered society, those who do not care about these rights, certainly do not care about yours. These things are not done underneath the cover of darkness, but rather are done in the open, yet the mindfulness of them neither come to mind, nor are a concern with those who are unable to pull away from the entrapments of their mind. They are being steered, controlled, unaware, but yet willfully blissful of the 'pleasures' that are for but a moment, yet they don't see the ultimate problem, the ultimate deception.

Ignorance is not bliss, though for a moment it may appear to be that way. Someone may be ignorant about the error of getting too close to a downed power line, but should they survive the onset of voltage to their body, they will not make that mistake twice. While there are those public service messages that provide warnings about the dangers of down-powered lines, where are those who are providing the warnings regarding the consequences of men who do not repent and believe into Jesus Christ as their Lord and Savior. For them there is no second chance, only a second death.

"But the cowardly, unbelieving, abominable, murderers, prostitutes, sorcerers, idolaters, and all liars shall have their part in the lake which burns with fire and brimstone, which is the second death." Revelation 21:8

I ponder as I see Americans who simply sit in front of the television, watching rerun after rerun of shows which truly do have what would be considered an entertainment value, in terms of society's thoughts, yet have no value, nor place to those who are citizens of Heaven. The world could be collapsing around them, yet if there television is on, there is food in the home, then to many, what else matters. Truly ignorant of the frails of society and even more so ignorant to the reality of God. The same could be said true of those who use their phones all day long, engaging in meaningless 'likes' and back and forth simple text messages, as they visit social media sites, tweet and gather the latest gossip from their pagan idols who wholeheartedly are examples of the damned. Harsh words? I think not.

The harshest words are reserved for those who do these things, those whose hearts are not right before their Creator, who have not became a Christian, yet with their mouth they confess Jesus Christ, in word only. When they stand before their Creator and hear the words, *"depart from me" (Matt. 7:23)*, there mouths will be shut, their eternal destination sealed, their hopes dashed and their hearts dismayed. So where are those who would plead with their fellow mankind that they need to awake out of their slumber, they need to unfog their glasses and simply understand that despite being surrounded by endless forms of entertainment, trinkets and other pleasures of this world, there are those who are in the earth who would tell you *(Luke 16:27-31)*, if they could, not to make the same error as them, to turn, turn to a merciful God who is willing to forgive, to cast all aside, to not only follow Jesus Christ, but to run the race diligently, as if to win, for this life and all of the pleasures that are found in it are not worth denying the reconciliation that God provided by sending His Son to die on the Cross for your sins, if only you were willing to accept the free gift of Salvation!

"Truly, these times of ignorance God overlooked, but now commands all men everywhere to repent, because He has established a day on which He will judge the world in righteousness by the Man whom He has appointed. He has given assurance of this to everyone by raising Him from the dead." Acts 17:30-31

The suggestion is not that one becomes a scholar or understands all of the geopolitical maneuvers being foisted upon an unsuspecting world, but rather that people earnestly seek their Creator and realize the frailties of themselves. Truly, without Christ, all mankind is dying, dying in their sin. Only by realizing their condition and repenting, believing into Jesus Christ, can they be made whole. Get your head out of the muck and pay attention. Just how much time do you have?

"And I saw a great white throne and Him who sat on it, from whose face the earth and the heavens fled away. And there was found no place for them. And I saw the dead, small and great, standing before God. And books were opened. And another book was opened, which is the Book of Life. And the dead were judged according to their works, out of the things which were written in the books. And the sea gave up the dead who were in it, and Death and Hades delivered up the dead who were in them. And they were judged, each one, according to their works. And Death and Hades were cast into the Lake of Fire. This is the second death. And anyone not found written in the Book of Life was cast into the Lake of Fire." Revelation 20:11-15

Amen!

Christians – Get Up!

Recently I had an exchange with the person who does the translating work for the Spanish language section of All Will Stand. In that exchange they made mention of *"what more can I do"*, the same thing is on my heart regarding the work of the Lord. Many Believers around the world have the same feeling that the *"time is at hand"* *(Rev. 22:10)* and the world doesn't have much time left. Truly we can't know how much time we have left *(Matt. 24:36)*, but we also must not slacken our work that Jesus has called us to do as Christians *(Matt. 28:19-20)*.

A radio show regarding this topic will be up online soon, but the issue really is pressing. Just how often do we as *"citizens of Heaven"* *(Phil. 3:20)*, forget just how important the task is that is presented before us. Not everyone is called to preach, not everyone is called to be a pastor of a church or a Sunday school teacher, etc., but often times just by our communication, we can have an effect on those who are lost and dying.

"In this regard, they think it strange that you do not run with them in the same overflow of dissipation, blaspheming. They will give an account to Him who is ready to judge the living and the dead." 1st Peter 4:4-5

We know that the apostasy *(2 Tim. 4:3)* that we are seeing was foretold prophetically, we see the evil fruits of this terrible thing throughout the world. In fact it will not get better, but only worse *(2 Tim. 3:13)* until Jesus comes to take us out of here, to be with Him *(Jn. 14:3)*. Knowing that eventually that time will happen, we not only need to be watching and ready *(Matt. 25:13)*, but we should also be diligently doing His work. Remember that there is a lost world out there, whom are doomed to the Judgment of the Most High, unless they repent and believe the Gospel *(Rev. 20:11-15)*. Without Christ as their Savior *(Jn. 14:6)*, they are lost, just as we were before we accepted the free gift of Salvation that God provided to all of mankind *(Eph. 2:8-9)*. This is serious business, though many are beat down, the world seemingly provides an excuse to sit on the sidelines, as for many it is -too late- in their minds to try to spread the Gospel. True, it can be exceedingly discouraging to see so little fruit for our endeavors, we must never forget that there is rejoicing in Heaven over one sinner who repents *(Lk. 15:7)*. We as Christians don't save people, God does.

"Do you not know that those who run in a race all run, but one receives the prize? Run in such a way that you may obtain it. And everyone who competes for the prize controls himself in all things. Now they do it to obtain a perishable crown, but we an imperishable. Therefore I run in this manner: not with uncertainty. Thus I fight: not as one who beats the air. But I discipline my body and bring it into subjection, lest, when I have preached to others, I myself should become disqualified." 1st Corinthians 9:24-27

There should be no 'notches' on our belts, but we are the body of Christ *(1st Cor. 12:12)*, the Church, doing as servants to Jesus should be doing. As Paul says:

"Who then is Paul, and who is Apollos, but ministers through whom you believe, as the Lord gave to each one? I planted, Apollos watered, but God made it grow. So then neither he who plants is anything, nor he who waters, but God who causes growth. Now he who plants and he who waters are one, and each one will receive his own reward according to his own labor. For we are God's fellow workers; you are God's field, God's building." 1st Corinthians 3:5-9

Walking in the Spirit *(Gal. 5:16)* and doing His will should be the goal for all Christians. Understand that we must listen to what God speaks to our heart. Perhaps you haven't been called to the ministry, but consider if you will an analogy.

A homeless man sits on the side of a gas station building, complete with a bottle of liquor. You feel that the Holy Spirit has laid it upon your heart to purchase the man a sandwich, some chips and a bottle of water from inside the gas station, to simply drop it off next to him and walk away. While it might not seem that a seed would be sowed for such an action, how do we know what God knows?

Perhaps the man had been sitting there drinking alcohol, yet cursing God in his heart, telling him that he behaves in this manner because he never provides anything for him and if God was truly there, he would provide a meal for him. Just then as you pull into the gas station and soon thereafter set a meal aside the man, who clearly isn't in the right mind to hear the Gospel anyway, yet walking away, that man would know, he would know, though you might never be none the wiser. Sometimes the things that God has us doing as Christians might seem to have no fruits, but God knows the heart *(Jer. 17:10)*.

Yet another example, same sort of thing. I remember walking through an East Side undeveloped area of Chicago and seeing a bunch of street kids hiding out there. Imagine if God laid it upon your heart to talk to these people, yet you couldn't think to actually do such a thing, but nonetheless you were obedient. Walking up to the group of kids you tell them about the Gospel. Sure, maybe they throw a drink in your face and curse at you. Perhaps then you walk away thinking how dumb that was and how you are not even sure if the Lord really spoke to your heart regarding talking to them. After all a lot of people find it hard to do such things. A few minutes later, after cleaning your self up in the restroom, you go to get in your car and see you the kids crossing the street illegally. Suddenly out of nowhere one of the cars refuses to stop (as I have seen first hand how often times kids will just walk where they want, irregardless of traffic flow) and one of the kids is struck down – dead.

Now this analogy could be looked at two different ways. One, if you hadn't been obedient to the *"small voice" (1st Kings 19:12)* you would be cut to the heart regarding having seen afterwards the purpose that God had in mind. On the other hand, by being obedient, you would have known that God had foreseen what would happen and had given them an opportunity to repent and believe into Jesus Christ as their Savior, yet their heart was against their Creator *(Jer. 17:9)*.

So should we worry about what results doing the Lord's work brings? No, rather we should be diligent as Christians to do the work of the Lord, not worrying about results, but knowing that we are doing as good servants should be doing.

"And we know that all things work together for good to those who love God, to those who are the called according to His purpose." Romans 8:28

A personal example regarding myself and All Will Stand. A month ago God spoke to my heart regarding helping Believers in Venezuela. My first thought was 'me?'. I searched out some independent fundamental Baptist churches in Venezuela and decided to email three separate churches down there, giving them a brief that I was looking to help, but also I presented a simple question, *"How can one be Saved?"*. One of the emails bounced back that I had found on some obscure list. I waited.

Three weeks went by and I began to ponder if I was correct in the Lord calling me to help out in Venezuela. I remained faithful in assuming so, but the lack of response did make me question my position. Finally I received an email from a pastor in Venezuela. A reply was sent, presumably the work of more than one Believer, regarding my question about Salvation and was spot on. God had indeed connected me to a true Church thousands and thousands of miles away. Project Venezuela was created and though I don't know what the fullness of such a thing will be, I do know it will be according to His will, that is all that matters.

We must not give up and get discouraged, going to the sidelines. We might have been beat down by the world, but we must get back up, we must continue on.

"The Lord is not slow concerning His promise, as some count slowness, but is longsuffering toward us, not purposing that any should perish but that all should come to repentance. But the day of the Lord will come as a thief in the night, in which the heavens will pass away with a loud noise, and the elements will be dissolved with intense burning; both the earth and the works that are in it will be burned up. Therefore, since all these things will be dissolved, of what sort ought you to be in holy behavior and godliness, looking for and earnestly hastening unto the coming of the Day of God,

through which the heavens will be dissolved, being set on fire, and the elements will melt with intense burning?" 2nd Peter 3:9-12

Let us never forget that doing the Lord's work is a great honor and privilege. Whether it simply helping an elderly neighbor by taking out the trash, giving a homeless person a meal, speaking to someone about Christ or simply living our lives holy and spotless *(Phil. 2:15)*, we are a light to the world. What did Jesus say about such a light?

"You are the light of the world. A city that is set on a hill cannot be hidden. Nor do they light a lamp and put it under a grain measure, but on a lampstand, and it shines for all who are in the house. Let your light so shine before men, so that they may see your good works and glorify your Father in Heaven." Matthew 5:14-16

There is still work to be done and I know many pastors know those who are true Christians in their churches sitting on the sidelines. We must encourage them, build them up *(1 Thes. 5:11)*, but we also ourselves must be examples, as we must always remember the greatness of what Christ did for us by dying on the Cross, paying the penalty for our sins, of which we are not worthy.

"Therefore, having been justified by faith, we have peace with God through our Lord Jesus Christ, through whom also we have access by faith into this grace in which we stand, and rejoice on the hope of the glory of God. And not only that, but we also exult in afflictions, knowing that affliction produces perseverance; and perseverance, proven character; and proven character, hope. And hope does not make ashamed, because the love of God has been poured out in our hearts through the Holy Spirit who was given to us. For when we were yet without strength, in due time Christ died for the ungodly. For scarcely for a righteous man will one die; yet perhaps for a good man some would even be bold enough to die. But God demonstrates His own love toward us, in that while we were yet sinners, Christ died for us." Romans 5:1-8

Amen!

Proud to Defy God?

Let's not let the media 'tell' us what to think and do, rather each American should turn to the Bible for knowledge of God and His standards. Yet if those who continue to push such propaganda, which is contrary to their Creator and the people continue to buy into the lies, then what will happen? Should celebrations be held by those who are proud to defy God?

"My people are destroyed for lack of knowledge... As they were increased, so they sinned against Me. I will change their glory into shame. They eat up the sin of My people, and they set their appetites on their iniquity. And it shall be: Like people, like priest. And I will visit their ways upon them and repay them for their deeds. For they shall eat and not have enough. They shall commit fornication and not bring forth, because they have ceased to take heed to Jehovah. Harlotry and wine and new wine snatch away the heart. My people seek advice from their wooden idols, and their magic wand expounds to them. For the spirit of harlotry has led them astray, and they have committed adultery against their God." Hosea 4:6a, 7-12

Though they may laugh, cheer and celebrate their blasphemous agendas, eventually such wickedness will turn into weeping and gnashing of teeth. Let each man be assured that God Almighty, the One to whom ALL will stand *(Rev. 20:12)* before, certainly does take notice.

"And in that day Jehovah of Hosts called for weeping and mourning, and for baldness, and for girding with sackcloth. But behold, joy and gladness, slaying oxen and killing sheep, eating flesh and drinking wine, saying, Let us eat and drink, for tomorrow we die!" Isaiah 22:12-13

"Then one said to Him, Lord, are there few who are saved? And He said to them, Strive to enter through the narrow gate, for many, I say to you, will seek to enter and will not be able. When once the Master of the house has risen up and shut the door, and you begin to stand outside and knock at the door, saying, Lord, Lord, open to us, and He will answer and say to you, I do not know you, where you are from, then you will begin to

say, We ate and drank in Your presence, and You taught in our streets. But He will say, I tell you I do not know you, where you are from. Depart from Me, all you workers of iniquity. There will be weeping and gnashing of teeth, when you see Abraham and Isaac and Jacob and all the prophets in the kingdom of God, and yourselves being thrust outside." Luke 13:23-28*

"May Jehovah take notice, and require it!" 2nd Chr. 24:22

Understand the conditioning that is taking place across this once great land called America. All across the country schools are telling lies against the Most High, jobs are pushing feel-good positivism propaganda and diversity training. The entertainment industry can take even what would appear to be benign television programming about real estate transactions and turn it into shows promoting the lusts of the world, covetousness and sodomy. These are traps, traps which try to push enough of society from coast to coast to walk contrary to their Creator *(Rev. 12:9)*.

Those who promote these things are against God and blaspheme Him with their words and actions. Understand that the origin of the positive thinking movement, which has changed names many times in the work place, but is still the same origin, is none other than someone who walked contrary to God. The world might see what is going on with Hollywood directors and the evil that has been going on behind the scenes for years and years, yet is this not simply a symptom of the real problem? Those who push this trash upon us are walking contrary to God – intentionally. Now as our country becomes more and more engrained in sexual perversities, many of those want God to take notice. Be assured, you can be absolutely assured that the God who Created the oceans on the edges of our land that we have taken for our country, the God who Created the Rocky Mountains that go from Canada to Panama, the God who Created you, will indeed take notice.

"Behold, Jehovah's hand is not shortened, that it cannot save; nor is His ear heavy, that it cannot hear. But your iniquities have separated between you and your God, and your sins have hidden His face from you, that He will not hear. For your hands are defiled with blood, and your fingers with iniquity; your lips have spoken lies, your tongue has uttered perverseness. No one calls for justice, nor does anyone plead for truth; they trust in vanity and speak lies. They conceive mischief and bring forth iniquity. They hatch vipers' eggs and weave the spider's web; he who eats their eggs dies, and that which is crushed breaks out into a viper. Their webs shall not become garments, nor shall they cover themselves with their works; their works are works of iniquity, and the act of violence is in their hands. Their feet run to evil, and they make haste to shed innocent blood; their thoughts are thoughts of iniquity; devastation and destruction are in their paths. The way of peace they have not known, and there is no justice in their paths. They have made crooked paths for themselves; whoever goes in them shall not know peace. Therefore justice is far from us; nor does righteousness overtake us. We wait for daylight, but behold, the night; for brightness, but we walk in darkness. We grope for the wall like the blind, and we grope as if we had no eyes. We stumble at noonday as in the night; we are in desolate places like dead men. We all roar like bears, and mourn with

moaning like doves; we look for justice, but there is none; for salvation, but it is far off from us. For our transgressions are multiplied before You, and our sins testify against us. For our transgressions are with us; and as for our iniquities, we know them; in transgressing and lying against Jehovah, and backsliding from our God, speaking oppression and revolt, conceiving and uttering from the heart words of falsehood. And justice is driven back, and righteousness stands afar off; for truth has fallen in the street, and uprightness cannot enter. Yea, truth fails; and he who departs from evil makes himself a prey. And Jehovah saw it, and it displeased Him that there was no justice. And He saw that there was no man, and wondered that there was no intercessor. Therefore His own arm brought salvation unto Him; and His righteousness, it sustained Him. For He put on righteousness like a breastplate, and a helmet of salvation on His head. And He put on the garments of vengeance for clothing, and was covered with zeal as a cloak. According to their deeds, accordingly He will repay; fury to His adversaries, recompense to His enemies. He will completely repay their deeds to the coastlands." Isaiah 59:1-18

"And they did not repent of their murders nor their sorceries nor their sexual perversions nor their thefts." Revelation 9:21

"The heavens declare the glory of the Mighty God; and the firmament proclaims His handiwork." Psalms 19:1

There is mercy with God, if one repents. Will we as a nation, as a people who still largely proclaim to be Christians, continue to behave as we do not know what His Word says regarding Truth? Will we allow those who invite us to join them in their rebellion against God to continue on with their agendas? Dear individual, please understand that the hour is late.

"The soul who sins shall die. The son shall not bear the guilt of the father, nor the father bear the guilt of the son. The righteousness of the righteous shall be upon himself, and the wickedness of the wicked shall be upon himself. But if a wicked man turns from all his sins which he has done, keeps all My statutes, and does what is lawful and right, he shall live life; he shall not die. None of the transgressions which he has done shall be remembered against him; because of the righteousness which he has done, he shall live. Do I delight with pleasure in the death of the wicked? says the Lord Jehovah, and not that he should turn back from his ways and live? But when a righteous man turns away from his righteousness and commits iniquity, and does according to all the abominations that the wicked man does, shall he live? All the righteousness which he has done shall not be remembered; because of the treachery of his unfaithfulness, and the sin which he has sinned, in them he shall die. Yet you say, The way of the Lord is not fair. Hear now, O house of Israel, is it not My way which is fair, and your ways which are not fair. When a righteous man turns away from his righteousness, commits iniquity, and dies in it, it is for the iniquity which he has done that he dies. Again, when a wicked man turns away from the wickedness which he has done, and does what is lawful and right, he preserves himself alive. Because he considers and turns away from all the transgressions which he has done, he shall live life; he shall not die... For I have no pleasure in the death of one who dies, declares the Lord Jehovah. Therefore turn and live!" Ezekiel 18:20-28, 32

While those of us who know God, who have repented and believed into Jesus Christ as our Savior, can only hope that our nation has some sort of repentance and recognizes that they are accountable to their Creator, understand that you too will individually stand before Him *(Ro. 14:12)*. Do you want to go along with the flow? Do you want to continue ignoring God and hope in your heart that the existence of Him is simply a lie? Or perhaps you want to continue on, either believing in a god, but not believing in who He is and what standards He has set in His Word, as well as that you are a sinner in need of repentance and a Savior, namely Jesus Christ, whom God sent to die on the Cross and who paid the penalty for your sins *(1st Peter 2:24)*, raised the third day *(1st Cor. 15:4)* should you accept it. Truly there is a choice in the matter, by making no decision, you have made a decision. By ignoring, refusing to understand the Gospel or openly defying your Creator, yes you, as you might join the masses in rebellion against God, but there will be no protest or group funding to try and save you as you are cast into the Lake of Fire for your sin *(Rev. 20:15)*.

"But now the righteousness of God apart from the Law is revealed, being witnessed by the Law and the Prophets, even the righteousness of God, through the faith of Jesus Christ, to all and upon all who believe. For there is no difference; for all have sinned and fall short of the glory of God, being justified freely by His grace through the redemption that is in Christ Jesus, whom God set forth as a propitiation through faith in His blood, to give evidence of His righteousness, because in His forbearance God had passed over the sins that were previously committed, to prove at the present time His righteousness, that He might be just and the justifier of the one who is of the faith of Jesus. Where is boasting then? It is excluded. By what law? Of works? No, but through the law of faith. Therefore we conclude that a man is justified by faith apart from the works of the Law. Or is He the God of the Jews only? Is He not also the God of the Gentiles? Yes, of the Gentiles also, since there is one God who will justify the circumcised by faith and the uncircumcised through faith." Romans 3:21-30

"Do you not know that to whom you present yourselves slaves to obey, you are that one's slaves whom you obey, whether of sin unto death, or of obedience unto righteousness? But God be thanked that though you were slaves of sin, yet you obeyed from the heart that form of doctrine which was delivered to you. And having been set free from sin, you became slaves to righteousness. I speak in human terms because of the weakness of your flesh. For just as you presented your members as slaves to uncleanness, and to iniquity unto iniquity, so now present your members as slaves to righteousness unto sanctification. For when you were slaves to sin, you were free in regard to righteousness. What fruit did you have then in the things of which you are now ashamed? For the end of those things is death. But now having been set free from sin, and having become slaves to God, you have your fruit unto sanctification, and the end, eternal life. For the wages of sin is death, but the gift of God is eternal life in Christ Jesus our Lord." Romans 6:16-23

"Now it was not written for his sake alone, that it was accounted to him, but also for us, to whom it shall be accounted, believing in Him who raised up Jesus our Lord from the

dead, who was delivered up because of our trespasses, and was raised for our justification." Romans 4:23-25

"Truly, these times of ignorance God overlooked, but now commands all men everywhere to repent, because He has established a day on which He will judge the world in righteousness by the Man whom He has appointed. He has given assurance of this to everyone by raising Him from the dead." Acts 17:30-31

Harsh words? Or perhaps you hope that they are lies, as certainly there is no end to the amount of so-called preachers who are eagerly awaiting your participation in your so-called churches or ministries, telling you what you desire to hear. Both the teacher and the willfully ignorant participants in their false ministries will stand before their Creator at the Judgment individually and be judged with equity and justice. Take heed!

"But He answered and said, Every plant which My Heavenly Father has not planted will be uprooted. Let them alone. They are blind leaders of the blind. And if the blind leads the blind, both will fall into the ditch." Matthew 15:13-14

"You have rebuked the nations, You have destroyed the wicked, You have blotted out their name forever and ever. The desolations of the enemy have come to an end forever, and You have destroyed the cities; the remembrance of them has perished with them. But Jehovah shall endure forever; He has prepared His throne for justice. And He shall judge the world in righteousness; He shall execute judgment to the people with equity. Jehovah also will be a refuge for the oppressed, a refuge in times of distress. And those who know Your name will put their trust in You; for You, Jehovah, have not forsaken those who seek You." Psalms 9:5-10

"Take heed to yourself and to the doctrine. Continue in them, for in doing this you will deliver both yourself and those who hear you." 1st Tim. 4:16

As far as our nation and our rebellion against our Creator, we got big words against God and actions that defy Him,ns yet we also have big words of war against many nations. Will God intervene to help a nation who refuses to repent and is bent on continuing in the rebellion against Him or will he defy us who refuse to obey His edicts and refuse to acknowledge the One true God?

"For the army of the Syrians came with a small company of men; but Jehovah delivered a very great army into their hand, because they had forsaken Jehovah the God of their fathers." 2nd Chr. 24:24a

"Thus says Jehovah, Let not the wise glory in his wisdom, nor let the mighty glory in his might; let not the rich glory in his riches; but let him who glories glory in this, that he understands and knows Me, that I am Jehovah, doing kindness, justice, and righteousness in the earth; for in these things I delight, says Jehovah." Jeremiah 9:23-24

"Lament and mourn and weep. Let your laughter be turned to mourning and your joy to shame. Humble yourselves in the sight of the Lord, and He will exalt you." Jacob (James) 4:9-10

Amen!

Unfortunate Ones

"If one of your brethren becomes poor, and his hand has become shaky, then you shall support him, like a stranger or a sojourner, that he may live with you." Leviticus 25:35

Many of the younger generation in America support being global citizens. Some of their beliefs include food, shelter, education and basic medical needs for all people, with little or no regard to borders or their own countries. While the idea, often mixed with flavors of both socialism and communism, might seem noble to some on the surface, undoubtedly they are being prepped for the *"time of Jacob's trouble" (Jer. 30:7)*, better known as the Tribulation.

Through the federal government strong arming against state sovereignty regarding controlling the content of our respective education systems in this country, they have over a generation of those who through moral relativism, humanistic and propaganda, as well as just plain old ignorance, prepared to accept the coming Antichrist. Let me place a note here that the Rapture will happen before this time period begins, despite what the naysayers proclaim.

A moral society could never go down this road. What we have is a society that is custom designed by those who knowingly have engineered the entire ordeal, one of which is full of wickedness, selfishness and evil. To put this into scope we must first consider where America really stands amidst our current party attitude, then we must consider also the evil that we as a society have allowed to happen worldwide. How can a society that overwhelmingly rejects God's Word and rejects Jesus Christ as their Savior assume to create a utopia? Quite easily, those who refuse to acknowledge their sin and repent to their Creator are the same as those who foster great evil upon unfortunate ones throughout the countries of the world.

First let's take a look at the real condition of America, one whereas Americans through self pride, self consumption, consumerism and a truly full fledge me-based society ignore the unfortunate ones found in our own country. We must consider and think about some of the large problems that we find in the United States.

1.) Many of our major cities in our country are full of violence and evil. I'm no stranger to having seen these things first hand and neither are a lot of others, despite the fact that their daily commute to work might have them passing through one of the zones of a city of the unfortunate ones.

In these areas violence prevails, murders happen on a regular basis. Injustice is common as police often plant drug evidence on suspects, just to get them off the street. Children can't even play safely in parks without being in the crosshairs of gunfire between street gangs. Women are ravaged, thefts are rampant and the rules of the street prevail, as those who are innocently stuck in an impoverished condition simply have to deal with the reality of the world around them. To them, a major city like Chicago, one of which I am very familiar with, is but a few blocks of their neighborhood where the fortunate ones travel to the Golden Mile, picking up their favorite brew from a local coffee shop on the way to their career.

The schools are not much safer, though they are locked down in a police state system of repression, they also harvest much violence, threatening those who refuse to align themselves with those who are actively participating in evil. With an education designed to create prisoners of the future, not only in the real system of derogatory economics, but also a system designed to make them unable to change their neighborhoods into a once again more flourishing society, instead of the current docile controlled godless society.

While these same conditions of repressions against the unfortunate ones in our communities are not simply limited to major cities, it is more prevalent and obvious to the eyes. As the government allows drugs to be shipped in, as the war in Afghanistan produces record amounts of opium that end up on our streets, let us never forget, though as much as those in power do not want us to look behind the curtain, that indeed a system of purposeful repression is in full play. A solution to counteract such measures is simply for those who are called to do so, to faithfully preach the Gospel in such areas as the ultimate solution, where those who are enslaved will truly be set free with the Truth that is found in Jesus Christ *(John 8:32)*, our Lord and Savior.

2.) For those who are far away from such neighborhoods and enjoy the greater things in life, they too are also entrapped by the guiles of society. Personal credit card debt, mortgages, student loans, auto payments and a skyrocketing cost for both medical insurance premiums, as well as the respective deductibles that go along with them, have enslaved them in yet another trap.

They scramble to and fro, too busy to acknowledge their Creator, with the majority unwilling to help out or even acknowledge the unfortunate ones that are in many cases just miles away from their comfortable, yet unaffordable, abode. Consumed with the luxuries of social media, entertainment and the next meet-up at a local club or coffee shop, there is no time to allow the realization that they are self centered, focusing on the things of this world, rather than the things of God. They are without self control, knowing certain things of God, but never willing to truly yield to Him, they refuse to repent and believe into Jesus Christ as their Savior. For just as they are unwilling to sacrifice their delicacies of life for those who are more unfortunate, they are unwilling to repent of their sins, their hearts just as wicked as those with less means.

"For men will be lovers of themselves, lovers of money, boasters, proud, blasphemers, disobedient to parents, unthankful, unholy, without natural affection, unyielding, slanderers, without self-control, savage, despisers of good, traitors, headstrong, haughty, lovers of pleasure rather than lovers of God, having a form of godliness but denying its power. And from such people turn away." 2nd Timothy 3:2-5

"Come now, you rich, weep and howl for your calamities that are coming upon you. Your riches are corrupted, and your garments are moth-eaten. Your gold and silver are corroded, and their corrosion will be a witness against you and will eat your flesh like fire. You have heaped up treasure in the last days. Indeed the wages of the laborers who reaped your fields, which you kept back by fraud, cry out; and the cries of the reapers have reached the ears of the Lord of Hosts. You have lived on the earth in pleasure and luxury; you have fattened your hearts as in a day of slaughter. You have condemned, you have murdered the just; he does not resist you. Therefore be patient, brethren, until the coming of the Lord. See how the farmer waits for the precious fruit of the earth, waiting patiently for it until it receives the early and latter rain. You also be patient. Make your hearts firm, for the coming of the Lord draws near. Do not grumble against one another, brethren, that you not be condemned. Behold, the Judge stands at the door. My brethren, take the prophets, who spoke in the name of the Lord, as an example of suffering affliction and endurance. Indeed we count them blessed who endure. You have heard of the endurance of Job and seen the outcome brought about by the Lord; that the Lord is very kind and merciful." Jacob (James) 5:1-11

3.) With a cry of making America great again, our nation looks to reap prosperity from the supposed benefits of simply 'being great', yet we never look behind the curtain, we simply don't care. The assumption is that food aid through the United Nations feeds the hungry. Instead we as Americans support the corporations who raise havoc over the unfortunate ones around the world, not knowing what those in the upper echelons of both corporations and our government are doing to keep the empire going, truly an unfortunate truth of imperialism being used as a mechanism of evil, without the knowledge or even caring of the America people. This, in and of itself is a great evil.

A nation that preys off of the unfortunate ones through corporate-government partnerships that align themselves with many nations of the world, of which foster horrific conditions for many people in many different countries. Like our major cities full of those in poverty and despair, around the world there are the unfortunate ones who cry out, many knowing more about what is going on in regards to the imperialistic goals of our corpotracy then our own people.

While such topics might open up controversy among our people, should they take the time to understand what the unfortunate ones in many nations already know, the reality is that this has already happened and continues to accelerate. Many in positions of power will argue that if the World Bank, along with corporations, funded by the Treasury

Department, in reality printed by the Federal Reserve, working with the government of the United States did not do these things than communism or Russia or China would simply come in and take over. So do those who follow the Manifest Destiny, popular in the 1800's, who lead many corporations and embody positions of power in our government truly condone that the ends justify the means? Should evil be done that good come?

"Woe to those who draw iniquity with cords of vanity, and sin with cart ropes; who say, Let Him hurry and hasten His work, so that we may see it; and let the purpose of the Holy One of Israel draw near and come, so that we may know it! Woe to those who call evil good and good evil; who put darkness for light and light for darkness; who put bitter for sweet and sweet for bitter! Woe to those who are wise in their own eyes, and understanding in their own sight!" Isaiah 5:18-21

Here we are, 2017, and most Americans are so wrapped up in a self centered world that not only would they not want to know about what is going on in the world, they also live in a society where the media is so controlled that it does take some diligent study to realize the mechanisms of our society, that is a far cry from the Constitutional Republic that was installed in this nations many years ago.

Our sin has engulfed us as many find it more entertaining to take selfies with a woman who is passed out on the street from having been punched in the face during a robbery, rather than call for help. Our young people randomly assault people for no reason, except a game that they play, as they taunt and laugh, while recording a video for YouTube, as a man drowns in the ocean, providing no help. There are those in our worse neighborhoods that are shot or stabbed or hit by a vehicle, laying on the ground, helpless, as many will walk over them, so self-centered, that after taking a picture for their phone, they go into the convenience store to pick up a 40. A society that is ripe for the just Judgment from the Most High.

"For judgment will be without mercy to the one who has shown no mercy. Indeed, mercy rejoices over judgment. What does it profit, my brethren, if someone says he has faith but does not have works? Is faith able to save him? If a brother or sister is naked and destitute of daily food, and one of you says to them, Depart in peace, be warmed and filled, but you do not give them the things which are needed for the body, what does it profit? Thus also faith, if it does not have works, being alone, is dead. But someone will say, You have faith, and I have works. Show me your faith without your works, and I will show you my faith from my works." Jacob (James) 2:13-18

As the debts continue to pile higher than ever for our nations, as our forest burn down to the ground, as hurricanes wreck billions and billions of dollar worth of damage, they continue, continue to puff themselves up before their Creator, refusing to acknowledge the blood on their hands and putting both hands to do evil. They call justice acceptance and allowing men to behave as women and vice versa. Justice is not for those who are unfortunate, but for those who refuse to repent of their sins and continue on promoting their agendas of sodomy that is clearly contrary to God's Word. They will stand accountable, yet let's not forget those of the world who have suffered greatly under our hand.

Ours you say? Certainly not ours? Yes, with absolutely certainly, whether without knowledge or not, we have allowed a system of repression, the same which is slowly coming for us also, gaining much ground, to repress the unfortunate ones throughout the world. Just go to many countries around the world, go to the very bottom of the income bracket and ask, I challenge you ask! Ask them why they live in such filth, ask them why they cannot afford to eat, ask them why their children don't have a proper education or medical care, just ask. I am certain, certain as the sun will come up tomorrow, that many will point to your country, yes they will point to the United States and deals that have been made through secret programs of repression, through the World Bank and through corporate-private partnerships, to their ills.

So what do we do, what can we do, what should we do? For if the realization of our nations sins are fully understood, both in our own borders and that done through certain mechanisms throughout the world, then we should stand in awe for the disastrous conditions that have been created. Yet how many would not want to take account for such things? For the realization of that, the full understanding of what truly oils the wheels of the United States to continue on would be the realization that by pulling the plug on these infamous systems, we would also pull the plug on our dissolving prosperity.

Adding in the fact that God is watching our nation, seeing what appears to already be judgments against our country, what should we do? Continue on in evil so good may come? Let it not be, rather let us look at our society and fall on our knees in repentance, hoping that God Almighty may have mercy on us. Though our standards of living would decrease greatly, could we not be satisfied if God had mercy on our land, to at least the extent of allowing us the very basic necessities of life, shelter, food, education and basic medical care? Will we not accept that which we proclaim to have as a goal for the countries around the world here at home or would we simply continue on in ignorance as our sins continue to pile up to the heavens?

Now for those of you who can hear, for those of you who are part of the unfortunate ones in the world, please pay attention. While many, even true Christians, do not have an understanding of what is done in America's name amongst the nations of the world, truly our society is turning into a nightmare scenario, where even in the small town of Kalispell, Montana, we are not immune to the ills of our society caused by the sins of our nation.

To me it makes no difference what race or nation one belongs to, if they are in Christ, certainly they are part of the body of Believers and indeed our Home is all the same. So what can we do, what can people of the world do? What can we as Americans do? Essentially they have us trapped, essentially they have won. They didn't win through the measures of repressive means setup among the nations, but the won through the refusal of Americans to accept God's guidelines to humanity in the Holy Scriptures. They won through Americans reviling in their sin, so self centered that most all refuse to repent and accept the Gospel. Yet Jesus provided the solution, a solution to the inhabitants of the world.

Even if we lived in a society where indeed there was some sort of global utopia, where nearly every inhabitant of the earth had their basic needs covered, each individual is still going to stand before a holy and righteous God. Unless their name is written in the Book of Life, unless they have repented and believed into Jesus Christ, they will inherit eternal hellfire. The world isn't going to change, even during the Tribulation, while multitudes are Saved *(Rev. 7:9)*, the world as a whole refuses to repent of their sin *(Rev. 16:11)*. While those in Libya are in cages, being sold as slaves, those in Australia push for same-sex marriage, those in Venezuela feel the effects of ill policies from the United States, as well as many nations around the world, understand that the noose is certainly being put around America's neck and if the Lord doesn't come back to take those who are Believers to be with Him, Rapturing them prior to the *"time of Jacob's trouble" (Jer. 30:7)*, I fear that we could be in for some serious trouble beforehand, albeit deserving.

"Truly, these times of ignorance God overlooked, but now commands all men everywhere to repent, because He has established a day on which He will judge the world in righteousness by the Man whom He has appointed. He has given assurance of this to everyone by raising Him from the dead." Acts 17:30-31

"And I saw a great white throne and Him who sat on it, from whose face the earth and the heavens fled away. And there was found no place for them. And I saw the dead, small and great, standing before God. And books were opened. And another book was opened, which is the Book of Life. And the dead were judged according to their works, out of the things which were written in the books. And the sea gave up the dead who were in it, and Death and Hades delivered up the dead who were in them. And they were judged, each one, according to their works. And Death and Hades were cast into the Lake of Fire. This is the second death. And anyone not found written in the Book of Life was cast into the Lake of Fire." Revelation 20:11-15

What really needs to be done, is for those of the world who truly are Christians, we need to not forget about the unfortunate ones. While our hands might be able to provide some aid, what the world really needs is to hear the Gospel. God hasn't forgotten the unfortunate ones and He will Judge appropriately.

"He sits in the lurking places of the villages; in the secret places he murders the innocent; his eyes are hidden against the unfortunate ones. He lies in wait secretly, like a lion in his den. He lies in wait to catch the poor; he catches the poor when he draws him into his net. He lies low and crouches, and the poor unfortunate ones have fallen by his might. He has said in his heart, the Mighty God has forgotten; He hides His face; He will never see it! Arise, O Jehovah! O Mighty God, lift up Your hand! Forget not the lowly poor. Why have the wicked spurned God? He has said in his heart, You will not investigate. But You have seen it, for You pay attention to trouble and provocation; to repay it with Your hand. The poor commits himself to You; You are the Helper of the

fatherless. Break the arm of the wicked and the evil one; investigate his wickedness, until You find no more. Jehovah is King forever and ever; the nations have perished out of His land. Jehovah, You have heard the desire of the lowly; You will prepare their heart, You will cause Your ear to hear, to vindicate the fatherless and the oppressed, so that the man of the earth may terrify no more." Psalms 10:8-18

"God stands in the congregation of the mighty; He judges among the gods. How long will you judge unjustly, and show partiality to the wicked? Selah Defend the poor and fatherless; do justice to the afflicted and needy. Deliver the poor and needy; rescue them out of the hand of the wicked. They do not know, nor do they understand; they walk about in darkness; all the foundations of the earth are shaken. I have said, You gods, all of you are sons of the Most High. But you shall die like men, and fall like one of the princes. Arise, O God, judge the earth; for You shall inherit all nations." Psalms 82

Please understand, dear reader, that God did not intend for society to go down this road, but He knew beforehand what would happen. This is why He provided Salvation as a free gift to all, through Jesus Christ *(John 3:16)*. Hold on! Seek Salvation while you can, put your faith in Him and tarry on, even unto death *(Psalms 48:14)*. For the time will come where it becomes increasingly likely that the only solution to the ails of the world will supposedly be fixed by the Antichrist. Then the world can look at the systems of repression that have happened in the history of the world and that are currently ongoing nowadays and understand that what has happened will not even compare with the horrific future that that time will hold *(Matt. 24:22)*.

If only, if only the world, the unfortunate ones, could have hope in Jesus Christ, that despite the fact that their lives might not be such a great thing in the eyes of men, they would have the true riches that are only found in Jesus Christ *(Phil. 4:19)*. With that they would be satisfied, knowing that the things of this world are passing away *(1st John 2:17)*. My thoughts and my prayers are with you.

"There was a certain rich man who was clothed in purple and fine linen and fared sumptuously every day. And there was a certain beggar named Lazarus, full of sores, who was laid at his gate, desiring to be fed with the crumbs which fell from the rich man's table. Moreover the dogs came and licked his sores. So it happened that the beggar died, and was carried by the angels into Abraham's bosom. The rich man also died and was buried. And being in torments in Hades, he lifted up his eyes and saw Abraham afar off, and Lazarus in his bosom. Then he cried and said, Father Abraham, have mercy on me, and send Lazarus that he may dip the tip of his finger in water and cool my tongue; for I am tormented in this flame. But Abraham said, Son, remember that in your lifetime you received your good things, and likewise Lazarus evil things; but now he is comforted and you are tormented. And besides all this, between us and you there is a great chasm fixed, so that those who want to pass from here to you are not able, nor can those from there pass to us. Then he said, I beg you therefore, father, that you would send him to my father's house, for I have five brothers, that he may testify to them, that they not also come to this place of torment. Abraham said to him, They have Moses and the Prophets; let them hear them. And he said, No, father Abraham; but if one goes to

them from the dead, they will repent. But he said to him, If they do not hear Moses and the Prophets, neither will they be persuaded though one should rise from the dead." Luke 16:19-31

"But whoever has this world's goods, and sees his brother in need, and shuts up his heart from him, how does the love of God abide in him?" 1st John 3:17

Amen!

Lights Out?

"Seek Jehovah while He may be found; call upon Him while He is near. Let the wicked forsake his way, and the unrighteous man his thoughts; and let him return to Jehovah, and He will have mercy on him; and to our God, for He will abundantly pardon." Isaiah 55:6-7

In Montana, Kalispell is one of the big cities, but in the scope of the nation, it is but a small quiet town. Having lived in Orlando, Phoenix, Chicago and even a bit of time in Toledo, there is no comparison. Driving the other night between two small Montana towns, the realization of the scope of potential trouble on the horizon, thinking of how America is so backslidden before God, my spirit was deeply troubled.

Imagine for a moment, if you will, your respective city. Whether it be a small town on the plains of America, a big hustling urban center of a major city, a medium sized city or even the rural countryside, miles away from the nearest gas station, if the lights went out. As we were driving between the small city of Kalispell to the very small town of Bigfork, the glistening lights of rural houses and the glimmering of communities approaching against the black night sky was a reminder that we were surrounded by people, who were getting ready for bed in the late evening. What if as we were driving suddenly and without warning all of the lights went out?

What if the dark black sky of night soon became even darker and our headlights on our car became more powerful as they cut through more darkness, without the aid of the light from rural homes we were passing? This thought was pondered and glancing at my fuel gauge, it was noted that the tank was nearly full. What would be done, what would happen if such a scenario as North Korea has been threatening, an EMP weapon had just been deployed, even a thousand miles to the east, with the effects now covering the great state of Montana?

What could be done? How would one even know soon enough what had happened? Certainly the emergency broadcast system should be working, but could we count on the government to deploy the message of what exactly happened soon enough? Would we know right away the truth, or simply be told that there is a temporarily blackout? Could the government be trusted? At that moment, the moment the lights went out, those who would act immediately would gain very much, than those who waited and acted afterwards.

How would someone even rush to the grocery store, assuming they had some cash on them, not just a plastic credit card, to fill up carts of food? Wouldn't they have locked their doors, no power, no way to effectively ring up the food? Certainly they would not be privy to knowing what had happened, assuming it was just a power outage, but by time the general populace found out, would not the doors of the grocery store be ripped off and the shelves bare? With nearly a full tank of gas, our range would be around 250 miles, shouldn't we have had some gas cans with extra gas to extend that to 500? Not that 500 miles in Montana will get you very far.

If at least we had a 500 mile range we could make a run for Canada. Would the borders even be opened? They have no power, how will they scan the passports? Certainly the Canadian government would know what had happened, even if it was not publicly spoken about yet, perhaps they have a contingency plan to lock all of their borders to keep out a potential unknown enemy. This would certainly seem sensible. How would one know just what had happened soon enough?

Certainly a blackout could be caused for many different reasons, perhaps a cyber attack on our electrical infrastructure that could be repaired soon, a major earthquake that may not have even been felt in the local area or some other reason, but time would be of essence. A nighttime blackout would be the best scenario and give those who happened to be up, quite an edge. Without cell phones working, many would simply sleep through the first few hours. For a daytime blackout those who live in major metropolitan areas would find there travel home to be quite difficult as the traffic lights would not work, causing traffic jams that only, as of yet, Hollywood has made up with their scenarios in movies. Either way, once the population learned that this was not a short term event, but an EMP had knocked out the majority of the power to the United States, chaos as has never been seen before would ensue.

My heart has been troubled by the great sinful behavior of our nation. Is it not becoming more apparent that we have the wounds of Judgment by God Almighty? Does not the party today for tomorrow we die attitude of this country *(Is. 22:13)* strike fear in the hearts of men who otherwise fear Him who Created them? Will God simply take notice of what our nation has done to other nations, creating poverty, death and war throughout the world? Will God ignore the fact that America has murdered over 50 million babies? Will He who created the heavens and the earth not take note that we continue to promote sexual immoralities to a level that has not been seen on the face of this once great land until now? Will He hold our nation accountable for blaspheming His Word and calling ourselves a Christian nation, despite the fact that we walk contrary to Him? Given these thoughts, my heart ponders whether or not our success in North Korea is guaranteed.

Did not our government administration give North Korea the technology? Has there not been talk about the "Phoenix" and how out of the ashes of America the new world order will arise? Why, with the recent major uptick in military spending has our government ignored the threats of an EMP or even a super-EMP weapon from North Korea, even as other countries have testified before Congress that they believe North Korea might be in possession of a super-EMP weapon. A space based weapon in the hands of North Korea?

The same government, ours, who denied that North Korea had the technology for a three stage fuel system to launch a medium to long range ICBM, is also the same government who didn't, at least publicly, foresee that North Korea would also have been able to create a miniaturized hydrogen bomb, capable of being placed on top of an ICBM. Do we really trust in aid from our enemies, Russia and China, in reaching a diplomatic solution regarding North Korea? Would it not benefit them if North Korea did the job they can't do without receiving the recompense for their deed? Why did the House disband the EMP Commission recently? If we can upgrade our electrical system to become EMP proof for $400 billion, then why are we not actively pursuing it as we continue to taunt and threaten North Korea? If we are going to show them the fire and fury of the United States, as the world has never seen, then why are we giving them so long to prepare for a conflict? Why are we allowing them time to continue to create more ready to fire missiles, increasing the odds that an EMP will hit the mainland, as well as hydrogen bombs? Does North Korea not understand that we would absolutely cause mass death and destruction on their country? Would they not then prepare to launch as many missiles into the sky before they are unable to do so? Questions, questions, then comes my very troubling thought on my heart regarding this ordeal.

Can we be assured of success, despite our obvious military superiority, against North Korea? With being so backslidden against our Creator, with walking contrary to His ways, should we even risk such a battle? While we certainly could wipe them out, they have the potential to do much damage and kill most Americans through an EMP attack, plus whatever cities might be hit by incoming nuclear missiles. Do not Americans realize that our missile defense system is not as accurate as they want us to believe? Can a nation such as us, who does so much evil within and outside our borders, continue to flex our muscles, rebel against our Creator and assume that we will be successful in our endeavors?

"For though you had smitten the whole army of the Chaldeans who fight against you, and there remained only wounded men among them, they would rise up, each man in his tent, and burn this city with fire." Jeremiah 37:10

Looking over comments that people leave regarding North Korea, one voice is pushed to the top. That voice is that we are going to wipe them out, we are going to destroy them. Those who speak of such things, speak as ignorant ones, not knowing the capabilities of what is indeed a rogue regime, but not another Libya or Syria. North Korea has been preparing for years and years, both with the aid of Russian scientists and at the border of their ally, China. Let's not forget history and why Americans did not win the war against North Korea, they had an endless supply of Chinese solders.

Perhaps our country has technology that is not known to the populace. We might pull it off, without any major problems. Indeed we might go in and bomb them out, ending the supposed threat, one that is often instigated by our policies. One might question if we didn't have such measures against North Korea, whether or not this would even be an issue. Maybe this is just another rumor of war *(Matt. 24:6)*, one that will never come into action. Just as we have went years and years with such threats, albeit less than today, more years will come and go. If we were to take such military actions, if such an endeavor is launched against this rogue nation, if we were a nation whom is God fearing, one who holds His Words in reverence, one who does not walk contrary, then we could simply say *"may God be with us"*. Let us not say that and walk contrary to Him.

"And the Philistine said to David, Am I a dog, that you are coming to me with sticks? And the Philistine cursed David by his gods. And the Philistine said to David, Come to me, and I will give your flesh to the birds of the heavens and the beasts of the field! Then David said to the Philistine, You are coming to me with a sword, with a spear, and with a javelin. But I am coming to you in the name of Jehovah of Hosts, the God of the ranks of Israel, whom you have reproached. This day Jehovah will deliver you into my hand, and I will strike you and take your head from you. And this day I will give the carcasses of the camp of the Philistines to the birds of the heavens and the wild beasts of the earth, that all the earth may know that there is a God in Israel. Then all this assembly shall know that Jehovah does not save with sword and spear; for the battle is Jehovah's, and He has given you into our hands." 1st Samuel 17:43-47

Oh…but you say, look at how evil the regime of North Korea is, certainly God would want us to destroy a nation that kills and maims their citizens. Certainly God would be on our side as they have gulags throughout the country, propaganda and strict governmental controls, fear in the hearts of all of their citizens. Have they murdered as many innocent as us? Have they oppressed as many people as our fiscal and military policies throughout the world have oppressed? Do they claim to be a Christian people doing these things or do they simply refuse to acknowledge God? Which is worse, to claim to be a Christian nation and walk contrary to Him or to claim to be an atheist nation? Certainly the first, as we blaspheme God before the nations by calling upon Him and then pushing poverty, death and destruction unto millions and millions of the unfortunate ones, victims of our empire.

Israel was warned:

"If you walk in My statutes and keep My commandments, and do them, then I will give you rain in its season, the land shall yield its produce, and the trees of the field shall yield their fruit. Your threshing shall last till the time of vintage, and the vintage shall last till the time of sowing; you shall eat your bread to the full, and dwell in your land safely. I will give peace in the land, and you shall lie down, and no one shall make you afraid; I will rid the land of evil beasts, and the sword shall not go through your land. You shall chase your enemies, and they shall fall by the sword before you. Five of you shall chase a hundred, and a hundred of you shall put ten thousand to flight; your enemies shall fall by the sword before you. For I will look on you favorably and make you fruitful, multiply you and establish My covenant with you. You shall eat the old harvest, and clear out the old because of the new. I will set My tabernacle among you,

and My soul shall not abhor you. I will walk among you and be your God, and you shall be My people. I am Jehovah your God, who brought you out of the land of Egypt, that you should not be their slaves; I have broken the bands of your yoke and made you walk upright. But if you do not obey Me, and do not do all these commandments, and if you despise My statutes, or if your soul abhors My judgments, so that you do not do all My commandments, but break My covenant, I also will do this to you: I will even appoint terror over you, wasting disease and fever which shall consume the eyes and cause pining away of soul. And you shall sow your seed in vain, for your enemies shall eat it. I will set My face against you, and you shall be smitten by your enemies. Those who hate you shall reign over you, and you shall flee when no one pursues you. And after all this, if you do not obey Me, then I will chastise you seven times more for your sins. I will break the pride of your power; I will make your heavens like iron and your earth like bronze. And your strength shall be spent in vain; for your land shall not yield its produce, nor shall the trees of the land yield their fruit. And if you walk contrary to Me, and are not willing to obey Me, I will bring upon you seven times more plagues, according to your sins. I will also send wild beasts among you, which shall rob you of your children, destroy your livestock, and make you few in number; and your highways shall be desolate. And if by these things you do not let yourselves be corrected by Me, but walk contrary to Me, then I also will walk contrary to you, and I will punish you yet seven times for your sins. And I will bring a sword against you that shall execute the vengeance of the covenant; when you are gathered together within your cities I will send pestilence among you; and you shall be delivered into the hand of the enemy. And when I have cut off your supply of bread, ten women shall bake your bread in one oven, and they shall bring back your bread by weight, and you shall eat and not be satisfied. And after all this, if you do not obey Me, but walk contrary to Me, then I also will walk contrary to you in fury; and I, even I, will chastise you seven times for your sins. And you shall eat the flesh of your sons, and you shall eat the flesh of your daughters. And I will destroy your high places, cut down your incense altars, and cast your carcasses upon the carcasses of your idols; and My soul shall abhor you. And I will lay your cities waste and bring your sanctuaries to desolation, and I will not smell your soothing aromas. I will bring the land to desolation, and your enemies who dwell in it shall be astonished at it. I will scatter you among the nations and draw out a sword after you; your land shall be desolate and your cities waste." Leviticus 26:3-33

Yet you say that we are a moral nation, one who does not deserve the punishment from God Almighty? Consider and consider diligently the ways of our nation. If such a scenario unfolded, if in but a moment, the lights went out in this country, how would you fare? Would our government who, unlike other governments of the nations, such as South Korea and Russia, who have a full fledge plan in place to shelter millions and millions of people in the event of a nuclear attack, come to our aid? Where is your local nuclear shelter for the people in your city? Those who live in Seoul know, those who live in Moscow know, where or where is yours?

If our nation is so moral, then would not there be a system of equitable groceries distributed to each family, according to the amount of supplies and need? Would not the government be providing truck loads of food to cities across the country to continue feeding the public? While we do have some warehouses with food, we could not deal with such a large event. Would the grocery stores doors be ripped off and the shelves emptied or people calmly picking up food, leaving some behind for the next family to also be able to eat? Wouldn't at that moment you see your fears, that it is each man for themselves, violence, blood shed and murder would be rampant, the police overwhelmed and unable to protect, themselves stuck in traffic jams, running out of gas and simply too busy? Would your fellow moral citizens allow you to eat as well?

When night came, would the street remain quiet and peaceful or a certain fear overtake your family as you have to push the couch near the front door to barricade it from the bands of thieves and murderers who suddenly walk the streets, with little or no fear of the overwhelmed police? Just how well would our supposed God fearing society look in your eyes at that moment? Where are those morals you talk about? Where are those of this supposed Christian nation to provide aid?

Are the works of allowing sodomite marriage in this country moral before an Almighty God *(1st Cor. 6:9-10)*? Are the policies of pushing transgender rights throughout this country not contrary to His Word *(Duet. 22:5)*? Do even states, like Montana, who are pushing for birth certificates to no longer simply state male or female, all with the beckoning and cheering on of the ACLU, have a fear of their Creator who Created them male and female *(Gen. 5:2)*? Does our rampage against innocent countries for fiscal dominance, policies that most Americans can not even comprehend, that has lead to death, destruction and absolute poverty for millions and millions around the globe align with bringing the hope of Christ to nations who are ravaged? Is not already the fruit of our deeds being realized with the ever increasing debt of both our personal household and nation, as well as the catastrophes that have been decimating our nation?

You say that we are a moral society, then go for a walk through the South Side of Chicago. You say that we are a moral society than take a drive through inner Detroit on a Friday night. You say that we are a moral society than quit walking past your fellow man sitting on the sidewalk in pure poverty. You say that we are a moral society than quit defying your Creator, by walking contrary to Him. You say that we are a moral society, then ask those unfortunate ones of nations who will tell you otherwise. You say that we are a moral society, then if the lights went out in this country, you should have nothing to fear.

Yet understand this and understand this well. While it is not for man to know the future, and while we can simply state something as a scenario of an EMP attack from North Korea, understand that eventually a time will come when those who have refused to repent will be Left Behind. Those who refuse to repent and believe the Gospel, to accept Jesus Christ as their Savior, will be left destitute. Then even a scenario as is outlaid here, will not even be in comparison to what God's Word has outlaid in the Holy Scriptures, one that is certain to come to pass, for the Most High God has spoken it. Why or why should we take and defy our Creator and walk contrary to Him?

"I, Jehovah, have spoken it; it shall come to pass, and I will do it; I will not hold back, nor will I spare, nor will I have compassion; according to your ways and according to your deeds they will judge you, declares the Lord Jehovah." Ezekiel 24:14

Why as a nation should we call ourselves good, yet we have both hands on the plow to do evil? Why should we assume that our nation is under the blessing of Him, when we refuse to repent of our wickedness? Consider diligently, for the time is come, indeed it will come, as a thief in the night, and then what will you do o man? Who will you go to, who will you turn to for your aid? Turn now to your Creator *(Ez. 33:11)*, seek God while he may be found *(Is. 55:6)*. Comprehend His works *(Job 37:14)*, understand His free gift *(Jn. 3:16)* and repent and believe into Jesus Christ, that you might be Saved. I fear greatly for this country, not because of threats from abroad, not because of a potential economic crisis, but because our nation no longer fears God, our nation walks contrary to Him. What makes me fear most of all is that we call upon His name while our hearts are far from Him *(Is. 29:13)*. That should make you tremble. Then again, if it is as you say, that we are a moral nation who would never come under the Judgment of an Almighty God, for you say our deeds are righteous and we walk accordingly, then I suppose if the lights go out we shall see how moral and God fearing of a society we really are.

"Woe to those who draw iniquity with cords of vanity, and sin with cart ropes; who say, Let Him hurry and hasten His work, so that we may see it; and let the purpose of the Holy One of Israel draw near and come, so that we may know it! Woe to those who call evil good and good evil; who put darkness for light and light for darkness; who put bitter for sweet and sweet for bitter! Woe to those who are wise in their own eyes, and understanding in their own sight!" Isaiah 5:18-21

"Both hands are on evil, to do it well. Both the ruler and the judge ask for a bribe. And the great one speaks the lust of his soul; and they weave it together." Micah 7:3

"For you yourselves know perfectly that the day of the Lord so comes as a thief in the night." 1st Corinthians 5:2

"The prophets prophesy falsely, and the priests bear rule by their own power; and my people love to have it so, and what will you do in the end?" Jeremiah 5:31

"Truly, these times of ignorance God overlooked, but now commands all men everywhere to repent, because He has established a day on which He will judge the world in righteousness by the Man whom He has appointed. He has given assurance of this to everyone by raising Him from the dead." Acts 17:30-31

For those of you who can hear, seek God while He may be found. Put your faith in trust in Him, knowing that He certainly is able to deliver those who are His, in Christ, throughout whatever trials and tribulations might come upon the world.

"For the Lord Jehovah will help Me; therefore I have not been ashamed. Therefore I have set My face like flint, and I know that I shall not be ashamed. He is near who

justifies Me; who will contend with Me? Let us stand together; who is the master of My judgment? Let him come near Me. Behold, the Lord Jehovah will help Me; who is he who shall condemn Me? Lo, they all shall wear out like a garment; the moth shall eat them. Who among you fears Jehovah? Who obeys the voice of His Servant? Who walks in darkness and has no light? Let him trust in the name of Jehovah and rest on his God." Isaiah 50:7-10

Amen!

Where have all of the Preachers Gone?

"I say then, has God cast away His people? Let it not be! For I also am an Israelite, of the seed of Abraham, of the tribe of Benjamin. God has not cast away His people whom He foreknew. Or do you not know what the Scripture says of Elijah, how he pleads with God against Israel, saying, Lord, they have killed Your prophets and torn down Your altars, and I alone am left, and they seek my life. But what does the Divine response say to him? I have reserved to Myself seven thousand men who have not bowed the knee to Baal. Even so then, at this present time there is a remnant according to the election of grace." Romans 11:1-5

Certainly there are still preachers who are faithfully doing the work of the Lord throughout the world. Yet it wasn't that long ago that in America we had some preachers whom were used by God to proclaim His truth to many, many people across our once great land. Billy Sunday comes to mind immediately.

Less than a hundred years ago Billy Sunday was preaching to crowds from coast to coast. It is said that he preached to over a 100 million people directly during the ministry that God had given him to do. While he was one of the most outspoken opponents of alcohol, he also preached against playing cards, dance halls, theatres and immoral reading material. Billy Sunday did not shy away from telling the truth about God, proclaiming His truth regarding Creation, a literal devil, a literal Hell and also the Gospel, that Salvation is only through Jesus Christ. That was then, this is now.

Here we sit in this country approximately a hundred years from his the peak portion of his ministry, a time when major cities' newspapers would print his sermon in full on their front page. Many people heard his sermons and repented of their sins, believing into Jesus Christ as their Lord and Savior. Where are all the preachers who are faithfully preaching the Word? Why do we live in a time were such truth seems like fiction or nonsense to a world who is dying?

"For the message of the cross is foolishness to those who are perishing, but to us who are being saved it is the power of God." 1st Corinthians 1:18

Instead we have preachers who speak to masses of people through both their programs that other churches institute, as well as their well published books, to the destruction of many. We have entered a time of full blown apostasy, a sad portion of our history. The people do not want to hear the truth, they would rather turn off their ears and close their eyes and be told lies, believing in demonic doctrines.

"Now the Spirit expressly says that in latter times some will depart from the faith, being devoted to corrupting spirits and doctrines of demons, speaking lies in hypocrisy, having their own conscience seared..." 1st Timothy 4:1-2

"But know this, that in the last days perilous times will come: For men will be lovers of themselves, lovers of money, boasters, proud, blasphemers, disobedient to parents, unthankful, unholy, without natural affection, unyielding, slanderers, without self-control, savage, despisers of good, traitors, headstrong, haughty, lovers of pleasure rather than lovers of God, having a form of godliness but denying its power. And from such people turn away." 2nd Timothy 3:1-5

"But there were also false prophets among the people, even as there will be false teachers among you, who will secretly bring in destructive heresies, even denying the Lord who bought them, and bring on themselves swift destruction. And many will follow their destructive ways, through whom the way of truth will be blasphemed. By covetousness they will exploit you with well-turned words; whose judgment of old is not idle, and their destruction does not slumber." 2nd Peter 2:1-3

"Enter by the narrow gate; for wide is the gate and broad is the way that leads to destruction, and there are many entering in through it. Because narrow is the gate and distressing is the way which leads unto life, and there are few who find it. Beware of false prophets, who come to you in sheep's clothing, but inwardly they are ravenous wolves. You will know them from their fruits. Do men gather grapes from thornbushes or figs from thistles? Even so, every good tree produces excellent fruit, but a corrupt tree produces evil fruit. A good tree is not able to produce evil fruit, nor is a corrupt tree able to produce excellent fruit. Every tree that does not produce excellent fruit is cut down and thrown into the fire. Therefore from their fruits you will know them. Not everyone who says to Me, Lord, Lord, will enter the kingdom of Heaven, but he who does the will of My Father in Heaven. Many will say to Me in that day, Lord, Lord, have we not prophesied in Your name, cast out demons in Your name, and done many works of power in Your name? And then I will declare to them, I never knew you; depart from Me, you who work out lawlessness!" Matthew 7:13-23

This is serious business! We live in a society that would think it is foolishness to call playing poker sin. We live in a society that would find it ridiculous to tell them to burn their romance novels. We live in a society that would scoff at the notion of turning off the garbage they view on their television sets. Yet God has standards, His standards haven't changed *(Mal. 3:6)*, the Gospel message is still the same and these exact times that we live in have been prophesied beforehand, as well as what will come upon the world afterwards *(Jer. 30:7)*.

Rather then continuing on in the sins of this nation, as we now have crimes from coast to coast that are mind boggling, sodomite relationships ruled legal and a transgender movement that is growing in acceptance everyday, we need to get down on our knees, realizing the wickedness of our nation and repent to a holy and righteous God, the One to whom every individual will stand before!

"Therefore God also has highly exalted Him and given Him a name which is above every name, that at the name of Jesus every knee should bow, of those in Heaven, and of those on earth, and of those under the earth, and that every tongue should confess that Jesus Christ is Lord, to the glory of God the Father." Philippians 2:9-11

"And I saw a great white throne and Him who sat on it, from whose face the earth and the heavens fled away. And there was found no place for them. And I saw the dead, small and great, standing before God. And books were opened. And another book was opened, which is the Book of Life. And the dead were judged according to their works, out of the things which were written in the books. And the sea gave up the dead who were in it, and Death and Hades delivered up the dead who were in them. And they were judged, each one, according to their works. And Death and Hades were cast into the Lake of Fire. This is the second death. And anyone not found written in the Book of Life was cast into the Lake of Fire." Revelation 20:11-15

For those who truly know the Lord, do not forget the following:

"Yes, and all who desire to live godly in Christ Jesus will suffer persecution. But evil men and pretenders will grow worse and worse, leading astray and being led astray. But you continue in the things which you have learned and been assured of, knowing from whom you have learned them, and that from childhood you have known the Holy Scriptures, which are able to make you wise for salvation through faith which is in Christ Jesus." 2nd Timothy 3:12-15

"Heaven and earth will pass away, but My words will by no means pass away. But take heed to yourselves, lest your hearts be weighed down with giddiness, drunkenness, and cares of this life, and that Day come upon you unexpectedly. For it will come as a snare on all those who dwell on the face of the whole earth. Watch therefore, and pray always that you may be counted worthy to escape all these things that will come to pass, and to stand before the Son of Man." Luke 21:33-36

Amen!

Alarm Bells

"The burden against the Valley of Vision. What ails you now, that you have gone up to the housetops? The noisy city, the joyous city, is filled with turbulence. Your slain ones are not slain with the sword, nor dead in battle. All your rulers have fled together; they have been captured without the bow; all who are found in you have been captured together; they have fled from afar. Therefore I said, Look away from me; I will weep bitterly; do not insist on comforting me because of the devastation of the daughter of my people. For it is a day of trouble, and of trampling down, and of perplexity by Jehovah of Hosts in the Valley of Vision; of breaking down the walls, and of crying to the mountains. And Elam carried the quiver with chariots of men and horsemen, and Kir uncovered the shield. And it shall come to pass that your choicest valleys shall be full of chariots; and the horsemen shall surely be set in array at the gate. And he uncovered Judah's covering, and you looked in that day to the armor of the House of the Forest. You have also seen the breaks in the city of David, that they are many; and you gathered the waters of the lower pool. And you have counted the houses of Jerusalem, and you have broken down the houses to fortify the wall. You also made a reservoir between the two walls for the water of the old pool; but you have not looked to its Maker, nor had regard for Him who formed it long ago. And in that day Jehovah of Hosts called for weeping and mourning, and for baldness, and for girding with sackcloth. But behold, joy and gladness, slaying oxen and killing sheep, eating flesh and drinking wine, saying, Let us eat and drink, for tomorrow we die!" Isaiah 22:1-13

The other day I was sitting in a busy restaurant in Kalispell, Montana, with my family, awaiting the lunch we ordered to be brought to the table. Looking around, as people were busily chatting with others, the noise somewhat deafening, I was reminded of the sadness of just how godless of a society we have become. All around people were self consumed, oblivious to the reality of how our world is quickly being prepared for the *"time of Jacob's trouble" (Jer. 30:7)*, better known as the Tribulation.

Afterwards we went to Walmart where people were scurrying around, back and forth, slowly making their way to the long holiday lines, while seemingly unaware of the changes in the world around them. Our society, long having abandoned the Way of Life

(John 14:6), continuing on in their daily routines, on a path that is not good, one that has denied their Creator.

"God looked down from Heaven upon the children of mankind to see if any was circumspect, seeking God. Every one of them has turned back; they have all together become corrupt; not one is doing good, no, not even one." Psalms 53:2-3

If we were to compare the general acceptance of moral standards by our society, verses God's Word, we would see that we are far off of the mark. When we take a look at what goes on in this country (and indeed in the world) regarding our apostate churches, LGBT agendas, crime, covetousness, drunkenness, drug usage, wickedness and every other abominable thing that could be imagined, things that happen on a daily basis, to the point that no one even takes to heart the condition of the sins of this nation, then alarm bells should be going off.

Alarms are put in place in buildings all throughout the world. If your family happened to be sleeping and a fire alarm went off, it would provide a warning and a chance to escape the horrors of being consumed in a fire. Such alarms are in place in hospitals, schools and other businesses throughout the world, indeed in most places they are required to be.

In tornado alley, the constant siren of a tornado alarm gives people time to take shelter before the storm hits. In the costal states that deal with hurricanes, there are emergency messages displayed or played on air. In other cities around the world, such as Mexico City, there are alarms for earthquakes, one which recently went off and probably saved scores of lives. Many cities around the world have alarms for incoming missiles or other major catastrophes.

Certainly from time to time there are false alarms. There are instances were a fire alarm goes off and there is no fire. Other times an earthquake alarm could go off, but the earthquake is simply a minor tremor. Oftentimes a tornado alarm is given, but no tornado is ever seen or heard by those who react to it. Even hurricanes often dissipate in strength and cause minor damage in comparison to their original capability. Yet in each of these cases, when the alarm is not a false warning, those who listen and adheed to the alarm's warning are thankful, oftentimes the alarm has saved their lives and the lives of their family members.

Who goes and plans a vacation to Miami when a Category 5 hurricane warning is in effect? Who takes and tells the local school baseball team to begin the game when lightning is striking in the near distance? Who hears a fire alarm in the middle of the night and simply takes out the battery, going back to sleep? So then, who hears the Word of God read from the pulpit and ignores His warnings?! Would anyone hear an air raid siren and send their children out to play?

Do we not warn children to avoid a hot stove? Are not people crossing a street to check to make sure it is first safe to do so? Do we jump into a lake to swim without knowing how to swim or having a life preserver? Why then to we forsake God's Word, no longer believing what He has told us? What we need to have are alarm bells going off in every church, in every home across this once great nation, knowing that eventually time will run out!!

"The harvest is past, the summer is ended, and we are not saved." Jeremiah 8:20

The alarm should warn that eventually there will come a time when those who are not Saved will be Left Behind. Such an alarmingly message should be proclaimed from the mountaintops! From coast to coast, people should dust off their bibles that are somewhere in their homes and read the Word. Christians should be knocking on the doors of their neighbors, telling them about the Gospel. A call for repentance and believing into Jesus Christ, should be proclaimed boldly from every pulpit in this land! The seriousness of the situation could not even begin to be understated.

We have a land full of people and indeed around the world, of those who are in ignorance of the things of God. We have those who proclaim to believe in Him, yet they DO NOT believe what the Holy Scriptures say. Certainly God provided a solution to sin, through His Son Jesus, yet people ignore His Word wholeheartedly. In fact they do just the opposite of seeking Him, seeking the things of this world.

"For what profit is it to a man if he gains the whole world, and loses his own soul? Or what will a man give in exchange for his soul?" Matthew 16:26

But you, dear reader, understand that it should not be like this. We might watch as the mad throngs of people continue on the broad path that leads to destruction, but Jesus Christ paid the price for our sins *(1st Peter 3:18)* on the Cross *(Gal. 3:13)* and through Him we can have eternal life *(1st John 5:11-12)*, we can inherit Salvation *(Heb. 5:9)*, indeed we can be on the narrow and winding path which leads to life. So consider and consider carefully, do you want to continue on being part of the mad throngs or do you want to diligently seek God, while He may still be found.

"Enter by the narrow gate; for wide is the gate and broad is the way that leads to destruction, and there are many entering in through it. Because narrow is the gate and distressing is the way which leads unto life, and there are few who find it." Matthew 7:13-14

"Seek Jehovah while He may be found; call upon Him while He is near. Let the wicked forsake his way, and the unrighteous man his thoughts; and let him return to Jehovah, and He will have mercy on him; and to our God, for He will abundantly pardon. For My thoughts are not your thoughts, nor are your ways My ways, says Jehovah. For as the heavens are higher than the earth, so are My ways higher than your ways, and My thoughts than your thoughts." Isaiah 55:6-9

"For He says: In an acceptable time I have heard you, and in a day of salvation I have helped you. Behold, now is the accepted time; behold, now is the day of salvation." 2nd Corinthians 6:2

Remember…

"So the great dragon was cast out, that serpent of old, called the Devil and Satan, who leads the whole world astray; he was cast out onto the earth, and his angels were cast out with him." Revelation 12:9

"And the devil, who led them astray, was cast into the Lake of Fire and brimstone where the beast and the false prophet are. And they will be tormented day and night forever and ever. And I saw a great white throne and Him who sat on it, from whose face the earth and the heavens fled away. And there was found no place for them. And I saw the dead, small and great, standing before God. And books were opened. And another book was opened, which is the Book of Life. And the dead were judged according to their works, out of the things which were written in the books. And the sea gave up the dead who were in it, and Death and Hades delivered up the dead who were in them. And they were judged, each one, according to their works. And Death and Hades were cast into the Lake of Fire. This is the second death. And anyone not found written in the Book of Life was cast into the Lake of Fire." Revelation 20:10-15

Amen!

The Broad Path

"Therefore, whatever you want men to do to you, do also to them, for this is the Law and the Prophets. Enter by the narrow gate; for wide is the gate and broad is the way that leads to destruction, and there are many entering in through it. Because narrow is the gate and distressing is the way which leads unto life, and there are few who find it." Matthew 7:12-14

Everywhere people set goals for themselves. Many of those goals are focused on finances. There are goals to pay for college, goals to own transportation, goals to buy a house, goals to save for retirement. Lives are planned based upon certain interpretations of how to achieve these goals. Yet for many a goal of becoming rich is upon their hearts.

All around this nation financial bubbles are exploding in growth. The amount of student loan debt acquired by those who are studying for a career to obtain such goals has hit a record amount. Auto loans have exploded, reaching new highs in indebtedness of our American society. Home buying in many places has created bubbles of unsustainable pricing and debt that is piling up in a manner that is neither sustainable or realistic. The stock market is increasing often by three digit figures per day, far surpassing common sense and then there is Bitcoin.

Bitcoin and other cryptocurrencies are exploding in value as hand joins to hand across this once great nation, with those who are investing hoping for a landslide of profits to materialize in front of them. The false security in these bubbles has further seduced our society to take bigger risks than ever before. Credit card debt is skyrocketing as those who promise prosperity from the helms of society continue to preach their false doctrine of riches for all.

All over the goals of obtaining a piece of the American Dream, a slice of the pie continue to increase month after month. As the holiday shopping is in full swing, with each credit card swipe or click of a button, the insanity of living for today without worrying about tomorrow increases. Just who will hold the cards when it crashes and who will pay those bills when they are due?!

Constantly, as a wind blows, people are pointed in a direction that is not wise. Did society already forget about the housing bubble? Have people forgotten the lessons from the tech boom? Indeed their goals are set, they are actively trying to obtain them, but for most they are ill-focused, on the broad path that leads to destruction.

With the future in mind, the cars, the houses, the nice and elegant things to fill the home, the keeping up with the Joneses, planning for a sound retirement, focusing on their glamorous lives, just where is the planning for one's own soul? Where is the focus on their eternal destinations, rather than material items and wealth to achieve superficial goals?

"Come now, you rich, weep and howl for your calamities that are coming upon you. Your riches are corrupted, and your garments are moth-eaten. Your gold and silver are corroded, and their corrosion will be a witness against you and will eat your flesh like fire. You have heaped up treasure in the last days. Indeed the wages of the laborers who reaped your fields, which you kept back by fraud, cry out; and the cries of the reapers have reached the ears of the Lord of Hosts. You have lived on the earth in pleasure and luxury; you have fattened your hearts as in a day of slaughter. You have condemned, you have murdered the just; he does not resist you. Therefore be patient, brethren, until the coming of the Lord. See how the farmer waits for the precious fruit of the earth, waiting patiently for it until it receives the early and latter rain. You also be patient. Make your hearts firm, for the coming of the Lord draws near. Do not grumble against one another, brethren, that you not be condemned. Behold, the Judge stands at the door." Jacob (James) 5:1-9

"And to the angel of the church of the Laodiceans write, These things says the Amen, the Faithful and True Witness, the Beginning of the creation of God: I know your works, that you are neither cold nor hot. I would that you were cold or hot. So then, because you are lukewarm, and neither cold nor hot, I will vomit you out of My mouth. Because you say, I am rich, have become wealthy, and have need of nothing; and do not know that you are wretched and miserable and poor and blind and naked; I counsel you to buy from Me gold refined in the fire, that you may be rich; and white garments, that you may be clothed, that the shame of your nakedness may not be revealed; and anoint your eyes with eye salve, that you may see. As many as I love, I rebuke and chasten. Therefore be zealous and repent. Behold, I stand at the door and knock. If anyone hears My voice and opens the door, I will come in to him and dine with him, and he with Me. To him who overcomes I will grant to sit with Me on My throne, as I also overcame and sat down with My Father on His throne. He who has an ear, let him hear what the Spirit says to the churches." Revelation 3:14-22

All will stand before their Creator and quite simply if an individual has not repented and believed the Gospel their name is not written in the Book of Life. Only through faith in Jesus Christ can an individual be Saved.

"And I saw a great white throne and Him who sat on it, from whose face the earth and the heavens fled away. And there was found no place for them. And I saw the dead,

small and great, standing before God. And books were opened. And another book was opened, which is the Book of Life. And the dead were judged according to their works, out of the things which were written in the books. And the sea gave up the dead who were in it, and Death and Hades delivered up the dead who were in them. And they were judged, each one, according to their works. And Death and Hades were cast into the Lake of Fire. This is the second death. And anyone not found written in the Book of Life was cast into the Lake of Fire." Revelation 20:11-15

"Nor is there salvation in any other, for there is no other name under Heaven given among men that is required for us to be saved." Acts 4:12

"Truly, these times of ignorance God overlooked, but now commands all men everywhere to repent, because He has established a day on which He will judge the world in righteousness by the Man whom He has appointed. He has given assurance of this to everyone by raising Him from the dead." Acts 17:30-31

"Jesus said to him, I am the Way, the Truth, and the Life. No one comes to the Father except through Me." John 14:6

So why goals for what will only be obtainable for years?

"For we brought nothing into this world, and it is evident that we can carry nothing out." 1st Timothy 6:7

"For what will it profit a man if he gains the whole world, and loses his own soul? Or what will a man give in exchange for his soul?" Mark 8:36-37

Consider for a moment, if you will, your goals, your priorities. Why all of these goals, health care to try to take care of one's medical needs, money for a home and retirement, families, etc.; when there is no or little thought into the afterlife?

"And Death and Hades were cast into the Lake of Fire. This is the second death. And anyone not found written in the Book of Life was cast into the Lake of Fire." Revelation 20:14-15

What will you do when you stand before the Judge and you are cast into the Lake of Fire? Of what value will these goals, without Salvation, be to you? Of what good will it be if you were able to obtain the things of this world, but have nothing but empty pockets for the next? For without the eternal riches, of which are only found in Christ, you are poor, blind and naked.

"And you being dead in trespasses and sins, in which you formerly walked according to the course of this world, according to the ruler of the authority of the air, the spirit who now works in the sons of disobedience, among whom also we all formerly conducted ourselves in the lusts of our flesh, fulfilling the desires of the flesh and of the mind, and were by nature children of wrath, just as the others; but God, who is rich in mercy, because of His great love with which He loved us, even when we were dead in trespasses, made us alive together with Christ (by grace you are saved), and raised us up together, and made us sit together in the heavenlies in Christ Jesus, that in the ages to come He might display the exceeding riches of His grace in His kindness toward us in Christ Jesus. For by grace you are saved through faith; and that not of yourselves, it is the gift of God; not of works, that no one should boast. For we are His workmanship, created in Christ Jesus unto good works, which God prepared beforehand that we should walk in them. Therefore remember that you, being Gentiles in the flesh; who are called uncircumcision by what is called the circumcision made in the flesh by hands; that at that time you were without Christ, being aliens from the commonwealth of Israel and strangers from the covenants of promise, having no hope and without God in the world. But now in Christ Jesus you who once were far off have been made near by the blood of Christ. For He Himself is our peace, who has made both one, and has broken down the middle wall of separation, having abolished in His flesh the enmity, that is, the Law of commandments contained in ordinances, that He might create in Himself one new man from the two, thus making peace, and that He might reconcile them both to God in one body through the cross, thereby putting to death the enmity. And He came and preached peace to you who were afar off and to those who were near. For through Him we both have access by one Spirit to the Father. Now, therefore, you are no longer strangers and foreigners, but fellow citizens with the saints and members of the household of God, having been built on the foundation of the apostles and prophets, Jesus Christ Himself being the chief corner stone, in whom the whole building, being joined together, grows into a holy temple in the Lord, in whom you also are being built together into a dwelling place of God in the Spirit." Ephesians 2*

"But now the righteousness of God apart from the Law is revealed, being witnessed by the Law and the Prophets, even the righteousness of God, through the faith of Jesus Christ, to all and upon all who believe. For there is no difference; for all have sinned and fall short of the glory of God, being justified freely by His grace through the redemption that is in Christ Jesus, whom God set forth as a propitiation through faith in His blood, to give evidence of His righteousness, because in His forbearance God had passed over the sins that were previously committed, to prove at the present time His righteousness, that He might be just and the justifier of the one who is of the faith of Jesus." Romans 3:21-26

"Do you not know that to whom you present yourselves slaves to obey, you are that one's slaves whom you obey, whether of sin unto death, or of obedience unto righteousness? But God be thanked that though you were slaves of sin, yet you obeyed from the heart that form of doctrine which was delivered to you. And having been set free from sin, you became slaves to righteousness. I speak in human terms because of the weakness of your flesh. For just as you presented your members as slaves to uncleanness, and to iniquity unto iniquity, so now present your members as slaves to righteousness unto sanctification. For when you were slaves to sin, you were free in regard to righteousness. What fruit did you have then in the things of which you are now ashamed? For the end of those things is death. But now having been set free from sin, and having become slaves to God, you have your fruit unto sanctification, and the end,

eternal life. For the wages of sin is death, but the gift of God is eternal life in Christ Jesus our Lord." Romans 6:16-23

Is it wrong to want to obtain a car, a home and a sound retirement? No, but without Jesus Christ as your Savior, these goals are fruitless.

"There is a way which seems right to a man, but the end of it is the ways of death." Proverbs 14:12

"If then you are raised with Christ, seek those things which are above, where Christ is, sitting at the right hand of God. Set your mind on things above, not on the things of the earth; for you died, and your life is hidden with Christ in God. When Christ who is our life is revealed, then you also will be revealed with Him in glory." Colossians 3:1-4

The goal of any individual should be Salvation through faith in Jesus Christ as their Lord and Savior. There one may rest comfortably, one may be secure, knowing that their eternal destination is secure in Christ Jesus. Focusing on superficial things that will ultimately be parted with at death is a fruitless endeavor, one that many follow on the broad path that leads to destruction.

"Do not love the world or the things in the world. If anyone loves the world, the love of the Father is not in him. For all that is in the world; the lust of the flesh, the lust of the eyes, and the pride of life; is not of the Father but is of the world. And the world is passing away, and its lust; but he who does the will of God abides forever." 1st John 2:15-17

Amen!

Pounding the Pulpit

"If you refrain from delivering those being led away to death, those about to die; if you say, Behold, we did not know it; does not He who ponders the heart consider it? And the Keeper of your soul, does He not know it? And shall He not repay to a man according to his deeds?" Proverbs 24:11-12

Here we are in the end of 2017, a year that in my opinion that seemed to go by quite quickly. Yet, as the remainder of the year plays out and the next year begins, I realize just how horrible of times we really live in, as a nation, as a world. Why?

"The harvest is past, the summer is ended, and we are not saved." Jeremiah 8:20

We live in a time where bible prophecy has clearly been fulfilled. What else has to be fulfilled before Christ appears to take Home His bride, prior to the *"time of Jacob's trouble" (Jer. 30:7)*…nothing. That's right, nothing. Nothing else has to happen on the prophetic timeline.

We live in a time where people, so-called evangelical Christians, often from fully apostate churches are pleased to see Jerusalem recognized as the capital of Israel. While I am also happy that finally someone did what should have always been done, recognizing Jerusalem as the capital, the very thought that people are pushing so hard for Israel and peace, without realizing that the fulfillment of that very peace deal might as well be the beginning of the Tribulation.

While it is certainly possible that a peace treaty could be signed that is not the prophetic one that is signed by the Antichrist, it is also possible that it is. Most of these deals are done in secret, agreed upon prior to being publicly released. Is not a deal often complete upon an agreement, even before the ink is placed on the paper? I don't think that those who truly know Christ will witness such an event, I believe that the Rapture will have taken place.

"And he shall confirm a covenant with many for one week." Daniel 9:27a

"And then the lawless one will be unveiled, whom the Lord will consume with the breath of His mouth and destroy with the brightness of His coming." 2nd Thessalonians 2:8

We live in a time where preachers, true men called by God to preach His Word, should be pounding the pulpit, speaking His Truth. They should be pounding the pulpit, reminding those who are Saved to get busy in some regard of doing the Lord's work. They should be pounding the pulpit, warning those who are not saved, that time is running out!

Instead, what do we often see? Compromise and more compromise, apostasy full blown, blowing it's false doctrine at those who refuse to compromise, those who are truly separated and serving Jesus Christ, their Lord and Savior. We have preachers who preach a prosperity doctrine, a self doctrine, indeed doctrines of demons.

"Now the Spirit expressly says that in latter times some will depart from the faith, being devoted to corrupting spirits and doctrines of demons"... 1st Timothy 4:1

For those who are true Christians, for those who have truly repented and by faith believed into the Lord Jesus Christ as their Savior, are you watching and ready?

"Watch therefore, for you do not know what hour your Lord comes. But know this, that if the master of the house had known what hour the thief comes, he would have watched and not allowed his house to be dug through. Therefore you also be ready, for the Son of Man comes at an hour you do not expect." Matthew 24:42-44

Has the Lord laid upon your heart to speak to some individuals? Have you done so? Has the Lord given you something else to do? Have you done it? Have you told your neighbors, your family and your friends the Gospel? Do you continue to support your pastor and help with biblical ministry projects and missionary support that you Church is involved in? Certainly we all should consider the following verses:

"Therefore gird up the loins of your mind, be sober, and rest your hope fully upon the grace that is to be brought to you at the revelation of Jesus Christ; as obedient children, not conforming yourselves to the former lusts in your ignorance; but as He who called you is holy, you also become holy in all conduct, because it is written, Be holy, because I am holy." 1st Peter 1:13-16

"And you shall love the Lord your God with all your heart, with all your soul, with all your mind, and with all your strength. This is the first commandment. And the second, like it, is this: You shall love your neighbor as yourself. There is no other commandment greater than these." Mark 12:30-31

"Do you not know that those who run in a race all run, but one receives the prize? Run in such a way that you may obtain it." 1st Corinthians 9:24

Now for those who have been sitting on the fence, not having actually repented and believed into Jesus Christ, just how long can you wait? What will you do if the Trumpet sounds *(1st Cor. 15:52)* and you are Left Behind? What will you do if you die in your sins before you accept Jesus Christ as your Savior? What will you do when you stand before your Creator, not having been washed in the blood of Christ *(1st Cor. 6:11)*, not having your name written in the Book of Life *(Rev. 20:11-15)* and you are condemned for eternity to the Lake of Fire? This is serious stuff, certainly should not be taken lightly!

Whatever it is that seems to stand in your way, consider this and consider it carefully…

"For what will it profit a man if he gains the whole world, and loses his own soul? Or what will a man give in exchange for his soul?" Mark 8:36-37

Plus also consider this one thing, for those who have been sitting on the fence and assume to become Saved after the Rapture takes place:

"The coming of the lawless one is according to the working of Satan, with all power, signs, and lying wonders, and with all unrighteous deception among those who are perishing, because they did not receive the love of the truth, that they might be saved. And for this reason God will send them strong delusion, that they should believe the lie, that they all may be judged who did not believe the truth but had pleasure in unrighteousness." 2nd Thessalonians 2:9-12

Not a chance, if you fully knew the Gospel and denied accepting it.

"For this let everyone who is godly pray unto You, in a time when You may be found; surely in the floods of great waters they shall not come near him." Psalms 32:6

"Seek Jehovah while He may be found; call upon Him while He is near. Let the wicked forsake his way, and the unrighteous man his thoughts; and let him return to Jehovah, and He will have mercy on him; and to our God, for He will abundantly pardon." Isaiah 55:6-7

While the world looks towards Israel, mostly with disdain, understand this:

"Behold, I will make Jerusalem a cup of trembling to all the peoples all around, and it shall also be against Judah in the siege against Jerusalem." Zechariah 12:2

In all reality, if you, dear reader, are not Saved, then you should be trembling for your soul. Knowing that without Jesus Christ as your Savior, you are lost, doomed and without hope.

It does not have to be like that, you can certainly seek God, you can believe the Gospel, you can repent and by faith accept the free gift of Salvation. But will you, before it is too late?

"For He says: In an acceptable time I have heard you, and in a day of salvation I have helped you. Behold, now is the accepted time; behold, now is the day of salvation." 2nd Corinthians 6:2

Amen!

Slaves to Sin

"Jesus answered them, Truly, truly, I say to you, Everyone practicing sin is a slave of sin." John 8:34

The other day I stopped into a local restaurant to pick up some food. Around me were the emotionless faces of those also waiting, as well as the staff of the restaurant who had some heavy rock music blaring in the background. Business as usual as people were picking up their food, with blank stares. Looking around, knowing that most of the world's population are unsaved, the shackles of sin were apparent to those around me. I was standing amongst slaves, slaves to sin.

Was there anything remarkable about these customers and employees? Was there anything that made them worse than any other sinner, who is lost without Christ as their Savior? No, but at that moment as I was in there picking up dinner, the realization that there are so many lost, so many people who are slaves to sin, who desperately need Jesus as their Savior, hit my soul hard.

Having worked in the restaurant industry for many years, I can attest that much of the people whom I have worked with over the years have serious consequences from the sin that is in their lives. Yet, all mankind, irregardless of how many consequences they face from sin in their current states, have the most serious consequence awaiting them, should they not repent and by faith believe into Jesus Christ as their Lord and Savior.

Perhaps you are one of those who are reading this. Maybe you realize that you have so many issues, that sin has entrapped you, that you are being led astray by Satan and there are times in your life where you wish you could simply break free. For some the evidence is more apparent than others, but irregardless the result will be the same, eternity in the Lake of Fire.

"Some men's sins are clearly evident, preceding them to judgment, but those of some men follow later." 1st Timothy 5:24

How many times do many people seem to 'snap' out of it for a moment, pondering their ways? How many times does the drunkard wake up in the morning, regretting the night before, wishing it weren't so, but by evening again they are once again continuing on in their daily routine? How many times does the person who can't stop gambling away their money or pushing their debt higher, hope to simply hit it big and walk away from their sin? Is it that simple?

I once heard a story from a security guard at a casino that a woman had hit the jackpot on a slot machine. They had one slot machine in a high dollar slot room, this was a $100 or nothing. One hundred for each time the machine was played. The woman diligently played the machine and suddenly the lights went off, she had won the maximum prize, $100,000. Relieved, she took her earnings, yet her sin did not disappear. The very next day she was in the same casino and fed over $35,000 back into that same slot machine, trying to win again. Just as someone who might only drink excessively once in awhile, cannot yet (and hopefully never) contemplate the life of someone who is addicted to alcohol, others who only play a slot machine in passing would not understand those who were found dead in the parking lot or down by the lake, near this same casino. The thrills of potentially winning were outdone by the losses that were actually achieved, the sin that they committed became too great for them to handle and they sinned more, taking their own lives, sealing their eternal destination.

How many people who are trapped by Satan in their sins, drinking away their lives, have a significant event happen? They get into a bad car accident, abuse their spouse or children or some other serious injury occurs to someone or one of their pets. For a moment they ponder their ways, for a moment they try to break free from their sin, they try to end the enslavement to their vice, but alas, they return.

Do you ever ponder, perhaps this is your circumstance, dear reader, those who have apparent problems, those whom often are seen in the late hours of the night, whose sin has enslaved them so much, that the addiction to these terrible drugs that are so common on our streets, have someone who once had a bright future, scouring through trash cans, sleeping on sidewalks or benches, prostituting on the corner or their future hopes having been dashed to pieces as their children have been taken by the state, their home gone, their job gone and they, as often as they might try, are such a slave to sin that they seemingly have no hope and are unable to break free from the addiction of the drugs that they are on.

Do we look at them as less of a person. Do we call them trash and speak behind their back, telling others who might be in the car with us, 'did you see that person?' Or rather do we realize as we might drive to an affluent neighborhood (perhaps you live there), where there are nice cars parked outside of newer homes, as the inhabitants of those homes have no room to park their car in their garage, due to their excessive consumerism, that they too (perhaps you) are the same? That both will stand individually before their Creator, that they too will be judged. While their sins might not be as apparent as those unfortunate ones who have taken the bait of the fringes of society, likewise they will all call the Lake of Fire their eternal destination without repenting and believing the Gospel.

So what if you look at your life and realize that you are a slave to sin and you want to break free from it? Well first we must realize one thing, every man must realize this, that without repenting and by faith believing into Jesus Christ, whether your life seems to be glorious, or as most people you have some deep regrets in regards to sin in your life, both are equally lost, both will be cast into the Lake of Fire for eternity. Of course, God doesn't want it to be like that, He desires that you would become Saved, truly seek His Salvation and rather that you would become a servant of the Lord Jesus Christ, of where you would spend eternity with Him.

"Say to them: As I live, declares the Lord Jehovah, I take no delight in the death of the wicked, but that the wicked turn from his way and live." Ezekiel 33:11a

Over the years, working in the restaurant industry, I've had the opportunity to share the Gospel with many people and have found that oftentimes there are some main thoughts that people have regarding it that prevents them from being freed from their sins and brought to repentance and faith in Jesus Christ, receiving the free gift of Salvation. Perhaps you have some of these same arguments:

1.) I'm already a Christian, I believe in Jesus and was saved in such and such a church.

    a.) Did you just repeat a prayer, that a pastor had you repeat?

Unless you truly repented and by faith believed into Jesus Christ, then they were empty words. A sinner's prayer is not laid out in the Bible, but should come from the heart. Truly it is possible for one to be Saved through such a prayer, but it is truly a heart issue and most will be told by the pastor if they repeated those words they are now a Christian, most will find that there was no change, they are still lost in their sins. The sadness will occur when they stand before God Almighty at the Great White Throne and are cast into the Lake of Fire. Is this not the most horrific doctrine that is preached by false teachers, and sometimes those who are truly called by God?

"Examine yourselves as to whether you are in the faith. Test yourselves. Do you not know, yourselves, that Jesus Christ is in you; unless indeed you are ones failing the test?" 2nd Corinthians 13:5

    b.) You believe in Jesus and therefore it is a settled manner.

We must remember that repentance is necessary also. Repentance is not a work, but is a condition of the heart, one where the sinner realizes their guilt before our holy God and realizes that they are guilty and worthy of hellfire. They no longer want to do those things and are sorrowful, as such they realize there is nothing they can do, then the great gift of Salvation through Jesus Christ is realized, that He paid the price for our sins on the Cross.

"You believe that God is One. You do well. Even the demons believe, and shudder." Jacob (James) 2:19

"For Christ also suffered for sins once for all, the just for the unjust, that He might bring us to God, being put to death in the flesh but made alive by the Spirit"... 1st Peter 3:18

... *"who was delivered up because of our trespasses, and was raised for our justification."* Romans 4:25

"For He made Him who knew no sin to be sin for us, that we might become the righteousness of God in Him." 2nd Corinthians 5:21

2.) They simply don't believe the Gospel.

   a.) Many people simply refuse to believe. They tell you what they think, they often pick bits and pieces from other religions, including Christianity, adding in demonic doctrines of ideas that man have come up with regarding life after death, UFO's, evolution, etc. In essence they make up their own religion.

"If anyone among you thinks he is religious, and does not bridle his tongue but beguiles his own heart, this one's religion is vain. Pure and undefiled religion before God and the Father is this: to visit orphans and widows in their distress, and to keep oneself unspotted from the world." Jacob (James) 1:26-27

   b.) They don't believe in a literal Hell. They don't believe God would send them there. Yet often these same people, when they have a loved family member or friend who dies will say such things as 'they are in heaven now' or 'they are looking down on me', yet they want to accredit such things to a life that they assume is now sealed in some sort of eternal goodness apart from God? How is it that the same Bible that tells us about Heaven, also warns more about Hell and people choose to believe the one and not the other?

"And these will go away into everlasting punishment, but the righteous into eternal life." Matthew 25:46

"For when you were slaves to sin, you were free in regard to righteousness. What fruit did you have then in the things of which you are now ashamed? For the end of those things is death. But now having been set free from sin, and having become slaves to God, you have your fruit unto sanctification, and the end, eternal life. For the wages of sin is death, but the gift of God is eternal life in Christ Jesus our Lord." Romans 6:20-23

"There was a certain rich man who was clothed in purple and fine linen and fared sumptuously every day. And there was a certain beggar named Lazarus, full of sores, who was laid at his gate, desiring to be fed with the crumbs which fell from the rich man's table. Moreover the dogs came and licked his sores. So it happened that the beggar died, and was carried by the angels into Abraham's bosom. The rich man also

died and was buried. And being in torments in Hades, he lifted up his eyes and saw Abraham afar off, and Lazarus in his bosom. Then he cried and said, Father Abraham, have mercy on me, and send Lazarus that he may dip the tip of his finger in water and cool my tongue; for I am tormented in this flame. But Abraham said, Son, remember that in your lifetime you received your good things, and likewise Lazarus evil things; but now he is comforted and you are tormented. And besides all this, between us and you there is a great chasm fixed, so that those who want to pass from here to you are not able, nor can those from there pass to us. Then he said, I beg you therefore, father, that you would send him to my father's house, for I have five brothers, that he may testify to them, that they not also come to this place of torment. Abraham said to him, They have Moses and the Prophets; let them hear them. And he said, No, father Abraham; but if one goes to them from the dead, they will repent. But he said to him, If they do not hear Moses and the Prophets, neither will they be persuaded though one should rise from the dead." Luke 16:19-31

3.) They don't think that they can be saved because of their enslavement to sin.

    a.) This is another very common theme amongst people. They might assume that they need to break free from sin, whether drinking, drugs, homosexuality, lies, etc. They don't think they can be give it up, whatever it may be. They don't realize that Salvation is a supernatural work of God and He is able to break free their bonds to sin and they are able to rest securely in Jesus Christ. What they must do is repent of these things and put their trust in God.

"For by grace you are saved through faith; and that not of yourselves, it is the gift of God; not of works, that no one should boast." Ephesians 2:8-9

"being confident of this very thing, that He who has begun a good work in you will complete it unto the day of Jesus Christ"... Philippians 1:6

"For godly sorrow produces repentance leading to salvation, not to be regretted; but the sorrow of the world produces death." 2nd Corinthians 7:10

    b.) There are also those who want to try and get all of these things worked out on their own and come before God afterwards. They assume that they will clean up their lives of their sins and then seek God. Rather they are deceived by Satan and don't realize that if they could rectify themselves on their own, what need would it have been for Jesus Christ to lay down His life so that we might be Saved? Why did Jesus die on the Cross for your sins?

"I am the Good Shepherd; and I know My sheep, and am known by My own. As the Father knows Me, even so I know the Father; and I lay down My life for the sheep. And other sheep I have which are not of this fold; them also I must lead, and they will hear My voice; and there will be one flock and one Shepherd. Therefore My Father loves Me, because I lay down My life that I may take it again. No one takes it from Me, but I lay it

down of Myself. I have authority to lay it down, and I have authority to take it again. This precept I have received from My Father." John 10:14-18

c.) Another category are those who seemingly agree with the Gospel, yet they need to get things 'worked out' in their life first. Whether it is a family relationship issue, a job problem or even time management, the excuses are never-ending. Yet how many seem to ever get there? Would not Satan like to continue to procrastinate problem after problem to ensure that the soul who believes in such lies, instead of the great works of God, would be sealed to eternal doom in the Lake of Fire? They don't see clearly or don't believe that God can resolve each of those situations that they think need to be resolved beforehand. They don't believe in the power of their Creator to break free their bonds and set them on the narrow and winding path *(Matt. 7:13-14)*.

"Therefore, if anyone is in Christ, he is a new creation; the old things have passed away; behold, all things have become new." 2nd Corinthians 5:17

4.) They refuse to repent, they would rather have their sin than Jesus.

a.) There are more in this group than one can imagine and it would seem that often some of the others in the fore mentioned categories of people I often had spoken to also fall into this category. While they do not like the consequences of their sin that they have to deal with in this life, they refuse to get rid of the sin. They have made their choice and unless they repent, they have chosen their path, indeed in sin they will die and they will be judged accordingly.

Jesus said, *"I tell you, no; but unless you repent you will all likewise perish." Luke 13:3*

"Truly, these times of ignorance God overlooked, but now commands all men everywhere to repent, because He has established a day on which He will judge the world in righteousness by the Man whom He has appointed. He has given assurance of this to everyone by raising Him from the dead." Acts 17:30-31

"And I saw a great white throne and Him who sat on it, from whose face the earth and the heavens fled away. And there was found no place for them. And I saw the dead, small and great, standing before God. And books were opened. And another book was opened, which is the Book of Life. And the dead were judged according to their works, out of the things which were written in the books. And the sea gave up the dead who were in it, and Death and Hades delivered up the dead who were in them. And they were judged, each one, according to their works. And Death and Hades were cast into the Lake of Fire. This is the second death. And anyone not found written in the Book of Life was cast into the Lake of Fire." Revelation 20:11-15

Now these lists are not comprehensive or exclusive, certainly sin is sin. Whether it is a hardcore meth addict or the nice old lady who bakes goods for those poor children at the orphanage, without repenting and believing into Jesus Christ as their Lord and Savior, both are equally lost. Both will be cast into the Lake of Fire, both will regret their decision regarding refusing to believe the Gospel when they stand before their Judge.

Understand, dear reader, if you are reading this, if you are seeking after God, if you are looking into Salvation, it is very simple. Understand that this life of sin can be broken immediately, that you might accept Jesus Christ as your Savior and from that VERY MOMENT that you do so, you will be changed.

"Seek Jehovah while He may be found; call upon Him while He is near. Let the wicked forsake his way, and the unrighteous man his thoughts; and let him return to Jehovah, and He will have mercy on him; and to our God, for He will abundantly pardon." Isaiah 55:6-7

"For He says: In an acceptable time I have heard you, and in a day of salvation I have helped you. Behold, now is the accepted time; behold, now is the day of salvation." 2nd Corinthians 6:2

Things will brighten, the joy of the Lord will enter your heart. There is hope, no matter how destitute of a situation or how great of circumstances you find yourself in. Don't put it off until it is too late. If you want to break free from being a slave to sin, the choice is very simple, repent and believe the Gospel and you will be free.

"And you shall know the truth, and the truth shall set you free." John 8:32

"Jesus said to him, I am the Way, the Truth, and the Life. No one comes to the Father except through Me." John 14:6

"For God so loved the world that He gave His only begotten Son, that everyone believing into Him should not perish but have eternal life. For God did not send His Son into the world to judge the world, but that the world through Him might be saved. The one believing into Him is not judged; but the one not believing is judged already, because he has not believed in the name of the only begotten Son of God. And this is the judgment, that the Light has come into the world, and men loved darkness rather than the Light, for their deeds were evil. For everyone practicing evil hates the Light and does not come to the Light, lest his deeds should be reproved. But the one doing the truth comes to the Light, that his deeds may be clearly seen, that they have been worked in God." John 3:16-21

"And he brought them out and said, Sirs, what must I do to be saved? So they said, Believe on the Lord Jesus Christ, and you will be saved, you and your household." Acts 16:30-31

"Then Peter said to them, Repent, and let every one of you be immersed in the name of Jesus Christ to the remission of sins; and you shall receive the gift of the Holy Spirit." Acts 2:38

"Nor is there salvation in any other, for there is no other name under Heaven given among men that is required for us to be saved." Acts 4:12

Amen!

To the Oppressed of the World

"For the oppression of the poor, for the sighing of the needy, I will now arise, says Jehovah; I will set him in the safety for which he pants." Psalms 12:5

All over the world there are those who are oppressed. How often does man's system of oppression, through various means, affect a large amount of people through greed and a desire of control? How often are people struggling throughout their entire lives, just trying to make a life for themselves and their family?

While those who reside in the United States have such plights, those numbers are nothing in comparison with those throughout the world, those who are the oppressed of the world. Literally what was God's original intention has become rotten through the consequences of sin entering the world. The curse has made things to where they are today.

Let's just be frank about the state of our societies of the world. Quite often the focus has recently been on the ridiculous amount of increase in bubbles, as well as debt throughout the world. The focus is often on those who are in the midst of this system, putting their treasures of the world *(Matthew 6:19-21)*, before seeking God Almighty, their Creator, of whom they will give an account to *(1st Peter 4:5)*. Yet there is a world, one of which I have seen with my own eyes, that is outside of the scope of those same people who literally live for the moment and blow with every wind of doctrine that comes their way or joining in movements or trendy events as they come. This is written not towards those, but this is written to the oppressed of this world.

To you, you know who you are, if you will just give me a moment of your time, if you would just bear with this article and contemplate the solution, I will lay it out in simple terms.

Whether you are Chinese and you are struggling in your ever changing economical conditions, feeling as a slave against an industry that is bent on pricing manufactured goods so low that many are left enslaved, unrecognized as part of the system of oppression by those who purchase the end products. Whether or not you live in a place like Venezuela, where a struggle for economic independence, amongst other things, has led to harsh and impoverished conditions of a former bright future. Whether or not you are in an Islamic country that prohibits your seeking faith in the Lord, threatening to punish you for doing as you should. Whether or not you are in Africa, watching as upheavals constantly bring about regime changes, already living in oppressive conditions. Understand that there is a solution.

First and foremost one must realize that there is a God. Not only is there a God, but there is only one God. Even if your culture, which often does, mandates a certain religion or you are stuck in the midst of a culture of which you have religion, but you know that you don't have a personal relationship with God. You might follow the motions of your traditions, you might do what is required of you, but you still feel an emptiness about it, not knowing what to do or where to find out information. Then again, perhaps you live in a far away place, simply having never heard about God or about His Son Jesus Christ.

"For even if there are so-called gods, whether in the heavens or on earth (as there are many gods and many lords), yet for us there is one God, the Father, of whom are all things, and we for Him; and one Lord Jesus Christ, through whom are all things, and we through Him." 1st Corinthians 8:5-6

"To whom will you compare Me, and make Me equal; and compare Me, that we may be alike? They pour gold out of the bag, and weigh silver out on the measuring rod, and hire a goldsmith; and he makes it into a god; they prostrate themselves, yea, they bow down. They carry it on the shoulder, they carry it and set it in its place, and it stands; it shall not move from its place. Yes, one shall cry unto it, yet it cannot answer, nor save him out of his trouble. Remember this, and be a man; refresh the memory of your heart, you who rebel. Remember the former things from a long time ago; for I am the Mighty God, and there is no other; I am God, and no one else is like Me, declaring the end from the beginning, and from antiquity things which are not yet done, saying, My counsel shall stand, and I will do all My pleasure; calling a bird of prey from the east, the man who executes my counsel from a distant land. Indeed, I have spoken it; I will also bring it to pass. I have formed it; I will also do it." Isaiah 46:5-11

"The fool has said in his heart, There is no God. They are corrupt, and have done abominable iniquity; there is no one who does good." Psalms 53:1

Aside from what naysayers, particularly in western culture, may say about the origins of the earth, understand that the Holy Scriptures, or the Bible, teaches us exactly what happened and how it happened. We know for sure the origins of our world and when we look into the mirror, we also know the origins of our own selves. We were Created.

"In the beginning God created the heavens and the earth. And the earth was without form, and void, with darkness on the face of the deep; and the Spirit of God was hovering over the face of the waters. Then God said, Let there be light! And there was light. And God saw the light, that it was good; and God divided between the light and darkness. God called the light, Day; and the darkness He called, Night. Thus, the evening and the morning: Day One. Then God said, Let there be a firmament in the midst of the waters, separating the waters from the waters. And God made the firmament, and separated the waters which were under the firmament from the waters which were above the firmament: thus. And God called the firmament, Heavens. Thus, the evening and the morning: Day Two. Then God said, Let the waters under the heavens be gathered together into one place, and let the dry land appear: thus. And God called the dry land, Earth; and the gathering together of the waters He called, Seas. And God saw that it was good. And God said, Let the earth sprout vegetation, plants yielding seed, and the fruit tree producing fruit according to its kind, whose seed is in itself, on the earth: thus. And the earth brought forth vegetation, plants yielding seed according to its kind, and the tree producing fruit, whose seed is in itself according to its kind. And God saw that it was good. Thus, the evening and the morning: Day Three. Then God said, Let there be luminaries in the firmament of the heavens, to distinguish the day from the night; and let them be for signs and seasons, and for days and years; and let them be for luminaries in the firmament of the heavens to give light upon the earth: thus. And God made two great luminaries: the greater luminary to rule the day, and the lesser luminary to rule the night, and also the stars. And God set them in the firmament of the heavens to shine upon the earth, and to rule over the day and over the night, and to separate the light from the darkness. And God saw that it was good. Thus, the evening and the morning: Day Four. Then God said, Let the waters swarm with swarming living creatures, and let flying creatures fly to and fro above the earth across the face of the firmament of the heavens. So God created great sea monsters and every living creature that moves, that swarmed in the waters according to their kind, and every winged flying creature according to its kind. And God saw that it was good. And God blessed them, saying, Be fruitful and multiply, and fill the waters in the seas, and let the flying creatures multiply on the earth. Thus, the evening and the morning: Day Five. Then God said, Let the earth bring forth the living creature according to its kind: beasts, creeping things and living things of the earth, each according to its kind: thus. And God made the living things of the earth according to its kind, beasts according to its kind, and everything that creeps on the earth according to its kind. And God saw that it was good. Then God said, Let Us make man in Our image, according to Our likeness; let them have dominion over the fish of the sea, over the flying creatures of the heavens, and over the beasts, over all the earth and over every creeping thing that moves on the earth. So God created man in His own image; in the image of God He created him; male and female He created them. And God blessed them, and God said to them, Be fruitful and multiply; fill the earth and subdue it; have dominion over the fish of the sea, over the flying creatures of the heavens, and over every living thing that moves on the earth. And God said, Behold, I have given you every plant that yields seed which is on the face of all the earth, and every tree whose fruit yields seed; to you it shall be for food. Also, to every living thing of the earth, to every flying creature of the heavens, and to everything that moves on the earth, living creatures, I have given the green plants for food: thus. And God saw everything that He had made, and indeed it was extremely good. Thus, the evening and the morning: Day Six.

Genesis 2

Thus the heavens and the earth, and all the host of them, were finished. And on the seventh day God completed His work which He had made, and He rested on the seventh day from all His work which He had made. And God blessed the seventh day and consecrated it, because in it He rested from all His work which God had created and made. These are the generations of the heavens and the earth when they were created, in the day that Jehovah God was making the earth and the heavens, before any shrub of the field was on the earth and before any green plant of the field had sprouted; for Jehovah God had not caused it to rain on the earth, and there was no man to till the ground; but a mist went up from the earth and watered the whole face of the ground. And Jehovah God formed man of the dust of the ground, and breathed into his nostrils the breath of life; and man became a living soul. And Jehovah God planted a garden eastward in Eden, and there He put the man whom He had formed. And out of the ground Jehovah God made to sprout every tree that is pleasant to the sight and good for food. The Tree of Life was also in the midst of the garden, and also the tree of the knowledge of good and evil. And a river went out of Eden to water the garden, and from there it divided and became four heads. The name of the first is Pishon; it is the one which circles around all the land of Havilah, where there is gold; and the gold of that land is good. Bdellium and the onyx stone are there. The name of the second river is Gihon; it is the one which circles around all the land of Cush. The name of the third river is Tigris; it is the one going toward the east of Assyria. The fourth river is Euphrates. Then Jehovah God took the man and put him in the garden of Eden to work it and keep it. And Jehovah God commanded the man, saying, Of every tree of the garden you may eat to feed; but of the tree of the knowledge of good and evil you shall not eat, for in the day that you eat of it you shall die the death. And Jehovah God said, It is not good for the man to be alone; I will make him a helper to complement him. Out of the ground Jehovah God formed every living thing of the field and every flying creature of the heavens, and brought them to the man to see what he would call them. And whatever the man called each living creature, that was its name. So the man gave names to all the animals, to the flying creatures of the heavens, and to every living thing of the field. But for the man there was not found a helper to complement him. And Jehovah God caused a deep sleep to fall on Adam, and he slept; and He took one of his ribs, and closed up the flesh in its place. And the rib which Jehovah God had taken out of the man He rebuilt into a woman, and He brought her to the man. And the man said: This now at last is bone from my bones and flesh from my flesh; she shall be called Woman, because she was taken out of man. Therefore a man, leaving his father and mother, and having cleaved to his wife, they are one flesh. And they were both naked, the man and his wife, and were not ashamed."
Genesis 1 & 2

"For the wrath of God is revealed from Heaven against all ungodliness and unrighteousness of men, who suppress the truth in unrighteousness, because what may be known of God is clearly recognized by them, for God has revealed it to them. For ever since the creation of the world the unseen things of Him are clearly perceived, being understood by the things that are made, even His eternal power and Godhead, so that they are without excuse, because, although they know God, they do not glorify Him as God, nor are thankful, but become vain in their reasonings, and their stupid hearts are darkened. Professing to be wise, they become foolish, and change the glory of the incorruptible God into an image made like corruptible man, and birds and four-footed animals and creeping things. Therefore God also gives them up to uncleanness, in the lusts of their hearts, to dishonor their bodies among themselves, who change the truth of God into the lie, and fear and serve the created things more than the Creator, who is blessed forever. Amen. For this reason God gives them up to vile passions. For even their women change the natural use for what is contrary to nature. Likewise also the men, abandoning the natural use of the woman, burned in their lust toward one another, men with men performing what is shameful, and receiving the retribution within themselves, the penalty which is fitting for their error. And even as they do not like to have God in their full true knowledge, God gives them over to a reprobate mind, to do those things which are not fitting; being filled with every unrighteousness, sexual perversion, wickedness, covetousness, maliciousness; full of envy, murder, strife, deceit, depravity; whisperers, defamers, haters of God, insolent, proud, boasters, inventors of evil things, disobedient to parents, without understanding, untrustworthy, without natural affection, unforgiving, unmerciful; who, knowing the righteous judgment of God, that those who practice such things are deserving of death, not only do them, but also approve of those who practice them." Romans 1:18-32

"Truly I know it is so; but how can a man be just before the Mighty God? If one wished to contend with Him, he could not answer Him one time out of a thousand. He is wise in heart and mighty in strength. Who has hardened himself against Him and been at peace? He removes the mountains, and they do not know when He overturns them in His anger; He shakes the earth out of its place, and its pillars tremble; He commands the sun, and it does not rise; He seals up the stars; He alone spreads out the heavens, and treads upon the waves of the sea; He made the Ursa Major, Orion, and the Pleiades, and the chambers of the south; He does great things past finding out, yea, wonders without number." Job 9:2-10

"The heavens declare the glory of the Mighty God; and the firmament proclaims His handiwork." Psalms 19:1

"Woe to him who strives with the One who formed him, a potsherd among the potsherds of the earth! Shall the clay say to the one who forms it, What are you making? Or your work, He has no hands?" Isaiah 45:9

So I want you to consider and consider well for a moment, there is a God. This same God created you. Here you are in the midst of oppression, in whatever respective country it is that you live in, and you must realize that this same God has provided a choice regarding your eternal destination, this same God also cares about those who are His and watches over them.

"Behold, all souls are Mine; the soul of the father as well as the soul of the son is Mine; the soul who sins shall die. But if a man is righteous and does what is just and right; if he has not eaten on the mountains, nor lifted up his eyes to the idols of the house of Israel, nor defiled his neighbor's wife, nor approached a menstruating woman; if he has not oppressed anyone, but has restored to the debtor his pledge; has plundered no one by robbery, but has given his bread to the hungry and covered the naked with clothing; if he has not given with usury nor taken any increase, but has withdrawn his hand from iniquity and executed true judgment between man and man; if he has walked in My statutes and kept My judgments faithfully; he is righteous. He shall live life, says the Lord Jehovah. If he begets a son who is a robber or who sheds blood, who does any of these things, and does none of those duties, but has eaten on the mountains or defiled his neighbor's wife; if he has oppressed the poor and needy, plundered by robbery, not restored the pledge, has lifted his eyes to the idols, or committed abomination; if he has exacted usury or taken increase; shall he then live? He shall not live! If he has done any of these abominations, he shall die the death; his blood shall be upon him. If, however, he begets a son who sees all the sins which his father has done, and considers but does not do likewise; who has not eaten on the mountains, nor lifted his eyes to the idols of the house of Israel, nor defiled his neighbor's wife; has not oppressed anyone, nor withheld a pledge, nor plundered by robbery, but has given his bread to the hungry and covered the naked with clothing; who has withdrawn his hand from the poor and not received usury or increase, but has executed My judgments and walked in My statutes; he shall not die for the iniquity of his father; he shall live life! As for his father, because he cruelly oppressed, plundered his brother by robbery, and did what is not good among his people, behold, he shall die in his iniquity. Yet you say, Why? Does not the son bear the guilt of the father? When the son has done what is lawful and right, and has kept all My statutes and done them, he shall live life. The soul who sins shall die. The son shall not bear the guilt of the father, nor the father bear the guilt of the son. The righteousness of the righteous shall be upon himself, and the wickedness of the wicked shall be upon himself. But if a wicked man turns from all his sins which he has done, keeps all My statutes, and does what is lawful and right, he shall live life; he shall not die. None of the transgressions which he has done shall be remembered against him; because of the righteousness which he has done, he shall live. Do I delight with pleasure in the death of the wicked? says the Lord Jehovah, and not that he should turn back from his ways and live? But when a righteous man turns away from his righteousness and commits iniquity, and does according to all the abominations that the wicked man does, shall he live? All the righteousness which he has done shall not be remembered; because of the treachery of his unfaithfulness, and the sin which he has sinned, in them he shall die. Yet you say, The way of the Lord is not fair. Hear now, O house of Israel, is it not My way which is fair, and your ways which are not fair. When a righteous man turns away from his righteousness, commits iniquity, and dies in it, it is for the iniquity which he has done that he dies. Again, when a wicked man turns away from the wickedness which he has done, and does what is lawful and right, he preserves himself alive. Because he considers and turns away from all the transgressions which he has done, he shall live life; he shall not die." Ezekiel 18:4-28

What are you dealing with?

If one considers and ponders why things are the way they are, irregardless of what you might be facing, you know that it is wrong. It is wrong to have to work endlessly for an enslavement pay. It is wrong to have to be under a regime that oppresses people. It is wrong to be stuck in a situation where you can not provide for your family. Why is it wrong? Is not those who enslave people, often through the direct or indirect influence of a giant corporation or those who oppress people through various means, doing wrong because it simple seems wrong? This feeling of wrong is the conscience that God placed in every man *(Rom. 2:15)*, it is sin, it is what separates you from God Almighty.

Even in poor countries, a man might justify stealing a loaf of bread to eat, but when he is punished, he is guilty, because it is wrong. Likewise, is not the system of oppression that will not provide an opportunity to him who thinks to justify the wrong, by taking the loaf of bread, also wrong? Why not have a method where a man could earn the money or keep the labor of his own hard work? So to the oppressed of the world, you are oppressed because of sin, sin and the evil that comes with it, is the unseen mechanism that fosters such oppression.

There is a problem for them though, one that you must consider. God, the one and only God, also sees. He knows what is going on and He will repay.

"And He shall judge the world in righteousness; He shall execute judgment to the people with equity. Jehovah also will be a refuge for the oppressed, a refuge in times of distress." Psalms 9:8-9

"He who oppresses the poor reproaches his Maker, but he who honors Him has mercy upon the needy." Proverbs 14:31

"He shall execute justice for the lowly of the people; He shall save the children of the needy, and shall crush in pieces the oppressor." Psalms 72:4

"Listen, my beloved brethren: Has God not chosen the poor of this world to be rich in faith and heirs of the kingdom which He promised to those who love Him? But you have dishonored the poor. Do not the rich oppress you and drag you to the judgment seats?" Jacob (James) 2:5-6

However, a problem also exists and that is that you, dear reader, also will have to stand before God Almighty. God is holy, righteous, but He is also merciful and kind to those who will seek Him.

"And I saw a great white throne and Him who sat on it, from whose face the earth and the heavens fled away. And there was found no place for them. And I saw the dead, small and great, standing before God. And books were opened. And another book was opened, which is the Book of Life. And the dead were judged according to their works, out of the things which were written in the books. And the sea gave up the dead who were in it, and Death and Hades delivered up the dead who were in them. And they were

judged, each one, according to their works. And Death and Hades were cast into the Lake of Fire. This is the second death. And anyone not found written in the Book of Life was cast into the Lake of Fire." Revelation 20:11-15

"For thus says the high and lofty One who inhabits eternity, whose name is Holy: I dwell in the high and consecrated place, even with the contrite and humble spirit, to revive the spirit of the humble, and to revive the heart of the contrite ones." Isaiah 57:15

"For You, Lord, are good, and ready to forgive, and abounding in mercy unto all those who call upon You." Psalms 86:5

Sin, the curse that began in the Garden of Eden, is still ongoing. What happened there?

"Now the serpent was more cunning than any living thing of the field which Jehovah God had made. And he said to the woman, Has God indeed said, You shall not eat of every tree of the garden? And the woman said to the serpent, We may eat the fruit of the trees of the garden; but of the fruit of the tree which is in the midst of the garden, God has said, You shall not eat it, nor shall you touch it, lest you die. And the serpent said to the woman, You shall not die the death. For God knows that in the day you eat of it your eyes will be opened, and you will be as God, knowing good and evil. So when the woman saw that the tree was good for food, that it was pleasant to the eyes, and a tree to be desired to make one wise, she took of its fruit and ate. She also gave to her husband with her, and he ate. And the eyes of both of them were opened, and they knew that they were naked; and they sewed fig leaves together and made themselves loin coverings. And they heard the sound of Jehovah God walking around in the garden in the cool of the day, and the man and his wife hid themselves from the presence of Jehovah God among the trees of the garden. And Jehovah God called to the man and said to him, Where are you? And he said, I heard the sound of You in the garden, and I was afraid because I was naked; and I hid myself. And He said, Who told you that you were naked? Have you eaten from the tree of which I commanded you not to eat? And the man said, The woman whom You gave to be with me, she has given to me of the tree, and I ate. And Jehovah God said to the woman, What is this you have done? And the woman said, The serpent deceived me, and I ate. So Jehovah God said to the serpent: Because you have done this, you are cursed more than all beasts, and more than every living thing of the field; on your belly you shall go, and you shall eat dust all the days of your life. And I will put enmity between you and the woman, and between your seed and her Seed; He shall bruise your head, and you shall bruise His heel. To the woman He said: I will greatly multiply your sorrow and your conception; in pain you shall bring forth children; your desire shall be for your husband, and he shall rule over you. And to Adam He said, Because you have heeded the voice of your wife, and have eaten from the tree of which I commanded you, saying, You shall not eat of it: Cursed is the ground for your sake; in toil you shall eat of it all the days of your life. Both thorns and thistles it shall bring forth for you, and you shall eat the plants of the field. In the sweat of your face you shall eat bread till you return to the ground, for out of it you have been taken; for dust you are, and to dust you shall return. And the man called his wife's name Eve, because she was the mother of all living. Also for the man and his wife Jehovah God made tunics of skins, and clothed

them. And Jehovah God said, Behold, the man has become as one of Us, to know good and evil. And now, that he not put forth his hand and take also of the Tree of Life, and eat, and live forever; therefore Jehovah God sent him out of the garden of Eden to till the ground from which he was taken. So He drove out the man; and He placed cherubim at the east of the Garden of Eden, and a flaming sword turning this way and that, to guard the way to the Tree of Life." Genesis 3*

Likewise, even as your oppressors are doing wrong, truly you also are dead in your sins. Your sins separate you from God Almighty, One who wishes that you would not perish, but that you would have eternal life through Jesus Christ, His Son. First, let's speak about the seriousness of sin.

"for all have sinned and fall short of the glory of God"... Romans 3:23

"For the wages of sin is death, but the gift of God is eternal life in Christ Jesus our Lord" Romans 6:23

"Do not be led astray, God is not mocked; for whatever a man sows, that he will also reap. For he who sows to his flesh will of the flesh reap corruption, but he who sows to the Spirit will of the Spirit reap eternal life." Galatians 6:7-8

"Behold, Jehovah's hand is not shortened, that it cannot save; nor is His ear heavy, that it cannot hear. But your iniquities have separated between you and your God, and your sins have hidden His face from you, that He will not hear. For your hands are defiled with blood, and your fingers with iniquity; your lips have spoken lies, your tongue has uttered perverseness. No one calls for justice, nor does anyone plead for truth; they trust in vanity and speak lies. They conceive mischief and bring forth iniquity. They hatch vipers' eggs and weave the spider's web; he who eats their eggs dies, and that which is crushed breaks out into a viper. Their webs shall not become garments, nor shall they cover themselves with their works; their works are works of iniquity, and the act of violence is in their hands. Their feet run to evil, and they make haste to shed innocent blood; their thoughts are thoughts of iniquity; devastation and destruction are in their paths. The way of peace they have not known, and there is no justice in their paths. They have made crooked paths for themselves; whoever goes in them shall not know peace. Therefore justice is far from us; nor does righteousness overtake us. We wait for daylight, but behold, the night; for brightness, but we walk in darkness. We grope for the wall like the blind, and we grope as if we had no eyes. We stumble at noonday as in the night; we are in desolate places like dead men. We all roar like bears, and mourn with moaning like doves; we look for justice, but there is none; for salvation, but it is far off from us." Isaiah 59:1-11

"Therefore, just as through one man sin entered the world, and death through sin, and thus death spread to every person, because everyone sinned. For until the Law sin was in the world, but sin is not accounted when there is no law. Nevertheless death reigned from Adam to Moses, even over those who had not sinned according to the likeness of the transgression of Adam, who is a type of Him who was to come. But the free gift is not

like the offense. For if by the one man's offense many died, much more the grace of God and the gift by the grace of the one Man, Jesus Christ, abounded to many. And the gift is not like it was through the one who sinned. For the judgment from one offense was unto condemnation, but the free gift from many offenses is unto justification. For if by the one man's offense death reigned through the one, much more those who are receiving abundance of grace and of the gift of righteousness will reign in life through the One, Jesus Christ. Therefore, as through one man's offense judgment was to every person unto condemnation, even so through one Man's righteous act the free gift is to every person unto justification of life. For as through one man's disobedience many were declared sinners, so also through one Man's obedience many will be declared righteous. Moreover the Law entered that the offense might abound. But where sin abounded, grace abounded much more, so that as sin reigned in death, even so grace might reign through righteousness unto eternal life through Jesus Christ our Lord." Romans 5:12-21*

"There is a way which seems right to a man, but the end of it is the ways of death." Proverbs 14:12*

I want you to consider and consider well that every bit of oppression that you face would be nothing compared to what will come if you do not change from your ways, if you do not realize that you are deserving of Hell, a place of eternal torment for those who do not seek God and die in their sins.

"But he does not know that the spirits of the dead are there; the ones she summons are in the depths of Sheol." Proverbs 9:18* — Note: Sheol is another name for Hell.

"If anyone does not abide in Me, he is cast out as a branch and is dried up; and they gather them and throw them into the fire, and they are burned." John 15:6*

"And many of those sleeping in the earth's dust shall awake, some to everlasting life, and some to reproach and everlasting abhorrence." Daniel 12:2*

"As the cloud vanishes and goes away, so he who goes down to Sheol does not come up." Job 7:9*

"And do not fear those who kill the body but are not able to kill the soul. But rather fear Him who has power to destroy both soul and body in Gehenna." Matthew 10:28*

Think about it for a moment, if you were in a dark dungeon of a prison, a horrific place with hungry, cold, diseases, etc., at least you might have hope that one day the door would open and they would let you out. If you were in an oppressive government, following the status quo of how things are supposed to be done, what will you gain in the end when you stand before Him who Created you? If you were stuck barely surviving your entire life and dying in poverty, of what would it advantage you if the afterlife is far worse than the current life, and for that eternally. Imagine a million years go by and knowing that there is no end!!! Yet, though man is undeserving God provided the Way for us to be rectified with Him. He sent His Son to die on the Cross, who rose again from the dead to be with the Almighty God.

"For God so loved the world that He gave His only begotten Son, that everyone believing into Him should not perish but have eternal life. For God did not send His Son into the world to judge the world, but that the world through Him might be saved. The one believing into Him is not judged; but the one not believing is judged already, because he has not believed in the name of the only begotten Son of God. And this is the judgment, that the Light has come into the world, and men loved darkness rather than the Light, for their deeds were evil. For everyone practicing evil hates the Light and does not come to the Light, lest his deeds should be reproved. But the one doing the truth comes to the Light, that his deeds may be clearly seen, that they have been worked in God." John 3:16-21

"Jesus said to him, I am the Way, the Truth, and the Life. No one comes to the Father except through Me." John 14:6

This same Jesus is God, God in the flesh. God is one, yet in three parts.

"In the beginning was the Word, and the Word was with God, and the Word was God. He was in the beginning with God. All things were made through Him, and without Him nothing was made that was made. In Him was life, and the life was the light of men. And the light shines in the darkness, and the darkness did not lay hold of it." John 1:1-5

"For there are three that bear witness in Heaven: the Father, the Word, and the Holy Spirit; and these three are one." 1st John 5:7

Imagine working in horrific conditions, perhaps you do, of where it is simply pure poverty or near pure poverty. A rich man who has a nice place in a skyscraper, complete with cars, food, nice furniture and a large bank account stops by one day. He looks at you and says, you know what, 'I am going to move my family here, immediately. Give us your clothes, give us your work, give us your things. You will take everything we own, our place, our cars, our furniture, our clothing and all of our money. We will switch lives, I desire to take the place for you so that you might have a better life, so you might inherit good things. Please do so now, go and let us trade immediately, then drive away, we will continue on with your life.'

Imagine begin stuck in a horrific prison, as I described above. Clothes torn, destitute, without hope. Suddenly a man from a foreign country arrives. He asks to see one of the prisoners, it turns out to be you. There he talks with the government and makes an arrangement that he will take your place and you can go free. He will simply spend the rest of his life in that prison, so that you can go and live yours.

Certainly this seems so far fetched. Who in their right mind would do such a thing? Who would do that? Of how much more unlikely would it be for someone to do such a thing for a person who had been wronged by that person?! Well that is what God ordained, this is what Jesus did for you. He died on the Cross for your sins, He paid the penalty for your sins on the Cross. If you are willing to accept that, if you are willing to repent and believe into Him as your Lord and Savior.

"For Christ also suffered for sins once for all, the just for the unjust, that He might bring us to God, being put to death in the flesh but made alive by the Spirit"... 1st Peter 3:18

"By this we know the love of God, because He laid down His life for us." 1st John 3:16a

"And you know that He was manifested in order to take away our sins, and in Him there is no sin." 1st John 3:5

"Who has believed our report? And to whom has the arm of Jehovah been revealed? For He grows up before Him as a tender plant, and as a root out of the dry ground. He has no form nor splendor that we should regard Him, nor anything spectacular that we should desire Him. He is despised and rejected by men; a Man of pain, and knowing infirmity; a hiding of faces; being despised, we have esteemed Him not. Truly He has borne our sicknesses, and carried our pain; yet we esteemed Him stricken, smitten by God, and afflicted. But He was wounded for our transgressions; He was bruised for our iniquities; the chastisement for our peace was upon Him; and with His stripes we are healed. All we like sheep have gone astray; we have turned, each one to his own way; and Jehovah has laid upon Him the iniquity of us all. He has been oppressed, and He was afflicted; yet He opens not His mouth. He is brought as a lamb to the slaughter; and as a sheep before its shearers is mute, so He opens not His mouth. He was taken from prison and from judgment; and who shall declare His generation? For He was cut off out of the land of the living; for the transgression of My people He was stricken. And His grave was assigned with the wicked, and with the rich in His death; although He had done no violence, nor was any deceit in His mouth. Yet it pleased Jehovah to crush Him; to grieve Him; that He should give His soul as a sin-offering. He shall see His seed, He shall prolong His days, and the delight of Jehovah shall prosper in His hand. He shall see the travail of His soul, and shall be fulfilled. By His knowledge shall My righteous Servant justify many; for He shall bear their iniquities. Therefore I will apportion to Him with the great, and He shall divide the spoils with the strong; because He has poured out His soul unto death; and He was reckoned among the transgressors; and He bore the sin of many, and made intercession for the transgressors." Isaiah 53

"For when we were yet without strength, in due time Christ died for the ungodly. For scarcely for a righteous man will one die; yet perhaps for a good man some would even be bold enough to die. But God demonstrates His own love toward us, in that while we were yet sinners, Christ died for us." Romans 5:6-8

"Moreover, brethren, I declare to you the gospel which I preached to you, which also you received and in which you stand, by which also you are being kept safe, if you hold fast that Word which I preached to you; unless you believe in vain. For I delivered to you first of all that which I also received: that Christ died for our sins according to the Scriptures, and that He was buried, and that He was raised the third day according to

the Scriptures, and that He was seen by Cephas, then by the twelve. After that He was seen by over five hundred brethren at once, of whom the greater part remain until the present time, but some have fallen asleep. After that He was seen by Jacob, then by each of the apostles. Then last of all He was seen by me also, as by one of untimely birth." 1st Corinthians 15:1-8

"But Christ came as High Priest of the good things to come, with the greater and more perfect tabernacle not made with hands, that is, not of this creation. Not with the blood of goats and calves, but with His own blood He entered the Holy of Holies once for all, having obtained eternal redemption. For if the blood of bulls and goats and the ashes of a heifer, sprinkling the unclean, sanctifies for the purifying of the flesh, how much more shall the blood of Christ, who through the eternal Spirit offered Himself without blemish to God, cleanse your conscience from dead works to serve the living God. And for this reason He is the Mediator of the new covenant, by means of death, for the redemption of the transgressions under the first covenant, that those who are called may receive the promise of the eternal inheritance." Hebrews 9:11-15

One might look at their life, they might hold out hope, but in the end there is no hope without Jesus Christ as your Savior, none whatsoever.

"Let this mind be in you which was also in Christ Jesus, who, being in the form of God, did not consider clinging, to be equal with God, but emptied Himself, taking the form of a bondservant, and coming in the likeness of men. And being found comprised as a man, He humbled Himself and became obedient unto death, even the death of the cross. Therefore God also has highly exalted Him and given Him a name which is above every name, that at the name of Jesus every knee should bow, of those in Heaven, and of those on earth, and of those under the earth, and that every tongue should confess that Jesus Christ is Lord, to the glory of God the Father." Philippians 2:1-11

"Now if Christ is preached that He has been raised from the dead, how do some among you say that there is no resurrection of the dead? But if there is no resurrection of the dead, neither has Christ been raised. And if Christ has not been raised, then our preaching is vain and your faith is also vain. Yes, and we are found to be false witnesses of God, because we have testified of God that He raised up Christ, whom He did not raise up; if in fact the dead are not raised. For if the dead are not raised, then Christ has not been raised. And if Christ has not been raised, your faith is vain; you are still in your sins. Then also those who have fallen asleep in Christ have perished. If in this life only we have hope in Christ, we are of all men the most pitiable. But now Christ has been raised from the dead, and has become the firstfruits of those who have fallen asleep." 1st Corinthians 15:12-20

"And you being dead in trespasses and sins, in which you formerly walked according to the course of this world, according to the ruler of the authority of the air, the spirit who now works in the sons of disobedience, among whom also we all formerly conducted ourselves in the lusts of our flesh, fulfilling the desires of the flesh and of the mind, and were by nature children of wrath, just as the others; but God, who is rich in mercy, *because of His great love with which He loved us, even when we were dead in trespasses, made us alive together with Christ (by grace you are saved), and raised us up together, and made us sit together in the heavenlies in Christ Jesus, that in the ages to come He might display the exceeding riches of His grace in His kindness toward us in Christ Jesus. For by grace you are saved through faith; and that not of yourselves, it is the gift of God; not of works, that no one should boast. For we are His workmanship, created in Christ Jesus unto good works, which God prepared beforehand that we should walk in them. Therefore remember that you, being Gentiles in the flesh; who are called uncircumcision by what is called the circumcision made in the flesh by hands; that at that time you were without Christ, being aliens from the commonwealth of Israel and strangers from the covenants of promise, having no hope and without God in the world. But now in Christ Jesus you who once were far off have been made near by the blood of Christ. For He Himself is our peace, who has made both one, and has broken down the middle wall of separation, having abolished in His flesh the enmity, that is, the Law of commandments contained in ordinances, that He might create in Himself one new man from the two, thus making peace, and that He might reconcile them both to God in one body through the cross, thereby putting to death the enmity. And He came and preached peace to you who were afar off and to those who were near. For through Him we both have access by one Spirit to the Father. Now, therefore, you are no longer strangers and foreigners, but fellow citizens with the saints and members of the household of God, having been built on the foundation of the apostles and prophets, Jesus Christ Himself being the chief corner stone, in whom the whole building, being joined together, grows into a holy temple in the Lord, in whom you also are being built together into a dwelling place of God in the Spirit." Ephesians 2*

So you might consider your life, the life of your family, your struggles, your oppression, whatever your situation might be. Maybe you live in a place where the country has a religion, that you might even be a part of. Perhaps it is Hindu, Islam, Roman Catholicism or some other religion, but it is in vain. While some might hold virtues of truth, these virtues fall short from the true and living God.

"But Jehovah is the true God, He is the living God, and the eternal King. At His wrath the earth shall tremble, and the nations shall not be able to endure His indignation. So you shall say to them, The gods who have not made the heavens and the earth, they shall perish from the earth and from under these heavens. He has made the earth by His power; He has established the world by His wisdom, and has stretched out the heavens by His understanding. When He utters His voice, there is the noise of much water in the heavens. He causes the vapors to ascend from the ends of the earth; He makes lightnings with the rain, and brings forth the wind out of His treasures. Every man is stupid in his knowledge; every refiner is dried up by the graven image; for his molten image is a lie, and no breath is in them. They are vanity, the work of delusion; in the time of their judgment they shall perish." Ephesians 10:10-15

So how does one get Saved, what must one do? Well the Bible speaks for itself, the explanation is quite simple. If you seek God, He will be found by you.

"Seek Jehovah while He may be found; call upon Him while He is near. Let the wicked forsake his way, and the unrighteous man his thoughts; and let him return to Jehovah, and He will have mercy on him; and to our God, for He will abundantly pardon." Isaiah 55:6-7

Consider this carefully, read through these verses and seek Him! God is willing to forgive, He is merciful. You must be willing to repent and by faith believe into Jesus Christ, as your Lord and Savior.

"Then Peter said to them, Repent, and let every one of you be immersed in the name of Jesus Christ to the remission of sins; and you shall receive the gift of the Holy Spirit. For the promise is to you and to your children, and to all who are afar off, as many as the Lord our God will call." Acts 2:38-39

"Truly, these times of ignorance God overlooked, but now commands all men everywhere to repent, because He has established a day on which He will judge the world in righteousness by the Man whom He has appointed. He has given assurance of this to everyone by raising Him from the dead." Acts 17:30-31

Jesus said, "I tell you, no; but unless you repent you will all likewise perish." Luke 13:3

"Nor is there salvation in any other, for there is no other name under Heaven given among men that is required for us to be saved." Acts 4:12

"Behold, I stand at the door and knock. If anyone hears My voice and opens the door, I will come in to him and dine with him, and he with Me." Revelation 3:20

"He who is unjust, let him be unjust still; he who is filthy, let him be filthy still; he who is righteous, let him be righteous still; he who is holy, let him be holy still. And behold, I am coming quickly, and My reward is with Me, to give to every one according to what his work shall be. I am the Alpha and the Omega, the Beginning and the Ending, the First and the Last. Blessed are those who do His commandments, that they may have the right to the Tree of Life, and may enter through the gates into the city. But outside are dogs and sorcerers and prostitutes and murderers and idolaters, and whoever loves and produces a lie. I, Jesus, have sent My angel to testify these things to you, to the churches. I am the Root and the Offspring of David, the Bright and Morning Star. And the Spirit and the bride say, Come. And let him who hears say, Come. And let him who thirsts come. Whoever desires, let him take of the Water of Life freely." Revelation 22:11-17

"And he brought them out and said, Sirs, what must I do to be saved? So they said, Believe on the Lord Jesus Christ, and you will be saved, you and your household." Acts 16:30-31

"But what does it say? The Word is near you, in your mouth and in your heart (that is, the Word of Faith which we preach): that if you confess with your mouth the Lord Jesus *and believe in your heart that God has raised Him from the dead, you will be saved. For with the heart one believes unto righteousness, and with the mouth confession is made unto salvation. For the Scripture says, Everyone believing on Him will not be put to shame. For there is no distinction between Jew and Greek, for the same Lord over all is rich toward all who call upon Him. For everyone, whoever calls on the name of the Lord shall be saved." Romans 10:8-13*

In the end, no matter whether or not God intervenes in resolving whatever oppressive situation you might be in, certainly He does provide, according to His will, but either way you will be rich, with the riches and joy that are only found in Christ!

"And my God shall supply all your need according to His riches in glory in Christ Jesus." Philippians 4:19

"For this reason I bow my knees to the Father of our Lord Jesus Christ, of whom the whole family in Heaven and earth is named, that He would grant you, according to the riches of His glory, to be strengthened with might through His Spirit in the inner man, that Christ may dwell in your hearts through faith; that you, being rooted and grounded in love, may be able to grasp with all the saints what is the width and length and depth and height; to know the surpassing knowledge and love of Christ; that you may be filled with all the fullness of God. Now to Him who is able to do exceedingly abundantly above all that we ask or think, according to the power that works in us, to Him be glory in the church in Christ Jesus to all generations, forever and ever. Amen." Ephesians 3:14-21

"But if anyone loves God, this one is known by Him." 1st Corinthians 8:3

Amen!

Garbage Heap

"And I will make Jerusalem a heap of ruins, a den of dragons; and I will make the cities of Judah a desolation, without inhabitant. Who is the wise man who may understand this? And who is he to whom the mouth of Jehovah has spoken, that he may declare it? Why does the land perish and burn up like a wilderness, so that no one passes through? And Jehovah says, Because they have forsaken My Law which I set before them, and have not obeyed My voice, and have not walked in it, but they have walked after the stubbornness of their own heart, and after the Baals, which their fathers taught them." Jeremiah 9:11-14

"Therefore, on account of you, Zion shall be plowed as a field, and Jerusalem shall become heaps, and the mountain of the house like the high places of the forest." Micah 3:12

Recently my family had watched part of a documentary showing where much of the 'recycled' plastic from the United States (as well as much of the world) goes. To our horror we watched as a Chinese family worked one of the thousands of recycling 'factories' in a town that specializes in receiving barges of plastic junk. Their children, including infants, grow up in horrible conditions, living amongst a stinking heap of filthy, partially sorted plastic trash. Then the news hit here in Kalispell, Montana about our plastic.

Apparently our plastic recycling also goes to China. China has had enough and will no longer accept the plastic of the world, due to the contamination it is causing on their land. They also cited the poor quality of the plastic they were receiving, as well as the grime. So starting immediately there is no where for the plastic to go. A resolution is being sought.

I had also seen another documentary showing electronics from the world being dumped in a country in Africa. There a hard working advocate was trying to stop this sort of pollution in his country. Literally fields and fields of discarded electronics from around the world, with children burning the plastic components to try and salvage any metal they might sell for a few cents at the scrap yard. These children are breathing the air of all of this melting plastic, as well as heavy metals, as they are collecting the metal. Terrible.

I pondered these things. Here we have a society that pretends to push environmental causes, particularly corporations, yet apparently their green only goes as far as the money it costs to do so. In other words, the question now is what to do with the barges that have delivered Chinese goods to the United States. Should they return empty, instead of full of our recycled garbage? Truly a burden, not only the United States, but other countries as well, places on those whom they can. One that causes people to live in absolute filth and the heavy risk of disease, both from dealing with such garbage, but also the hazards of the work required.

Certainly those in the know try to hide such things from the general public. Does the public want to know that those who are manufacturing their expensive goods in far away countries do so under impoverished conditions? Does the public want to know what really happens to much of the recycling? Just as they do not want to know the things of God, preferring to ultimately be ignorant towards the great gift that God has given to mankind, should they choose to accept it, they would rather not deal with it, as they do not want to change their ways.

"For the wrath of God is revealed from Heaven against all ungodliness and unrighteousness of men, who suppress the truth in unrighteousness, because what may be known of God is clearly recognized by them, for God has revealed it to them. For ever since the creation of the world the unseen things of Him are clearly perceived, being understood by the things that are made, even His eternal power and Godhead, so that they are without excuse, because, although they know God, they do not glorify Him as God, nor are thankful, but become vain in their reasonings, and their stupid hearts are darkened. Professing to be wise, they become foolish, and change the glory of the incorruptible God into an image made like corruptible man, and birds and four-footed animals and creeping things." Romans 1:18-23

"For God so loved the world that He gave His only begotten Son, that everyone believing into Him should not perish but have eternal life. For God did not send His Son into the world to judge the world, but that the world through Him might be saved. The one believing into Him is not judged; but the one not believing is judged already, because he has not believed in the name of the only begotten Son of God. And this is the judgment, that the Light has come into the world, and men loved darkness rather than the Light, for their deeds were evil. For everyone practicing evil hates the Light and does not come to the Light, lest his deeds should be reproved. But the one doing the truth comes to the Light, that his deeds may be clearly seen, that they have been worked in God." John 3:16-21

We can ignore these things as a society. We can ignore such places as Detroit, as well as filthy places around the world. Our societies can place our burdens upon the poorer countries of the world, yet as we sit in our cities, even those in the same countries that have much impoverishment, looking at the works of our hands, we must realize that all will be a gigantic garbage heap.

Think of places like the Golden Mile in Chicago. Travel to even Latin America and behold the skyscrapers in places like Panama City. Even in Mexico, the resort areas are full of what appears to be abundance luxury and wealth. Travel to Shanghai and look at the impressive cityscape. Look upon the city of Paris, or the cities of London, Moscow, Montreal, New York City, Miami, San Diego, Seattle, Brussels, Buenos Aires, Tel Aviv and many others and see the works of men's hands. Sprawling cities of intense complexity, noting that the complexity is nothing compared to that which our Creator has worked in regarding His Creation.

"He removes the mountains, and they do not know when He overturns them in His anger; He shakes the earth out of its place, and its pillars tremble; He commands the sun, and it does not rise; He seals up the stars; He alone spreads out the heavens, and treads upon the waves of the sea; He made the Ursa Major, Orion, and the Pleiades, and the chambers of the south; He does great things past finding out, yea, wonders without number." Job 9:5-10

"The heavens declare the glory of the Mighty God; and the firmament proclaims His handiwork." Psalms 19:1

"Thus says Jehovah the Mighty God, He who created the heavens and stretched them out, spreading out the earth and its offspring; Who gives breath to the people on it and spirit to those who walk on it." Isaiah 42:5

"He who sits in the Heavens shall laugh; Jehovah shall have them in derision." Psalms 2:4

Yet from the fancy houses that adorn Whitefish Lake, Harbor Springs, Bar Harbor and many other resort towns for the rich around the country, understand that even those will be laid waste, a garbage heap.

Why do men try to prevail and ignore God's warnings to mankind? Why do they not seek their Creator? Why do they not repent and believe by faith into Jesus Christ as their Lord and Savior, forsaking their wicked ways and focusing on their heavenly home? Certainly they do not have citizenship in Heaven *(Phil. 3:20)*, their names are not written in the Book of Life.

"This is the purpose that is purposed upon all the earth; and this is the hand that is stretched out upon all the nations. For Jehovah of Hosts has purposed, and who shall annul it? And His hand is stretched out, and who shall turn it back?" Isaiah 14:26-27

"But if you do not do so, behold, you have sinned against Jehovah; and recognize that your sin will find you out." Numbers 32:23

"Truly, these times of ignorance God overlooked, but now commands all men everywhere to repent, because He has established a day on which He will judge the world in righteousness by the Man whom He has appointed. He has given assurance of this to everyone by raising Him from the dead." Acts 17:30-31

"He makes nations great, and destroys them; He spreads out nations, and guides them. He takes away the heart of the heads of the people of the earth, and makes them wander in a wilderness with no path. They grope in the darkness without light, and He makes them stagger like a drunkard." Job 12:23-25

"And I saw a great white throne and Him who sat on it, from whose face the earth and the heavens fled away. And there was found no place for them. And I saw the dead, small and great, standing before God. And books were opened. And another book was opened, which is the Book of Life. And the dead were judged according to their works, out of the things which were written in the books. And the sea gave up the dead who were in it, and Death and Hades delivered up the dead who were in them. And they were judged, each one, according to their works. And Death and Hades were cast into the Lake of Fire. This is the second death. And anyone not found written in the Book of Life was cast into the Lake of Fire." Revelation 20:11-15

One day the great skyscrapers of the cities of the world will come down. One day the fancy houses that adorn cities throughout all of the world, will be nothing more than a garbage heap. One day the luxury resorts will be abandoned and laid waste. One day the works of man's hands upon the whole earth will be the biggest gigantic garbage heap possible.

The dams will break, the nuclear power plants will be destroyed. The awesome freeway systems of big cities will come down, being rendered junk. Cars will sit abandoned, the bodies of the dead will be left decomposing on the earth, with no one to bury them. One day the women who dress in the latest fashions will find themselves looking dreadful and pathetic, their beauty turned into shame. One day men will be scarce on the earth. One day humankind will see the full wrath of God, towards those who refuse to repent of their iniquities.

"And I looked when He opened the sixth seal, and behold, there was a great earthquake; and the sun became black as sackcloth of hair, and the moon became like blood. And the stars of heaven fell to the earth, as a fig tree drops its untimely figs when it is shaken by a mighty wind. And the heavens separated as a scroll when it is rolled up, and every mountain and island were moved out of their places. And the kings of the earth, the great men, the rich men, the commanders, the mighty men, every slave and every free man, hid themselves in the caves and in the rocks of the mountains, and said to the mountains and rocks, Fall on us and hide us from the face of Him who sits on the throne

and from the wrath of the Lamb! For the great day of His wrath has come, and who is able to stand?" Revelation 6:12-17

"Speak, Thus says Jehovah, Even the carcasses of men shall fall as dung on the open field, and as the fallen grain after the reaper; and no one shall gather them. Thus says Jehovah, Let not the wise glory in his wisdom, nor let the mighty glory in his might; let not the rich glory in his riches; but let him who glories glory in this, that he understands and knows Me, that I am Jehovah, doing kindness, justice, and righteousness in the earth; for in these things I delight, says Jehovah. Behold, the days are coming, says Jehovah, that I will punish all the circumcised along with the uncircumcised;" Jeremiah 9:22-25

"Furthermore Jehovah says, Because the daughters of Zion are haughty, and walk with stretched out necks and wanton eyes, walking and mincing as they go, and make a tinkling with their feet; therefore Jehovah will attach scabs to the top of the head of the daughters of Zion; and Jehovah will lay bare their secret parts. In that day the Lord will take away the beauty of their anklets, and their headbands, and their crescents of the moon, the pendants, and the bracelets, and the veils; the turbans, and the leg ornaments, and the sashes, and the perfume boxes, and the amulets; the rings and nose jewels; the festal apparel and the outer garments; and the mantles, and the purses; the mirrors and the fine linen; and the turbans and the veils. And it shall be, instead of a smell of perfume, there shall be an odor of decay. And instead of a belt, a rope. And instead of well set hair, baldness. And instead of a rich robe, a girding of sackcloth; and branding instead of beauty. Your men shall fall by the sword, and your mighty in the war. And her gates shall lament and mourn; and she shall sit desolate on the ground. And in that day seven women shall take hold of one man, saying, We will eat our own bread and wear our own clothing; only let us be called by your name, to take away our reproach." Isaiah 3:16-4:1

"Howl! For the day of Jehovah is at hand! It shall come as a destruction from the Almighty. Therefore all hands shall be faint, and every man's heart shall melt; and they shall be afraid. Pangs and sorrows shall take hold of them. They shall writhe like a woman giving birth. They shall be amazed at one another; their faces like flames. Behold, the day of Jehovah comes, cruel and with wrath and fierce anger, to lay the land waste; and He shall destroy its sinners out of it. For the stars of the heavens and their constellations shall not give light; the sun shall be darkened in its going forth, and the moon shall not shine its light. And I will punish the world for its evil, and the wicked for their iniquity. And I will put an end to the arrogance of the proud, and will lay low the haughtiness of the tyrants. I will make mortal man more precious than refined gold; even mankind than the pure gold of Ophir. Thus I will shake the heavens, and the earth shall move out of its place, in the wrath of Jehovah of Hosts, and in the day of His fierce anger. And it shall be as a hunted gazelle, and as a sheep that no man takes up; each man shall turn to his own people, and everyone flee into his own land. Everyone who is found shall be thrust through; and everyone who is captured shall fall by the sword. Their children shall be dashed to pieces before their eyes; their houses shall be plundered, and their wives ravished." Isaiah 13:6-16

"And they did not repent of their murders nor their sorceries nor their sexual perversions nor their thefts." Revelation 9:21

"And men were scorched with great heat, and they blasphemed the name of God who has authority over these plagues; and they did not repent to give Him glory." Revelation 16:9

Look not upon the things of this world, but rather the things of God. Seek Him while He may be found!

"Do not love the world or the things in the world. If anyone loves the world, the love of the Father is not in him. For all that is in the world; the lust of the flesh, the lust of the eyes, and the pride of life; is not of the Father but is of the world. And the world is passing away, and its lust; but he who does the will of God abides forever." 1st John 2:15-17

"Seek Jehovah while He may be found; call upon Him while He is near. Let the wicked forsake his way, and the unrighteous man his thoughts; and let him return to Jehovah, and He will have mercy on him; and to our God, for He will abundantly pardon. For My thoughts are not your thoughts, nor are your ways My ways, says Jehovah. For as the heavens are higher than the earth, so are My ways higher than your ways, and My thoughts than your thoughts. For as the rain comes down, and the snow from heaven, and does not return there, but waters the earth, and makes it bring forth and bud, and gives seed to the sower and bread to the eater; so shall My Word be, which goes forth from My mouth; it shall not return to Me void, but it shall accomplish what I please, and it shall succeed in that for which I have sent it." Isaiah 55:6-11

Lest you also be Left Behind during that time period. For one day the Lord will restore the garbage heap that is left when He returns with His Saints. Where will you be in that day? Will you have been killed during the *"time of Jacob's trouble" (Jer. 30:7)* or will you watch in amazement to see your end, taking part of the final rebellion against your Creator?

"And I saw Heaven opened, and behold, a white horse. And He who sat on him was called Faithful and True, and in righteousness He judges and makes war. His eyes were like a flame of fire, and on His head were many crowns. He had a name written that no one knew except Himself. And He was clothed with a robe dipped in blood, and His name is called The Word of God. And the armies in Heaven, clothed in fine linen, white and pure, followed Him on white horses. And out of His mouth goes a sharp sword, that with it He might strike the nations. And He Himself will rule them with a rod of iron. He Himself treads the winepress of the fierceness and wrath of Almighty God. And He has on His robe and on His thigh a name written: KING OF KINGS AND LORD OF LORDS." Revelation 19:11-16

Take heed, God is not mocked!

"Do not be led astray, God is not mocked; for whatever a man sows, that he will also reap. For he who sows to his flesh will of the flesh reap corruption, but he who sows to the Spirit will of the Spirit reap eternal life." Galatians 6:7-8

Amen!

Don't Wait

"He who is unjust, let him be unjust still; he who is filthy, let him be filthy still; he who is righteous, let him be righteous still; he who is holy, let him be holy still." Revelation 22:11

The recent false missile alert in Hawaii certainly delivered fear to those who are living there. All over and for good reason, people were panicking, crying, screaming, trying to figure out what to do. After all what can one do?

From what I have heard, the traffic in Honolulu is terrible. Imagine being stuck in traffic, getting an alert that there is an incoming ballistic missile and there is no where to go. You are literally at ground zero, stuck. Fortunately I haven't heard any reports of injuries or deaths regarding this false alert. From my understanding there were some who were driving very erratically, trying to get home to there loved ones, disregarding all traffic laws.

There is also a video of a family lowering their children in the sewer drain, as a place for them to go. Truly that is an interesting take on a bomb shelter, one that would make one ponder if it would actually be effective or not. There is also a popular video out there showing university students running to take cover. Of course there are numerous more videos of people's last words, even one man who just continued to play golf.

However, one reaction, one article truly got my attention. A woman in the midst of the chaos prayed to God and asked for forgiveness of her sins, as well as protection. If only, if only there were a warning prior to the Rapture, to those who will be Left Behind!

There is. With an incoming ballistic missile, my understanding is that from the actual time the alert is activated, the average citizen in Hawaii would have 12-17 minutes before the missile actually hit. With the ensuing chaos that occurred after the false alert, it is apparent that most people are completely ill prepared for such a crisis. After all, without a hardened bomb shelter, what could most people do anyway?

Yet when the Trumpet sounds, truly it will be too late for those who haven't repented and believed into Jesus Christ as their Lord and Savior, they will have been Left Behind.

"For the Lord Himself will descend from Heaven with a shouted command, with the voice of the archangel, and with the trumpet of God. And the dead in Christ will rise first. Then we who are alive and remain shall be caught up together at the same time with them in the clouds to meet the Lord in the air. And thus we shall always be with the Lord." 1st Thessalonians 4:16-17

Without Warning

Unlike a potential incoming ballistic missile, the Rapture will happen without warning. The warning has been given in God's Word and been proclaimed by those whom God has called to proclaim His truth from pulpits across the world. There will be no 12-17 minutes to determine what to do, it will simply be too late.

"But of that day and hour no one knows, not even the angels of Heaven, but My Father only. But as the days of Noah were, so also will the coming of the Son of Man be. For as in the days before the flood, they were eating and drinking, marrying and giving in marriage, until the day that Noah entered into the ark, and did not realize until the flood came and took them all away, so also will the coming of the Son of Man be. Then two will be in the field: one is taken and the other is left. Two will be grinding at the mill: one is taken and the other is left. Watch therefore, for you do not know what hour your Lord comes. But know this, that if the master of the house had known what hour the thief comes, he would have watched and not allowed his house to be dug through. Therefore you also be ready, for the Son of Man comes at an hour you do not expect. Who then is a faithful and wise servant, whom his master made administrator over his household, to give them food in due season? Blessed is that servant whom his master, when he comes, will find so doing. Truly, I say to you that he will appoint him as administrator over all his possessions. But if that wicked servant says in his heart, My master delays his coming, and begins to beat his fellow servants, and to eat and drink with the drunkards, the master of that servant will come on a day when he is not expecting him and in an hour he does not know, and will cut him in two and appoint him his portion with the hypocrites. There shall be weeping and gnashing of teeth." Matthew 24:36-51

Right now people who experienced the false alert are very angry with the government for not only the false alert, but also the fact that it took nearly 40 minutes for them to rectify it. Nearly 40 minutes of mass panic across the region, before the message got out that it was a false alert! Perhaps those in power simply wanted to see what the reaction would be?

Imagine if you will, for a moment, if it were not a drill, if in fact a missile had come from North Korea. North Korea claims to have mastered miniaturizing hydrogen warheads. Let's assume that there bluff is no longer called, but indeed what they had stated was certain, the proof was there, Honolulu was the target. They hit their target. The results would be the same in any major metropolitan city.

In a moment, in an instance, life is shattered. Many miles of pure destruction lie in wake of the targeted city, heavy destruction goes further out, beyond that there the destruction continues, with death at the door. In a moment a million lives are evaporated, dreams are ended, hopes are gone. Indeed the last game of golf is played by those who witness a flash, the last moments recorded and sealed on social media of those who didn't make it.

In the wake of such a realization, it is but too late. There is no amount of preparation that could have been had for the vast majority. The basements of the high rise buildings prove to be too close to the vicinity of ground zero, even if a portion has survived, the inhabitants are now full of toxicity from the radioactive disaster, they are the walking dead, soon they will meet the grave. Who will come into ground zero and save them? Who will walk through the radioactive disaster and provide aid to those who were targeted? Of what good would it be? Are they not marked for death already, are they not counted as the dead, though alive?

What could have been done differently? What more preparations could have been had? Certainly should the anger not be at the government who should have been preparing non-stop real solutions? Should the anger not be at the government who should have been building nuclear bomb shelters to hold masses of people? Should the anger not be at the government who underestimated the threat and did not prevent such a disaster from occurring, but rather pushed their enemy with both words and actions?

Did our government ever mock the Soviet Union and badger them to no end during the height of the cold war? Did our government not run drills throughout the entire United States of what to do should the Soviets fire nukes at our soil? Were not shelters prepared throughout the United States, fully stocked with food and other non perishable goods? Did not a threat linger and the government at least pretended to take necessary precautions?

Where are our precautions now? Where are the shelters being built now? Are they not the same as those who preach from the pulpits, those who do not proclaim the truth of God's Word and explain the Gospel, including repentance, not just faith? Do the pastors of this country and indeed the world proclaim the security that is found only in Jesus Christ? Where does the soul go to for shelter, to whom do they look towards? The Creator or some man made religious object of false praise and false security? A Jesus who supposedly accepts everyone as they are, one who allows gay pastors, one who allows homosexual marriage, one who will not come with wrath, one who will not judge the world, one in which would not place people in a literal hell, one who will simply accept mankind as they are, without any need of change, one who needed not die on the

Cross, as they preach of no penalty having been necessary to have been paid, as they teach that man can simply believe in Jesus, without repentance.

"In whom also, after you heard the Word of Truth, the gospel of your salvation, in whom also, believing, you were sealed with the Holy Spirit of promise, who is the earnest of our inheritance until the redemption of the purchased possession, to the praise of His glory." Ephesians 1:13-14

"God is our refuge and strength, a very present help in trouble. Therefore we will not fear when the earth changes, when mountains are slipping into the midst of the seas. Let its waters roar and foam; let the mountains shake with the swelling of it. Selah. There is a river whose streams cause rejoicing in the city of God, the consecrated place of the tabernacle of the Most High. God is in the midst of her; she shall not be moved; God shall help her at the break of day. The nations raged, the kingdoms were shaken; He uttered His voice, the earth melted. Jehovah of Hosts is with us; the God of Jacob is our refuge. Selah. Come, behold the works of Jehovah, who has made desolations on the earth; who makes wars to cease to the ends of the earth; He breaks the bow and cuts the spear in two; He burns the chariots in the fire. Be still, and know that I am God! I will be exalted among the nations, I will be exalted in the earth! Jehovah of Hosts is with us; the God of Jacob is our refuge. Selah." Psalms 46

"Truly, these times of ignorance God overlooked, but now commands all men everywhere to repent, because He has established a day on which He will judge the world in righteousness by the Man whom He has appointed. He has given assurance of this to everyone by raising Him from the dead." Acts 17:30-31

"Do you not know that the unrighteous will not inherit the kingdom of God? Do not be led astray. Neither prostitutes, nor idolaters, nor adulterers, nor effeminate, nor sodomites, nor thieves, nor covetous, nor drunkards, nor revilers, nor extortioners will inherit the kingdom of God. And such were some of you. But you were washed, but you were sanctified, but you were justified in the name of the Lord Jesus and by the Spirit of our God." 1st Corinthians 6:9-11

"Let the sea roar, and all its fullness, the world and those who dwell in it; let the rivers clap their hands; let the hills be joyful together before Jehovah, for He is coming to judge the earth. With righteousness He shall judge the world, and the peoples with equity." Psalms 98:7-9

"And these will go away into everlasting punishment, but the righteous into eternal life." Matthew 25:46

"And He said to them, Thus it is written, and thus it was necessary for the Christ to suffer and to rise from the dead the third day, and that repentance and remission of sins be preached in His name to all nations, beginning out of Jerusalem." Luke 24:46-47

"But now the righteousness of God apart from the Law is revealed, being witnessed by the Law and the Prophets, even the righteousness of God, through the faith of Jesus Christ, to all and upon all who believe. For there is no difference; for all have sinned and fall short of the glory of God, being justified freely by His grace through the redemption that is in Christ Jesus, whom God set forth as a propitiation through faith in His blood, to give evidence of His righteousness, because in His forbearance God had passed over the sins that were previously committed, to prove at the present time His righteousness, that He might be just and the justifier of the one who is of the faith of Jesus." Romans 3:21-26

They preach a false gospel, they preach what is not correct, they have forsaken the right way and instead preach what the people want to hear. They do not want to preach repentance, they deny His Creation, they deny the Rapture and ridicule those who proclaim that true Christians are not appointed to wrath *(1st Thes. 5:9)*. They laugh at the doctrine of Hell, they mock a supposed Judgment, they have neglected to preach the full Gospel, there is no power in their gospel to save, but rather only to collect souls and try to maintain them until sin has conceived its full end, filling up the Lake of Fire with souls who are willingly manipulated.

"I marvel that you are turning away so soon from Him who called you into the grace of Christ, to a different gospel, which is not another; but there are some who trouble you, even determined to pervert the gospel of Christ. But even if we, or an angel from Heaven, preach any other gospel to you than what we have preached to you, let him be accursed. As we have said before, so now I say again, if anyone preaches any other gospel to you than what you have received, let him be accursed." Galatians 1:6-9

"They have forsaken the right way and gone astray, following the way of Balaam the son of Beor, who loved the wages of unrighteousness; but he was rebuked for his iniquity: a dumb donkey speaking with a man's voice restrained the madness of the prophet. These are wells without water, clouds being driven by a tempest, for whom is reserved the blackness of darkness forever. For when they speak great swelling words of vanity, they allure through the lusts of the flesh, through wantonness, the ones who have actually escaped from those living in error. While they promise them liberty, they themselves are slaves of corruption; for by whom a person is overcome, by him also he is brought into bondage. For if, after they have escaped the defilements of the world through the full true knowledge of the Lord and Savior Jesus Christ, they are again entangled in them and overcome, the end is worse for them than the beginning. For it would have been better for them not to have known the way of righteousness, than having known it, to turn from the holy commandment delivered to them. But it has happened to them according to the true proverb: A dog returns to his own vomit, and, a sow, having been washed, to her wallowing in the mire." 2nd Peter 2:15-22

"For the time will come when they will not endure sound doctrine, but according to their own lusts, desiring to hear pleasant things, they will heap up for themselves teachers; and they will turn their ears away from the truth, and be turned aside to myths." 2nd Timothy 4:3-4

"For ever since the creation of the world the unseen things of Him are clearly perceived, being understood by the things that are made, even His eternal power and Godhead, so that they are without excuse, because, although they know God, they do not glorify Him as God, nor are thankful, but become vain in their reasonings, and their stupid hearts are darkened. Professing to be wise, they become foolish, and change the glory of the incorruptible God into an image made like corruptible man, and birds and four-footed animals and creeping things." Romans 1:20-23

"Because you have kept the Word of My perseverance, I also will keep you from the hour of trial which shall come upon the whole world, to test those who dwell on the earth." Revelation 3:10

Indeed a burning anger goes out against the government of Hawaii for such supposed ridiculous actions to have scared much of the population. Yet how much of a burning anger does God have for those who call themselves pastors, who preach from the pulpits of this world and twist His words to the destruction of the hearers?! How much of an anger will those who stand before the Almighty God have at the Great White Throne Judgment *(Rev. 20:11-15)* regarding have been sucked into the lies of false teachers! Yet they will be without excuse, yet they will be guilty.

"Thus says Jehovah of Hosts, Do not listen to the words of the prophets who prophesy to you. They fill you with vanities; they speak a vision from their own heart, not out of the mouth of Jehovah. They speak to those who despise Me, promising, Jehovah has said, You shall have peace! And they say to everyone who walks after the stubbornness of his own heart, No evil shall come upon you! For who has stood in the counsel of Jehovah, and has perceived and heard His Word? Who has paid attention to His Word and heeded it? Behold, a tempest from Jehovah has gone forth in fury, a whirling tempest. It shall whirl upon the head of the wicked. The anger of Jehovah shall not turn back, until He has executed and until He has fulfilled the purposes of His heart; in the latter days you shall diligently consider it with understanding. I have not sent these prophets, yet they ran; I have not spoken to them, yet they prophesied. But if they had stood in My counsel and had caused My people to hear My Words, then they would have turned them from their evil way and from the evil of their doings. Am I a God near by, says Jehovah, and not a God afar off? Can anyone hide himself in secret places so that I shall not see him? says Jehovah. Do I not fill the heavens and earth? says Jehovah. I have heard what the prophets have said, who prophesy lies in My name, saying, I have dreamed, I have dreamed. How long shall this be in the heart of the prophets who prophesy lies? Indeed, they are prophets of the deceit of their own heart, who think to cause My people to forget My name by their dreams which they tell, each one to his neighbor, as their fathers have forgotten My name for Baal. The prophet who has a dream, let him tell a dream. And he who has My Word, let him speak My Word faithfully. What is the chaff to the wheat? says Jehovah. Is not My Word like a fire? says Jehovah; and like a hammer that breaks the rock in pieces? Therefore thus says Jehovah, Behold, I am against the prophets who steal My Words each one from his neighbor. Jehovah says, Behold, I am against the prophets who use their tongues and say, He says. Jehovah says, Behold, I am against

those who prophesy false dreams and tell them, and cause My people to go astray by their lies and by their foolishness. Yet I did not send them nor command them; therefore they shall not profit this people at all, says Jehovah." Jeremiah 23:16-32

"Therefore, beloved, looking forward to these things, be diligent to be found by Him in peace, spotless and without blemish; and consider that the longsuffering of our Lord is salvation; as also our beloved brother Paul, according to the wisdom given to him, has written to you, as also in all his epistles, speaking in them of these things, in which are some things hard to understand, which the unlearned and unstable twist, as they do also the rest of the Scriptures, to their own destruction. You therefore, beloved, since you know this beforehand, beware also that you not be led away with the error of the wicked, and fall from your own steadfastness. But grow in the grace and knowledge of our Lord and Savior Jesus Christ. To Him be the glory both now and forever. Amen." 2nd Peter 3:14-18

"So the great dragon was cast out, that serpent of old, called the Devil and Satan, who leads the whole world astray; he was cast out onto the earth, and his angels were cast out with him." Revelation 12:9

For those who can hear, for those who are willing to listen. Why or why do you wait? Don't wait! For what will you do when the Trumpet sounds and you are Left Behind? Do you not know, has your ear not heard that God is not mocked. Indeed, do not assume to see such marvelous things with your eyes and assume that you will then yield. Certainly there is a time to be Saved, a time to finally repent and by faith believe into Jesus Christ as your Lord and Savior. He who bore your sins on the Cross *(1st Pet. 2:24)*, He who is the Son of God *(John 3:16)*, who sits at the right hand of the Father *(Ro. 8:34)*, for He conquered death *(2nd Tim. 1:10)* and rose again *(1st Cor. 15:20)*.

"He who has ears to hear, let him hear." Matthew 11:15

"Then Jesus said to the twelve, Do you also want to go away? Then Simon Peter answered Him, Lord, to whom shall we go? You have the Words of eternal life. And we have believed and understood that You are the Christ, the Son of the living God." John 6:67-69

"For He says: In an acceptable time I have heard you, and in a day of salvation I have helped you. Behold, now is the accepted time; behold, now is the day of salvation." 2nd Corinthians 6:2

"Do not be led astray, God is not mocked; for whatever a man sows, that he will also reap. For he who sows to his flesh will of the flesh reap corruption, but he who sows to the Spirit will of the Spirit reap eternal life." Galatians 6:7-8

"For this let everyone who is godly pray unto You, in a time when You may be found; surely in the floods of great waters they shall not come near him." Psalms 32:6

"The coming of the lawless one is according to the working of Satan, with all power, signs, and lying wonders, and with all unrighteous deception among those who are perishing, because they did not receive the love of the truth, that they might be saved. And for this reason God will send them strong delusion, that they should believe the lie, that they all may be judged who did not believe the truth but had pleasure in unrighteousness." 2nd Thessalonians 2:9-12

No one knows when that time will be *(Matt. 24:36)*. It could be today, it could be tomorrow, it could be further down the road, but the warnings have been provided. Why gamble with your soul? Why are you waiting, why are you not concerned about your eternal destination? Why do your eyes see your life now, as you do this and that, but your heart forsakes the right way?

"For what will it profit a man if he gains the whole world, and loses his own soul? Or what will a man give in exchange for his soul?" Mark 8:36-37

This is not the will of God. God provided the free gift of Salvation for all who would believe.

"For God so loved the world that He gave His only begotten Son, that everyone believing into Him should not perish but have eternal life. For God did not send His Son into the world to judge the world, but that the world through Him might be saved. The one believing into Him is not judged; but the one not believing is judged already, because he has not believed in the name of the only begotten Son of God. And this is the judgment, that the Light has come into the world, and men loved darkness rather than the Light, for their deeds were evil. For everyone practicing evil hates the Light and does not come to the Light, lest his deeds should be reproved. But the one doing the truth comes to the Light, that his deeds may be clearly seen, that they have been worked in God." John 3:16-21

Take heed! Don't wait! Your warning is now. Just as there could be an enemy that secretly smuggled in a nuclear weapon, hidden somewhere unknown, there would be no warning when that went off. There will be no warning, only sadness and the knowledge of having been Left Behind. The woman did the right thing in the wake of such a supposed imminent disaster, such an expectation of a violent end to life, she asked for forgiveness for her sins, she trusted in God. Certainly those who repent and believe into Jesus Christ will not be ashamed.

Should it have not been a drill, should Hawaii have actually had an incoming ICBM, then know that those who perished and truly knew the Lord, those who were true Christians, their plight on this earth would have been over, the gates of Heaven opened to receive them to their eternal destination, to be with the Lord. Though violence ended their life, their lives were Saved.

"For whoever desires to save his life will lose it, but whoever loses his life for My sake and the gospel's will save it." Mark 8:35

"But I do not want you to be ignorant, brethren, concerning those who are asleep, that you sorrow not as others who have no hope. For if we believe that Jesus died and rose again, even so God will bring with Him those who sleep in Jesus." 1st Thessalonians 4:13-14

"We are confident, yes, preferring rather to be absent from the body and to be at home with the Lord." 2nd Corinthians 5:8

Just as the Flood can unaware to those who dwelt on the Earth *(Matt. 24:39)*, so too will the wrath of God come unexpectedly upon the world. Understand that destruction during that time will be widespread, while the mercy of God will still abound to those who will accept Christ and become martyrs, most of the world's population will perish due to the wrath of God *(Matt. 24:22)*. Then the horror of it all will be apparent as they stand before their Creator, whom they rejected, as their names are not written in the Book of Life.

"And when He opened the fifth seal, I saw under the altar the souls of those who had been slain because of the Word of God and because of the testimony which they held. And they cried with a loud voice, saying, How long, O Lord, holy and true, until You judge and avenge our blood on those who dwell on the earth? And a white robe was given to each one of them; and it was said to them that they should rest a little while longer, until both the number of their fellow servants and their brethren, who were about to be killed as they were, was filled up." Revelation 6:9-11

"And the devil, who led them astray, was cast into the Lake of Fire and brimstone where the beast and the false prophet are. And they will be tormented day and night forever and ever. And I saw a great white throne and Him who sat on it, from whose face the earth and the heavens fled away. And there was found no place for them. And I saw the dead, small and great, standing before God. And books were opened. And another book was opened, which is the Book of Life. And the dead were judged according to their works, out of the things which were written in the books. And the sea gave up the dead who were in it, and Death and Hades delivered up the dead who were in them. And they were judged, each one, according to their works. And Death and Hades were cast into the Lake of Fire. This is the second death. And anyone not found written in the Book of Life was cast into the Lake of Fire." Revelation 20:10-15

Amen!

In a Moment

"The harvest is past, the summer is ended, and we are not saved." Jeremiah 8:20

Driving home from the sleepy town of Bigfork, Montana the other night, my family and I were listening to a CD. Suddenly the CD went silent then resumed. Ahead the yellow flashing caution traffic light had went out, the CD went silent again, once again resuming. As we turned on the highway heading towards Kalispell, I looked just to make sure the glow of lights from Kalispell was still apparent in the distance, presumably the CD probably has a scratch or a fingerprint on it.

Heading down the highway I began to contemplate the reality of the world we live in, the uncertainty of a normal tomorrow, the unknown lying ahead. As a Christian, I know that if the Rapture occurs I will meet Lord in the air, along with my wife and son. Yet the troublesome times that we live in often has my thoughts comprehending the possibility of disaster striking the United States before that awesome Day.

"But I do not want you to be ignorant, brethren, concerning those who are asleep, that you sorrow not as others who have no hope. For if we believe that Jesus died and rose again, even so God will bring with Him those who sleep in Jesus. For this we say to you by the Word of the Lord, that we who are alive and remain until the coming of the Lord will by no means precede those who are asleep. For the Lord Himself will descend from Heaven with a shouted command, with the voice of the archangel, and with the trumpet of God. And the dead in Christ will rise first. Then we who are alive and remain shall be caught up together at the same time with them in the clouds to meet the Lord in the air. And thus we shall always be with the Lord. Therefore encourage one another with these words." 1st Thessalonians 4:13-18

As I continued driving down the highway, watching out for deer as it was well past evening and into the late night hours, I wondered what would happen if a major city had just been nuked or an EMP had struck the United States. Yes, while I certainly don't know the future, my mind is occasionally troubled at the prospect of such horror. There are so many unanswered questions and concerns regarding the direction that the United States has taken in the past many years that simply don't get addressed. I've addressed those questions before and won't do so again now.

Last year was the most costly year on record for natural disasters in the history of the United States. I ponder, why wasn't it worse during previous administrations, why now? While I will stick to the sound thought that in order for America to be great again we need to repent and return to our Creator, still hasn't some common sense from the current administration been implemented?

"O Israel, return to Jehovah your God, for you have stumbled by your iniquity." Hosea 14:1

"Go and proclaim these words toward the north, and say, Return, O backsliding Israel, says Jehovah; and I will not cause My anger to fall upon you; for I am merciful, says Jehovah, and I will not keep anger forever." Jeremiah 3:12

Could not the same be said about any country that abhors their ways and returns to their Creator?

Is not the federal mandate taken away that all public schools have to allow so-called transgenders to use the bathroom of the opposite sex, as well as shower with the opposite sex? Is not some of the rules regarding forcing private non-profit organizations to provide the day after pill through medical insurance relaxed? Are not transgenders banned from signing up to the military, at least until the courts make up their final decision? Did the United States not bow out of the Paris Accord, in regards to the ridiculous climate change treaty, one that defies what the Bible says about the end of this world? Did not Jerusalem just get recognized as the Capital of Israel? What gives? Perhaps it is that 'price' that Israel had to agree to in order for President Trump to declare Jerusalem the Capital?

"Behold, I will make Jerusalem a cup of trembling to all the peoples all around, and it shall also be against Judah in the siege against Jerusalem. And in that day I will make Jerusalem a heavy stone for all the peoples; all who lift it shall be slashed; cut to pieces. And all the nations of the earth will be gathered against it." Zechariah 12:2-3

"Yet I have chosen Jerusalem, that My name may be there; and I have chosen David to be over My people Israel." 2nd Chronicles 6:6

Certainly if I were in the position to be able to have declared Jerusalem the Capital of Israel, I would have done so, agreeing with the Bible, yet with absolutely no stipulations whatsoever. Who is man to mess with God's chosen land, His chosen people?! Certainly not a wise thing to do.

"I will also gather all nations, and will bring them down into the valley of Jehoshaphat. And I will enter into judgment with them there, on account of My people and My possession, Israel, whom they have scattered among the nations; and divided up My land." Joel 3:2

I'm not the only one who has looked upon these major natural disasters that we have had over the past several decades, on average getting worse and worse. This, seeing first hand with the horrific fire seasons of recent in Montana. Yet I can't declare that these are definitely God's judgment upon this country, though the evidence strongly suggests that they are. The moral decline and the rebellion against our Creator has surged, just as the annual average cost of natural disasters.

"Beware that you do not forget Jehovah your God by not keeping His commandments, His judgments, and His statutes which I am commanding you today, lest, when you have eaten and been filled, and have built beautiful houses and dwelt in them; and when your herds and your flocks multiply, and your silver and your gold are multiplied, and all that you have is multiplied; when your heart is lifted up, and you forget Jehovah your God who brought you out of the land of Egypt, from the house of bondage; who led you through the great and terrible wilderness, with the fiery serpents and scorpions and thirsty land with no water; who has brought water for you out of the rock of flint; who fed you in the wilderness with manna, which your fathers had not known, to humble you and to test you, to do you good in the end; you say in your heart, My power and the might of my hand have acquired me this wealth. But you shall remember Jehovah your God, for it is He who gives you power to acquire wealth, that He may establish His covenant which He has sworn to your fathers, as it is this day. And it shall be, if you cease caring, to forget Jehovah your God, and have walked after other gods, and have served them and bowed down to them, I testify against you this day that you shall perish to extermination. As the nations which Jehovah is destroying before you, so you shall perish, because you would not obey the voice of Jehovah your God." Deuteronomy 8:11-20

We could look at our now debtor nation, and the immense amount of household debt held by the average American. We could look at many different things, but one thing would be certain, in a moment things will change.

Perhaps one day the lights will go out, even in Montana. Perhaps one day millions will have been killed in a war from abroad, and it might not be North Korea that fires the first shot, we have other countries who knowingly despise us. Maybe one day the Trumpet will sound, before any major catastrophic events hit the United States? With the recent earthquake activity along the West Coast, maybe the big one will final hit? Even here in Montana we had a decent shaking not too long along. Man doesn't know the future in such terms, but in regards to knowing that one day those who are alive and remain and those who sleep will meet the Lord in the air, we do know that to be certain *(1 Thes. 4:17)*.

We know that absolutely one day the Lord is going to appear and take us Home. We have confidence in this, we know we won't be here during the *"time of Jacob's trouble" (Jer. 30:7)*, better known as the Tribulation. I simply can't stress the importance of the seriousness of this situation enough!

As the opening verse states, there were come a time where those who are not saved are just that, not saved. What exactly will you do? Why do you refuse to repent and by faith believe into the Lord Jesus Christ as your Savior? What is it that you are placing more importance to, than repenting before your Creator?

"For whoever desires to save his life will lose it, but whoever loses his life for My sake and the gospel's will save it. For what will it profit a man if he gains the whole world, and loses his own soul? Or what will a man give in exchange for his soul?" Mark 8:35-37

"Do not lay up for yourselves treasures on earth, where moth and rust destroy and where thieves dig through and steal; but lay up for yourselves treasures in Heaven, where neither moth nor rust destroys and where thieves do not dig through and steal. For where your treasure is, there your heart will be also." Matthew 6:19-21

"Truly, these times of ignorance God overlooked, but now commands all men everywhere to repent, because He has established a day on which He will judge the world in righteousness by the Man whom He has appointed. He has given assurance of this to everyone by raising Him from the dead." Acts 17:30-31

Who knows what the future may hold in regards to the United States, war, natural disasters or economic troubles? In a moment things will eventually change, whether it be the starting gun of the Rapture or another major problem faced by the world or this country. Will you be ready? Will you be watching and waiting? Or will you be one of those who will only have deep regret or caught off guard, having squandered your opportunity to avoid such troubling time?

"Watch therefore, for you do not know what hour your Lord comes. But know this, that if the master of the house had known what hour the thief comes, he would have watched and not allowed his house to be dug through. Therefore you also be ready, for the Son of Man comes at an hour you do not expect." Matthew 24:42-44

"Then the kingdom of Heaven shall be likened to ten virgins who took their lamps and went out to meet the bridegroom. And five of them were wise, and five foolish. Those who were foolish took their lamps and took no oil with them, but the wise took oil in their vessels with their lamps. But while the bridegroom was delayed, they all nodded and fell asleep. And at midnight there was a cry: Behold, the bridegroom is coming; go out to meet him! Then all those virgins arose and prepared their lamps. And the foolish said to the wise, Give us some of your oil, for our lamps are going out. But the wise answered, saying, No, lest there should not be enough for us and you; but go rather to

those who sell, and buy for yourselves. And while they went to buy, the bridegroom came, and those who were ready went in with him to the wedding feast; and the door was shut. Afterward the other virgins came also, saying, Lord, Lord, open to us! But he answered and said, Truly, I say to you, I do not know you. Watch therefore, for you know neither the day nor the hour in which the Son of Man comes." Matthew 25:1-13

There may come a night when my family is traveling across Montana where the car simply ceases to operate, the lights from homes and ranches in the distance go out. The sparks from the transformers fly into the air, a sure sign an EMP has went off somewhere. There may come a time when I wake up in the morning and turn on the news, only to find that a major war has erupted or millions are presumed dead in a single or many major cities in the United States. There may be a day when my home begins to shake again, this time in a more violent fashion, causing extreme damage. These things I do not know for certain and hope that none will come to pass, but I do know that there will be a Day when either I sleep awaiting my Lord or being alive I meet Him in the air. This I know for certainty, can you say the same?

"But let us who are of the day be sober, putting on the breastplate of faith and love, and as a helmet the hope of salvation. For God did not appoint us to wrath, but to obtain salvation through our Lord Jesus Christ, who died for us, that whether we watch or sleep, we should live together with Him. Therefore encourage each other and build up one another, just as you also are doing." 1st Thessalonians 5:8-11

Amen!

Warn Them!

"I tell you, no; but unless you repent you will all likewise perish." Luke 13:3

I want to take a moment to stress the importance of Biblical Salvation, which all Believers know. Biblical salvation is repentance and by faith believing into Jesus Christ as Lord and Savior. So true Believers, true Christians, those who have repented and believed into Jesus have their names written in the Book of Life *(Rev. 20:15)*.

We know that Christ died for all.

"For the love of Christ holds us, because we judge thus: that if One died for all, then all died; and He died for all, that those who live should no longer live unto themselves, but unto Him who died for them and rose again." 1st Corinthians 5:14-15

We know that God wishes that none would perish.

"The Lord is not slow concerning His promise, as some count slowness, but is longsuffering toward us, not purposing that any should perish but that all should come to repentance." 2nd Peter 3:9

"Do I delight with pleasure in the death of the wicked? says the Lord Jehovah, and not that he should turn back from his ways and live?" Ezekiel 18:23

Consider Christ, He gave His life so that we may have life in Him.

"In this the love of God was revealed in us, that God has sent His only begotten Son into the world, that we might live through Him. In this is love, not that we loved God, but that He loved us and sent His Son to be the propitiation for our sins. Beloved, if God so loved us, we also ought to love one another." 1st John 4:9-11

We are servants of Jesus, as His servants, what are we doing to further spread the Gospel? What about our loved ones, our friends, our neighbors and our coworkers. This was addressed last week, about what we as Christians are doing to store up treasures in Heaven *(Matt. 6:20)*, but let's take some additional time to consider our family and friends.

No one knows the day nor the hour that the Lord is going to appear to take those who are His to be with Him.

"But of that day and hour no one knows, not even the angels of Heaven, but My Father only." Matthew 24:36

"Then we who are alive and remain shall be caught up together at the same time with them in the clouds to meet the Lord in the air. And thus we shall always be with the Lord." 1st Thessalonians 4:17

Yet most Christians would seemingly agree that it appears to be much sooner than later. Even if it were later, should our attitude change towards His work?

Take a look around at what is going on. We have the Israeli peace treaty in the forefront of political discussions. While this certainly has been an issue with many previous administrations, one must consider that things are being done different this time. Finally Jerusalem has been recognized by the United States as the capital on Israel.

With this bargaining chip off the table, apparently with some sort of yet unknown concession having been made on Israel's part, a peace deal seems more viable than in times past. What if the Palestinians started mass terror attacks against Israel? We have seen before that Israel will respond. What if Israel does what they are considering and goes after portions of Syria and Iran? Then again, what if none of these things happen, but peace proceeds.

So many so-called evangelical Christians look forward to this sort of advancement. As has been said before, if they are not Saved and the Rapture happens, there is nothing to look forward to, they will have been Left Behind. Yet with all of this going on, how much longer do we have?

With cryptocurrencies becoming popular, could this not perhaps be a predecessor for a one world currency??? Look at how hard it is to find a Church that preaches biblical Salvation. To take it one step further, how many that even do so are becoming quickly apostate themselves. It is apparent that the apostasy is in full bloom, getting worse seemingly by the year.

"For the time will come when they will not endure sound doctrine, but according to their own lusts, desiring to hear pleasant things, they will heap up for themselves teachers;

and they will turn their ears away from the truth, and be turned aside to myths." 2nd Timothy 4:3-4

Last time we took a look at how Christians ought to be doing the work of the Lord, this time let's take a more personal look at the Lord's work in regards to our family. Truly we can not save people, Jesus Saves them, but we may plant the seed, we may water, ultimately it is in God's hand.

"Who then is Paul, and who is Apollos, but ministers through whom you believe, as the Lord gave to each one? I planted, Apollos watered, but God made it grow. So then neither he who plants is anything, nor he who waters, but God who causes growth. Now he who plants and he who waters are one, and each one will receive his own reward according to his own labor. For we are God's fellow workers; you are God's field, God's building. According to the grace of God which was given to me, as a wise master builder I have laid the foundation, and another builds on it. But let each one take heed how he builds on it. For no one is able to lay any other foundation than that which is laid, which is Jesus Christ. Now if anyone builds on this foundation with gold, silver, precious stones, wood, hay, straw, each one's work will be revealed; for the Day will declare it, because it will be disclosed by fire; and the fire will test each one's work, of what sort it is. If anyone's work which he has built on it remains, he will receive a reward. If anyone's work is consumed, he will suffer loss; but he himself will be saved, yet so as through fire." 1st Corinthians 3:5-15

Men are not guaranteed a breath from the one they are taking now. So we can not necessarily assume that we can put off doing such things.

"As water evaporates from the sea, and a river wastes away and dries up, so man lies down and does not rise. Until the heavens are no more, they shall not awake nor be aroused from their sleep." Job 14:11-12

Yes in times past I have spoken to my family members. Even though most are not receptive, does that simply mean that if the Lord provides the opportunity to further speak to them, I should automatically write them off?

Do you not know that a loved family member or friend could get in a car accident today? Imagine the horror to receive a phone call or a text message that someone who you truly care about is now dead or on life support, struggling to stay alive. Once they are dead or unable to hear you and respond, what can you say? Should you have not already said such things, should not the heart be content in regards to you knowing that you had warned them diligently?

How much sadder is the death of a loved one when you know they are not Saved? How much worse is it knowing that they are going to stand before the Great White Throne Judgment and be condemned to the Lake of Fire *(Rev. 20:11-15)*.

If you will, imagine for a moment that you would be able to be a spectator of such an event. Certainly if the person was very bad, one could imagine, as the family of the victims often watch the man on death row being executed. However, imagine if it were your mother, your brother, your sister, your best friend, your grandpa or grandma or someone else held very dear in your heart.

As you stood there, unable to intercede to God's just judgment, and you heard the verdict, of which you already knew beforehand, that their name was not written in the Book of Life, would you cry out to the Most High, would you beg for mercy because that soul is one whom you care greatly about? As they are cast into Hell, would you burst into tears asking them to forgive you for not telling them about Jesus Christ?

Would you tell them that you knew you needed to warn them, but you didn't want them because you didn't want them to think less of you? Would you tell them that if you weren't so busy you would have had time to make the Bible study with them, that you had thought about doing? Would you tell them that you loved them, but not enough to forsake your selfish ways and warn them?

If you dug a hole in your back yard, to look for buried treasure and you had some nieces and nephews over, would you warn them about the hole as they are running around your yard? If not, if one fell in the hole and broke their leg, this would be bad, this would be irresponsible, but the leg would heal, the bills would eventually get paid, the child would tarry on. Not warning those whom you care about, about the truth of the matter regarding life, sin and Salvation, about God's just judgment, the need for repentance *(Acts 17:30-31)*, the great gift of God *(John 3:16)*, the sacrifice of Jesus Christ who died on the Cross for our sins *(Rom. 4:25)* and rose again from the dead *(1 Cor. 15:14)* to sit at the right hand of the Almighty *(Mark 16:19)*, of which there is no other name of which to be Saved *(Acts 4:12)*, this is another matter.

For the child with the broken leg, some flowers, a sincere apology and perhaps a gift would suffice. Though the ill sentiment of the situation may far outlast the consequences of the broken leg, the situation could be tamed down, the relationship could be restored to where it was prior. With those loved ones who die, without Christ, there is no restoration, there is nothing that can be done. They are lost, they will spend eternity in the Lake of Fire.

Jesus died for our sins, He did not live doing what He pleased, but rather did the will of God the Father *(Luke 22:42)*. As Christians do we continue doing what we please or do we follow in our Lord and Savior's example, doing the will of Him who died for us?

"For to this you were called, because Christ also suffered for us, leaving us an example, that you should follow His steps: Who committed no sin, nor was deceit found in His mouth; who, when He was reviled, did not revile in return; when He suffered, He did not threaten, but gave Himself over to Him who judges righteously; who Himself bore our sins in His own body on the tree, that we, having died to sins, might live unto righteousness; by whose stripes you were healed." 1st Peter 2:21-24

Rather than this just being something that can be nodded in agreement. As Believers, if you are not actively telling those whom you love about the Gospel or if you haven't already, you know what I am saying is true. You can nod in agreement, but if you don't actually get out there and warn them, would they nod in agreement as they stand before God Almighty at the Great White Throne Judgment, when it comes to remembrance that you had warned them or if they could, would they cast a look wondering why you didn't love them enough to tell them, to try and fully explain the Gospel, as they are cast into the Lake of Fire for eternity.

My friends, this is serious business, one which requires due diligence on the part of every Believer. Someone took the time to tell you about the Gospel, someone took the time to tell you about Christ's love for you. You must go and do the same. Do not keep your Salvation a secret, do not prevent the world from knowing that indeed you rest securely in Jesus Christ, your Lord and Savior.

While Christ will wipe away the tears, we have an opportunity right now to not have so many tears when we stand before Jesus at the Judgment Seat of Christ.

"And God will wipe away every tear from their eyes; there shall be no more death, nor sorrow, nor crying. There shall be no more pain, for the former things have passed away." Revelation 21:4

"For we must all appear before the judgment seat of Christ, that each one may receive the things done in the body, according to what he has done, whether good or bad. Knowing, therefore, the terror of the Lord, we persuade men; and we are well known to God, and I also hope are well known in your consciences." 2nd Corinthians 5:10-11

Certainly it may very well be that they simply won't listen, that they don't want to hear. Unfortunately these are the truths that we may have to experience, yet remember that we might have planted a seed, we may have watered and the time could come that God will cause it to grow. We can't always assume that the worst will happen, but we do know that without their names being written in the Book of Life, through biblical Salvation, there is no hope.

"He who testifies to these things says, Surely I am coming quickly. Amen. Even so, come, Lord Jesus." Revelation 22:20

Amen!

Set in Order

"Then the kingdom of Heaven shall be likened to ten virgins who took their lamps and went out to meet the bridegroom. And five of them were wise, and five foolish. Those who were foolish took their lamps and took no oil with them, but the wise took oil in their vessels with their lamps. But while the bridegroom was delayed, they all nodded and fell asleep. And at midnight there was a cry: Behold, the bridegroom is coming; go out to meet him! Then all those virgins arose and prepared their lamps. And the foolish said to the wise, Give us some of your oil, for our lamps are going out. But the wise answered, saying, No, lest there should not be enough for us and you; but go rather to those who sell, and buy for yourselves. And while they went to buy, the bridegroom came, and those who were ready went in with him to the wedding feast; and the door was shut. Afterward the other virgins came also, saying, Lord, Lord, open to us! But he answered and said, Truly, I say to you, I do not know you. Watch therefore, for you know neither the day nor the hour in which the Son of Man comes." Matthew 25:1-13

When king Hezekiah was going to die, the prophet Isaiah told him to set his house in order.

"In those days Hezekiah had become sick unto death. And Isaiah the prophet, the son of Amoz, came to him and said to him, Thus says Jehovah: Set your house in order, for you are dying, and shall not live." 2nd Kings 20:1

Certainly when a man knows that his days are numbered, when he can see that the end of his life is in the near future, the time to ensure that all things are set in order come into play. For each person who has this opportunity to foresee their end here on the earth, they have various things that they want to accomplish and set in order before their death.

How much more should those who are Believers ensure that their lives are set in order before Jesus appears to take us to be with Him *(1 Thes. 4:17)*? How much more should the Church ensure that things are orderly and admonish those who are the bride of Christ *(Rev. 21:9)* to make sure things are set in order?

Are you watching and ready?

"Watch therefore, for you do not know what hour your Lord comes." Matthew 24:42

"Therefore you also be ready, for the Son of Man comes at an hour you do not expect." Matthew 24:44

Have you warned your loved ones, friends, neighbors and coworkers? Have you got these things set in order?

Have you ever considered leaving behind the Gospel message and your personal testimony for those who will be Left Behind and go through your belongings after we depart from this world? Is your Christianity set in order so that those who know you would know that you went to be with the Lord or is it such that they would file a missing persons report, not knowing what happened to you or where you went after you are Raptured?

For those who don't know Christ as their Savior, for those who have not repented and by faith believed into Jesus Christ as their Lord and Savior, why are you putting off getting these things set in order? Do you not realize that you are not guaranteed to live yet another day and if you do not have Salvation set in order, you will be Left Behind?!

The time will come when whatever order things are set in, that is it. It is over, those who are Saved will go to be with the Lord, those who are unsaved will have been Left Behind. At that moment, those who do not have Jesus Christ as their Lord and Savior and pondered doing so, will have to deal with the consequences of not having done so.

"But of that day and hour no one knows, not even the angels of Heaven, but My Father only. But as the days of Noah were, so also will the coming of the Son of Man be." Matthew 24:36-37

"And he said to me, Do not seal the Words of the Prophecy of this Book, for the time is at hand. He who is unjust, let him be unjust still; he who is filthy, let him be filthy still; he who is righteous, let him be righteous still; he who is holy, let him be holy still. And behold, I am coming quickly, and My reward is with Me, to give to every one according to what his work shall be. I am the Alpha and the Omega, the Beginning and the Ending, the First and the Last. Blessed are those who do His commandments, that they may have the right to the Tree of Life, and may enter through the gates into the city. But outside are dogs and sorcerers and prostitutes and murderers and idolaters, and whoever loves and produces a lie. I, Jesus, have sent My angel to testify these things to you, to the churches. I am the Root and the Offspring of David, the Bright and Morning Star. And

the Spirit and the bride say, Come. And let him who hears say, Come. And let him who thirsts come. Whoever desires, let him take of the Water of Life freely." Revelation 22:10-17

Just as a dying man might not get things set in order, so too those who do not repent and believe into Jesus Christ as their Lord and Savior will have to deal with the consequences of that situation. No one can tell you how long before Jesus comes *(Matt. 24:36)* to take those who are truly His to be with Him. Just as no one can declare to you how long you shall live.

"There are many plans in a man's heart; nevertheless the counsel of Jehovah shall stand." Proverbs 19:21

If you take a look around you, is it not apparent that this world is going in the wrong direction. Yet another school shooting, just one larger example of the violence seen throughout America on a daily basis.

The other day I was reading a story to my child. The book is an old one and in there a woman gets into the wrong color car, her families car is parked behind. My son asked how she was able to get into the car, my response is simple, people used to not have to lock their car doors.

While we fortunately have some small cities scattered here and there, where people can generally leave their car doors unlocked, in some cases even their homes, in most cities, even in Kalispell, Montana, one would have to assume the risk for not locking their car doors or homes. On a regular basis, even here, we have people going through parking lots, looking for those who didn't lock their car doors. We also have people breaking into homes and stealing goods, often to purchase drugs. This is the unfortunate reality, we live in a very broken world, a very broken society, one where safety is not guaranteed, even in the best of the neighborhoods.

Just as half of virgins were not prepared, how many people focus on setting in order things of this world, rather than storing up treasures in Heaven?

"Vanity of vanities, says the preacher, vanity of vanities! All is vanity. What is the profit to a man in all his labor which he labors under the sun? A generation passes away, and a generation comes; but the earth stands perpetually." Ecclesiastes 1:2-4

"Do not lay up for yourselves treasures on earth, where moth and rust destroy and where thieves dig through and steal; but lay up for yourselves treasures in Heaven, where neither moth nor rust destroys and where thieves do not dig through and steal. For where your treasure is, there your heart will be also." Matthew 6:19-21

How many people make sure to set in order purchasing a home, a couple of cars, ensuring a solid retirement and great vacations from time to time? How many people set in order trying to ensure that their children are able to participate in numerous extra curricular activities, in order to supposedly give them a well-rounded education, as well as more opportunities later in life, but do not have them set in order the things of God in their hearts, of which true prosperity would exist, the true riches that are found only in Christ?

"And my God shall supply all your need according to His riches in glory in Christ Jesus." Philippians 4:19

How much time do even Christians spend in trying to set in order the things of this world rather than having everything set in order in a biblical manner before their Creator? Consider and consider carefully whether or not your heart is in order before your Creator? Just how much time do we have?

"If then you are raised with Christ, seek those things which are above, where Christ is, sitting at the right hand of God. Set your mind on things above, not on the things of the earth; for you died, and your life is hidden with Christ in God. When Christ who is our life is revealed, then you also will be revealed with Him in glory. Therefore put to death your members which are on the earth: sexual perversion, uncleanness, passion, evil lusts, and covetousness, which is idolatry. Because of these things the wrath of God is coming upon the sons of disobedience; in which you yourselves once walked when you lived in them. But now you yourselves are to put off all these: anger, wrath, malice, blasphemy, filthy language out of your mouth. Do not lie to one another, since you have put off the old man with his practices, and have put on the new man who is renewed in full true knowledge according to the image of the One who created him, where there is neither Greek nor Jew, circumcised nor uncircumcised, barbarian, Scythian, slave nor free, but Christ is all things and in all. Therefore, as the elect of God, holy and beloved, put on a heart of compassion, kindness, humility, meekness, longsuffering; bearing with one another, and forgiving one another, if anyone has a complaint against another; even as Christ forgave you, so you also do. And above all these things put on love, which is the bond of perfectness. And let the peace of God rule in your hearts, to which also you were called in one body; and be thankful. Let the Word of Christ dwell in you richly in all wisdom, teaching and admonishing one another in psalms and hymns and spiritual songs, singing with grace in your hearts to the Lord. And whatever you do in word or deed, do all in the name of the Lord Jesus, giving thanks to God, even the Father, through Him." Colossians 3:1-17

Do not be like the five foolish virgins, be prepared, be ready, have things set in order before God. Get those things done you know you should do, clean up what you know you should. Go! Get things set in order!

"Therefore gird up the loins of your mind, be sober, and rest your hope fully upon the grace that is to be brought to you at the revelation of Jesus Christ; as obedient children, not conforming yourselves to the former lusts in your ignorance; but as He who called you is holy, you also become holy in all conduct, because it is written, Be holy, because I am holy." 1st Peter 1:13-16

Amen!

Place of Torment

"But the cowardly, unbelieving, abominable, murderers, prostitutes, sorcerers, idolaters, and all liars shall have their part in the lake which burns with fire and brimstone, which is the second death." Revelation 21:8

Personal responsibility is a concept that is disappearing quickly. Nowadays there are people who look towards others to bail them out of troubles that oftentimes they have gotten themselves into. Whether it is trouble with the law, troubles with finances or a host of other issues.

In all reality men and women, by and large, need to have the personal responsibility, when they are capable, to provide for their own families and obey the laws of the land. Failure to do so results in consequences. Likewise, preachers also have a responsibility to God to preach His truth regarding the condition of man, Salvation and declaring what God says about the ultimate destiny of mankind and their personal responsibility regarding their sin.

"There was a certain rich man who was clothed in purple and fine linen and fared sumptuously every day. And there was a certain beggar named Lazarus, full of sores, who was laid at his gate, desiring to be fed with the crumbs which fell from the rich man's table. Moreover the dogs came and licked his sores. So it happened that the beggar died, and was carried by the angels into Abraham's bosom. The rich man also died and was buried. And being in torments in Hades, he lifted up his eyes and saw Abraham afar off, and Lazarus in his bosom. Then he cried and said, Father Abraham, have mercy on me, and send Lazarus that he may dip the tip of his finger in water and cool my tongue; for I am tormented in this flame. But Abraham said, Son, remember that in your lifetime you received your good things, and likewise Lazarus evil things; but now he is comforted and you are tormented. And besides all this, between us and you there is

a great chasm fixed, so that those who want to pass from here to you are not able, nor can those from there pass to us. Then he said, I beg you therefore, father, that you would send him to my father's house, for I have five brothers, that he may testify to them, that they not also come to this place of torment. Abraham said to him, They have Moses and the Prophets; let them hear them. And he said, No, father Abraham; but if one goes to them from the dead, they will repent. But he said to him, If they do not hear Moses and the Prophets, neither will they be persuaded though one should rise from the dead." Luke 16:19-31

Let's get this straight and with boldness let the Word of God be proclaimed *(Eph. 6:19)*. There is a place of torment, Hell is a real place. You are separated from God due to your sin, you have a personal responsibility for your sin unless you repent and by faith believe into the Lord Jesus Christ as your Savior, you will ultimately end up in the Lake of Fire, a real place of torment.

"And these will go away into everlasting punishment, but the righteous into eternal life." Matthew 25:46

"For the wages of sin is death, but the gift of God is eternal life in Christ Jesus our Lord." Romans 6:23

"And do not fear those who kill the body but are not able to kill the soul. But rather fear Him who has power to destroy both soul and body in Gehenna." Matthew 10:28

"For certain men have crept in unnoticed, who long ago were set forth to this condemnation, ungodly men, who turn the grace of our God into licentiousness and deny the only Lord God, even our Lord Jesus Christ. But I want to remind you, though you once knew this, that the Lord, having saved the people out of the land of Egypt, afterward destroyed those who did not believe. And the angels who did not keep their proper domain, but left their own abode, He has reserved in everlasting bonds under darkness for the judgment of the Great Day; as Sodom and Gomorrah, and the cities around them in a similar manner to these, having given themselves over to sexual immorality and gone after other flesh, are set forth as an example, suffering the vengeance of eternal fire." Judas (Jude) 1:4-7

"Behold, Jehovah's hand is not shortened, that it cannot save; nor is His ear heavy, that it cannot hear. But your iniquities have separated between you and your God, and your sins have hidden His face from you, that He will not hear." Isaiah 59:1-2

"Truly, these times of ignorance God overlooked, but now commands all men everywhere to repent, because He has established a day on which He will judge the world in righteousness by the Man whom He has appointed. He has given assurance of this to everyone by raising Him from the dead." Acts 17:30-31

"For Christ also suffered for sins once for all, the just for the unjust, that He might bring us to God, being put to death in the flesh but made alive by the Spirit, by whom also He

went and preached to the spirits in prison, who formerly were disobedient, when once the Divine longsuffering waited in the days of Noah, while the ark was being prepared, in which a few, that is, eight souls, were saved through water. There is also an antitype which now saves us; immersion (not the removal of the filth of the flesh, but the answer of a good conscience toward God), through the resurrection of Jesus Christ, Who has gone into Heaven and is at the right hand of God, angels and authorities and powers having been made subject to Him." 1st Peter 3:18-22

"Then Peter said to them, Repent, and let every one of you be immersed in the name of Jesus Christ to the remission of sins; and you shall receive the gift of the Holy Spirit." Acts 2:38

"And he brought them out and said, Sirs, what must I do to be saved? So they said, Believe on the Lord Jesus Christ, and you will be saved, you and your household." Acts 16:30-31

Who believes in Hell anymore? So many preachers for many years have either sideswiped the issue or wholesale deny the existence of a literal place of torment, a literal Hell. Why?

Why? Do they not believe in a Holy and Righteous God who has warned all of humanity? Do not believe in the necessity of Christ to die on the Cross for our sins? Do they not believe that without the blood of Christ, no one could be Saved? Do they not realize the fullness of the great gift of God, who sent His Son that all might not perish, but have everlasting life?

"Do I delight with pleasure in the death of the wicked? says the Lord Jehovah, and not that he should turn back from his ways and live?" Ezekiel 18:23

"The Lord is not slow concerning His promise, as some count slowness, but is longsuffering toward us, not purposing that any should perish but that all should come to repentance. But the day of the Lord will come as a thief in the night, in which the heavens will pass away with a loud noise, and the elements will be dissolved with intense burning; both the earth and the works that are in it will be burned up." 2nd Peter 3:9-10

"For to this you were called, because Christ also suffered for us, leaving us an example, that you should follow His steps: Who committed no sin, nor was deceit found in His mouth; who, when He was reviled, did not revile in return; when He suffered, He did not threaten, but gave Himself over to Him who judges righteously; who Himself bore our sins in His own body on the tree, that we, having died to sins, might live unto righteousness; by whose stripes you were healed. For you were like sheep going astray, but have now returned to the Shepherd and Overseer of your souls." 1st Peter 2:21-25

"And according to the Law almost all things are purified with blood, and without shedding of blood there is no remission. Therefore it was necessary that the copies of the things in the heavens should be purified with these, but the Heavenly things themselves

with better sacrifices than these. For Christ has not entered the holy places made with hands, which are copies of the true, but into Heaven itself, now to appear in the presence of God on our behalf; not that He should offer Himself often, as the high priest enters the Holy of Holies every year with blood of others; He then would have had to suffer often since the foundation of the world; but now, once for all, at the end of the ages, He has been manifested to put away sin through the sacrifice of Himself. And as it is appointed for men to die once, and after this the judgment, so Christ was offered once to bear the sins of many. To those who eagerly wait for Him He will appear a second time, without sin, unto salvation." Hebrews 9:22-28

"For God so loved the world that He gave His only begotten Son, that everyone believing into Him should not perish but have eternal life. For God did not send His Son into the world to judge the world, but that the world through Him might be saved. The one believing into Him is not judged; but the one not believing is judged already, because he has not believed in the name of the only begotten Son of God. And this is the judgment, that the Light has come into the world, and men loved darkness rather than the Light, for their deeds were evil. For everyone practicing evil hates the Light and does not come to the Light, lest his deeds should be reproved. But the one doing the truth comes to the Light, that his deeds may be clearly seen, that they have been worked in God." John 3:16-21

Do they like to get up on the pulpits and pound their nonsense, their sensational doctrine of lies *(1 Tim. 4:1)*, leading their listeners to nothing more than a vain faith in God *(2 Tim. 3:7)*, where what they preach about Him, but they do not speak of the attributes of the Most High, the God of Abraham, Isaac and Jacob *(Ex. 3:6)*? Do they love to tell of the golden streets in Heaven *(Rev. 21:21)* and how there are so many wonderful things there *(John 14:2-3)*? Do they love to tell of those lost loved ones who look down upon you, despite the fact that they might never have repented and believed the Gospel *(Heb. 4:12-13)*? Do they love to tell you how God loves you and wants you to be successful in every economic endeavor in this world? Do they love to tell you how much you are worth, pumping your self esteem through the roof?

"If then you are raised with Christ, seek those things which are above, where Christ is, sitting at the right hand of God. Set your mind on things above, not on the things of the earth; for you died, and your life is hidden with Christ in God. When Christ who is our life is revealed, then you also will be revealed with Him in glory. Therefore put to death your members which are on the earth: sexual perversion, uncleanness, passion, evil lusts, and covetousness, which is idolatry. Because of these things the wrath of God is coming upon the sons of disobedience; in which you yourselves once walked when you lived in them. But now you yourselves are to put off all these: anger, wrath, malice, blasphemy, filthy language out of your mouth. Do not lie to one another, since you have put off the old man with his practices, and have put on the new man who is renewed in full true knowledge according to the image of the One who created him, where there is neither Greek nor Jew, circumcised nor uncircumcised, barbarian, Scythian, slave nor free, but Christ is all things and in all. Therefore, as the elect of God, holy and beloved, put on a heart of compassion, kindness, humility, meekness, longsuffering; bearing with one

another, and forgiving one another, if anyone has a complaint against another; even as Christ forgave you, so you also do. And above all these things put on love, which is the bond of perfectness. And let the peace of God rule in your hearts, to which also you were called in one body; and be thankful. Let the Word of Christ dwell in you richly in all wisdom, teaching and admonishing one another in psalms and hymns and spiritual songs, singing with grace in your hearts to the Lord. And whatever you do in word or deed, do all in the name of the Lord Jesus, giving thanks to God, even the Father, through Him." Colossians 3:1-17

"Do not lay up for yourselves treasures on earth, where moth and rust destroy and where thieves dig through and steal; but lay up for yourselves treasures in Heaven, where neither moth nor rust destroys and where thieves do not dig through and steal. For where your treasure is, there your heart will be also. The lamp of the body is the eye. If therefore your eye is sound, your whole body will be full of light. But if your eye is bad, your whole body will be full of darkness. If therefore the light that is in you is darkness, how great is that darkness! No one is able to serve two masters; for either he will hate the one and love the other, or else he will hold to the one and despise the other. It is not possible to serve God and mammon. Therefore I say to you, do not be anxious about your life, what you will eat or what you will drink; nor about your body, what you will put on. Is not life more than food and the body more than clothing? Observe the birds of the air, for they neither sow nor reap nor gather into barns; yet your Heavenly Father feeds them. Are you not of more value than they? Which of you by being anxious is able to add one cubit to his stature? So why are you anxious about clothing? Consider the lilies of the field, how they grow: they neither toil nor spin; and yet I say to you that even Solomon in all his glory was not arrayed like one of these. Now if God so clothes the grass of the field, which today is, and tomorrow is thrown into the furnace, will He not much more clothe you, O you of little faith? Therefore do not be anxious, saying, What shall we eat? or What shall we drink? or What shall we wear? For after all these things the Gentiles seek. For your Heavenly Father knows that you need all these things. But seek first the kingdom of God and His righteousness, and all these things shall be added to you. Therefore do not be anxious about tomorrow, for tomorrow will worry about its own things. Sufficient for the day is its own trouble." Matthew 6:19-24

"Let nothing be done through selfish ambition or self-glory, but in lowliness of mind let each esteem others as surpassing himself. Let each of you not look out for his own interests, but also for the interests of others. Let this mind be in you which was also in Christ Jesus, who, being in the form of God, did not consider clinging, to be equal with God, but emptied Himself, taking the form of a bondservant, and coming in the likeness of men. And being found comprised as a man, He humbled Himself and became obedient unto death, even the death of the cross. Therefore God also has highly exalted Him and given Him a name which is above every name, that at the name of Jesus every knee should bow, of those in Heaven, and of those on earth, and of those under the earth, and that every tongue should confess that Jesus Christ is Lord, to the glory of God the Father. Therefore, my beloved, as you have always obeyed, not as in my presence only, but now much more in my absence, cultivate your salvation with fear and trembling; for it is God who works in you both to will and to do for His good pleasure." Philippians 2:3-13

Indeed! And they love to pump the world's music, under the guise of 'Christianity', as you grab a coffee from the bar, your heart filled with the false sensations of the deceptive moment. They love for you to leave their meetings full of the deception to think that God is there to help you fulfill your desires! Why would they tell you to die to self and live to God? Why would they tell you to love the Lord your God with all of your being?! Why would they preach hellfire to their congregation where they might upset the masses and realize that they are indeed politically incorrect? Would not the social justice warriors pounce upon such a notion?

"But He answered and said, Every plant which My Heavenly Father has not planted will be uprooted. Let them alone. They are blind leaders of the blind. And if the blind leads the blind, both will fall into the ditch." Matthew 15:13-14

"I have been crucified with Christ; it is no longer I who live, but Christ lives in me; and the life which I now live in the flesh I live by the faith of the Son of God, who loved me and gave Himself for me." Galatians 2:20

"So he answered and said, You shall love the Lord your God with all your heart, with all your soul, with all your strength, and with all your mind, and your neighbor as yourself. And He said to him, You have answered rightly; do this and you will live." Luke 10:27-28

"For the message of the cross is foolishness to those who are perishing, but to us who are being saved it is the power of God. For it is written: I will destroy the wisdom of the wise, and bring to nothing the understanding of the intelligent. Where is the wise? Where is the scribe? Where is the disputer of this age? Has not God made foolish the wisdom of this world? For since, in the wisdom of God, the world through wisdom did not know God, it pleased God through the foolishness of the message preached to save those who are believing. For Jews request a sign, and Greeks seek after wisdom; but we preach Christ crucified, truly to the Jews a stumbling block and to the Greeks foolishness, but to those who are called, both Jews and Greeks, Christ the power of God and the wisdom of God. Because the foolishness of God is wiser than men, and the weakness of God is stronger than men." 1st Corinthians 1:18-25

"And you will be hated by everyone on account of My name. But he who endures to the end will be kept safe." Matthew 10:22

Would the preacher indeed call sodomy a sin that is an abomination to their Creator *(Lev. 18:22)*? Would the preacher tell the hearer that they are deserving of going to Hell due to their sin *(Rom. 6:23)* and that all have sinned *(Rom. 3:23)*? Would the preacher tell people to stop chasing the world's goods and store up treasures in Heaven *(Matt. 6:19)*? Would the preacher tell the congregation to stop thinking about yourself and think of others *(Phil 2:3)*, to follow the example of Christ *(Gal 2:20)*? Would the preacher tell the congregation of the doomed that unless they repent they will ultimately end up in a place of torment? That their future is the Lake of Fire, where they will be cast for all eternity because of their sin! Will he tell those who attend that they will be personal responsible as they stand before their Creator at the Great White Throne Judgment and their will be no bailing them out at that time? Will he let them know that the bailout is readily available and found in no other name than Jesus Christ, the Son of God, who sits at the right hand of the Father *(Mark 16:19)*?!

"And I saw a great white throne and Him who sat on it, from whose face the earth and the heavens fled away. And there was found no place for them. And I saw the dead, small and great, standing before God. And books were opened. And another book was opened, which is the Book of Life. And the dead were judged according to their works, out of the things which were written in the books. And the sea gave up the dead who were in it, and Death and Hades delivered up the dead who were in them. And they were judged, each one, according to their works. And Death and Hades were cast into the Lake of Fire. This is the second death. And anyone not found written in the Book of Life was cast into the Lake of Fire." Revelation 20:11-15

"Nor is there salvation in any other, for there is no other name under Heaven given among men that is required for us to be saved." Acts 4:12

"Jesus said to him, I am the Way, the Truth, and the Life. No one comes to the Father except through Me." John 14:6

Why not?! Why should not a man who is truly called by God Almighty preach what God has called him to preach?! Why should not that man be in fear before His Creator to do what he is called to do and do it appropriately? Why should he not fall on his knees before His Maker, instead of falling prey to those who hold the checkbooks that fund the ministry, if God has indeed called him? Who is he held accountable to, the congregation or the Most High?

"Be diligent to present yourself approved to God, a worker who does not need to be ashamed, rightly dividing the Word of Truth." 2nd Tim. 2:15

"Take heed to yourself and to the doctrine. Continue in them, for in doing this you will deliver both yourself and those who hear you." 1st Tim. 4:16

"Therefore, take heed to do as Jehovah your God has commanded you; do not turn aside to the right hand or to the left." Deuteronomy 5:32

"For there is nothing covered that will not be uncovered, nor hidden that will not be known. Therefore whatever you have spoken in the dark will be heard in the light, and what you have spoken in the ear in inner rooms will be proclaimed on the housetops. And I say to you, My friends, do not be afraid of those who kill the body, and after that have no more that they can do. But I will show you whom you should fear: Fear Him

who, after He has killed, has authority to cast into Gehenna; yes, I say to you, Fear Him!" Luke 12:2-5

The personal responsibility of a Believer is to be doing the work of God through Jesus Christ *(Matt. 24:46)*. The responsibility of the Church is to remain faithful *(1 Cor. 4:2)* and separate unto Christ *(2 Cor. 6:17)*. The responsibility of the preacher is to be faithful and speak the truth *(1 Tim. 4:16; 2 Tim. 2:15)*, according to the Gospel *(Jud. 1:3)*.

"Enter by the narrow gate; for wide is the gate and broad is the way that leads to destruction, and there are many entering in through it. Because narrow is the gate and distressing is the way which leads unto life, and there are few who find it. Beware of false prophets, who come to you in sheep's clothing, but inwardly they are ravenous wolves. You will know them from their fruits. Do men gather grapes from thornbushes or figs from thistles? Even so, every good tree produces excellent fruit, but a corrupt tree produces evil fruit. A good tree is not able to produce evil fruit, nor is a corrupt tree able to produce excellent fruit. Every tree that does not produce excellent fruit is cut down and thrown into the fire. Therefore from their fruits you will know them. Not everyone who says to Me, Lord, Lord, will enter the kingdom of Heaven, but he who does the will of My Father in Heaven. Many will say to Me in that day, Lord, Lord, have we not prophesied in Your name, cast out demons in Your name, and done many works of power in Your name? And then I will declare to them, I never knew you; depart from Me, you who work out lawlessness! Therefore whoever hears these sayings of Mine, and does them, I will liken him to a wise man who built his house on the rock; and the rain descended, the floods came, and the winds blew and beat on that house; and it did not fall, for it was founded on the rock. And everyone who hears these sayings of Mine, and does not do them, will be likened to a foolish man who built his house on the sand; and the rain descended, the floods came, and the winds blew and beat upon that house; and it fell. And great was its fall." Matthew 7:13-27

Amen!

Threats

"And you will hear of wars and rumors of wars. See that you are not troubled; for all these things must come to pass, but the end is not yet. For nation will rise against nation, and kingdom against kingdom. And there will be famines, pestilences, and earthquakes in various places. All these are the beginning of travail." Matthew 24:6-8

Oh for the days of before where there wasn't so many supposed threats against our nation, both from inside and outside influences! This country has suffered from threats before.

We had the threat of a nuclear war during the Cold War with the Soviet Union. There the government increased the paranoia of the situation by telling people to duct tapes windows and school children to go underneath school desks. The horror was fully felt as Barry Goldwater apparently lost the presidential election after the influence of a commercial of a girl picking flower pedals as a mushroom cloud appears. We also had the oil crisis that caused a lot of strife, panic and problems for Americans from coast to coast.

There was a long period of threats from the outside world having disappeared during the 80's, 90's and 2000's. During that time the perceived threat rhetoric was changed from that of an outside threat to an interior threat. The nation took the bait hook, line and sinker, while those who were in the know began ringing the alarm bells. The threat had become an interior one.

Americans allowed wars to continue on around the globe, without any concern of the validity of such actions. With no concern to the millions displaced and starving citizens of foreign countries, nor the literally over a million men, women and children killed for presumed and purposely falsified information, that gained the supposed support of our country's citizens, in all the name of fighting terror. Our government had declared that the threats to our national security was an interior one, thus allowing for both the bombarding of propaganda towards Americans, as well as supposed justification to increase our global military dominance around the globe.

Growing poppy fields with no end in sight in Afghanistan, where the current Trump administration has yet increased troops, the opium crisis is now apparent. Poppies are used to make opiates, including heroin. With bases established in the Middle East the Obama administration managed to blow out the Arab governments, creating the Arab Spring, of which these countries are even more torn than before, with wars and instability. This also creates great discord with Russia, who is fighting to retain their Mediterranean port in Syria. In America the government declared war on freedom, under the guise of terrorism.

Starting with the Oklahoma City bombing, one that has evidence of collusion by the government, the battle began. Yet Americans still remained resilient towards taking away freedoms from the general public, yet all of this changed on 9/11.

In an instance a tragedy had happened. While the World Trade Center had an attack prior, via a bomb in the parking garage, Americans watched over and over again video and news commentary regarding the terrorist attack. Pictures of people jumping from the towers, to their death, the buildings free falling, as if they were imploded. Horrific images, deeply embedded, the images burned into the memory of those Americans who revisited over and over again the horror of what appeared to be a legitimate terrorist attack. Then there were those who started asking questions.

Professors, engineers and others wondered how the World Trade Center towers managed to freefall into their own footprint. People began to ask questions why so quickly all of the leftover steel from that tragic day was suddenly shipped off to China. With traces of thermite in scraps of steel, those who were in leadership positions and questioned the official story began to drop like flies, dying one after another. While the lines were full of Americans waiting to enlist in the Army, in order to fight back those who had done such a thing, those in power had done some curious things.

George W. Bush's own father had called for a new world order EXACTLY ten years before 9/11, when he was President. When President Bush was approached, while reading a book, he was reading a book about a goat, holding it upside down. The goat is symbolic to satanism. Larry Silverstein had purchased extra insurance prior to the attacks on 9/11. Fighter jets had been ordered to stand down on that fateful day, as well at the same time there were drills going on for such an event. Some had foretold that the rumor was that an attack was going to happen. The attack happened, but without writing a book of details, many of which are written, the evidence points correctly to 9/11 being an inside job. Who exactly pulled it off, remains a mystery.

With this the war on the people had begun. The Patriot Act, the Military Commissions Act, the John Werner Defense Authorization Act and many others, including executive orders by President Bush, stripped Americans of many of their rights, as well as unleashed the NSA (National Security Administration), the DOJ (Department of Justice) and created the ridiculous DHS (Department of Homeland Security). The FBI (Federal Bureau of Investigation) began compiling watchlists for terrorists, including the KST (Known or Suspected Terrorist). That list blew up to well over a million citizens.

People began to become complacent. Certainly there was a backlash and the Tea Party movement caught on. Soon enough there were enough Tea Party candidates who got elected, though they turned on their voters and refused to overturn the notorious Patriot Act. With some relief put in place, after the revelations of Edward Snowden, the Patriot Act has not only regained it's full power, but expanded it even further.

During that time a fair portion of Americans started to prepare for the inevitable to no end. Now the threat perceived by that portion of Americans was that they were the enemy and they were being targeted. Indeed my family can attest to what it is like to have been and be targeted by the Federal Government. You can read our story for free by clicking on the link on All Will Stand (allwillstand.org) or going directly to the Of Missing Persons website (ofmissingpersons.com). After time the amount of those who complain about such draconian measures begins to dwindle. Most people give up and certainly many more accept having to have their naked body scanned and treated as enemy combatants while traveling across the country.

They justify the necessity of dealing with such totalitarian measures by an 'ends justify the means' mentality. Some suggest that if you have nothing to hide, then why worry about it? Well, because our government can not be trusted, what government can? Do not the American people now see how big of a mess Washington D.C. is and the amount of deep rooted corruption found throughout, in both political parties? This same nonsense argument is now being used to try and take away guns from citizens who quite simply have a 2nd Amendment right, irregardless of the opinion of those who oppose. Just as there is supposed free speech, via the 1st Amendment, I assure you that you run a risk by having a genuine opinion. Rights are rights, simple as that.

Now with the precedent already set for a locked-down society, one that can declare a citizen an enemy combatant, removing them of their citizenship and placing them in a prison, a society that promotes torture, under the guise of 'enhanced-interrogation', here we are well into the 21st century. Don't expect these measures to lessen anytime soon, largely they simply get worse with time. So we have a full blown war on the American people, those whom the government declares to be enemies of the state, under the guise of the war on terrorism, of whom those unfortunate ones who end up on these ridiculous and nonsense lists have much company, with well over a million other American citizens. Those who are your neighbors, your co-workers, your friends and even family, our government has declared them to be potential terrorists, yet these same intelligence agencies can't stop a school shooting, even when the man openly declared, using his own name, that he is going to become a professional school shooter! That is not protected free speech.

Now threats are appearing on the outside. We have a government who has the ability to lock down this country, arrest and imprison those who they declare are enemies of the state, should they either choose to do so or if the conditions in this country supposedly merit such a measure. Over the past several years numerous foreign enemies have been appearing and our drastic policies towards these countries certainly are not of the isolationist sort.

China has been building their military nonstop, include new weaponry, tanks, fighter jets, etc. They are actively trying and so far successfully doing so, taking over the South China Sea, as well as placing military bases in different countries around the world. Together with Russia, their open ally, who also has been making alliances around the world. Of course the North Korea ordeal, that has been discussed before, has not went away, with recent threats of wars having been made. All around the world, America has become a joke, a byword, are we becoming a Banana Republic? How many of our supposed allies wouldn't care if North Korea were able to knock out our power grid with a super EMP weapon or hit some city with a nuclear warhead? Now Vladimir Putin, Russia's President, has just made threats that far outweigh those of our other enemies.

Showing off an array of new weaponry that could easily exterminate those who reside from sea to shining sea of this country, he mocks our forces that he claims are preparing for war against Russia via NATO. These new weapons are indeed powerful and likely could circumvent our missile defense system, of which there is no guarantee that even North Korea couldn't do the same. So here we are, as Americans living in the year 2018.

We watched as our country suffered the highest cost of natural disasters ever in our history last year. As our country continues down the moral decline, rebelling against our Creator, one can only ponder what other disasters, even a major disaster such as our power grid knocked out or nuclear war. While our American pride might be strong enough to go against other nations, certainly our pride is nothing compared to the Almighty God, who sees what we are doing.

"And the pride of man shall be bowed down; and the haughtiness of men shall be brought low; and Jehovah alone shall be exalted in that day." Isaiah 2:17

What type of stability is there in this world nowadays. Is now a good time to purchase a new home? Is now a good time to plan for expanding your family? Is now a good time to start a business endeavor? Is now a good time to move to a major city? Or rather is it a good time to ensure that one certainly has repented and by faith believed into Jesus Christ as their Lord and Savior? Indeed! We have threats that are both from the inside of our own government and also from the outside, often instigated by our own government.

There are wars and rumors of wars. The stock market bounces back and forth in what would only be another threat against the sensibility of money, as well as the stability of our nation. Of course we can not forget about the Federal Reserve, which is neither federal, nor a reserve, and has historical been proven to be financers of revolutions, wars, depressions and propping up financial markets, manipulating currencies throughout the nations.

Who can say what the future holds? Well God has told us the future, He has declared what happens to mankind. He tells us that those whose names are not written in the Book of Life will be cast for eternity in the Lake of Fire. Clearly these things are declared, clearly they are not threats, they are the reality, one which every man, woman and child on the face of the earth needs to know. The Gospel needs to be preached to all of them, whether or not they choose to accept this absolute Truth.

"Remember this, and be a man; refresh the memory of your heart, you who rebel. Remember the former things from a long time ago; for I am the Mighty God, and there is no other; I am God, and no one else is like Me, declaring the end from the beginning, and from antiquity things which are not yet done, saying, My counsel shall stand, and I will do all My pleasure; calling a bird of prey from the east, the man who executes my counsel from a distant land. Indeed, I have spoken it; I will also bring it to pass. I have formed it; I will also do it." Isaiah 46:8-11

"And I saw a great white throne and Him who sat on it, from whose face the earth and the heavens fled away. And there was found no place for them. And I saw the dead, small and great, standing before God. And books were opened. And another book was opened, which is the Book of Life. And the dead were judged according to their works, out of the things which were written in the books. And the sea gave up the dead who were in it, and Death and Hades delivered up the dead who were in them. And they were judged, each one, according to their works. And Death and Hades were cast into the Lake of Fire. This is the second death. And anyone not found written in the Book of Life was cast into the Lake of Fire." Revelation 20:11-15

"Go therefore and instruct all the nations, immersing them into the name of the Father and of the Son and of the Holy Spirit, teaching them to observe all things whatever I have commanded you; and lo, I am with you always, even to the end of the age. Amen." Matthew 28:19-20

While my hope is that none of these threats occur, while I would hope that the Lord would take us to be with Him prior to any potential threats actually occurring. We do know for certain from the Bible that indeed there will come a time where men will hide. There will come a time when most of humanity will be killed, their bodies littering the landscape. The Holy Scriptures teaches what happens to a world that has chosen to be disobedient to their Creator and the just Judgment of the Most High, who though with a heavy hand chastises the nations, He also has mercy towards those who would still, even then, repent and by faith believe into His Son Jesus Christ as Lord and Savior *(Rev. 7:9-17)*. While they will give their lives during that time for doing so, we can be certain that those of us who are true Christians, who have truly repented and believed the Gospel will not be here during that time, we will have been Raptured out of this world beforehand.

"For the Lord Himself will descend from Heaven with a shouted command, with the voice of the archangel, and with the trumpet of God. And the dead in Christ will rise first. Then we who are alive and remain shall be caught up together at the same time with them in the clouds to meet the Lord in the air. And thus we shall always be with the Lord." 1st Thessalonians 4:16-17

"For behold the days are coming in which they will say, Blessed are the barren, wombs that never bore, and breasts which never nursed. Then they will begin to say to the mountains, Fall on us! and to the hills, Cover us!" Luke 23:29-30

"A roaring noise shall come to the ends of the earth; for Jehovah has a controversy with the nations; He will enter into judgment with all flesh. He will give those who are wicked to the sword, says Jehovah. Thus says Jehovah of Hosts, Behold, evil shall go forth from nation to nation, and a great tempest shall be roused up from the recesses of the earth. And in that day the slain of Jehovah shall be from one end of the earth even to the other end of the earth. They shall not be mourned, nor gathered, nor buried. They shall be as dung on the ground." Jeremiah 25:31-33

"And they shall go into the caves of the rocks, and into the holes of the earth, for the terror of Jehovah, and from the glory of His majesty; when He rises up to make the earth tremble." Isaiah 2:19

"For God did not appoint us to wrath, but to obtain salvation through our Lord Jesus Christ, who died for us, that whether we watch or sleep, we should live together with Him." 1st Corinthians 5:9-10

What will you do when the future happens, when the *"time of Jacob's trouble" (Jer. 30:7)* begins, better known as the Great Tribulation? Then, when horror upon horror is inflicted upon the earth in its due time, where will you turn to o' man? To whom will you go or to what? Will you look towards earthly leaders? Will you join in with those who still continue to rebel and refuse to repent towards their Creator? Will you accept the mark of the beast *(Rev. 14:9-10)*, dooming yourself for all eternity? Will you look towards gods made with man's hands, gods of wood, gold and silver? Will you look towards the stars that were Created by the one and only God, as your refuge? Will you believe more falsehoods? Ultimately irregardless of what you choose, there is really only one choice. Either you repent and by faith believe into Jesus as your Savior or else you will with certainty stand before your Creator who will recompense you for all of your sins, indeed as your name is not written in the Book of Life, you will give Him who all men are accountable before, no choice but by His own holiness to cast you forever into the Lake of Fire where Satan and the False Prophet will reside.

"The great day of Jehovah is near; it is near and hastens greatly, the sound of the day of Jehovah. The mighty man shall cry out bitterly there. That day is a day of wrath, a day of trouble and distress, a day of desolation and ruin, a day of darkness and gloom, a day of clouds and thick darkness, a day of the shofar and alarm against the fortified cities, and against the high towers. And I will bring distress upon men, and they shall walk like

the blind, because they have sinned against Jehovah. And their blood shall be poured out as dust, and their flesh like dung. Their silver and their gold shall not be able to deliver them in the day of the wrath of Jehovah. But all the earth shall be devoured by the fire of His jealousy. For He shall make a complete and speedy end of all those who live in the land." Zephaniah 1:14-18

"And I saw another angel flying in the midst of heaven, having the eternal gospel to preach to those who dwell on the earth; to every nation, tribe, tongue, and people; saying with a loud voice, Fear God and give glory to Him, for the hour of His judgment has come; also, do homage to Him who made the heavens and the earth, the sea and springs of water. And another angel followed, saying, Babylon is fallen, is fallen, that great city, because she has made all nations drink of the wine of the wrath of her sexual perversion." Revelation 14:6-8

"But the rest of mankind, who were not killed by these plagues, did not repent of the works of their hands, that they should not do homage to demons, and idols of gold, silver, brass, stone, and wood, which are not able to see nor hear nor walk. And they did not repent of their murders nor their sorceries nor their sexual perversions nor their thefts." Revelation 9:20-21

"In that day a man shall throw his idols of silver and gold, which they made each man to bow down to, to the moles and to the bats; to go into the crevices of the rocks, and into the clefts of the cliffs, from the terror of Jehovah, and from the glory of His majesty; when He rises up to make the earth tremble. Leave off from such a man, whose breath is in his nostril; for how is he to be accounted?" Isaiah 2:20-22

"And the devil, who led them astray, was cast into the Lake of Fire and brimstone where the beast and the false prophet are. And they will be tormented day and night forever and ever." Revelation 20:10

This is no threat, this is the truth.

Amen!

Knowledge Shall Be Increased

"And at that time, Michael shall stand up, the great ruler who stands for the sons of your people. And there shall be a time of distress, such as has not been since there was a nation until that time. And at that time, your people shall be delivered, everyone that shall be found written in the Book. And many of those sleeping in the earth's dust shall awake, some to everlasting life, and some to reproach and everlasting abhorrence. And the prudent shall shine as the brightness of the firmament, and those who turn many to righteousness, as the stars forever and ever. But you, O Daniel, shut up the words and seal the book, to the time of the end. Many shall run to and fro, and knowledge shall be increased." Daniel 12:1-4

It is apparent that knowledge has been increased. As I write this article, just over a month shy of 40 years old, I have seen numerous changes in my lifetime.

This article is typed using software that will alert me to misspelled words, it's older software that I choose to use. Then I will take this article and I will post it up on the world wide web, a term that is barely used outside of geek squads nowadays. This will be posted on a website that was designed using software, hosted on a computer overseas. Afterwards the link to the article will make its way to three separate social media websites, finally it will be emailed to those who have subscribed to have these articles emailed to them. Then, as is usually the case, a radio show will be recorded using software and a semi-pro microphone, specifically for webcasting.

Afterwards the audio clip saved to the computer will be uploaded to where there is a subscription for hosting webcasts. Finally it will be made available to whomever might listen to it now or in the future. If one were to ponder the extent of ease of making information readily available, it would be immediately seen just how much knowledge has increased. Yes, with that increase there is a seemingly jungle of too much information, too many things, out there.

Of course there are autonomous vehicles, buses and trucks. Commercial jets have the capability to land themselves, medical science has made leaps and bounds, just to name a couple of more things. Now the latest military weapons of some countries are hypersonic missiles and jets. Quite honestly a very large and extensive list could be made of the increase of knowledge regarding these awesome technological advances. Yet where I ask is the increase of knowledge regarding the things of God? The Bible has a yet to be fulfilled prophecy regarding that also.

"Behold, the days are coming, declares the Lord Jehovah, that I will send a famine into the land, not a famine for bread, nor a thirst for water, but rather a famine for hearing the Words of Jehovah. And they shall wander from sea to sea, and from the north even to the east; they shall roam to and fro to seek the Word of Jehovah, and they shall not find it." Amos 8:11-12

I'm old fashioned in regards to having a preference of actual printed books, reference books to complete whatever task has been laid on my heart for All Will Stand. However, even though I have a printed dated edition of *Strongs*, as well as other resources, even I have a browser open as I write this article, to quickly pull up verses. All I have to do is know a couple of words of the verse and I can usually find it in a few seconds, much quicker than the old *Strongs* that is used less and less.

That particular prophecy has always amazed me at how choke full of information is really there. Think about it, imagine not being able to find God's Word, the Holy Scriptures! Sure right now there are many bad copies of translations everywhere, truly a shame, but even Walmart still sells the King James Version here in Kalispell, Montana. There is a link on the website to an online KJV. You can order one on a thousand different websites, you can go to the library, you can go to your neighbors, you can get one for free at our local Salvation Army. Imagine not being able to find a copy of the Bible!

Imagine the world seeking after the things of God! Is that not contrary to what we see going on in today's societies of the world? People during that time, during the *"time of Jacob's trouble" (Jer. 30:7)*, will actually be roaming to and fro to seek the Word of Jehovah! Talk about censorship during the Antichrist reign! Obviously if one considers the martyrs that are killed for proclaiming Christ during the Tribulation period, then you can seemingly understand the same spirit that is likely behind trying to seek the things of God. It is all anti-Christian, truly a terrible time for those dwelling on the earth.

"And when He opened the fifth seal, I saw under the altar the souls of those who had been slain because of the Word of God and because of the testimony which they held. And they cried with a loud voice, saying, How long, O Lord, holy and true, until You judge and avenge our blood on those who dwell on the earth? And a white robe was given to each one of them; and it was said to them that they should rest a little while

longer, until both the number of their fellow servants and their brethren, who were about to be killed as they were, was filled up." Revelation 6:9-11

As knowledge has increased, so also has the violence in this world. In my old neighborhood, just outside of Chicago, violence has become much more common. The street signs are covered with tagging and the last time I was in that neighborhood, one block away from where we used to live, there was drug dealing on the corner in broad daylight. Another spot that my family used to enjoy was Oklahoma City.

The last time we were there, same thing, there was drug dealing and hookers on the street corners during broad daylight, that being a city that we had known fairly well years prior. Even in Montana, where often we are what appears to be behind in the times, in terms of the latest technology, trends, etc., violence is becoming more common place. One can no longer safely leave a bicycle unlocked and expect it to be where they left it. Once again these violent times that not only the United States is suffering from, are prophesied.

"But evil men and pretenders will grow worse and worse, leading astray and being led astray." 2nd Timothy 3:13

"And as it was in the days of Noah, so it will be also in the days of the Son of Man: They ate, they drank, they married wives, they were given in marriage, until the day that Noah entered into the ark, and the flood came and destroyed them all. Likewise as it was also in the days of Lot: They ate, they drank, they bought, they sold, they planted, they built; but on the day that Lot went out of Sodom it rained fire and brimstone from heaven and destroyed them all. Even in the same way will it be in the day when the Son of Man is revealed. In that day, he who will be on the housetop, and his goods are in the house, let him not come down to take them away. And likewise the one who is in the field, let him not return back. Remember Lot's wife. Whoever seeks to save his life will lose it, and whoever loses his life will preserve it. I tell you, in that night there will be two in one bed: the one will be taken and the other will be left. Two will be grinding together: the one will be taken and the other left. Two will be in the field: the one will be taken and the other left. And they answered and said to Him, Where, Lord? And He said to them, Wherever the body is, there the eagles will be gathered together." Luke 17:26-37

"And Jehovah saw that the evil of man was great on the earth, and that every imagination of the thoughts of his heart was only evil all day long." Genesis 6:5

I'm well aware of the non-ending violence in South Africa, the horrific violence in Mexico, the increase of violence in Australia, as well as other parts of the world. You think that it is bad now? Well, let me tell you to understand clearly that those who are Left Behind, (because their name is not written in the Book of Life *(Rev. 20:15)*), at the Rapture, the violence that one sees now would be considered safety. Imagine what happens when the Holy Spirit who restrains is removed from this world?! If people just stab or shot people for now no reason, aside from wanting to kill someone, then what will they do when God's restraint is allowed to be removed?!

"For the mystery of lawlessness is already at work; only He is now restraining, until it is raised from out of the midst. And then the lawless one will be unveiled, whom the Lord will consume with the breath of His mouth and destroy with the brightness of His coming. The coming of the lawless one is according to the working of Satan, with all power, signs, and lying wonders, and with all unrighteous deception among those who are perishing, because they did not receive the love of the truth, that they might be saved. And for this reason God will send them strong delusion, that they should believe the lie, that they all may be judged who did not believe the truth but had pleasure in unrighteousness. But we owe thanks to God always for you, brethren beloved by the Lord, because God from the beginning chose you for salvation through sanctification of the Spirit and belief in the truth, to which He called you through our gospel, for the obtaining of the glory of our Lord Jesus Christ." 2nd Thessalonians 2:7-14

Yes we are certainly living in interesting times, but also very dangerous times. As we see such prophecies being fulfilled before our very eyes, we must remember those prophecies that were already fulfilled, numerous ones regarding Jesus Christ, the Lord and Savior. We must remember and look at this greatness of what God has already declared and how it has already come to pass and must remember what God declares will with absolute certainly come to pass EXACTLY as He has declared.

"Remember the former things from a long time ago; for I am the Mighty God, and there is no other; I am God, and no one else is like Me, declaring the end from the beginning, and from antiquity things which are not yet done, saying, My counsel shall stand, and I will do all My pleasure; calling a bird of prey from the east, the man who executes my counsel from a distant land. Indeed, I have spoken it; I will also bring it to pass. I have formed it; I will also do it." Isaiah 46:9-11

"The counsel of Jehovah stands forever, the thoughts of His heart from generation to generation." Psalms 33:11

"And all those living in the earth are counted as nothing. And He does according to His will in the army of Heaven, and among those living in the earth. And no one is able to restrain His hand or say to Him, What are You doing?" Daniel 4:35

We must consider these things and be diligent as Christians to let those who will listen know that all must repent and by faith believe into Jesus Christ as their Lord and Savior. We must remind the world and tell the world about the Gospel and about Salvation that is in no other name than Jesus Christ *(Acts 4:12)*. We must warn those who are sitting on the fence regarding making such a decision and answer those who have questions. Now is certainly the time.

"For He says: In an acceptable time I have heard you, and in a day of salvation I have helped you. Behold, now is the accepted time; behold, now is the day of salvation." 2nd Corinthians 6:2

"And he said to me, Do not seal the Words of the Prophecy of this Book, for the time is at hand. He who is unjust, let him be unjust still; he who is filthy, let him be filthy still; he who is righteous, let him be righteous still; he who is holy, let him be holy still. And behold, I am coming quickly, and My reward is with Me, to give to every one according to what his work shall be. I am the Alpha and the Omega, the Beginning and the Ending, the First and the Last. Blessed are those who do His commandments, that they may have the right to the Tree of Life, and may enter through the gates into the city. But outside are dogs and sorcerers and prostitutes and murderers and idolaters, and whoever loves and produces a lie." Revelation 22:10-15

For those of who ponder these things or postpone for whatever reason, understand that eventually it will be too late. Yes, if you have read such articles as these or heard such radio shows, you know that this is often times repeated. What will you do when you don't have to put up with such articles anymore? When you don't have to listen to such things anymore? Knowing that if you did not receive Christ as your Savior, you will have been Left Behind. Of course, one would simply mention the fact that there is no guarantee that one would live until tomorrow anyway. Yet take a clear look at the beginning passage of scripture to this article. Where will you awake?

"For thus says Jehovah who Created the heavens, God who has formed the earth and made it; who has established it, who has not created it void, but has formed it to be inhabited: I am Jehovah, and there is no other. I have not spoken in secret, in a dark place of the earth. I did not say to the seed of Jacob, Seek me in vain. I, Jehovah, speak righteousness, I declare things that are right. Assemble yourselves and come; draw near together, you who have escaped from the nations. Those who set up the wood of their graven image, and those that pray to a god that cannot save, they know nothing. Declare and approach; yea, let them take counsel together. Who has declared this from antiquity? Who has told it since then? Is it not I, Jehovah. And there is no other God besides Me; a just Mighty God and a Savior; there is no one besides Me. Turn to Me, and be saved, all the ends of the earth; for I am the Mighty God, and there is no other. I have sworn by Myself, the word has gone out of My mouth in righteousness, and shall not return, that to Me every knee shall bow, every tongue shall swear." Isaiah 45:18-23

Amen!

They Believe Others

"I have come in My Father's name, and you do not receive Me. If another comes in his own name, him you will receive." John 5:43

Certainly we know this to be a prophetic statement. Truly there will come a time where the Antichrist will arise and lead the world astray *(Rev. 13:14)*. Pretending to be God *(2 Thes. 2:4)*, he will become both the political and religious leader of the world *(Rev. 13:3)*. During that time, the *"time of Jacob's trouble" (Jer. 30:7)*, better known as the Great Tribulation, many will be deceived. That is a time like no other and Jesus warned about such a time.

"For then there will be great affliction, such as has not been since the beginning of the world until this time, no, nor ever shall be. And unless those days were shortened, no flesh would be kept safe alive; but for the elect's sake those days will be shortened. Then if anyone says to you, Look, here is the Christ; or, There; do not believe it. For false christs and false prophets will arise and show great signs and wonders to lead astray, if possible, even the elect. Behold, I have told you beforehand." Matthew 24:21-25

Yet we have seen precursors in many ways since Jesus went to sit at the Father's right hand *(Mk. 16:19)*. Already the mass majority believe others, instead of believing Jesus Christ, the author and finisher of our faith.

"Therefore we also, since we are surrounded by so great a cloud of witnesses, let us lay aside every weight, and the sin which so persistently harasses us, and let us run with perseverance the race that is set before us, looking unto Jesus, the author and finisher of our faith, who for the joy that was set before Him endured the cross, despising the shame, and has sat down at the right hand of the throne of God." Hebrews 12:1-2

We know that God does not change. Quite simply the character and moral standards set by God are the same.

"For I, Jehovah, change not." Malachi 3:6a

"Jesus Christ the same yesterday, today, and forever." Hebrews 13:8

So why has man changed the standards of God? Why has the simplicity of Salvation, for a sinner to repent and by faith believe into Jesus Christ as their Lord and Savior, become so watered down, that there are literally flocks of people who falsely name Jesus as their Savior, never having been Born Again, those who claim, but do not truly know Jesus in their hearts?

"All things have been delivered to Me by My Father, and no one knows the Son except the Father. Nor does anyone know the Father except the Son, and the one to whom the Son wills to reveal Him. Come to Me, all you who labor and are heavy laden, and I will give you rest. Take My yoke upon you and learn from Me, for I am meek and lowly in heart, and you will find rest unto your souls. For My yoke is easy and My burden is light." Matthew 11:27-30

"Truly, these times of ignorance God overlooked, but now commands all men everywhere to repent, because He has established a day on which He will judge the world in righteousness by the Man whom He has appointed. He has given assurance of this to everyone by raising Him from the dead." Acts 17:30-31

"And he brought them out and said, Sirs, what must I do to be saved? So they said, Believe on the Lord Jesus Christ, and you will be saved, you and your household." Acts 16:30-31

"Then Peter said to them, Repent, and let every one of you be immersed in the name of Jesus Christ to the remission of sins; and you shall receive the gift of the Holy Spirit. For the promise is to you and to your children, and to all who are afar off, as many as the Lord our God will call." Acts 2:38-39

"Jesus said to him, I am the Way, the Truth, and the Life. No one comes to the Father except through Me." John 14:6

"If we receive the testimony of men, the testimony of God is greater; for this is the testimony of God which He has witnessed about His Son. He who believes in the Son of God has the testimony in himself; he who does not believe God has made Him a liar, because he has not believed the testimony that God has given concerning His Son. And this is the testimony: that God has given us eternal life, and this life is in His Son. He who has the Son has life; he who does not have the Son of God does not have life. These things I have written to you who believe in the name of the Son of God, that you may know that you have eternal life, and that you may continue to believe in the name of the Son of God." 1st John 5:9-13

Jesus said, *"I tell you, no; but unless you repent you will all likewise perish."* Luke 13:3

Understand what has become a complex issue. Salvation is simple, repent and by faith believe into the Lord Jesus Christ as your Savior, truly an issue of the heart of a sinner before their Creator. Yet what we have is an extremely complex issue whereas many are on the broad path that leads to destruction, with the thought that they will be in Heaven after they die. Many are chasing after false religions that offer pretences based upon works or other unbiblical rites that they purport are the correct path to Heaven. These are not new ideas or a new problem, but what has confounded the simplicity that is found in Christ *(2 Cor. 11:3)* is that fact that nowadays there are all of these preachers who speak lies, who preach a dangerous doctrine, one that does not fit into the Word of God. They twist their words and proclaim that this is what God proclaims, yet He does not. He hasn't changed, they have changed, changed from the Truth, if they were ever even there, to spewing words of death to their unfortunate and often willingly participating congregation. They believe others, instead of believing Jesus Christ.

"Enter by the narrow gate; for wide is the gate and broad is the way that leads to destruction, and there are many entering in through it. Because narrow is the gate and distressing is the way which leads unto life, and there are few who find it. Beware of false prophets, who come to you in sheep's clothing, but inwardly they are ravenous wolves. You will know them from their fruits. Do men gather grapes from thornbushes or figs from thistles? Even so, every good tree produces excellent fruit, but a corrupt tree produces evil fruit. A good tree is not able to produce evil fruit, nor is a corrupt tree able to produce excellent fruit. Every tree that does not produce excellent fruit is cut down and thrown into the fire. Therefore from their fruits you will know them. Not everyone who says to Me, Lord, Lord, will enter the kingdom of Heaven, but he who does the will of My Father in Heaven. Many will say to Me in that day, Lord, Lord, have we not prophesied in Your name, cast out demons in Your name, and done many works of power in Your name? And then I will declare to them, I never knew you; depart from Me, you who work out lawlessness! Therefore whoever hears these sayings of Mine, and does them, I will liken him to a wise man who built his house on the rock; and the rain descended, the floods came, and the winds blew and beat on that house; and it did not fall, for it was founded on the rock. And everyone who hears these sayings of Mine, and does not do them, will be likened to a foolish man who built his house on the sand; and the rain descended, the floods came, and the winds blew and beat upon that house; and it fell. And great was its fall." Matthew 7:13-27

"Now the Spirit expressly says that in latter times some will depart from the faith, being devoted to corrupting spirits and doctrines of demons, speaking lies in hypocrisy, having their own conscience seared, forbidding to marry, and commanding to abstain from foods which God created to be partaken with thanksgiving by those who believe and know the truth." 1st Timothy 4:1-3

"But know this, that in the last days perilous times will come: For men will be lovers of themselves, lovers of money, boasters, proud, blasphemers, disobedient to parents,

unthankful, unholy, without natural affection, unyielding, slanderers, without self-control, savage, despisers of good, traitors, headstrong, haughty, lovers of pleasure rather than lovers of God, having a form of godliness but denying its power. And from such people turn away. For of this sort are those who creep into households and make captives of gullible women loaded down with sins, led away by various lusts, always learning, but never able to come to the full true knowledge of the truth." 2nd Timothy 3:1-7

"For the time will come when they will not endure sound doctrine, but according to their own lusts, desiring to hear pleasant things, they will heap up for themselves teachers; and they will turn their ears away from the truth, and be turned aside to myths." 2nd Timothy 4:3-4

Dangerous times, dangerous times indeed! For now the preacher from the pulpit likes to tell lies. They enjoy their large buildings, their full congregations of the doomed, who seem to portray the rightness of their false doctrine, just by the mere numbers of people who sit amongst the spiritually dead week after week. Certainly who will rise up against them and speak the truth?! Who will dare tell those wealthy, those in high positions, those with respect amongst the leaders of their respective community, that indeed their doctrine of self, wealth and relative morals are lies that they enjoy hearing, because their companions certainly say it is so?!

Just as Stephen Hawking will now have his confidence in a scientific formula of there being no God shattered, that which he preached, as the unnamed king of the atheists, tested, so too they will stand before their Creator, not in joy, not with the gates of Heaven being opened, but in fear of knowingly that whether willingly or unwittingly, they are doomed for all eternity to the Lake of Fire. For all will stand before their Creator, if your name is not written in the Book of Life, then the judgment against you is known already.

"And I saw a great white throne and Him who sat on it, from whose face the earth and the heavens fled away. And there was found no place for them. And I saw the dead, small and great, standing before God. And books were opened. And another book was opened, which is the Book of Life. And the dead were judged according to their works, out of the things which were written in the books. And the sea gave up the dead who were in it, and Death and Hades delivered up the dead who were in them. And they were judged, each one, according to their works. And Death and Hades were cast into the Lake of Fire. This is the second death. And anyone not found written in the Book of Life was cast into the Lake of Fire." Revelation 20:11-15

"The coming of the lawless one is according to the working of Satan, with all power, signs, and lying wonders, and with all unrighteous deception among those who are perishing, because they did not receive the love of the truth, that they might be saved. And for this reason God will send them strong delusion, that they should believe the lie, that they all may be judged who did not believe the truth but had pleasure in unrighteousness." 2nd Thessalonians 2:9-12

These issues have been addressed in the past. The reality of the situation that more than ever nowadays, we as Americans, and indeed much of the world face, is that the amount of preachers who are called by God to preach and indeed do not water down God's Word is becoming more and more sparse. As a preacher is called to be faithful, so to must those who are Believers in this dark age.

"All Scripture is breathed by God, and is profitable for doctrine, for reproof, for correction, for instruction in righteousness, that the man of God may be complete, thoroughly equipped for every good work." 2nd Timothy 3:16-17

"I charge you therefore before God and the Lord Jesus Christ, who will judge the living and the dead at His appearing and His kingdom: Preach the Word. Be ready in season and out of season. Convict, rebuke, exhort, with all longsuffering and teaching." 2nd Timothy 4:1-2

"Moreover it is required in stewards that one be found faithful." 1st Corinthians 4:2

"Therefore we strive, whether at home or away, to be well pleasing to Him. For we must all appear before the judgment seat of Christ, that each one may receive the things done in the body, according to what he has done, whether good or bad. Knowing, therefore, the terror of the Lord, we persuade men; and we are well known to God, and I also hope are well known in your consciences." 2nd Corinthians 5:9-11

We certainly live in world where they believe others.

They believe others rather than God who Created the heavens and earth.

"In the beginning God created the heavens and the earth." Genesis 1:1

"Professing to be wise, they become foolish, and change the glory of the incorruptible God into an image made like corruptible man, and birds and four-footed animals and creeping things." Romans 1:22-23

They believe others rather than God who says there are two genders.

"But from the beginning of the creation, God made them male and female." Mark 10:6

They believe others rather than God who states that sodomy is an abomination.

"For this reason a man shall leave his father and mother and cleave to his wife, and the two shall become one flesh; so then they are no longer two, but one flesh." Mark 10:7-8

"You shall not lie with a male as with a female. It is an abomination." Leviticus 18:22

They believe others rather than God and continue on in their sexual perversions.

"Flee sexual perversion. Every sin that a man does is outside the body, but he who commits sexual immorality sins against his own body." 1st Corinthians 6:18

"Do you not know that the unrighteous will not inherit the kingdom of God? Do not be led astray. Neither prostitutes, nor idolaters, nor adulterers, nor effeminate, nor sodomites, nor thieves, nor covetous, nor drunkards, nor revilers, nor extortioners will inherit the kingdom of God." 1st Corinthians 6:9-10

"And they did not repent of their murders nor their sorceries nor their sexual perversions nor their thefts." Revelation 9:21

The list could go on and on, nonetheless, for those who know Christ, for those who have repented and by faith believed into the Lord Jesus Christ, remember and keep this close to your heart.

"And if it seems evil to you to serve Jehovah, choose for yourselves this day whom you will serve, whether the gods which your fathers have served that were on the other side of the River, or the gods of the Amorites, in whose land you are living. But as for me and my house, we will serve Jehovah." Joshua 24:15

For those who believe others and like to listen to soothing words from the preacher, take to heart these words of warning from Jesus.

"And to the angel of the church of the Laodiceans write, These things says the Amen, the Faithful and True Witness, the Beginning of the creation of God: I know your works, that you are neither cold nor hot. I would that you were cold or hot. So then, because you are lukewarm, and neither cold nor hot, I will vomit you out of My mouth. Because you say, I am rich, have become wealthy, and have need of nothing; and do not know that you are wretched and miserable and poor and blind and naked; I counsel you to buy from Me gold refined in the fire, that you may be rich; and white garments, that you may be clothed, that the shame of your nakedness may not be revealed; and anoint your eyes with eye salve, that you may see. As many as I love, I rebuke and chasten. Therefore be zealous and repent. Behold, I stand at the door and knock. If anyone hears My voice and opens the door, I will come in to him and dine with him, and he with Me. To him who overcomes I will grant to sit with Me on My throne, as I also overcame and sat down with My Father on His throne. He who has an ear, let him hear what the Spirit says to the churches." Revelation 3:14-22

Amen!

Slothful

"Be diligent to present yourself approved to God, a worker who does not need to be ashamed, rightly dividing the Word of Truth." 2nd Timothy 2:15

The other day there was a knock on the door. At the door was someone who is from the Jehovah Witnesses. With information in hand they were trying to get me to attend their meeting. After our brief conversation, at which I let them know that I was not interested at all and that were neither of Jehovah or a witness to the Truth, they made their way to the neighbors home.

Two by two members of both the Jehovah Witnesses and Mormons go out into the world with their false doctrine, propagating their lies. Though one would understand that indeed those knocking on doors are also deceived, their diligence is something to be commended, if only they were really doing the work of Christ in spreading the Gospel message.

In times past I have had tracts left by what would be considered conservative Independent Fundamental Baptist churches. While the tract would be a breath of fresh air in comparison to some of the bizarre and unbiblical teachings left by others, it too fell short of the full Gospel message. Even then repentance was not mentioned and nearly all tracts that I have run across, except on a rare occasion, include a sinner's prayer for one to repeat, also absent of repentance. In most cases if someone repeated those words they are instructed to call or write and let the church that handed out the tract know that they are now saved, that they have accepted Jesus Christ as their Lord and Savior, of which the Holy Scriptures is silent on a so-called 'sinner's prayer'.

So we have the diligence of those cults, yes there is no other term as they have made up a religion, no matter how many people seemingly make it acceptable; and we also have those who do not rightfully divide the Word *(2 Tim. 2:15)*, those who do not search the Scriptures, those who do not separate themselves to the Lord. The Bible speaks of these things also:

"These were more noble than those in Thessalonica, in that they received the Word with all readiness, and searched the Scriptures daily, to see whether these things are so." Acts 17:11

"Do not be unequally yoked together with unbelievers. For what fellowship has righteousness with lawlessness? And what communion has light with darkness? And what agreement has Christ with Belial? Or what part has a believer with an unbeliever? And what agreement has the temple of God with idols? For you are the temple of the living God. As God has said: I will dwell in them and walk among them. I will be their God, and they shall be My people. Therefore, Come out from among them and be separate, says the Lord. Do not touch what is unclean, and I will receive you. And I will be a Father to you, and you shall be My sons and daughters, says the Lord Almighty." 2nd Corinthians 6:14-18

Here we are in the year 2018. Our societies are a mess, sin is rampant and getting worse. Those who are Christians, true Believers, who have repented and by faith believed into Jesus Christ as their Lord and Savior are too often slothful. The pastors of these churches know that oftentimes they have a hard enough time to get their congregation to live holy and separate lives, read the Bible, spend time in prayer, let alone help in the churches ministries to spread the Gospel to those willing to hear. They are slothful.

Certainly God be thanked for those who are diligent to spread the Gospel, those who set up guards against false doctrine coming into their congregations, those who rightly divide the Word, those who stick to biblical separation. There are those churches out there who certainly are diligently doing the work of Christ, to these, this is not written.

For those who are diligent, you know that most congregations would rather water down God's Word in order to grow their supposed God-honoring church, yet what they are doing is destroying the foundation. They are not building wisely.

"Therefore whoever hears these sayings of Mine, and does them, I will liken him to a wise man who built his house on the rock; and the rain descended, the floods came, and the winds blew and beat on that house; and it did not fall, for it was founded on the rock. And everyone who hears these sayings of Mine, and does not do them, will be likened to a foolish man who built his house on the sand; and the rain descended, the floods came, and the winds blew and beat upon that house; and it fell. And great was its fall." Matthew 7:24-27

"According to the grace of God which was given to me, as a wise master builder I have laid the foundation, and another builds on it. But let each one take heed how he builds on it. For no one is able to lay any other foundation than that which is laid, which is Jesus Christ. Now if anyone builds on this foundation with gold, silver, precious stones, wood,

hay, straw, each one's work will be revealed; for the Day will declare it, because it will be disclosed by fire; and the fire will test each one's work, of what sort it is. If anyone's work which he has built on it remains, he will receive a reward. If anyone's work is consumed, he will suffer loss; but he himself will be saved, yet so as through fire." 1st Corinthians 3:10-15

Certainly preaching the true Gospel is not popular with the masses, but it is what has been given to those whom God has called. Also it is apparent that each Believer also has a part in the Great Commission. Each Believer should be a light unto the world.

"For the message of the cross is foolishness to those who are perishing, but to us who are being saved it is the power of God. For it is written: I will destroy the wisdom of the wise, and bring to nothing the understanding of the intelligent. Where is the wise? Where is the scribe? Where is the disputer of this age? Has not God made foolish the wisdom of this world? For since, in the wisdom of God, the world through wisdom did not know God, it pleased God through the foolishness of the message preached to save those who are believing. For Jews request a sign, and Greeks seek after wisdom; but we preach Christ crucified, truly to the Jews a stumbling block and to the Greeks foolishness, but to those who are called, both Jews and Greeks, Christ the power of God and the wisdom of God." 1st Corinthians 1:18-24

"And Jesus came and spoke to them, saying, All authority is given to Me in Heaven and on earth. Go therefore and instruct all the nations, immersing them into the name of the Father and of the Son and of the Holy Spirit, teaching them to observe all things whatever I have commanded you; and lo, I am with you always, even to the end of the age. Amen." Matthew 28:18-20

"You are the light of the world. A city that is set on a hill cannot be hidden. Nor do they light a lamp and put it under a grain measure, but on a lampstand, and it shines for all who are in the house. Let your light so shine before men, so that they may see your good works and glorify your Father in Heaven." Matthew 5:14-16

Certainly there are times that preaching the Gospel can seem fruitless. All Will Stand is not a big organization, nor never has any intention on becoming such. What God's will is regarding this ministry will be done. What God intends to happen, will happen.

If I were to take a look at the numbers of people who visit the website, if I were to take a look at the amount of people who listen to the radio show or the amount of people who visit the Spanish website, I could quickly become discouraged. I could look at the fruit of the ministry and declare 'what is the point' and simply cease doing what the Lord leads me to do. Yet in such would be great folly, in these instances I would be in a grave sin, for if the Lord calls you to do His bidding, regarding His work, then we are commanded to be diligent, not slothful.

"Do you not know that those who run in a race all run, but one receives the prize? Run in such a way that you may obtain it. And everyone who competes for the prize controls

himself in all things. Now they do it to obtain a perishable crown, but we an imperishable. Therefore I run in this manner: not with uncertainty. Thus I fight: not as one who beats the air. But I discipline my body and bring it into subjection, lest, when I have preached to others, I myself should become disqualified." 1st Corinthians 9:24-27

"Therefore we also, since we are surrounded by so great a cloud of witnesses, let us lay aside every weight, and the sin which so persistently harasses us, and let us run with perseverance the race that is set before us, looking unto Jesus, the author and finisher of our faith, who for the joy that was set before Him endured the cross, despising the shame, and has sat down at the right hand of the throne of God. For consider Him who endured such opposition from sinners against Himself, that you not become weary and faint in your souls." Hebrews 12:1-3

Rather we should consider those examples given to us in the Holy Scriptures, of men called by God to proclaim His truth and realize that the results our God's, not ours. It makes no difference whether or not one person gets Saved, one person has a seed planted, one person is watered or if the ministry is a so-called success in man's eyes, as we live in a day and age where nearly every success story has the apparent threads of deception mixed in with the truth of God's Word.

"Who then is Paul, and who is Apollos, but ministers through whom you believe, as the Lord gave to each one? I planted, Apollos watered, but God made it grow. So then neither he who plants is anything, nor he who waters, but God who causes growth. Now he who plants and he who waters are one, and each one will receive his own reward according to his own labor. For we are God's fellow workers; you are God's field, God's building." 1st Corinthians 3:5-9

Consider Elijah,

"And he said, I have been very zealous for Jehovah the God of Hosts; for the children of Israel have forsaken Your covenant, torn down Your altars, and killed Your prophets with the sword. I alone am left; and they seek my soul, to take it away." 1st Kings 19:10

Anyone who studies the Bible knows that Elijah was certainly a great prophet. How many people did he proclaim God's truth to? Yet we can clearly see in his day and age, no one would listen, rather they killed God's prophets. Yet God replies:

"Yet I have left in Israel seven thousand, all whose knees have not bowed to Baal, and every mouth that has not kissed him." 1st Kings 19:18

Consider Jeremiah

"O Jehovah, You have deceived me, and I was deceived. You are stronger than I, and You have prevailed. I am in derision all the day; everyone mocks me. For whenever I speak, I cry out, I cry violence and devastation; for the Word of Jehovah has been a reproach and a derision to me all the day. Then I said, I will not make mention of Him, nor speak in His name any more. But His Word was in my heart like a burning fire shut up in my bones, and I was weary with holding it in, and I could not. For I have heard the whisperings of many, terror is all around. Proclaim, they say, and we will report it. Everyone at peace with me is watching for me to stumble and fall, saying, Perhaps he will be lured away, and we shall prevail against him, and shall take our revenge on him. But Jehovah is with me like a mighty, awesome one. Therefore my persecutors shall stumble, and they shall not prevail. They shall be greatly ashamed; for they shall not succeed. Their everlasting reproach shall never be forgotten. But, O Jehovah of Hosts, who tries the righteous and sees the soul and the heart, let me see Your vengeance on them. For I have made my cause known to You. Sing to Jehovah! Praise Jehovah! For He has delivered the soul of the poor from the hand of evildoers. Cursed be the day in which I was born; let not the day in which my mother bore me be blessed. Cursed be the man who brought news to my father, saying, A male child has been born to you; making him very glad. And let that man be as the cities which Jehovah overthrew without compassion; and let him hear the cry in the morning, and the shouting at noon; because he did not kill me from the womb; or that my mother might have been my grave, and her womb always pregnant. Why did I come forth from the womb to see labor and sorrow, that my days should be consumed with shame?" Jeremiah 20:7-18

Yet God was for him,

"And Nebuchadnezzar king of Babylon gave charge concerning Jeremiah to Nebuzaradan the captain of the guard, saying, Take him and look after him, and do him no evil; but do with him even as he says to you." Jeremiah 39:11-12

Consider Paul

"When Silas and Timothy had come from Macedonia, Paul was compelled by the Spirit, and testified to the Jews that Jesus is the Christ. But when they opposed him and blasphemed, he shook his garments and said to them, Your blood be upon your own heads; I am clean. From now on I will go to the Gentiles." Acts 18:5-6

Yet the Lord responded,

"Then the Lord spoke to Paul in the night by a vision, Do not be afraid, but speak, and do not keep silent; for I am with you, and no one will attack you to harm you; for I have many people in this city." Acts 18:9-10

As Christians what we need to be doing is the work of the Lord. The necessity in this day and age is apparent, irregardless of what the results may be. Our only responsibility to our Savior is that we be doing what we should, not the results of that.

"Blessed is that servant whom his master will find so doing when he comes." Luke 12:43

What we want to hear is 'well done good and faithful servant' *(Matt. 25:23)* when we stand before Christ at the Judgment seat *(2 Cor. 5:10)*.

Don't give up! Keep going! Let the Lord find those who are His, doing what we are supposed to do. While we may certainly get discouraged, remember the results are God's, we simply are to be faithful.

"Moreover it is required in stewards that one be found faithful." 1st Corinthians 4:2

Amen!

Word by Word

"To whom shall He teach knowledge? And whom shall He make to understand the message? Those weaned from the milk and removed from the breasts. For precept must be upon precept, precept upon precept; line upon line, line upon line; here a little, there a little"... Isaiah 28:9-10

We live in a world, where word by word things are being changed. Mass deceptions, as defined as words that are contrary to the Holy Scriptures, are being placed as snares upon the whole world, word by word. This tactic has been deployed on unsuspecting masses for quite a time. The purpose of this article is to make people, including Believers, aware of such tactics, not to actually break down the principles of how the deception works.

Truly there is an easy way to overcome these deceptions. For Christians, for those who have truly repented and by faith believed into Jesus Christ as their Lord and Savior, simply believe God, believe His Word, believe what He says and anything that is contrary to what our Creator has declared, then we can easily see through the deception. Really it is that simple.

"Finally, my brethren, be strong in the Lord and in the power of His might. Put on all the armor of God, that you may be able to stand against the wiles of the devil. For we do not wrestle against flesh and blood, but against rulers, against authorities, against the world's rulers of the darkness of this age, against spiritual wickedness in the heavenlies. Therefore take up all the armor of God, that you may be able to resist in the evil day, and having done all, to stand. Stand firm therefore, having girded your waist with truth, having put on the breastplate of righteousness, and having shod your feet with the preparation of the gospel of peace; above all, taking the shield of faith with which you will be able to quench all the fiery darts of the wicked one. And take the helmet of

salvation, and the sword of the Spirit, which is the Word of God; praying always with all prayer and supplication in the Spirit, being watchful to this end with all perseverance and supplication for all the saints;" Ephesians 6:10-18

"These were more noble than those in Thessalonica, in that they received the Word with all readiness, and searched the Scriptures daily, to see whether these things are so." Acts 17:11

This article is going to touch on a potentially very serious subject. While I by no means claim to have any special insight regarding prophecy, I am seeing what may very well be a huge snare in our midst, one of biblical proportions of deception. Could this be tied into the Antichrist system, perhaps, then again perhaps not? Jesus makes quite clear no one knows the day nor the hour and I doubt that Believers would know who the Antichrist is prior to the pretribulation Rapture. We might suspect, we could guess it correctly, but I would think the verification of such a thing would not be prior to the Lord taking us to be with Him.

"But of that day and hour no one knows, not even the angels of Heaven, but My Father only." Matthew 24:36

"For the mystery of lawlessness is already at work; only He is now restraining, until it is raised from out of the midst." 2nd Thessalonians 2:7

With that said, also understand that I do not find it my duty or the duty of the Christian Church to try and guess exactly what mechanism will be used for the mark of the beast, or who the Antichrist will be. While certainly these subjects make for interesting conversations, with that said, our faith should be solid enough to know that these things will happen and ultimately what we have been called to do, as Believers, is to further the Gospel, by doing the Lord's will individually in regards to this work of His. Certainly there are those who are needed to, at least on occasion, preach against false doctrines *(2 Tim. 4:2)*, which do oftentimes include a post-trib rapture theory, some who claim that we are in the Tribulation now, etc. Yet I must be reminded that there are always those who proclaim that such and such a person is the Antichrist, by either naming every recent President of the United States or speculating future leaders of Israel. Due to this, someone will eventually have guessed it correctly, though I do not believe that the Lord would actually give insight into such things, as that is not for the Church *(Rev. 4:1)*, who at that time will be removed, for we are not appointed to wrath *(1 Cor. 5:9)*.

"And he causes all, both small and great, rich and poor, free and slave, to receive a mark on their right hand or on their foreheads, so that no one may buy or sell except one who has the mark or the name of the beast, or the number of his name. Here is wisdom. Let him who has understanding calculate the number of the beast, for it is the number of a man, and his number is 666." Revelation 13:16-18

"And then the lawless one will be unveiled, whom the Lord will consume with the breath of His mouth and destroy with the brightness of His coming." 2 Thessalonians 2:8

"Heaven and earth will pass away, but My Words will by no means pass away." Matthew 24:35

"And this gospel of the kingdom will be preached in all the world as a testimony to all the nations, and then the end will come." Matthew 24:14

Nonetheless I do not shy away from discussing such things, especially if the burden is laid on my heart, but I tell all to exercise caution in such discussions that only lead to speculation, without any absolute proof. Eventually a time will come when the Rapture has happened *(Rev. 22:10-12)* and those who had heard of some of these things and been Left Behind will take to the internet. Those who happened, by chance of the moment, to have guessed who the Antichrist was correctly will have their writings and doctrines that they teach being promoted, yet further dissuading the masses of people from the simplicity that is in Christ. This will only render the deception greater and as such will cause people to believe the person's false doctrine, who logically would also have been Left Behind, heaping even more deception, in many cases justly.

"But I fear, lest somehow, as the serpent deceived Eve by his craftiness, so your minds may be corrupted from the simplicity that is in Christ. For if he who comes preaches another Jesus whom we have not preached, or if you receive a different spirit which you have not received, or a different gospel which you have not accepted; you may well put up with it." 2nd Corinthians 11:3-4

"The coming of the lawless one is according to the working of Satan, with all power, signs, and lying wonders, and with all unrighteous deception among those who are perishing, because they did not receive the love of the truth, that they might be saved. And for this reason God will send them strong delusion, that they should believe the lie, that they all may be judged who did not believe the truth but had pleasure in unrighteousness." 2nd Thessalonians 2:9-12

We have discussed many issues regarding what the world teaches verses what God says. There is a big difference here. The Creator of this world *(Is. 42:5)*, your Creator *(Gen. 1:27)*, has given His Words to all humanity, has provided His Son Jesus Christ as the means of Salvation for every man and quite simply as for me and my family we will firmly adheed to what God says. There will be no compromise regarding what the Bible states regarding God's truth in my family.

"All Scripture is breathed by God, and is profitable for doctrine, for reproof, for correction, for instruction in righteousness, that the man of God may be complete, thoroughly equipped for every good work." 2nd Timothy 3:16-17

"Nor is there salvation in any other, for there is no other name under Heaven given among men that is required for us to be saved." Acts 4:12

"And if it seems evil to you to serve Jehovah, choose for yourselves this day whom you will serve, whether the gods which your fathers have served that were on the other side of the River, or the gods of the Amorites, in whose land you are living. But as for me and my house, we will serve Jehovah." Joshua 24:15

So we will start here. What we see is mass deception on various scales. When the deception happens then there are tons of people who propagate the lies and further the deception. In fact such things often even happen in so-called churches where God's truth is so watered down, that their status is either clearly evident to those who know Christ or their compromising has made the saving power of the Gospel *(Ro. 1:16)* virtually ineffective. Let's look at a few examples of what has happened throughout the years.

The first example we will look at will be regarding Creation verses man's lies of evolution. Clearly, as a Believer, and we have discussed this issue in detail in the past, as well as addressed this on radio shows, God is the Creator and the world was Created in six, twenty-four hour days *(Gen. 1:31-2:1)*. This is an absolute fact. Yet word by word they have caused God's Creation to go astray from this great truth, to me a very important truth, to the point where even those who believe what God's Word clearly states are often embarrassed to the point where they won't even speak up when the opportunity presents itself, due to knowing they will be ridiculed.

The second example we will look at will be regarding marriage and sexual immortality. Clearly, as we have discussed before, the Bible is not silent in any regard *(1 Cor. 6:9-10)*, regarding what God's states about these things. Yet man has changed what God has stated word by word. Now we live in a nation with rampant sexual immorality and unbiblical marriage, in contrary to what the Bible teaches.

The last example given will be regarding the doctrine of the Rapture. Years ago many churches used to preach a pretribulation Rapture doctrine, as the Bible clearly states, yet now it is becoming less and less prominent. Word by word the preachers have changed what God's Word clearly teaches about the future of this world and the hope of all Believers *(1 Thes. 5:11)* and instead teach that Believers will go through the Tribulation. Why then, not also preach enthusiastically, as I am sure some do, for all of their listeners to dig a cave, buy supplies, etc., for the seven year period that they are going to endure? I ask you, why not?

"For God did not appoint us to wrath, but to obtain salvation through our Lord Jesus Christ, who died for us, that whether we watch or sleep, we should live together with Him." 1st Thessalonians 5:9-10

Now I will give an example of how this is done. Our education system and our entertainment industry work very hard to slowly take and change the morals of this nation, as well as around the world. Recently I came across the word homosexual. The example sentence for the word was *"Why are homosexuals discriminated against."* Right here might seem like not much, but word by word ideas are entered into the public's mind and eventually ideas start corrupting those who are not Saved, even sometimes those who do know the Lord *(2 Cor. 11:3-4)*.

To further on this topic, I remember attending a Southern Baptist Church (SBC) years ago when I was in high school. The SBC had decided that after Ellen had the first gay kiss on prime time television that ABC and Disney should be boycotted. Where are they now? Shouldn't the boycott continue? Another example was the *Roseanne* television hit series, now apparently coming back with a redone show. If the witch on a broomstick at the end of the show, in the credits, wasn't convincing enough that the show, which promotes moral relativism as the world's education system does, wasn't a big enough hint to the immorality, then after the show had captivated the hearts of their audience, probably some who knew they shouldn't have been watching it, but it wasn't that 'bad' in their minds; the appearance of characters whom had become part of the show suddenly, over time and slowly, come out of the closet as being gay and defying God's standards. This was not the only popular show to do such things, Rosie O'Donnell comes to mind also.

As was stated, the purpose is not to break down the mechanisms used by such people to change the viewpoints of their listeners, the problem truly starts when the world doesn't believe God and His Word. Yet, as many change agents across the country, have jobs were they press people into the predetermined position, manipulating them, the same mechanisms are introduced and effectively what we see now is what we see.

If you don't think this is correct, a few things should point out otherwise. First, Elvis records were burned by Christian groups at massive events throughout the United States, yet it was only a little while longer that groups like Led Zeppelin hit the top of the music charts. Women and men wore bathing suits that covered much more of their bodies, compared to the skimpy or sometimes none, depending on where one lives nowadays. Homosexuality was deemed wrong by society, now it is accepted and gay marriage is the law of the land. I guarantee you, that given enough time, the transsexual movement will become even more profound and if accepted enough, something more sinister and evil, yes even worse, will be around the corner, waiting to creep in. *The Sound of Music* was the first movie that I am aware of to use a swear word. I would ponder whether or not it would be acceptable to even type that word in this article, compared to the garbage mouths in the entertainment industry nowadays, even our politicians are often foul mouthed, truly a reflection of our values as a nation, that are contrary to God. Yet I know that God's standards don't change, they are the same. Therefore it is still wrong to type such things, just as it were, even if it would seem so mild in comparison to what else is out there.

"For I, Jehovah, change not." Malachi 3:6a

"Jesus Christ the same yesterday, today, and forever." Hebrews 13:8

Now I present something that has troubled my heart. I have watched on the sidelines regarding President Donald Trump. I even had a very dear Christian brother who had convinced me that I should vote for him, under an argument that I normally don't accept, the lesser of two evils. Certainly Hillary Clinton was a bad choice, a very bad one, yet I don't ever vote for those who support abortion anyway. I never did get around to voting for Donald Trump, but I have been watching him carefully since his inauguration.

Certainly there are a lot of things I agree with him on and applaud him on. Fair trade, getting rid of the Paris Accord, etc. I'm not against a wall with Mexico, countries have the right to their borders, yet I also have seen other things in regards to the amount of Goldman Sachs individuals, other named heads of departments, as well as just the overall immorality. Did I expect for America to elect a Christian in office? Of course not, but in a country that already appears by all means to be under God's judgment, we certainly should exercise caution regarding what we are doing in the world and in our own society. For instance, additional funding for abortion is not a step in the right direction. I stated beforehand and I will state it again. If America wants to be great again then America needs to repent. Quite honestly we, as a nation, are setting ourselves up for a heap of trouble when God decides to no longer be patient and merciful, whether this is before or after the Rapture happens.

"And after all this, if you do not obey Me, but walk contrary to Me, then I also will walk contrary to you in fury; and I, even I, will chastise you seven times for your sins." Leviticus 26:27-28

Remember God doesn't change, neither does His character.

Now if I were to tie in the word by word, that has been explained here, I must say that recently everything seemed to click. A theory has been developed, one that will either hold water or not, regarding what appears to be a deception on a biblical scale. What we might be seeing is one of the biggest deceptions in all of history, one that could or just as well could not, have something to do with the rise of the Antichrist. As a clear disclaimer, I am not proclaiming that this is going to be or that this theory is completely correct, but I am issuing it as a warning that something that doesn't seem right, probably isn't right and by time it becomes apparent whether President Trump will make the history books as one of the best Presidents of all time or if he turns out to be a monstrous man, it will be too late. The inklings of evidence have begun to show up and after over a year sitting on the sidelines, trying to see if I could clearly see a problem with the overall current administration, there is now enough evidence to present this theory, that while appears to be of such a great deception that it would seem impossible, I think of it in terms as a reminder of how the devil will deceive the entire world during the *"time of Jacob's trouble." (Jer. 30:7)*

"For we do not wrestle against flesh and blood, but against rulers, against authorities, against the world's rulers of the darkness of this age, against spiritual wickedness in the heavenlies." Ephesians 6:12

"So the great dragon was cast out, that serpent of old, called the Devil and Satan, who leads the whole world astray; he was cast out onto the earth, and his angels were cast out with him." Revelation 12:9

Will not during that time the deception be so great that the one who is literally possessed by Satan, the Antichrist, will at first seem genuine in wanting to fix the world's problem, to help humanity? Think about it, this man is going to cause peace in the Middle East, he is going to fix the world's financial problems, he is going to be a great leader. Truly, as a student of history, having studied Hitler, Mao, Lenin, Stalin, Mussolini and Pol Pot, I can tell you that they all started off the same, men with extreme ideologies. There needs to be something different about them, they have to be charismatic, a leader, normally those who end up turning out to be horrific dictators, start with a movement, unfortunately much like we have seen. This isn't the first time, certainly former President Obama would also have fit this bill, yet he did not turn out to be a dictator. When is the last time a dictator turns out to be someone like former President Bush or President Clinton? Generally no, it is always someone who is a bit extreme.

"And he shall confirm a covenant with many for one week. And in the middle of the week he shall cause the sacrifice and the grain offering to cease. And on a corner will be abominations that cause horror, even until the end. And that which was decreed shall be poured out on the desolate." Daniel 9:27

"And in the latter time of their kingdom, when the transgressors have come to the full, a king shall stand forth, having fierce countenance and understanding sinister schemes. And his power shall be mighty, but not by his own power. And he shall destroy extraordinarily, and he shall prosper, and work, and destroy the mighty and the holy people. And also through his cunning he will cause deceit to prosper in his hand. And he will magnify himself in his heart, and through prosperity shall destroy many. He shall also stand up against the Ruler of rulers, but he shall be broken in pieces without hands." Daniel 8:23-25

I admit there is a bit of entertainment to the whole ordeal. The fake news and a sitting President yelling at news companies that they are fake news, really states what a lot of Americans already believe. Yet what if that is part of the deception, what if it goes so deep that the media is in on it, setting up America for the fall?

When it came to 9/11 the fundamental question of why fighter jets came from across the country, rather than from local bases, was what raised my questions regarding the official story, likewise, when Henry Ford had addressed the issue of the lack of Americans understanding the Federal Reserve banking system, I was intrigued by that idea also and looked into his quote that I had found. Could it be that what we are witnessing is truly perhaps the biggest deception placed on the American people and indeed the people of the world? Could the presidency of Donald Trump be a huge deception of biblical proportions, perhaps even regarding the rise of the Antichrist in some way or another?

I've seen evidence contrary to what was spoken on in the campaign trail. Yet with what President don't we see this after they get elected. Remember former President Bush and his 'read my lips, no new taxes' quote. Really it would be a shock and surprise if a President actually kept all or even most of what they campaigned on, thus American politics, thus politics in general. So I watched as missiles flew into Syria, I watched as more weapons were sold to anti-Russia countries, I watched as NATO became more aggressive, I watched as more troops went to Afghanistan, I even watched as the swamp was getting put into positions of power.

On the other hand I watched as the Trans Pacific Partnership deal was shredded, I watched (and am still watching) as the Clinton Foundation and Hillary Clinton are under federal investigation. I watched as the federal transgender rules put in place by President Obama regarding the schools became garbage. I watched as the Paris Accord was backed out of and not signed by the United States. I watch as trade tariffs are coming into effect to bring back American jobs, as well as the immigration issues being addressed, etc. Very confusing, some good things, some bad things. In all reality, some really good things and some really bad things. Just as with 9/11, the Federal Reserve, etc., there comes a point where, for Trump supporters, one could say that I am on the wrong side of the fence. No more fence straddling, but rather I wish to be proven wrong, I hope this country gets better, I hope things are not as bad as I am proposing they could be. I hope that all goes well and our economy becomes booming, not on bubbles, but on real American wealth. I wish I am proven wrong and would be happy the day that someone says, see 'I told you so', but with good conscience I must go forth and present this theory that something is wrong here and it may be very detrimental to the United States, in fact it could possibly, not saying it will or would, but could possibly have something to do with the rise of the Antichrist government.

When I thought that the evidence was clear that there was something wrong, hardcore Trump supporters and advocates would present a theory, that while somewhat fascinating, was their reason to excuse Trump's behavior for the betterment of America. I've never been for and as a Christian can never agree with the do evil that good may come mentality that some hold. No rather do good to those who hate you, not evil.

"Woe to those who draw iniquity with cords of vanity, and sin with cart ropes; who say, Let Him hurry and hasten His work, so that we may see it; and let the purpose of the Holy One of Israel draw near and come, so that we may know it! Woe to those who call evil good and good evil; who put darkness for light and light for darkness; who put bitter for sweet and sweet for bitter! Woe to those who are wise in their own eyes, and understanding in their own sight! Woe to those mighty to drink wine, and men of strength to mix strong drink; who justify the wicked for a bribe, and take away justice from the righteous! Therefore, as the fire devours the stubble, and the flame consumes the chaff, so their root shall be like rottenness, and their blossoms shall go up like dust, because they have cast away the Law of Jehovah of Hosts, and despised the Word of the Holy One of Israel." Isaiah 5:18-24

"You have heard that it was said, You shall love your neighbor and hate your enemy. But I say to you, Love your enemies, bless those who curse you, do good to those who hate you, and pray for those who abuse you and persecute you, that you may become sons of your Father in Heaven; for He makes His sun rise on the evil and on the good, and sends rain on the just and on the unjust. For if you love those who love you, what reward have you? Do not even the tax collectors the same? And if you greet your brethren only, what do you do more than others? Do not also the tax collectors so? Therefore you shall be perfect, just as your Father in Heaven is perfect." Matthew 5:43-48

A lot of the alternative media was discussing various theories for why President Trump was doing these things. For instance the appointment of so many Goldman Sachs representatives was so that Trump could use their own system against them. The massive stock market and debt bubbles in this country is so that Trump can create as much wealth as possible before taking out the Federal Reserve and ultimately making America great again, basically a landing pad of real wealth, real jobs, when the economy bottom falls out. They would be quick to point at the success of the supposed summit coming up with Kim Jong-un and Donald Trump. Truly either a situation that would deserve the Nobel Peace Prize, if done correctly or would likely lead into immediate war, as the newest appointees of the President, getting rid of seemingly decent people, in terms of man, and replacing them with known neocons and bad people. That for me was the last straw.

Years ago I had listened to Alex Jones quite a bit and read news from his website. While I didn't agree with everything he stated, quite simply he was spot on on many things. However, now I see that if it doesn't line up with the Trump narrative then these same things spoken of in the past do not get proper attention. Case in point, google YouTube videos of the alternative media's take on John Bolton and see, while there is criticism, that criticism by hardcore Trump supporters is mild in comparison to what it was years ago when Bolton was in power in the Bush administration. In fact the excuse given by Infowars, of which they have a huge audience, was that Trump was trying to show that he is tough to North Korea to bring peace. What? Is not already peace coming? I don't buy it.

Yet these people have never had the whole picture. While they are quick to point out the history and oftentimes reality of things passed by Congress, the evil embedded within the system, how things really work, etc., when it comes to things from the Bible they certainly are fully compromised. They do not do the work of Christ, despite often claiming to be Christians, in fact their doctrine doesn't have the morals of God's Word as their hate filled speech is full of profanity and blatant evil, oftentimes digging deep into the depths of Satan, contrary to the Bible *(Rev. 2:24)*. In fact they vehemently criticize Christians who believe in Creation, as their human nature theories can't address a Biblical worldview, and go one step further, in all cases I have seen of the 'big ones' of the alternative media, in denying that the Rapture is true, instead lumping this doctrine into another conspiracy of the elite. While supporting Trump, even Alex Jones will compare Trump with the prophet Moses and state to his listeners that he is using the new world order system against them to create a new 'new world order'. Hmmm…I don't know the truth in such a matter, but realize that making America great again and changing the world order into something else is highly suspicious. Does not one exist during the Tribulation, are they ever in full agreement?

"The ten horns which you saw are ten kings who have received no kingdom as yet, but they receive authority for one hour as kings with the beast. These are of one mind, and they will give their power and authority to the beast. These will make war with the Lamb, and the Lamb will overcome them, for He is Lord of lords and King of kings; and those who are with Him are called, elect, and faithful. Then he said to me, The waters which you saw, where the harlot sits, are peoples, multitudes, nations, and tongues. And the ten horns which you saw on the beast, these will hate the harlot, make her desolate and naked, eat her flesh and consume her with fire. For God has put it into their hearts to fulfill His purpose, to be of one mind, and to give their kingdom to the beast, until the words of God are fulfilled. And the woman whom you saw is that great city which reigns over the kings of the earth." Revelation 17:12-18

"And the fourth kingdom shall be as strong as iron. Inasmuch as iron breaks in pieces and shatters all things, and like iron that crushes all these, it will break in pieces and crush. And whereas you saw the feet and the toes, partly of potters' clay and partly of iron, the kingdom shall be divided. But there shall be in it the strength of iron, just as you saw the iron mixed with miry clay. And as the toes of the feet were partly of iron and partly of clay, so the kingdom shall be partly strong and partly broken. And as you saw the iron mixed with the miry clay, they shall become mixed with the seed of men. But they shall not cleave to one another, even as iron does not fellowship with clay. And in the days of these kings, the God of Heaven shall set up a kingdom which shall never be destroyed. And the kingdom shall not be left to other people. It shall break in pieces and bring all these kingdoms to an end, and it shall stand forever." Daniel 2:40-44

"And after this I was looking in the night visions. And, behold, the fourth beast was frightening and terrifying, and very strong! And it had great iron teeth. It devoured, and broke in pieces, and stamped what was left with its feet. And it was different from all the beasts before it; and it had ten horns. I was contemplating the horns. And behold, another little horn came up among them, and three of the first horns were uprooted before it. And behold, in this horn were eyes like the eyes of a man, and a mouth speaking great things. I watched until the thrones were cast down, and the Ancient of Days sat, whose robe was white as snow and the hair of His head like pure wool. His throne was like flames of fire, its wheels like burning fire. A stream of fire went out and came out from before Him. A thousand thousands served Him, and a vast innumerable number stood before Him. The judgment was set and the books were opened. Then I was watching because of the voice of the great words which the horn spoke. I was watching until the beast was killed, and his body was destroyed and given to the burning flame. As for the rest of the beasts, their dominion was taken away. Yet their lives were prolonged for a season and a time. I saw in the night visions. And behold, one like the Son of Man came with the clouds of the heavens. And He came to the Ancient of Days. And they brought Him near before Him. And dominion was given to Him, and glory, and a kingdom, that all peoples, nations, and languages should serve Him. His dominion is an

everlasting dominion which shall not pass away, and His kingdom that which shall not be destroyed. I, Daniel, was distressed in my spirit within my body, and the visions of my head troubled me. And I came near one of those who stood by and asked him the truth of all this. So he told me and made me know the interpretation of the things. These great beasts which are four, are four kings which shall rise up out of the earth. But the saints of the Most High shall receive the kingdom and possess the kingdom forever, even forever and ever. Then I wanted to know the truth of the fourth beast, which was different from all of the others, very frightening, with its teeth of iron and its nails of bronze; which devoured and broke in pieces, and trampled what was left with its feet, also of the ten horns that were on its head, and the other which came up, and before whom three fell, even that horn that had eyes, and a mouth speaking great things, whose appearance was greater than his fellows. I was watching, and the same horn made war with the saints and prevailed against them, until the Ancient of Days came. And judgment was given to the saints of the Most High, and the time came that the saints possessed the kingdom. And he said, The fourth beast shall be the fourth kingdom on earth, which shall be different from all other kingdoms, and shall devour the whole earth, and shall trample it down and break it in pieces. And the ten horns out of this kingdom are ten kings; they shall rise, and another shall rise after them. And he shall be different from the first, and he shall abase three kings. And he shall speak words against the Most High, and shall continually harass the saints of the Most High. And he shall intend to change times and law. And they shall be given into his hand for a period of a time and times and one half time. But the court shall sit, and they shall take away his dominion, to consume and to destroy until the end. And the kingdom and dominion, and the greatness of the kingdoms under the whole heavens shall be given to the people of the saints of the Most High, whose kingdom is an everlasting kingdom. And all dominions shall serve and obey Him. Thus far is the end of the matter. As for me, Daniel, my thoughts terrified me much, and my countenance changed in me. But I kept the matter in my heart." Daniel 7:7-28

So when Mike Pompeo is named by Trump to be the Secretary of State, I must admit that all I can say about Pompeo is he certainly fits into the CIA. In fact, that is what he was and is what you would expect. But when I saw the alternative media playing up Gina Haspel, the first women to run the CIA and with their original articles, instead of telling people that she was in charge of the secret CIA torture blacksites, they touted that this defied those who say Trump doesn't like women, the whole thing began to stink. I made my choice on what side of the fence I was going to be on. To make matters worse, John Bolton came into view and then there are those alternative freedom minded people still out there, who haven't changed their viewpoints, who declare exactly what appears to be happening, that President Trump seems to be creating a war cabinet.

Well just how deep does this go? Now armed with some evidence and realizing that these main talking heads of the alternative media could no longer hold off my decision with their rationalizing of Trump's bad behavior for the ultimate good, I was off in my search to see what was going on. Then I ran across some very disturbing things. Inklings of a potential deception of biblical proportions became clearer and clearer, with still not knowing it, but neither will the public before it is too late or clearly debunked. No one will know whether or not President Trump is truly for the people or against, until it is too late. We will either wake up seeing the disastrous consequences having happened to a society that is deserving of God's just Judgment, if the Rapture hasn't happened yet, or we will see the wheels of the greatness of America turning forcefully, rebuilding wealth that truly ended with our grandparents generations, about the same time they quit burning those Elvis records, after they had been pressed word by word to deny God's standards and truth laid out in the Holy Scriptures.

Some have suggested that the elite, those who are really in control, decided that they needed a Republican to get gun control, a Democrat wouldn't work. Has not some of the comments that Trump has made caused this newest word by word idea in America where states are now taking guns from those who are deemed dangerous, with supposed due process that the average man could never afford to undertake? Do you really think they are going to get rid of the Second Amendment at this moment? Would it not take a monumental crisis first? Rather, get rid of it selectively, by those whom the government hates, those on their secret watchlists, those like me who pry off the lids of their lies and go against the official narrative. That is certainly in play at this moment.

Others suggested that Hillary Clinton was never meant to win the Whitehouse. They knew Bernie Sanders probably could have beat Trump, so they allowed Hillary to run, using the media supposedly against him, in order that Trump would win. While this certainly may not be the case, it is interesting enough to note that they are tons of pictures out there of Trump with the Clintons and they have friendly relations together. Yet the media, this seems to be where the potential mass deception is at.

The media has been largely controlled by four corporations for quite some time. Certainly the distrust of the media in many regards is well known, at least suspect by many. The internet is a different ball park, a large majority is controlled by a handful, but there are also alternative news options. The rise of these alternative news options was the fuel that accelerated the disbelief in the mainstream media. Then again, the American people being lied to time and time again certainly didn't help. What happens if there is collusion amongst those in the mainstream media, as well as the popular talking heads in the alternative media. While Twitter played an active role in allowing Donald Trump to get his viewpoints out there, without censorship, in all reality the media and their nonstop coverage also played a very active role.

Certainly it could be said that without non stop coverage of Donald Trump, even negative coverage, which was most networks solution, we could use the adage that no publicity is bad publicity. Even the regular news anchors of major networks were wondering why they were covering Donald Trump all day long. Could it be that this still nonstop barrage of anti-Trump news by most networks, with the exception of Fox News, could actually be part of a huge deception being placed by the global elite unto an unsuspecting population? The American people, especially so called conservatives, have been upset by getting blundered time and time again. With an American rising to the scene, that is Trump, going against or appearing to go against the establishment; and the media responding, as one would properly think they would, against Trump, this would only further the movement and accelerate the popularity of the built in rebellious American people, a trait that this country has held from its inauguration.

With this being said, most of the alternative media pushed this exact narrative and promoted Trump by pointing out how the mainstream media were and are against him. This only further activated those who sit on the benches to begin to push for Donald Trump to become President. After all Hillary Clinton, the alternative, was known as not being trustworthy and more of the same establishment that we have seen time after time again, even many Democrats do not like Clinton. Now if Donald Trump truly is the real deal, truly a man who is anti establishment, draining the swamp, etc., then we have nothing to worry about. Yet the concern here is that this is part of a potential deception of biblical proportions, perhaps one that could lead into the rise of the Antichrist government or not.

The markings of deception are starting to become clear. As a note it should be mentioned that, with a stern warning as All Will Stand does not make predictions about who/what/how regarding who the Antichrist is, etc., a current large push for peace deal with Israel has gotten new teeth. Certainly we know that the Antichrist confirms a covenant regarding Israel *(Dan. 9:27)*, so as a Believer this is going to rightfully so cause me to ponder what ulterior motives the administration of the United States might be involved in. Do we know if the United States will be involved in this? The Bible is silent regarding aiding countries, we do know that Israel will be involved.

With the Trump administration we have seen Jerusalem recognized as the capital of Israel, rightfully so. Yet, as mentioned in a previous article, Israel had to make some not-yet-known concessions to President Trump in order for that to have happened. Personally I would never consider any motive other than simply doing what is right and recognizing Jerusalem as the capital of Israel and moving the embassy there, which would just make sense. For this is God's land that they are dealing with and the Holy Scriptures is not silent on those who divide up God's land.

"I will also gather all nations, and will bring them down into the valley of Jehoshaphat. And I will enter into judgment with them there, on account of My people and My possession, Israel, whom they have scattered among the nations; and divided up My land." Joel 3:2

Some interesting things regarding Jared Kushner, the President's son-in-law who is at the center of brokering a peace deal with Israel.

1) He is Jewish and practices Judaism.

2). He owns 666 Fifth Ave. in New York City, New York.

3.) He has so far gotten further in peace negotiations within the Middle East than any other predecessor.

4.) He has great relations with Benjamin Netanyahu, who used to be friends with his father and stayed at his house when he was a child.

Now as far as I know, Kushner could be ousted from his position of power at any time. This seems to be quite popular to have purges nowadays. Truly at one point in the future, someone connected with a peace covenant and Israel will be the Antichrist. I doubt anyone will know for certain prior and I assume that the Rapture will likely have happened around that time that the covenant is confirmed.

Also it could be that 100 years from now, when we no longer traverse on this earth and are with the Lord *(2 Cor. 5:8)*, that then the Antichrist rises. We do not know the day nor the hour, nor will we. Certainly a man on a website is not going to be able to proclaim such things, when Jesus doesn't even know *(Matt. 24:36)*.

To add credence to this potential mass deception, it should be noted that a largely underreported article appeared in The Guardian that had a former Google software engineer who created software that analyzed the algorithms on YouTube, also owned by Google. These algorithms during the election year showed what videos were recommended by YouTube, a very popular website, with searches for both Trump and Clinton. Despite the claims of censorship, which likely has happened in the past to Infowars, Infowars was promoted as the number one in searches for Trump. In fact Trump was promoted over and over again in the sheer number and volume. Make no mistake this was not a small thing, as Infowars alone was promoted by YouTube over 15,000,000,000 times with just searches relating to Trump in 2016 alone! Make no mistake, and I sincerely hope that Trump turns out to be a great President who will bring good jobs back to this country and fix many of the ills of our society, but this is solid evidence that there appears to be collusion amongst both the mainstream media, the online media and the alternative media to promote Trump. This and other tidbits, point to Donald Trump being the choice of the so-called swamp, of whom it is now apparent that President Trump is putting in positions of high power. How does one drain the swamp by placing them in positions of high power *(Eph. 6:12)*?

Moving along, it also must be noted that Trump's penthouse in NYC is full of occultic items, some that have to deal with the rising of Apollo. Does this fit into the conspiracy theory that America was created as a free country, by those who are in positions of high power, in order to allow it to become what it has, then destroy it and allow the Antichrist system arise? Certainly things would only be in God's timing not man's, but it is of interest that our Capital was setup in an evil manner, supposedly the United States is the Phoenix rising and out of the ashes of this country the new world order will arise. I also take note of the 1988 article from the Economist magazine that shows a Phoenix standing on burning American currency with a coin around its neck, stating that a new currency will come about on or around 2018, with 2018 being the year on the coin on the Phoenix's neck. I could also point out that the The Temple in Zion has a golden coin issued that has Trump on the backside. Why would they think that Trump would rebuild the Temple? Quoting from them..., *"The Trump Declaration must continue with a declaration of the role of the Jews in establishing the Temple in its place. Only then will President Trump's international ambitions come true in the Middle East."*

"For the mystery of lawlessness is already at work; only He is now restraining, until it is raised from out of the midst." 2nd Thessalonians 2:7

"The burden of the Word of Jehovah for Israel, says Jehovah, who stretches forth the heavens, and lays the foundation of the earth, and forms the spirit of man within him. Behold, I will make Jerusalem a cup of trembling to all the peoples all around, and it shall also be against Judah in the siege against Jerusalem. And in that day I will make Jerusalem a heavy stone for all the peoples; all who lift it shall be slashed; cut to pieces. And all the nations of the earth will be gathered against it. In that day I will strike every horse with bewilderment and his rider with madness, says Jehovah. And I will open My eyes on the house of Judah, and will strike every horse of the people with blindness. And the governors of Judah shall say in their heart, The inhabitants of Jerusalem shall be my strength in Jehovah of Hosts, their God. In that day I will make the governors of Judah like a hearth of fire among the wood, and like a torch of fire among cut grain. And they shall devour all the peoples all around, on the right hand and on the left. And Jerusalem shall be inhabited again in her own place, in Jerusalem. Jehovah also shall save the tents of Judah first, so that the glory of the house of David and the glory of the inhabitants of Jerusalem may not be magnified above Judah. In that day Jehovah shall defend the inhabitants of Jerusalem. And he who is feeble among them in that day shall be like David, and the house of David shall be like God, like the Angel of Jehovah before them. And it shall be in that day, that I will seek to destroy all the nations that come against Jerusalem. And I will pour on the house of David, and on the inhabitants of Jerusalem, the Spirit of grace and supplication. And they shall look on Me whom they have pierced; and they shall mourn for Him, as one mourns for an only son, and they shall be bitter over Him, like the bitterness over the firstborn." Zechariah 12:1-10

What we do know is that at some point in the future the Antichrist will arise *(2 Thes. 2:9)*. We do know that there will be *"the time of Jacob's trouble" (Jer. 30:7)*, we do know that there will be a one-world currency *(Rev. 13)*, we do know the Rapture will happen prior to these events *(Rev. 4:1)*, we do know that most of the world's population will die . We also know that multitudes will be Saved during that time, but that by doing so they will become martyrs of Christ. Furthermore we know that in order for these things to happen, logically some ground work would be laid.

"For, lo, I am beginning to bring evil on the city which is called by My name; and should you be found clean and free from guilt? You shall not be without guilt, for I will call for a sword upon all the inhabitants of the earth, says Jehovah of Hosts. Therefore prophesy against them all these Words, and say to them, Jehovah shall roar from on high, and utter His voice from His holy habitation. He shall mightily roar over His dwelling place. He shall give a shout, like those who tread out grapes, against all the inhabitants of the earth. A roaring noise shall come to the ends of the earth; for Jehovah has a controversy with the nations; He will enter into judgment with all flesh. He will give those who are wicked to the sword, says Jehovah. Thus says Jehovah of Hosts, Behold, evil shall go

forth from nation to nation, and a great tempest shall be roused up from the recesses of the earth. And in that day the slain of Jehovah shall be from one end of the earth even to the other end of the earth. They shall not be mourned, nor gathered, nor buried. They shall be as dung on the ground. Howl, you shepherds, and cry! Wallow in the ashes, you majestic ones of the flock! For the days of your slaughter and of your scattering are fulfilled; and you shall fall like a delightful vessel. And the shepherds shall have no way to flee, nor the majestic ones of the flock to escape. A voice of the cry of the shepherds, and a howling of the majestic ones of the flock shall be heard; for Jehovah has spoiled their pasture, and the peaceful pastures are cut down because of the fierce anger of Jehovah. He has left His den like a lion; for their land is wasted at the presence of His fierce violence, and before His fierce anger." Jeremiah 25:29-38

Truly I believe, rightfully so, that every generation of Believers should have had the hope of the immediate appearing of Christ, the Rapture, to take them to be with the Lord. I do ask how in a seven year period a one would currency and other prophetic events could have happened in places like Latin America in the 1600's. Yet with the knowledge of man at that time, no one would have considered it, therefore Believers are always right in their zeal to be watching and ready, as we are commanded to do so.

"But I do not want you to be ignorant, brethren, concerning those who are asleep, that you sorrow not as others who have no hope. For if we believe that Jesus died and rose again, even so God will bring with Him those who sleep in Jesus. For this we say to you by the Word of the Lord, that we who are alive and remain until the coming of the Lord will by no means precede those who are asleep. For the Lord Himself will descend from Heaven with a shouted command, with the voice of the archangel, and with the trumpet of God. And the dead in Christ will rise first. Then we who are alive and remain shall be caught up together at the same time with them in the clouds to meet the Lord in the air. And thus we shall always be with the Lord. Therefore encourage one another with these words." 1 Thessalonians 4:13-18

"Watch therefore, for you do not know what hour your Lord comes. But know this, that if the master of the house had known what hour the thief comes, he would have watched and not allowed his house to be dug through. Therefore you also be ready, for the Son of Man comes at an hour you do not expect." Matthew 24:42-44

Here we are, living in a time where the technology exists, Israel once again exists, peace is trying to be had, people are behaving more and more as in the days of Noah, and we have these strange movements in political systems around the world. While a lot of people would be quick to point out the great thing of people so-called waking up to how the world really works, I would also be quick to point out that it would make more sense for the masses to realize corruption on a huge scale, powers behind the scenes of their respective government, in order for them to accept the Antichrist as the so-called solution to their countries.

"But as the days of Noah were, so also will the coming of the Son of Man be. For as in the days before the flood, they were eating and drinking, marrying and giving in

marriage, until the day that Noah entered into the ark, and did not realize until the flood came and took them all away, so also will the coming of the Son of Man be. Then two will be in the field: one is taken and the other is left. Two will be grinding at the mill: one is taken and the other is left." Matthew 24:37-41

While I firmly believe that nothing else, absolutely nothing, needs to happen prophetically before the Rapture, it should be noted that it would make sense, with the United States holding the world's reserve currency, thus the source of our ill gained wealth, that a tragedy of huge proportions could happen that would destroy the economic systems of not only this country but the entire world. With that said, it would make sense that out of that chaos a man would arise who would deceive the world, the Antichrist, along with the False Prophet, who would fix these problems. Certainly there seems to be no need at the moment. Yet this could just as easily be something that hastens immediately after the Rapture of the Saints, not something that would necessarily have to happen prior.

Does one expect that the mass deception regarding end times events, the Tribulation, the Antichrist world government system is just all going to appear out of nowhere? Would it not make sense that these things would already be ongoing, just not yet unveiled, because it is not in man's timing, but in God's timing? I have often said that if it were up to man, we would already be gone, done with. Does not the Holy Spirit restrain men?

"Let no one deceive you by any means; for that Day will not come unless the falling away comes first, and the man of sin is unveiled, the son of perdition, who opposes and exalts himself above all that is called God or that is honored, so that he sits as God in the temple of God, declaring of himself that he is God. Do you not remember that when I was still with you I told you these things? And now you know what is restraining, that he may be unveiled in his own time. For the mystery of lawlessness is already at work; only He is now restraining, until it is raised from out of the midst. And then the lawless one will be unveiled, whom the Lord will consume with the breath of His mouth and destroy with the brightness of His coming. The coming of the lawless one is according to the working of Satan, with all power, signs, and lying wonders, and with all unrighteous deception among those who are perishing, because they did not receive the love of the truth, that they might be saved. And for this reason God will send them strong delusion, that they should believe the lie, that they all may be judged who did not believe the truth but had pleasure in unrighteousness." 2nd Thessalonians 2:3-12

Just how does America expect to be made great again, without God, without repentance? If one were to diligently consider, would America be primed for God's mercy, raining wealth down upon us all, or for God's just Judgment? Does a country that uses a rotten international banking scheme to control the world, to overthrow countries, to use our means as a method of repression, rather than helping, deserve to be judged by the Most High? Does our country that has killed way over 50,000,000 babies via abortion deserve to be judged by the Most High? Does the country that houses the Federal Reserve system that financed World War 2, Mao and Stalin, deserve to be judged by the Most High? Does a country that thinks it is alright to walk contrary to God and His standards, while proclaiming to be His people, deserve to be judged by the Most High? How well did that go for Israel, as they clung onto their idols of Baal? Woe to the country that forgets God. Worse yet, the country that claims to be a Christian people yet walk contrary to Him. Will He not walk contrary to us or will He rain down blessings and make this country great again?

"I create the fruit of the lips: Peace, peace, to him who is far off, and to him who is near, says Jehovah; and I will heal him. But the wicked are like the troubled sea, which cannot rest, whose waters cast up mire and dirt. There is no peace, says my God, to the wicked." Isaiah 57:19-21

No man knows the future, yet when I see the possibility of a grand deception of biblical proportions potentially taking place, it would only seem to be wise to act as a watchman and warn the people of potential disaster. While I hope to be proven wrong and will gladly accept it, if such a sinister scheme equating the destruction of America is on the verge of being effected, then it should be pointed out. What I do know is all will stand before God Almighty *(Ro. 14:12)* and unless you repent and by faith believe into the Lord Jesus Christ as your Savior, you will be cast forever into the Lake of Fire *(Rev. 20:15)*. Without Jesus as your Savior, your name is not written in the Book of Life.

"When I say to the wicked, You shall die the death, and you give him no warning, nor speak to warn the wicked from his wicked way, to save his life, that same wicked man shall die in his iniquity; but his blood I will require at your hand. Yet, if you warn the wicked, and he does not turn from his wickedness, nor from his wicked way, he shall die in his iniquity; but you have delivered your soul. Again, when a righteous man turns from his righteousness and commits iniquity, and I lay a stumbling block before him, he shall die. Because you did not give him warning, he shall die in his sin, and his righteousness which he has done shall not be remembered; but his blood I will require at your hand. Nevertheless if you warn the righteous man that the righteous should not sin, and he does not sin, he shall live life because he took warning; and you have delivered your soul." Ezekiel 3:18-21

As explained prior, the greatest deception of all is that people are being pushed away from God's truth, the Gospel and that is an eternal deception. They might be able to trick us in regards to what goes on in this world politically, but do not let them trick you regarding your soul. God is merciful and will forgive, He will grant Salvation to all that call upon Him *(Acts 2:21)*, through Jesus Christ His Son *(John 14:6)*. This same Jesus who died on the Cross for your sins and who rose again from the dead to sit at the right hand of the Father *(Ro. 8:34)*.

"For when we were yet without strength, in due time Christ died for the ungodly." Romans 5:6

"Then Peter said to them, Repent, and let every one of you be immersed in the name of Jesus Christ to the remission of sins; and you shall receive the gift of the Holy Spirit." Acts 2:38

"Repent therefore and be converted, that your sins may be blotted out, so that times of refreshing may come from the presence of the Lord, and that He may send Jesus Christ, who was preached to you before, whom Heaven must receive until the times of restoration of all things, of which God has spoken through the mouth of all His holy prophets since the past ages." Acts 3:19-21

"Truly, these times of ignorance God overlooked, but now commands all men everywhere to repent, because He has established a day on which He will judge the world in righteousness by the Man whom He has appointed. He has given assurance of this to everyone by raising Him from the dead." Acts 17:30-31

If such a scheme is upon the America people, with whatever method might be used, understand that the only potential solution would be for the American people to repent and ask for the mercies of God. For America to be made great again, not in the eyes of man, but in the eyes of the Lord. For then, whatever He who Created us deems appropriate would be worthy of all people. Certainly better for us to accept fault, repent and have the mercy of God, even if our country falls, rather than reap the horrors for our sins, by refusing to repent. Better a meal with our family under the warmth of our homes, without all of the bells and whistles, rather than a broken down society where lawlessness and death are outside our doors. Where men are being carted away to these camps that no one talks about anymore, when those whose names are on watchlists disappear in the night, of which is seldom mentioned anymore.

"Come now and let us reason together, says Jehovah: Though your sins are as scarlet, they shall be as white as snow; though they are red like crimson, they shall be as wool." Isaiah 1:18

Better to serve the Lord and truly seek His mercy with a repentant heart then continue to rebel against the Most High. Yet I fear for now that will be the case with America, that we continue to rebel as a society and will not change. For those who know the Lord, know that He cares about you *(1 Pet. 5:7)* and is your great help in times of distress. If our society is being tricked, understand that God certainly has mercy on those who have a contrite heart, those who are truly Saved and have repented. Understand that either way individually we will all stand before God, we are responsible for ourselves, we can not wait on society to fix its ails, Salvation is on an individual basis.

"God is our refuge and strength, a very present help in trouble. Therefore we will not fear when the earth changes, when mountains are slipping into the midst of the seas. Let its waters roar and foam; let the mountains shake with the swelling of it. Selah. There is a river whose streams cause rejoicing in the city of God, the consecrated place of the tabernacle of the Most High. God is in the midst of her; she shall not be moved; God shall help her at the break of day. The nations raged, the kingdoms were shaken; He uttered His voice, the earth melted. Jehovah of Hosts is with us; the God of Jacob is our refuge. Selah. Come, behold the works of Jehovah, who has made desolations on the earth; who makes wars to cease to the ends of the earth; He breaks the bow and cuts the

spear in two; He burns the chariots in the fire. Be still, and know that I am God! I will be exalted among the nations, I will be exalted in the earth! Jehovah of Hosts is with us; the God of Jacob is our refuge. Selah." Psalms 46

"The sacrifices of God are a broken spirit; a broken and a contrite heart, O God, You will not despise." Psalms 51:17

"And the devil, who led them astray, was cast into the Lake of Fire and brimstone where the beast and the false prophet are. And they will be tormented day and night forever and ever. And I saw a great white throne and Him who sat on it, from whose face the earth and the heavens fled away. And there was found no place for them. And I saw the dead, small and great, standing before God. And books were opened. And another book was opened, which is the Book of Life. And the dead were judged according to their works, out of the things which were written in the books. And the sea gave up the dead who were in it, and Death and Hades delivered up the dead who were in them. And they were judged, each one, according to their works. And Death and Hades were cast into the Lake of Fire. This is the second death. And anyone not found written in the Book of Life was cast into the Lake of Fire." Revelation 20:10-15

Amen!

One Chance

"And I saw a great white throne and Him who sat on it, from whose face the earth and the heavens fled away. And there was found no place for them. And I saw the dead, small and great, standing before God. And books were opened. And another book was opened, which is the Book of Life. And the dead were judged according to their works, out of the things which were written in the books. And the sea gave up the dead who were in it, and Death and Hades delivered up the dead who were in them. And they were judged, each one, according to their works. And Death and Hades were cast into the Lake of Fire. This is the second death. And anyone not found written in the Book of Life was cast into the Lake of Fire." Revelation 20:11-15

Here another Easter Sunday goes by, today I'm going to skip going over the pagan origins of the name Easter. Today I am going to skip warning about incorporating the Easter Bunny and Easter egg hunts into your church service. Today I am going to skip the rock concert going on in the bigger, more modern churches. For once I am going to remain silent about all of the programs that you use to get people into your church. Today I'm going about how your service was in the eyes of the Most High.

You finally did it, you know, they come on Easter Sunday. In droves, families will pack churches all around in the United States. Faces that you only see once per year or faces that you have never seen will fill the pulpits or chairs of your church. These people in general will have spent more time shopping for this one event, going to your church, more time getting their hair done, putting on new clothes, their Sunday best, to appear in your church. Though they might forget about Christ the remainder of the year, at this moment, just the fact that they believe that He exists, they will flood your church.

Sure they may be antsy to get out of there, certainly they have their plans afterwards. Right now whether or not they want to be there, they feel obligated to be there. So here you are, what are you going to preach?

You have your reasons for your programs to get people into church. You have your reasons for making your messages to preach the way you do. You have your reasons for allowing a melting pot of ideas with the world and other churches. You have your reasons for softening the churches stances on many issues. Yet here you are, up on the pulpit or perhaps on a stage in some casual clothes, are you ready? Do you realize that you also stand before your Creator?

So what are you going to preach? You have compromised on nearly everything in the Bible regarding biblical separation. You have made excuses for having worldly programs in your church. You constantly change the churches stances on issues as the world changes. Now are you going to water this down? Are you going to ignore the truth? Are you going to tell them what they want to hear or are you going to tell them a message that will not offend anyone?

Are you going to allow those who may die before they have an opportunity to come again next year to go to their graves in sin, awaiting the Great White Throne judgment where if their name is not written in the Book of Life they will be cast into the Lake of Fire! Are you going to allow those who might never step foot into a church again to not hear the full Gospel message that they need to repent and by faith believe into Jesus Christ as their Lord and Savior?! Are you even called to preach?!

"Only, acknowledge your iniquity, that you have transgressed against Jehovah your God and have scattered your ways to strangers under every green tree, and you have not obeyed My voice, says Jehovah." Jeremiah 3:13

So there you are, Easter Sunday, your pulpits are full, those who may only have one chance are sitting there in front of you. You have ignored biblical warnings about separation, you have mixed God's Word with false doctrine, you have watered down God's Word. Yet there you are, doing exactly what you hoped, having used man's ways to fill your church, now are you going to tell them the truth? Do you even know the truth yourself?

While written to Israel, the same could just as well be said to the New Testament Church.

"Return, O backsliding children, says Jehovah; for I am married to you. And I will take you, one from a city, and two from a family; and I will bring you to Zion. And I will give you shepherds according to My heart, who shall feed you with knowledge and understanding." Jeremiah 3:14-15

Compromising on God's Word will get little or no results. What good is it to have the pews full of those who will stand before their Creator and hear these words?!

"Not everyone who says to Me, Lord, Lord, will enter the kingdom of Heaven, but he who does the will of My Father in Heaven. Many will say to Me in that day, Lord, Lord, have we not prophesied in Your name, cast out demons in Your name, and done many works of power in Your name? And then I will declare to them, I never knew you; depart from Me, you who work out lawlessness!" Matthew 7:21-23

Understand there is a very clear warning to the church nowadays.

"And to the angel of the church of the Laodiceans write, These things says the Amen, the Faithful and True Witness, the Beginning of the creation of God: I know your works, that you are neither cold nor hot. I would that you were cold or hot. So then, because you are lukewarm, and neither cold nor hot, I will vomit you out of My mouth. Because you say, I am rich, have become wealthy, and have need of nothing; and do not know that you are wretched and miserable and poor and blind and naked; I counsel you to buy from Me gold refined in the fire, that you may be rich; and white garments, that you may be clothed, that the shame of your nakedness may not be revealed; and anoint your eyes with eye salve, that you may see. As many as I love, I rebuke and chasten. Therefore be zealous and repent. Behold, I stand at the door and knock. If anyone hears My voice and opens the door, I will come in to him and dine with him, and he with Me. To him who overcomes I will grant to sit with Me on My throne, as I also overcame and sat down with My Father on His throne. He who has an ear, let him hear what the Spirit says to the churches." Revelation 3:14-22

Take heed, the Bible is not silent on these things.

"But know this, that in the last days perilous times will come: For men will be lovers of themselves, lovers of money, boasters, proud, blasphemers, disobedient to parents, unthankful, unholy, without natural affection, unyielding, slanderers, without self-control, savage, despisers of good, traitors, headstrong, haughty, lovers of pleasure rather than lovers of God, having a form of godliness but denying its power. And from such people turn away. For of this sort are those who creep into households and make captives of gullible women loaded down with sins, led away by various lusts, always learning, but never able to come to the full true knowledge of the truth." 2nd Timothy 3:1-7

"For the time will come when they will not endure sound doctrine, but according to their own lusts, desiring to hear pleasant things, they will heap up for themselves teachers; and they will turn their ears away from the truth, and be turned aside to myths." 2nd Timothy 4:3-4

"Now the Spirit expressly says that in latter times some will depart from the faith, being devoted to corrupting spirits and doctrines of demons, speaking lies in hypocrisy, having their own conscience seared, forbidding to marry, and commanding to abstain from

foods which God created to be partaken with thanksgiving by those who believe and know the truth." 1st Timothy 4:1-3

Listen and pay attention!

"Take heed to yourself and to the doctrine. Continue in them, for in doing this you will deliver both yourself and those who hear you." 1st Timothy 4:16

Hear the words of the prophet Jeremiah and consider them diligently.

"Run to and fro through the streets of Jerusalem, and see now, and know, and seek in her open places, if you can find a man, if there is one who does justice, who seeks the truth; and I will pardon her. And though they say, As Jehovah lives; surely they swear falsely. O Jehovah, are not Your eyes on the truth? You have stricken them, but they have not grieved; You have destroyed them, but they have refused to receive correction; they have made their faces harder than rock; they have refused to return. So I said, Surely these are poor; they are foolish; for they do not know the way of Jehovah, nor the judgment of their God. I will go to the great men, and will speak to them; for they have known the way of Jehovah and the judgment of their God. But these have broken the yoke together and have torn off the bonds! Therefore a lion out of the forest shall kill them, and a wolf of the deserts shall destroy them; a leopard shall watch over their cities. Everyone who goes out from there shall be torn in pieces, because their transgressions are many and their backslidings are increased. How shall I pardon you for this? Your children have forsaken Me, and have sworn by those that are not gods. When I adjured them, then they committed adultery, and gathered themselves by troops in a harlot's house. They were like lusty, well-fed stallions in the morning; every one neighing after his neighbor's wife. Shall I not punish for these things? says Jehovah. And shall not My soul be avenged on such a nation as this? Go up on her vine rows and destroy; but do not make a full end; take away her branches, for they are not Jehovah's. For the house of Israel and the house of Judah have dealt very treacherously against Me, says Jehovah. They have denied Jehovah and said, It is not He; neither shall evil come upon us; nor shall we see sword nor famine. And the prophets shall become wind, for the Word is not in them; thus it shall be done to them." Jeremiah 5:1-13

Amen!

Controversy with the Nations

A roaring noise shall come to the ends of the earth; for Jehovah has a controversy with the nations; He will enter into judgment with all flesh. He will give those who are wicked to the sword, says Jehovah. Thus says Jehovah of Hosts, Behold, evil shall go forth from nation to nation, and a great tempest shall be roused up from the recesses of the earth. And in that day the slain of Jehovah shall be from one end of the earth even to the other end of the earth. They shall not be mourned, nor gathered, nor buried. They shall be as dung on the ground." Jeremiah 25:31-33

Who knows where our world will have gone with actions that are going on in the Middle East, as well as our relations with Russia. By time this article is finished and the accompanying radio show is done, so much can change. Could we see the beginning of World War 3? Perhaps no action will have been taken in Syria, against the Russian holdings. One thing we do no for sure is that truth has been out the window for a long time now. The only thing the world has to hold onto as Truth is God's Word to humanity, the Bible. Even then one must take extreme caution to have a good copy, for the English speaking people, that would safely be the King James Version.

Recently it seems politics have been on the forefront of the discussion from All Will Stand. Yet, looking at them from a biblical perspective. What the future holds is not known to us in regards to what man is going to do or what war might or might not break out, but we do know that God's Word stands and what He has declared will come to pass, not an inkling of doubt regarding it. These things have been talked about before, but why stop now?

"And you will hear of wars and rumors of wars. See that you are not troubled; for all these things must come to pass, but the end is not yet. For nation will rise against nation, and kingdom against kingdom. And there will be famines, pestilences, and earthquakes in various places. All these are the beginning of travail." Matthew 24:6-8

"I am Jehovah; that is My name; and My glory I will not give to another, nor My praise to graven images. Behold, the former things have come to pass, and new things I declare; before they spring forth, I proclaim them to you." Isaiah 42:8-9

So are we going to strike North Korea? Will a war with North Korea break out? Will peace be brought through a summit of Kim Jong-un and Donald Trump? Will we attack Syria? Will that lead to war with Russia? Why are we surrounding Russia with NATO and arming their enemies? Why do some Pentagon generals assume that we will eventually have to fight both Russia and China? What about the South China Sea, will that situation continue to escalate out of control? What about Netanyahu's threat regarding taking out Syria, in terms of going after Iran? What is really going on? What will really happen?

So many questions, none of which I have the answer for. All I can say is it is certainly very disturbing times, times that make me think of some questions in my own life, yet I trust in God Almighty. While we wait to see what our current government administration, with the newly appointed people turn out to do and what their final character turns out to be, we also must be watching and ready for the Rapture, for those of us who are Saved. Those who have repented and by faith believed into Jesus Christ as their Lord and Savior, who have their names written in the Book of Life.

"Heaven and earth will pass away, but My Words will by no means pass away. But of that day and hour no one knows, not even the angels of Heaven, but My Father only. But as the days of Noah were, so also will the coming of the Son of Man be. For as in the days before the flood, they were eating and drinking, marrying and giving in marriage, until the day that Noah entered into the ark, and did not realize until the flood came and took them all away, so also will the coming of the Son of Man be. Then two will be in the field: one is taken and the other is left. Two will be grinding at the mill: one is taken and the other is left. Watch therefore, for you do not know what hour your Lord comes. But know this, that if the master of the house had known what hour the thief comes, he would have watched and not allowed his house to be dug through. Therefore you also be ready, for the Son of Man comes at an hour you do not expect." Matthew 24:35-44

"For if we believe that Jesus died and rose again, even so God will bring with Him those who sleep in Jesus. For this we say to you by the Word of the Lord, that we who are alive and remain until the coming of the Lord will by no means precede those who are asleep. For the Lord Himself will descend from Heaven with a shouted command, with the voice of the archangel, and with the trumpet of God. And the dead in Christ will rise

first. Then we who are alive and remain shall be caught up together at the same time with them in the clouds to meet the Lord in the air. And thus we shall always be with the Lord." 1st Thessalonians 4:14-17

"But there shall by no means enter it anything that defiles, or produces an abomination or a lie, but only those who are written in the Lamb's Book of Life." Revelation 21:27

Will President Trump take this country down a very bad wrong turn? Just how are we going to make America great again when we have women protesting about the takedown of Backpage.com, regarding their rights to do as they wish with their bodies? Such an immoral society, full of controlled opposition and mind boggling media censorship, that it is almost unfathomable that a country which proclaims to be a Christian nation, behaving as a backslidden, idolatrous nation, before the holy and Almighty God might even stand a chance of 1950's American dream lifestyles. If one can get past digesting their daily dose of horrific news and keeping up with the latest moves of all of the so-called 'stars', pulling their heads out of the sand, it really appears that America is more akin to Nazi Germany than to a true democracy or should I say republic.

The opening verse talks about a controversy that Jehovah has with the nations. While this is certainly describing the timeframe during the *"time of Jacob's trouble" (Jer. 30:7)*, known to most as the Tribulation, this isn't going to have come from nations who were obedient in the sight of God. Why would such a horrific event, as the Tribulation will be, occur if Israel were obedient to the Messiah, Jesus Christ? Why would such horrible times be coming to the world if they were doing as they should before their Creator? They wouldn't, for God is merciful, yet it is our nations, our people, who have turned their back on the things of God, who have rejected His truth, His warnings and forsaken Him.

"Seventy weeks are decreed regarding your people, and regarding your holy city, to finish the transgression, and to make an end of sins, and to make atonement for iniquity, and to bring in everlasting righteousness, and to seal up the vision and prophecy, and to anoint the Holy of Holies. Know, therefore, and understand that from the going forth of the word to restore and to rebuild Jerusalem, to Messiah the Prince, shall be seven weeks and sixty two weeks. The street shall be built again, and the wall, even in times of distress. And after sixty two weeks, Messiah shall be cut off, but not for Himself. And the people of a coming ruler shall destroy the city and the sanctuary. And its end shall be with a flood, and desolations are determined, and there shall be war until the end. And he shall confirm a covenant with many for one week. And in the middle of the week he shall cause the sacrifice and the grain offering to cease. And on a corner will be abominations that cause horror, even until the end. And that which was decreed shall be poured out on the desolate." Daniel 9:24-27

"And I will pour on the house of David, and on the inhabitants of Jerusalem, the Spirit of grace and supplication. And they shall look on Me whom they have pierced; and they shall mourn for Him, as one mourns for an only son, and they shall be bitter over Him, like the bitterness over the firstborn." Zechariah 12:10

"When I shut up the heavens and there is no rain, or command the locusts to devour the land, or send pestilence among My people, if My people who have been called by My name will humble themselves, and pray and seek My face, and turn from their wicked ways, then I will hear from the heavens, and will forgive their sin and heal their land." 2nd Chronicles 7:13-14

Now are we going to continue to be a nation that is on the wrong side of history? Is our people, our nation, going to lie, murder, destroy, conquer and set off suffering for people around the world and assume that no one is going to eventually stand up to us? Are we going to continue to have a President who calls for the execution of those who deal drugs, when our government sends more troops to Afghanistan, where the poppies are grown to create this opiate crisis that we have in this country?! Shouldn't those who are growing, guarding and shipping in these opiates be the ones who would first fall underneath any legal death penalty that is passed into law?!

"And why not say (as we are slanderously reported and as some affirm that we say), Let us do evil that good may come? Their condemnation is just." Romans 3:8

"Woe to those who desire the day of Jehovah! Of what good is this to you? The day of Jehovah is darkness, and not light. It is as if a man fled before a lion, and a bear met him. Or he goes into the house and leans his hand against the wall, and a snake bites him. Is not the day of Jehovah darkness, and not light; even very dark, and not any brightness in it?" Amos 5:18-20

Why has our government been caught over and over again shipping in cocaine from Colombia? Why is it that the CIA has the nickname cocaine importing agency?! Just ask Rick Ross where he got the crack from, he will tell you, the government! Are we going to pursue a harsh military response, killing untold numbers of people and perhaps setting of the beginning stages of war with Russia, over Syria? Are we to even believe that such an incident took place?

"Woe to those who draw iniquity with cords of vanity, and sin with cart ropes; who say, Let Him hurry and hasten His work, so that we may see it; and let the purpose of the Holy One of Israel draw near and come, so that we may know it! Woe to those who call evil good and good evil; who put darkness for light and light for darkness; who put bitter for sweet and sweet for bitter! Woe to those who are wise in their own eyes, and understanding in their own sight! Woe to those mighty to drink wine, and men of strength to mix strong drink; who justify the wicked for a bribe, and take away justice from the righteous!" Isaiah 5:18-23

Even if such an incident took place, are we to believe that the United States didn't stage another false flag attack, as an excuse to regain control of Syria from the hands of the Russians?! Why not just be honest about the situation, this is about control of Syria, it is a matter between us and the Russians, the United States don't care about 40 dead people.

Where were the whiners when George Bush went in and over a million Iraqi's died, including women and children, during the Gulf War?! The sad reality is more people care about the latest trends and ridiculous immoral television programs and movies than they do about those who live in countries where a good amount of American citizens couldn't find it on a map if their life depended on it. Yet they have an opinion on these wars, there opinion without education is simply parroting what talking media heads have said.

It is also of interest to note how this is taking place in the Middle East at a time where a peace treaty is also being heavily sought, where more ground have been had in resolving the long disagreement between Israel and the so-called Palestinian people. Will a regional war bring about that peace deal and the rise of the Antichrist? Is it possible that We The People will have to endure a destroyed Republic before the Tribulation? For Believers, we know that we will be Raptured prior to the Tribulation, but in general, things are looking to escalate out of control.

"But let us who are of the day be sober, putting on the breastplate of faith and love, and as a helmet the hope of salvation. For God did not appoint us to wrath, but to obtain salvation through our Lord Jesus Christ, who died for us, that whether we watch or sleep, we should live together with Him. Therefore encourage each other and build up one another, just as you also are doing." 1st Thessalonians 5:8-11

We could talk about the immorality issues in the United States of America, we could talk about the staggering debt, the financial bubbles, the rotting inner cities of America, we could go on and discuss our broken down infrastructure and the rampant decay of small town America, but why bother? We are seeing a full fledge 1984 style censorship, where even small websites like this one can be buried in algorithms, not to be found by the vast majority who will not search (90%) beyond the first page of google search results. So, think these claims are outlandish? Why does God have a controversy with the nations?

Certainly we are not the only ones at fault in running evil systems. Guarantee that if we started pulling out of countries that Russia and China would quickly take advantage and fill in the voids. Don't believe it, take a look at Venezuela with China moving in. The Panama Canal, the US gave control back to Panama, with China coming in to sign more contracts. The Bible speaks of ten kingdoms, they don't appear to all be in agreement. The Antichrist will reign above them all.

"Now brethren, concerning the coming of our Lord Jesus Christ, and of our gathering together to Him, we ask you not to be quickly disturbed in mind or alarmed, either by spirit or by word or by letter, as if from us, as though the Day of Christ has come. Let no one deceive you by any means; for that Day will not come unless the falling away comes first, and the man of sin is unveiled, the son of perdition, who opposes and exalts himself above all that is called God or that is honored, so that he sits as God in the temple of God, declaring of himself that he is God." 2nd Thessalonians 2:1-4

"And after this I was looking in the night visions. And, behold, the fourth beast was frightening and terrifying, and very strong! And it had great iron teeth. It devoured, and broke in pieces, and stamped what was left with its feet. And it was different from all the beasts before it; and it had ten horns. I was contemplating the horns. And behold, another little horn came up among them, and three of the first horns were uprooted before it. And behold, in this horn were eyes like the eyes of a man, and a mouth speaking great things. I watched until the thrones were cast down, and the Ancient of Days sat, whose robe was white as snow and the hair of His head like pure wool. His throne was like flames of fire, its wheels like burning fire. A stream of fire went out and came out from before Him. A thousand thousands served Him, and a vast innumerable number stood before Him. The judgment was set and the books were opened. Then I was watching because of the voice of the great words which the horn spoke. I was watching until the beast was killed, and his body was destroyed and given to the burning flame. As for the rest of the beasts, their dominion was taken away. Yet their lives were prolonged for a season and a time. I saw in the night visions. And behold, one like the Son of Man came with the clouds of the heavens. And He came to the Ancient of Days. And they brought Him near before Him. And dominion was given to Him, and glory, and a kingdom, that all peoples, nations, and languages should serve Him. His dominion is an everlasting dominion which shall not pass away, and His kingdom that which shall not be destroyed. I, Daniel, was distressed in my spirit within my body, and the visions of my head troubled me. And I came near one of those who stood by and asked him the truth of all this. So he told me and made me know the interpretation of the things. These great beasts which are four, are four kings which shall rise up out of the earth. But the saints of the Most High shall receive the kingdom and possess the kingdom forever, even forever and ever. Then I wanted to know the truth of the fourth beast, which was different from all of the others, very frightening, with its teeth of iron and its nails of bronze; which devoured and broke in pieces, and trampled what was left with its feet, also of the ten horns that were on its head, and the other which came up, and before whom three fell, even that horn that had eyes, and a mouth speaking great things, whose appearance was greater than his fellows. I was watching, and the same horn made war with the saints and prevailed against them, until the Ancient of Days came. And judgment was given to the saints of the Most High, and the time came that the saints possessed the kingdom. And he said, The fourth beast shall be the fourth kingdom on earth, which shall be different from all other kingdoms, and shall devour the whole earth, and shall trample it down and break it in pieces. And the ten horns out of this kingdom are ten kings; they shall rise, and another shall rise after them. And he shall be different from the first, and he shall abase three kings. And he shall speak words against the Most High, and shall continually harass the saints of the Most High. And he shall intend to change times and law. And they shall be given into his hand for a period of a time and times and one half time. But the court shall sit, and they shall take away his dominion, to consume and to destroy until the end. And the kingdom and dominion, and the greatness of the kingdoms under the whole heavens shall be given to the people of the saints of the Most High, whose kingdom is an everlasting kingdom. And all dominions shall serve and obey Him. Thus far is the end of the matter. As for me, Daniel, my thoughts terrified me much, and my countenance changed in me. But I kept the matter in my heart." Daniel 7:7-28

Don't be caught up in all of this. Seek God before it is too late! Do you want to be Left Behind? Repent and believe the Gospel. Certainly Jesus died on the Cross for your sins. God provided Salvation through His Son Jesus, who rose again from the dead and sits at the right hand of God. What we might witness in the near future, or might not, will not be known. One thing that is known is that there will come a time where God's controversy with the nations will come into play. You might not be in political power or ever aspire to be, yet all will stand before their Creator *(Rev. 20:12)* and you are individually responsible for your own actions. There is no amount of good that you can do to make up for your sins before the Most High, the gift of Salvation is free, all you must do is accept it. Will you accept the invitation before it is too late? Will you stand before the Great White Throne and be judged by the righteous Judge of the whole earth, our Creator, as He justly condemns you to the Lake of Fire for refusing to repent and by faith believe into Him?

"For He says: In an acceptable time I have heard you, and in a day of salvation I have helped you. Behold, now is the accepted time; behold, now is the day of salvation." 2nd Corinthians 6:2

"Truly, these times of ignorance God overlooked, but now commands all men everywhere to repent, because He has established a day on which He will judge the world in righteousness by the Man whom He has appointed. He has given assurance of this to everyone by raising Him from the dead." Acts 17:30-31

"But God demonstrates His own love toward us, in that while we were yet sinners, Christ died for us." Romans 5:8

"For God so loved the world that He gave His only begotten Son, that everyone believing into Him should not perish but have eternal life. For God did not send His Son into the world to judge the world, but that the world through Him might be saved. The one believing into Him is not judged; but the one not believing is judged already, because he has not believed in the name of the only begotten Son of God. And this is the judgment, that the Light has come into the world, and men loved darkness rather than the Light, for their deeds were evil. For everyone practicing evil hates the Light and does not come to the Light, lest his deeds should be reproved. But the one doing the truth comes to the Light, that his deeds may be clearly seen, that they have been worked in God." John 3:16-21

"Nor is there salvation in any other, for there is no other name under Heaven given among men that is required for us to be saved." Acts 4:12

"And I saw a great white throne and Him who sat on it, from whose face the earth and the heavens fled away. And there was found no place for them. And I saw the dead, small and great, standing before God. And books were opened. And another book was opened, which is the Book of Life. And the dead were judged according to their works, out of the things which were written in the books. And the sea gave up the dead who were in it, and Death and Hades delivered up the dead who were in them. And they were

judged, each one, according to their works. And Death and Hades were cast into the Lake of Fire. This is the second death. And anyone not found written in the Book of Life was cast into the Lake of Fire." Revelation 20:11-15

Will you ultimately be rightfully punished for your sin and rebellion of your own life or accept Jesus as your Savior? We can look at the nations, we can see the evil that is going on in the world today, but what about our own lives? Do we look at ourselves and continue to rebel and refuse to repent? Do we have idolatrous hearts that put our sins above God, by refusing to yield? Do we treasure the things of this world more than God who Created this world? How long will you stand idle, how long will you refuse to adheed to your Creator? Will you try and ignore, talk yourself out of it, listen to others who say otherwise, all for in the end to stand before your Creator and be condemned to an eternity in Hell?

"Then Peter said to them, Repent, and let every one of you be immersed in the name of Jesus Christ to the remission of sins; and you shall receive the gift of the Holy Spirit." Acts 2:38

"From that time Jesus began to preach and to say, Repent, for the kingdom of Heaven has drawn near." Matthew 4:17

"The Lord is not slow concerning His promise, as some count slowness, but is longsuffering toward us, not purposing that any should perish but that all should come to repentance. But the day of the Lord will come as a thief in the night, in which the heavens will pass away with a loud noise, and the elements will be dissolved with intense burning; both the earth and the works that are in it will be burned up. Therefore, since all these things will be dissolved, of what sort ought you to be in holy behavior and godliness, looking for and earnestly hastening unto the coming of the Day of God, through which the heavens will be dissolved, being set on fire, and the elements will melt with intense burning?" 2nd Peter 3:9-12

"Do not lay up for yourselves treasures on earth, where moth and rust destroy and where thieves dig through and steal; but lay up for yourselves treasures in Heaven, where neither moth nor rust destroys and where thieves do not dig through and steal. For where your treasure is, there your heart will be also." Matthew 6:19-21

"For whoever desires to save his life will lose it, but whoever loses his life for My sake and the gospel's will save it. For what will it profit a man if he gains the whole world, and loses his own soul? Or what will a man give in exchange for his soul?" Mark 8:35-37

You better consider and consider well what you are going to do. As for me, I rest securely knowing that my soul is secure in Him who died for me!

"And He said to me, It is finished! I am the Alpha and the Omega, the Beginning and the Ending. I will give of the fountain of the Water of Life freely to him who thirsts. He who

overcomes shall inherit all things, and I will be his God and he shall be My son. But the cowardly, unbelieving, abominable, murderers, prostitutes, sorcerers, idolaters, and all liars shall have their part in the lake which burns with fire and brimstone, which is the second death." Revelation 21:6-8

"For we walk by faith, not by sight. We are confident, yes, preferring rather to be absent from the body and to be at home with the Lord. Therefore we strive, whether at home or away, to be well pleasing to Him. For we must all appear before the judgment seat of Christ, that each one may receive the things done in the body, according to what he has done, whether good or bad. Knowing, therefore, the terror of the Lord, we persuade men; and we are well known to God, and I also hope are well known in your consciences." 2nd Corinthians 5:7-11

Amen!

Fearmongers

"Enter into the rock and hide in the dust from the terror of Jehovah, and from the glory of His majesty. The lofty eyes of man shall be humbled, and the haughtiness of men shall be bowed down; but Jehovah, He alone, shall be exalted in that day." Isaiah 2:10-11

So with much due expectation a Syrian missile strike by the United States, France and the UK ensued. The internet immediately blew up with tons of people going live on their YouTube channels and other media outlets. The warnings were largely the same from both the small and big alternative media, World War 3 had broken out.

In hindsight, Russia did not and has not responded militarily. While their S-200 units, ran by Russian trained Syrian solders managed to shoot down a reported 71 of approximately 105 incoming missiles, militarily there was no exchange of fire between the United States and Russia. While I wouldn't dismiss the possibility of such type of events leading into a hot war with Russia at some point in the future, the opinion on that night was that war had begun.

It's been stated before and should be restated again, eventually these people who call out everything are going to be right on some things. The problem is that they have usually been wrong on nearly everything. While we could definitely dig deeper into the whole Syria ordeal, the proxy war for control between the US and Russia, we won't. The point here is that the fearmongers are always ready to call every potential disastrous situation as having went from a threat to reality, while also blowing other political events out of proportion.

Such things that are done by these fearmongers are not new, there is just a lot more of them nowadays, due to the ease of accessibility of the internet and the low cost or often free for someone to broadcast live or post media afterwards. Shall a list be compiled of the potential threats and the never-ending amount of people who push these forward? Why bother, new problems will come up, some will happen, some won't. I'm reminded of these words that Jesus proclaimed:

"And you will hear of wars and rumors of wars. See that you are not troubled; for all these things must come to pass, but the end is not yet." Matthew 24:6

Some will be wars, some will be rumors. Yet I would ask, where are those who would rightfully warn about something that is certain, a time will come in the world will the worst fears of mankind will come true. A time will come when God's Judgment against the wickedness of mankind that fills the earth will become a reality. This is not a rumor, this is the Truth from our Creator.

"A roaring noise shall come to the ends of the earth; for Jehovah has a controversy with the nations; He will enter into judgment with all flesh. He will give those who are wicked to the sword, says Jehovah. Thus says Jehovah of Hosts, Behold, evil shall go forth from nation to nation, and a great tempest shall be roused up from the recesses of the earth. And in that day the slain of Jehovah shall be from one end of the earth even to the other end of the earth. They shall not be mourned, nor gathered, nor buried. They shall be as dung on the ground. Howl, you shepherds, and cry! Wallow in the ashes, you majestic ones of the flock! For the days of your slaughter and of your scattering are fulfilled; and you shall fall like a delightful vessel. And the shepherds shall have no way to flee, nor the majestic ones of the flock to escape. A voice of the cry of the shepherds, and a howling of the majestic ones of the flock shall be heard; for Jehovah has spoiled their pasture, and the peaceful pastures are cut down because of the fierce anger of Jehovah. He has left His den like a lion; for their land is wasted at the presence of His fierce violence, and before His fierce anger." Jeremiah 25:31-38

"Behold, Jehovah empties the earth and makes it bare, and distorts its face, and scatters its inhabitants. And as it is with the people, so it shall be with the priest; as with the servant, so with the master; as with the maid, so it is with her mistress; as with the buyer, so with the seller; as with the lender, so with the borrower; as with the creditor, so with the debtor. The land shall be completely emptied, and utterly plundered; for Jehovah has spoken this Word. The earth mourns and fades away; the world droops and fades away; the haughty people of the earth grow feeble. The earth is also defiled under its inhabitants; because they have transgressed the laws, changed the ordinance, and have broken the perpetual covenant. Therefore the curse has devoured the earth, and those who dwell in it are held guilty; therefore the inhabitants of the earth are burned, and few men are left. The new wine mourns, the vine droops, all the merry-hearted sigh. The mirth of the tambourines ceases; the tumult of the jubilant ends; the joy of the harp

ceases. *They shall not drink wine with a song; strong drink is bitter to those who drink it. The city of emptiness is broken down; every house is shut up so that no one may come in. There is a cry for wine in the streets; all joy is darkened, the mirth of the land has gone. Desolation is left in the city, and the gate is battered and destroyed. For so it is in the midst of the land among the people. It shall be like the shaking of an olive tree, and as gleanings of grapes when the vintage has been finished. They shall lift up their voice, they shall sing for the majesty of Jehovah, they shall cry aloud from the sea. Therefore glorify Jehovah in the light of the fire, the name of the Lord Jehovah of Israel from the seashores. From the ends of the earth we have heard songs, glory to the righteous. But I said, Leanness to me! Leanness to me! Woe to me! Deceivers deceive, even with treachery. Deceivers deceive! Terror and the pit and the snare are upon you, O inhabitant of the earth. And it shall be that he who flees from the sound of terror shall fall into the pit. And he who comes up out of the midst of the pit shall be caught in the snare. For the windows from on high are opened, and the foundations of the earth quake. The earth has been badly broken! The earth is split open and cracked through! The earth has shaken greatly and is tottering! Like a drunkard the earth is staggering back and forth! And it sways to and fro like a hut! Its transgressions have been heavy upon it; and it shall fall and not rise again. And it shall come to pass in that day that Jehovah will punish the host of the haughty ones on high; and on earth, the kings of the earth. And they shall be gathered, as prisoners are gathered in a dungeon. And they shall be shut up in the prison, and after many days they shall be visited. Then the moon shall be abashed, and the sun shall be ashamed, when Jehovah of Hosts shall reign on Mount Zion, in Jerusalem, and before His elders, in splendor." Isaiah 24*

A nuclear exchange between Russia and the United States would be horrifying. Could you imagine the calamity in the United States ensuing from the aftermath of such an attack? The survivors would face a country with all basic essentials of life completely evaporated, the entire system shook to its core. At least in Moscow they have bomb shelters with some food for their people. Where will you go if such a situation were to occur?

You want to discuss outrage of the prospect of nuclear war with Russia, why not outrage against the lack of preparing against such a momentous disaster in this country?! Why not harden our electrical infrastructure against an EMP attack? Why when the threat is still present, have the Cold War bomb shelters been all but decommissioned and no longer stocked with food? Serious questions, questions the American people should be demanding answers to.

The fearmongers have this right, if one is to prepare for such disasters, you best do any preparing for your own family beforehand, as the government doesn't appear to have plans to provide any more aid than rounding up dissidents into political concentration camps. Yet, let me pose a thought, a question, some serious critical thinking about the recent situation in Syria regarding a potential deception, something that I haven't seen put out there.

What if the government knows, and they do, that people assume taking over Syria will lead to World War 3 with Russia. In order to calm the effects and eventually undertake more action, with the prospect of war a potential, the government of the United States purposely has a mild show of force (which we saw). The inaction of the Russian government calms the nerves of many of those who saw this as leading into a hot war with Russia. Then the United States is able to begin a bigger and more direct campaign to regain ground from the Russians in Syria, with the thought being that the Russians will not react. The precedent is laid, the Russians stood down, so the assumption is that they will stand down again. What if they don't stand down that time? Just some critical thinking on what might be a mass propaganda tool being used to quiet the fearmongers. After all these people were correct that this could have led into a hot war with Russia.

Just answer this one question, and this is said rhetorically, what if it were a serious bombing campaign that was directed at Assad's forces (backed by Russia) and lasted several days with numerous casualties, etc.? See what I mean? Moving along…

So where are those who are warning that mankind need to repent and believe the Gospel in order to be Saved? Where are those who are warning that if you die in your sins you will be cast into the Lake of Fire for all of eternity? Where are those who are warning that without repenting and by faith believing into Jesus Christ as your Lord and Savior, your end is just a breath away?

"And Jesus came and spoke to them, saying, All authority is given to Me in Heaven and on earth. Go therefore and instruct all the nations, immersing them into the name of the Father and of the Son and of the Holy Spirit, teaching them to observe all things whatever I have commanded you; and lo, I am with you always, even to the end of the age. Amen." Matthew 28:18-20

"Therefore I said to you that you will die in your sins; for if you do not believe that I AM, you will die in your sins." John 8:24

"But those things which God foretold through the mouth of all His prophets, that the Christ would suffer, He has thus fulfilled. Repent therefore and be converted, that your sins may be blotted out, so that times of refreshing may come from the presence of the Lord, and that He may send Jesus Christ, who was preached to you before, whom Heaven must receive until the times of restoration of all things, of which God has spoken through the mouth of all His holy prophets since the past ages." Acts 3:18-21

"Truly, these times of ignorance God overlooked, but now commands all men everywhere to repent, because He has established a day on which He will judge the world in righteousness by the Man whom He has appointed. He has given assurance of this to everyone by raising Him from the dead." Acts 17:30-31

"Jesus said to him, I am the Way, the Truth, and the Life. No one comes to the Father except through Me." John 14:6

"Who has believed our report? And to whom has the arm of Jehovah been revealed? For He grows up before Him as a tender plant, and as a root out of the dry ground. He has no form nor splendor that we should regard Him, nor anything spectacular that we should desire Him. He is despised and rejected by men; a Man of pain, and knowing infirmity; a hiding of faces; being despised, we have esteemed Him not. Truly He has borne our sicknesses, and carried our pain; yet we esteemed Him stricken, smitten by God, and afflicted. But He was wounded for our transgressions; He was bruised for our iniquities; the chastisement for our peace was upon Him; and with His stripes we are healed. All we like sheep have gone astray; we have turned, each one to his own way; and Jehovah has laid upon Him the iniquity of us all. He has been oppressed, and He was afflicted; yet He opens not His mouth. He is brought as a lamb to the slaughter; and as a sheep before its shearers is mute, so He opens not His mouth. He was taken from prison and from judgment; and who shall declare His generation? For He was cut off out of the land of the living; for the transgression of My people He was stricken. And His grave was assigned with the wicked, and with the rich in His death; although He had done no violence, nor was any deceit in His mouth. Yet it pleased Jehovah to crush Him; to grieve Him; that He should give His soul as a sin-offering. He shall see His seed, He shall prolong His days, and the delight of Jehovah shall prosper in His hand. He shall see the travail of His soul, and shall be fulfilled. By His knowledge shall My righteous Servant justify many; for He shall bear their iniquities. Therefore I will apportion to Him with the great, and He shall divide the spoils with the strong; because He has poured out His soul unto death; and He was reckoned among the transgressors; and He bore the sin of many, and made intercession for the transgressors." Isaiah 53

So, this sort of analogy has been used before, but it stands its ground on truth. Let's assume that the fearmongers were right and World War 3 broke out. You being privy to such information and educated about how to survive, as well as having had funds to prepare beforehand, placed your emergency plan into play. Let's assume you lived in the hood of Los Angeles. There in your unassuming house, you had been doing everything that the alternative media had told you, you were prepped. Not only did you have your supplies, your bug out location and a plan, you also had become a cryptocurrency master, having made your share of the electronic wealth through Bitcoin, using that to prepare for just such a scenario. While a coffee shop lover during your days, you suddenly rip into action.

The warnings are there, the gunfire from battleships between the United States and Russia begin to fire. Soon torpedoes are being launched and not long after fighter jets are actively bombing each other. The situation begins to accelerate out of control, neither superpower is willing to back down at this point. Before the nukes start getting launched, you get into your car, with the extra cans of gas in the trunk (you know, those that you had in your garage, ready) and begin your road trip. Drinking coffee after coffee you make it up to Montana.

Here you calculated carefully that northwestern Montana was not likely to take a direct hit from a nuclear missile, the proximity is too close to Canada, of whom Russia would probably leave alone, with the missiles at least. Up in the mountains near Eureka you had picked out a parcel of land with a self sufficient cabin, one that is on a hard to access mountain road. Here you traveled many times, stocking the cabin with dry goods, fuel, batteries, a hand pump well. Your located close to a good fishing stream and game in abundant. You have cleared a portion of your acreage for growing vegetables. There you also have planted both plum and apple trees. You have a cellar built into the mountainside hill. Your property is unsuspecting and you can easily protect yourself up there against most threats.

After a nearly nonstop drive from LA to Eureka, Montana, you arrive. With your shortwave radio you tune into the world's stream and begin to listen. You've abandoned your job, your house, your life in LA, but as your tune into the radio you hear that missiles have been launched from Russia towards the United States and that the United States is preparing to retaliate. Soon thereafter information becomes hard to get, no one really knows exactly what happened, but after several days the truth begin to pour out.

Both the United States and Russia have destroyed each other. Those who survived are fighting amongst themselves, society has failed. You plant your garden from your survival stash of seeds and begin chopping wood for the nuclear winter that is coming. Years and years go by, you survive and though life is bleak, you remind yourself of the intelligence that you had, how you outsmarted the system, how you managed to survive. Yet your funds to pay your taxes, still being collected by what is left to the state government of Montana is getting slim. Reading one of your books that you had stored about life in the frontier of Montana, in the warmth of the fireplace in the frigid winter, you come across a historical account of placer gold not too far from where you now reside.

With spring now in full bloom, you gather your rifle and a backpack, outfitted for the occasion. As you make your way through rugged terrain that hasn't been touched in years, you find the remains of some old cabin foundations, a sure sign of a small gold camp that had been in the vicinity. As you make your way up to the pilings you are unaware of the danger that is covered by the forest overgrowth. Walking towards the prospect you suddenly feel the ground give beneath your feet. Falling down nearly 50 feet into a pit, plunged into darkness, except the glimmer of light at the top, you take your last breath. You never had thought much on Christianity, you had believed some, but never repented and by faith believed into Jesus Christ as your Savior. You were a man, but a lost man, a man who died in his sins, one who was not made a new creature through Jesus Christ.

As you stand before your Creator at the Great White Throne Judgment and you are justly Judged by your Creator, you realize the errors of your ways. However, it is too late. You were able to outsmart the evils of mankind, you had enough knowledge about how the world really worked, but this knowledge didn't include God. You listened to the warnings of the fearmongers, who prepared and thought you had it right when the reality came, but they neglected to tell you about your lost condition, your sin. They only preached a doctrine of fear and self survival, to the ultimate losing of your own soul due to rejecting Jesus Christ as your Lord and Savior.

"And I saw a great white throne and Him who sat on it, from whose face the earth and the heavens fled away. And there was found no place for them. And I saw the dead, small and great, standing before God. And books were opened. And another book was opened, which is the Book of Life. And the dead were judged according to their works, out of the things which were written in the books. And the sea gave up the dead who were in it, and Death and Hades delivered up the dead who were in them. And they were judged, each one, according to their works. And Death and Hades were cast into the Lake of Fire. This is the second death. And anyone not found written in the Book of Life was cast into the Lake of Fire." Revelation 20:11-15

"Therefore, if anyone is in Christ, he is a new creation; the old things have passed away; behold, all things have become new. Now all things are from God, who has reconciled us to Himself through Jesus Christ, and has given us the ministry of reconciliation, that is, that God was in Christ reconciling the world to Himself, not imputing their trespasses to them, and has committed to us the Word of reconciliation. Now then, we are ambassadors for Christ. As God is exhorting through us, we beseech you on Christ's behalf, Be reconciled to God. For He made Him who knew no sin to be sin for us, that we might become the righteousness of God in Him." 2nd Corinthians 5:17-21

God has foretold the future, God has stated what happens if mankind does not accept the free gift of Salvation. Take heed, you have been warned. Believe God over the fearmongers!

"For God so loved the world that He gave His only begotten Son, that everyone believing into Him should not perish but have eternal life. For God did not send His Son into the world to judge the world, but that the world through Him might be saved. The one believing into Him is not judged; but the one not believing is judged already, because he has not believed in the name of the only begotten Son of God. And this is the judgment, that the Light has come into the world, and men loved darkness rather than the Light, for their deeds were evil. For everyone practicing evil hates the Light and does not come to the Light, lest his deeds should be reproved. But the one doing the truth comes to the Light, that his deeds may be clearly seen, that they have been worked in God." John 3:16-21

"For He says: In an acceptable time I have heard you, and in a day of salvation I have helped you. Behold, now is the accepted time; behold, now is the day of salvation." 2nd Corinthians 6:2

"Let it not be! Indeed, let God be true but every man a liar. As it is written: That You may be found just in Your words, and may win the case when You are judged." Romans 3:4

Amen!

Know No Evil

"Love is longsuffering and is kind; love does not envy; love does not boast itself, is not puffed up; does not behave indecently, does not seek its own, is not easily provoked, thinks no evil; does not rejoice in iniquity, but rejoices in the truth; covers all things, believes all things, hopes all things, endures all things. Love never fails." 1st Corinthians 13:4-8a

The other day a group of us listened to a guest sermon of a pastor who has a Church in Australia. The speaker of the sermon went over several items dealing with apostasy in the churches, as well as the pagan origins of the Roman Catholic Church. As I sat there and listened, suddenly what had been on my mind to write about, this article, became firmly founded. Though this speaker would be ridiculed or shown the exit door in most any church in America, he was spot on, in fact he could have gone further.

If one thinks about it, and we are going to address those who call themselves Christians, to know no evil is a far cry from the direction that the apostate churches currently have headed. Let's set the foundation for this topic, let this argument sink down into your soul and understand just how far away from righteousness that those who call themselves Christians really are.

"For no one is able to lay any other foundation than that which is laid, which is Jesus Christ." 1st Corinthians 3:11

So we will start off with the firm foundation, which is Jesus Christ. In Him we are Saved, through repentance and by faith believing the Gospel. Let's explore this a moment more:

"Nor is there salvation in any other, for there is no other name under Heaven given among men that is required for us to be saved." Acts 4:12

"Truly, these times of ignorance God overlooked, but now commands all men everywhere to repent, because He has established a day on which He will judge the world in righteousness by the Man whom He has appointed. He has given assurance of this to everyone by raising Him from the dead." Acts 17:30-31

..."testifying both to Jews, and also to Greeks, repentance toward God and faith toward our Lord Jesus Christ." Acts 20:21

Now those who are in Christ, those who have truly repented and by faith believed into Jesus as their Lord and Savior, this is the foundation. Consider the opening verses regarding love and consider these as well.

"Whoever believes that Jesus is the Christ is born from God, and everyone who loves Him who begets also loves him who is begotten from Him. By this we know that we love the children of God, when we love God and keep His commandments. For this is the love of God, that we keep His commandments. And His commandments are not burdensome. For whatever is born from God overcomes the world. And this is the victory that has overcome the world; our faith." 1st John 5:1-4

"And one of the scribes came, and having heard them reasoning together, perceiving that He had answered them well, asked Him, Which is the first commandment of all? Jesus answered him, The first of all the commandments is: Hear, O Israel, the Lord our God, the Lord is one. And you shall love the Lord your God with all your heart, with all your soul, with all your mind, and with all your strength. This is the first commandment. And the second, like it, is this: You shall love your neighbor as yourself. There is no other commandment greater than these." Mark 12:28-31

So now California has pending legislation that would ban licensed counselors from telling men who think they are women, who come for counseling, that they are indeed a man. To make matters worse, if this legislation passes, they would also be banned from giving them a Bible. Nothing like letting the Word of God shed light on man's sins, so that they man clearly see the evidence of their deeds and the contradicting nature of it, perhaps repent and be Saved. Not in California if they get their way.

"For the wrath of God is revealed from Heaven against all ungodliness and unrighteousness of men, who suppress the truth in unrighteousness, because what may be known of God is clearly recognized by them, for God has revealed it to them. For ever since the creation of the world the unseen things of Him are clearly perceived, being understood by the things that are made, even His eternal power and Godhead, so that

they are without excuse, because, although they know God, they do not glorify Him as God, nor are thankful, but become vain in their reasonings, and their stupid hearts are darkened. Professing to be wise, they become foolish, and change the glory of the incorruptible God into an image made like corruptible man, and birds and four-footed animals and creeping things. Therefore God also gives them up to uncleanness, in the lusts of their hearts, to dishonor their bodies among themselves, who change the truth of God into the lie, and fear and serve the created things more than the Creator, who is blessed forever. Amen. For this reason God gives them up to vile passions. For even their women change the natural use for what is contrary to nature. Likewise also the men, abandoning the natural use of the woman, burned in their lust toward one another, men with men performing what is shameful, and receiving the retribution within themselves, the penalty which is fitting for their error. And even as they do not like to have God in their full true knowledge, God gives them over to a reprobate mind, to do those things which are not fitting; being filled with every unrighteousness, sexual perversion, wickedness, covetousness, maliciousness; full of envy, murder, strife, deceit, depravity; whisperers, defamers, haters of God, insolent, proud, boasters, inventors of evil things, disobedient to parents, without understanding, untrustworthy, without natural affection, unforgiving, unmerciful; who, knowing the righteous judgment of God, that those who practice such things are deserving of death, not only do them, but also approve of those who practice them." Romans 1:18-32

We talk about knowing no evil. So why are those who are professing Christians, why are the churches, most of who lead the way on the broad path to destruction, dabbling or even knowing evil? Think about it diligently for a moment, consider you ways and then we will consider where the world will ultimately go in rebellion against their Creator. We will diligently consider the Words of the Most High, who has declared, and it will certainly come to pass, what the future holds. We will see where all of this is going to go in the future.

So how about television. What about the standards there? Am I saying that Christians shouldn't own a television? No, but what I am saying is that those who are Christians should know no evil in regards to the content that they view on the television. God is holy, we are to be holy and separate unto Him.

"Therefore gird up the loins of your mind, be sober, and rest your hope fully upon the grace that is to be brought to you at the revelation of Jesus Christ; as obedient children, not conforming yourselves to the former lusts in your ignorance; but as He who called you is holy, you also become holy in all conduct, because it is written, Be holy, because I am holy." 1st Peter 1:13-16

"I beseech you therefore, brethren, by the mercies of God, that you present your bodies a living sacrifice, holy, acceptable to God, which is your reasonable service. And do not be conformed to this world, but be transformed by the renewing of your mind, that you may prove what is that good and acceptable and perfect will of God." Romans 12:1-2

Do we laugh and watch the raunchy content on television programs? Do we deal with watching 'safer' television like HGTV and train our minds to the covetousness, lust and gay couple after gay couple? Do we smile at the sly sexual overtones? Do we lust at the half dressed women? Do we mind the murders, beatings, cursings, foul mouthed programs that depict evil after evil?

When in the history of the world, aside from war torn, early stages of countries or countries with radical leaders, does the average man, in past times, go and see people getting murdered on a regular basis? Where did the average person watch lewd women walking about half dressed? Certainly it happens, certainly it has happened, but now let's be specific and talk about you.

I could imagine some will say, I have seen it, I have seen it. There are obvious bad neighborhoods throughout the United States, and indeed the world. In all of my life I have yet to witness a shooting, except on television, in all of my life I have yet to see the bodies of those just gunned down lying in the street. Yet, I am no stranger to the world, I have lived in places that are not safe. I have had a gun pulled on me, I have been shot at, I have seen a drive-by shooting happen on the next block, but yet if I turned on the television, I can see men shooting at each other on a regular basis, bloody bodies lying in the street, oftentimes justified by some sort of street justice, further lowering the moral values of the viewers and pushing moral relativism. Yet the Word of God clearly proclaims that those who are His should know no evil.

So think about it, you can't do nothing about what you run across, what happens in your neighborhoods or cities, but are you going to know evil by watching the absolute filth on your television? Are you going to mingle with the sodomites via the television? Are you going to listen to filthy trash music that frequently mixes satanic rituals in their music videos and the words of their lutes?! Know no evil!

Take a look at the Word of God, dust off you Bible and know what your Creator says.

"To whom then will you compare the Mighty God? Or what likeness will you compare to Him?" Isaiah 40:18

"Have you not known? Have you not heard? Has it not been told you from the beginning? Have you not understood from the foundations of the earth? It is He who sits upon the circle of the earth, and its inhabitants are like grasshoppers; Who stretches out the heavens like a curtain, and spreads them out like a tent to dwell in; Who brings the rulers to nothing; He makes the judges of the earth as nothing. Indeed, they shall not be planted; indeed, they shall not be sown. Indeed, their stump shall not take root in the earth. And He shall also blow upon them, and they shall wither, and the tempest shall take them away like stubble. To whom then will you compare Me, or with whom am I equal? says the Holy One. Lift up your eyes on high, and consider who has created these things, who brings out their host by number. He calls them all by name by the greatness of His might, for He is strong in power; not one is missing. Why do you say, O Jacob, and speak, O Israel, My way is hidden from Jehovah and my judgment is passed over by

God? Have you not known? Have you not heard, that the eternal God, Jehovah, the Creator of the ends of the earth, does not grow faint nor weary? His understanding is unsearchable." Isaiah 40:21-28

"But now thus says Jehovah who created you, O Jacob, and He who formed you, O Israel; Fear not, for I have redeemed you; I have called you by your name; you are Mine. When you pass through the waters, I will be with you; and through the rivers, they shall not overflow you. When you walk through the fire, you shall not be burned; nor shall the flame consume you. For I am Jehovah your God, the Holy One of Israel, your Savior; I gave Egypt for your ransom, Ethiopia and Seba for you. Since you were precious in My eyes, you have been honored, and I have loved you; therefore I will give men for you, and people for your life. Fear not, for I am with you. I will bring your seed from the east, and gather you from the west. I will say to the north, Give up; and to the south, Do not keep back; bring My sons from afar and My daughters from the ends of the earth; everyone who is called by My name; for I have created him for My glory, I have formed him; yea, I have made him. Bring out the blind people who have eyes, and the deaf who have ears. Let all the nations be gathered together, and let the people be assembled. Who among them can declare this and cause us to hear former things? Let them bring out their witnesses, that they may be justified; or let them hear, and say, It is true. You are My witnesses, says Jehovah, and My servant whom I have chosen; that you may know and believe Me, and understand that I am He. Before Me no god was formed, nor shall there be after Me. I, even I, am Jehovah; and there is no one to save besides Me. I have declared and have saved, and I have shown, when there was no strange god among you; therefore you are My witnesses, says Jehovah, that I am the Mighty God. Yea, before the day was, I am He; and no one can deliver out of My hand; I work, and who will reverse it? Thus says Jehovah, your Redeemer, the Holy One of Israel: For your sake I have sent to Babylon, and have brought them all down as fugitives, and the Chaldeans, who shout in their ships. I am Jehovah, your Holy One, the Creator of Israel, your King." Isaiah 43:1-15

Know what God says, know what His standards are, know no evil! Love the Lord, your Savior, if indeed you are Saved, if you are in Christ.

For the time will come when man will refuse to repent of their murders and sexual immoralities. They will refuse to repent, despite the just Judgments of the Almighty, who still has mercy to those who are willing to repent and believe, are coming in full. Instead the masses will gather, the nations will gather at Armageddon, to what, fight God!

"But the rest of mankind, who were not killed by these plagues, did not repent of the works of their hands, that they should not do homage to demons, and idols of gold, silver, brass, stone, and wood, which are not able to see nor hear nor walk. And they did not repent of their murders nor their sorceries nor their sexual perversions nor their thefts." Revelation 9:20-21

Then the truth of the matter will be fully known. Then the real reason behind the rebellion of this world will be clear for all to see. The nations will line up, they will be ready, they are so deluded with sin that they are preparing for battle with their Creator. Though man can't look at the sun, though man couldn't swim across and ocean, they will pretend they are strong. They will gather and prepare to fight God. God will respond.

"Proclaim this among the nations: Consecrate a war; wake up the mighty men; let all the men of war draw near; let them come up. Beat your plowshares into swords, and your pruning hooks into spears. Let the weak say, I am strong. Assemble yourselves and come, all you nations; and gather yourselves together all around. O Jehovah, bring down Your mighty ones. Let the nations be awakened and come up to the Valley of Jehoshaphat. For there I will sit to judge all the nations all around. Put in the sickle, for the harvest is ripe. Come, go down, for the press is full, the vats overflow, for their wickedness is great. Multitudes, multitudes in the valley of decision! For the day of Jehovah is near in the valley of decision." Joel 3:9-14

At that time, at that moment Jesus Christ will return with all of the Saints, myself included, the battle stage will be set, yet the nations will not be able to begin. Before the battle begins it is over, before the war starts, they are gone. As a vapor, so they are gone. The blood is deep and their sin has destroyed them, they too will be Judged by their Creator at the Great White Throne Judgment *(Rev. 20:11-15)*.

"Come near, you nations, to hear; and you people, pay attention; let the earth hear, and its fullness; the world, and all its offspring. For the wrath of Jehovah is upon all nations, and His fury upon all their armies. He has utterly destroyed them, He has delivered them to the slaughter. Also their slain shall be thrown out, and their stench shall come up out of their corpses, and the mountains shall be melted with their blood. And all the host of the heavens shall be dissolved, and the heavens shall be rolled up like a scroll; and all their host shall wither, as a leaf withers off the vine, and as fruit falling from the fig tree." Isaiah 34:1-4

"And I saw Heaven opened, and behold, a white horse. And He who sat on him was called Faithful and True, and in righteousness He judges and makes war. His eyes were like a flame of fire, and on His head were many crowns. He had a name written that no one knew except Himself. And He was clothed with a robe dipped in blood, and His name is called The Word of God. And the armies in Heaven, clothed in fine linen, white and pure, followed Him on white horses. And out of His mouth goes a sharp sword, that with it He might strike the nations. And He Himself will rule them with a rod of iron. He Himself treads the winepress of the fierceness and wrath of Almighty God. And He has on His robe and on His thigh a name written: KING OF KINGS AND LORD OF LORDS. And I saw an angel standing in the sun; and he cried with a loud voice, saying to all the birds that fly in the midst of the heavens, Come and gather together for the supper of the great God, that you may eat the flesh of kings, the flesh of commanders, the flesh of mighty men, the flesh of horses and of those who sit on them, and the flesh of all people, free and slave, both small and great. And I saw the beast, the kings of the earth, and their armies, gathered together to make war against Him who sat on the horse and

against His army. And the beast was captured, and with him the false prophet who worked signs in his presence, by which he led astray those who received the mark of the beast and those who did homage to his image. These two were cast alive into the Lake of Fire burning with brimstone. And the rest were killed with the sword which proceeded out of the mouth of Him who sat on the horse. And all the birds were filled with their flesh." Revelation 19:11-21

"So the angel thrust his sickle into the earth and gathered the vine of the earth, and threw it into the great winepress of the wrath of God. And the winepress was trampled outside the city, and blood came forth out of the winepress, up to the horses' bridles, by a distance of one thousand six hundred furlongs." Revelation 14:19-20

If you are a true Believer, look at the things in your life. Look at the television programs you watch, the websites you visit, the music you listen to, the things you own, the stuff you do in your free time and if there is any inkling of evil, throw it out. Pound it into dust and let it blow in the wind. For God will repay the unsaved for their ways, as Christians we should simply know no evil.

"Behold what manner of love the Father has bestowed on us, that we should be called children of God. Therefore the world does not know us, because it did not know Him. Beloved, now we are children of God; and it has not yet been revealed what we shall be, but we know that when He is revealed, we shall be like Him, for we shall see Him as He is. And everyone who has this hope in Him purifies himself, just as He is pure." 1st John 3:1-3

"Therefore submit to God. Resist the devil and he will flee from you. Draw near to God and He will draw near to you. Cleanse your hands, you sinners; and purify your hearts, you double-minded. Lament and mourn and weep. Let your laughter be turned to mourning and your joy to shame. Humble yourselves in the sight of the Lord, and He will exalt you." Jacob (James) 4:7-10

"Josiah was eight years old when he became king, and he reigned thirty-one years in Jerusalem. And he did what was right in the eyes of Jehovah, and walked in the ways of his father David; he did not turn aside to the right hand or to the left. For in the eighth year of his reign, while he was still young, he began to seek the God of his father David; and in the twelfth year he began to purge Judah and Jerusalem of the high places, the groves, the graven images, and the molten images. They broke down the altars of the Baals in his presence, and the incense altars which were above them he cut down; and the groves, the graven images, and the molten images he broke in pieces, and pulverized them and scattered them on the graves of those who had sacrificed to them. He also burned the bones of the priests on their altars, and cleansed Judah and Jerusalem; and also in the cities of Manasseh, Ephraim, and Simeon, as far as Naphtali and all around; with chopping tools. When he had broken down the altars and the groves, had beaten the carved images into powder, and cut down all the incense altars throughout all the land of Israel, he returned to Jerusalem." 2nd Chronicles 34:1-7

Amen!

**For more articles visit the ministry website at:
http://www.allwillstand.org.**